AFRICA

AFRICA

THE POLITICS OF
INDEPENDENCE AND UNITY

Immanuel Wallerstein

WITH AN INTRODUCTION BY THE AUTHOR

UNIVERSITY OF NEBRASKA PRESS
LINCOLN AND LONDON

Africa: The Politics of Independence © 1961 by Immanuel Wallerstein
Africa: The Politics of Unity © 1967 by Immanuel Wallerstein
Epilogue © 1971 by Immanuel Wallerstein
Introduction to the Bison Books Edition © 2005 by Immanuel Wallerstein
All rights reserved
Manufactured in the United States of America

First Nebraska paperback printing: 2005

Library of Congress Cataloging-in-Publication Data
Wallerstein, Immanuel Maurice, 1930–
Africa: the politics of independence and unity / Immanuel Wallerstein; with
an introduction by the author.
p. cm.
First work originally published: Africa, the politics of independence. New
York: Vintage Books, 1961; 2nd work originally published: Africa, the
politics of unity. New York: Vintage Books, 1967.
"A Bison book."
Includes bibliographical references and index.
ISBN-13: 978-0-8032-9856-9 (pbk.: alk. paper)
ISBN-10: 0-8032-9856-0 (pbk.: alk. paper)
1. Africa—Politics and government.   2. Nationalism—Africa.   3. Africa—
History—1960–.   4. Pan-Africanism.   I. Wallerstein, Immanuel Maurice,
1930– Africa, the politics of independence.   II. Wallerstein, Immanuel
Maurice, 1930– Africa, the politics of unity.   III. Title.
DT30.W34   2005
960—dc22   2005015324

This Bison Books edition follows the originals in beginning chapter 1 in
"Independence" on arabic page 3 and chapter 1 in "Unity" on arabic page
3; no material has been omitted.

IMMANUEL WALLERSTEIN

Introduction to the Bison Books Edition

At the end of World War II, almost all countries in Africa were still colonial territories. There were only four exceptions: Egypt, Liberia, Ethiopia (newly restored to sovereignty following Italian conquest in 1935), and South Africa (a state ruled by a White minority). In 2005, sixty years later, virtually all of Africa consists of sovereign states based on universal suffrage, and all are members of the United Nations. Clearly something has changed. The questions are, exactly what has changed, and what do these changes mean for Africans and for the rest of the world?

In the immediate aftermath of World War II, the colonial powers had no intention of granting independence to their African colonies, nor did any of them expect to be forced to do so, at least not until a very long time later. True, Italy, one of the powers that had lost the war, was divested of its colonies, and it was not feasible politically to substitute another European power in its place (as had been done with Germany's colonies after World War I). To be sure, both Great Britain and France, which between them governed most of the continent, thought it prudent and necessary to introduce reforms in colonial administration. But independence of their colonies was explicitly rejected as a conceivable goal by France and referred to as a very remote objective by the British. In South Africa the election of the Nationalist Party to power in 1948 led in the opposite direction: to the withdrawal of the few political rights the Black African majority had previously had, rather than introducing ameliorating reforms that would have augmented those political rights.

Nonetheless, the world after 1945 had changed more than the colonial powers were ready to appreciate or willing to acknowledge. The combination of at least three things—the Cold War competition between the United States and the Soviet Union; the successive independences in Asia of the Philippines, the Indian subcontinent, and Indonesia, followed by those of Southeast Asia (including the defeat of the French by the Viet Minh); and the Communist Party's coming to power in China—transformed the geopolitics of the world-system. Africa did not remain unaffected. A wave of African nationalism speedily swept the continent and, by 1960, the so-called Year of Africa, more than half of Africa's nations had become sovereign states with every expectation that the other half would soon follow. This is the story I told in *Africa: The Politics of Independence*, published in 1961. It was a wonderful story—full of passion and optimism. Africa believed in itself, in its future, and in its past, and the world took note.

Problems immediately arose that foreshadowed less optimistic times. The (erstwhile Belgian) Congo fell into crisis immediately after gaining independence in 1960, leading to a civil war, an attempt at secession by the wealthy mining area of Katanga, the murder of Congo's first prime minister and nationalist hero Patrice Lumumba, and, above all, massive foreign intervention in Congo's internal affairs (notably by the United States as well as Congo's ex-colonial power, Belgium). In a sense the Congo crisis is still going on in 2005.

In 1963, the president of Togo, Sylvanus Olympio, was assassinated in the first of what would become a long series of military coups across the continent. By then the remaining colonies located in southern Africa were largely those either with White settler populations or considerable mineral wealth, or both. As a result, a strong front of resistance to more African independences was constructed, uniting Portugal, the apartheid regime of South Africa, and the White settler government of (Southern) Rhodesia. On the other hand, a movement for African unity emerged at the same time, continuing the thrust for African self-assertion. The African unity movement was very strong, but not quite strong enough. What it achieved concretely was a compromise: the establishment of the Organization of African Unity in 1963, with an African Liberation Committee designed to aid the liberation movements in southern Africa. In 1965, however, the White government in Southern Rhodesia proclaimed its Unilateral Declaration of Independence, and Gen. Joseph Mobutu established a military dictatorship in the Congo that lasted for three decades. Finally, in February 1966 the leading voice in the movement for African unity, President Kwame Nkrumah of Ghana, was overthrown. The movement for African unity seemed stymied and the optimistic picture of 1960 was dimmed. This is the story I tried to tell in *Africa: The Politics of Unity*, published in 1967.

The period from 1965 to 1974 was one of harder times for the proponents of African self-assertion. The continent saw many military coups, a difficult civil war in Nigeria, an acute slowdown of economic development, and what seemed like a stalemate in liberating southern Africa. Then, suddenly, the dike broke. Portugal underwent its so-called revolution of the carnations in 1974. The Portuguese military, despairing of the endless wars against the African liberation movements, overthrew the fascist regime that had been in power for over forty years. Portugal divested itself of all its African colonies by 1975, which was followed by the dismantlement of the White Rhodesian regime in 1980, and the establishment of a government that was based on universal suffrage in what would be renamed Zimbabwe. South Africa experienced a transfer of power in 1994 to a government based on universal suffrage and the election of Nelson Mandela, the liberation movement's leader, as president. So, better years again—with African anticolonial aspirations seemingly fulfilled throughout the continent. However, already in 1960, at the moment of high hopes and generalized optimism, many voices insisted clearly that formal sovereignty was by no means enough to realize the aspirations of many African states for true self-government and equality on the world stage. These voices warned against what Kwame Nkrumah called neo-colonialism, meaning a situation in which, despite formal sovereignty, African states would remain economically subordinated in the world-system and their political independence would remain superficial. Seen from the perspective of 2005, Nkrumah's analysis has much to commend it. Africa has not at all been doing well economically. All statistics point to Africa as not only the poorest continent but, relative to the rest of the world, much poorer than it was fifty years ago (and, in many areas, in absolute terms as well). The question has become, what explains this? A question that cannot be answered in isolation without discussing the structure of the world-system as a whole in the post-1945 period.

The twenty years or so following 1945 saw three significant developments in the world-system: the hegemony of the United States and its Cold War with the Soviet Union; the unprecedented economic expansion of the world-economy; and the political reassertion of the non-European world. The three developments were linked in important ways.

World War II was the culmination of a vast and long struggle between the United States and Germany that had begun in the 1870s, a struggle about which country would be the successor hegemonic power to Great Britain, whose period of maximum power had passed. When the struggle finally ended in 1945 with the victory of the United States, the economic infrastructures of all the major industrial powers of Europe and Asia had been grievously damaged, whereas the United States, already very strong in 1939, far from being damaged, emerged much reinforced. Consequently, in 1945 the United States could produce manufactured goods more efficiently than all other industrial powers and compete with them successfully, even in their home markets. This economic strength enabled the United States to impose its political will virtually everywhere, and certainly to the new interstate structures that were being built on the African continent. As for military power, although the United States disbanded much of its standing army, it possessed nuclear weapons and an air force capable of making them an effective menace.

The only possible military competitor to the United States was the Soviet Union which, despite the economic and demographic damage caused by the war, had a very large army and, by 1949, nuclear weapons as well. The United States was forced to come to terms with the Soviet Union to be able to establish and maintain the kind of world order in which it was interested. The Soviet Union for its part felt incapable of confronting the United States militarily. The result was a de facto arrangement we often call by the metaphoric name Yalta.

The Yalta arrangement had in practice three components. First, the two powers entered into a division of spheres of influence, essentially along the lines of the location of their armed forces at the end of 1945. The Soviet Union thus had one-third of the world in its sphere (from the Elbe to the Yalu rivers) and the United States two-thirds. Africa was considered to be part of the U.S. sphere. The two powers agreed not to intrude into each other's sphere, an unwritten agreement that was repeatedly tested—by the civil war in Greece of 1946–49, the Berlin Blockade of 1949, the Korean War of 1951–53, the Quemoy-Matsu dispute of 1955, the Hungarian uprising of 1956, the Cuban missile crisis of 1962, the Czech spring of 1968—but each time the outcome was a return to the status quo ante, without any actual military engagement of the two powers.

The second Yalta component was in the realm of the economy. The United States declined to assist in the economic reconstruction of the

Soviet Union or in those parts of eastern Europe under its sway, while at the same time launching the Marshall Plan for zones within its own sphere in Europe and, indirectly, the African colonial territories. The United States aided its East Asian zone in comparable ways, especially once the Korean War began. In return, however, the Soviet Union was able to establish, unchallenged, a closed and relatively integrated economic market in its own sphere, one that had little interaction with the rest of the world-economy.

The third component was cultural and ideological. The United States and the Soviet Union entered into an ideological Cold War. The United States defined it as a conflict between the values of the free world and those of Communism and totalitarianism. The Soviet Union defined it as a conflict between bourgeois capitalism and proletarian socialism en route to the Communist utopia. Each side loudly vaunted its ideology and sought to convey the ideology's virtues and obtain adherents worldwide. But the primary function of the two messages was less to make converts than to maintain political strength in their own camps. That is why neither superpower would accept the possibility that there could be groups or states that refused to align themselves with one or the other ideology. "Neutralism is immoral," asserted U.S. secretary of state John Foster Dulles in the 1950s. The Soviet authorities felt the same.

The world economic upturn after 1945, a typical Kondratieff A-phase of expansion of the world-economy, was not unusual. But it was nonetheless spectacular in how far it extended and the rapid social transformations that it wrought everywhere. A vibrant world-economy was pump-primed in part by the economic and military expenditures occasioned by the Cold War and in part by the implementation of governmental policies that favored the expansion of consumer spending. Governmental policies took different forms in different parts of the world—the welfare state in the pan-European world, "socialism" in the Soviet sphere, development expenditures in the South. But for some twenty years at least, the world economic situation was an example of the aphorism that a rising tide lifts all boats. Things seemed to be improving everywhere.

The political assertiveness of the non-European world was also not new. It has been going on in various forms throughout the twentieth century. But World War II removed many obstacles. The defeats first of the colonial powers in Asia and then of Japan, which attempted to take over these colonies, exposed the political and military vulnerabilities of the erstwhile masters of the nineteenth-century world-system. In the years immediately following 1945, both the United States and the Soviet Union saw advantages in a reduction in the role of the erstwhile colonial powers in Asia (and then in Africa). The nationalist movements in Asia were primed to take full advantage of this modification of the *rapports de force* in the world-system and, as already noted, the pattern caught on rapidly in Africa. The colonial powers tried to slow down the process by providing new kinds of economic assistance and expanding educational opportunities, but these only fed the flames. This is why, by 1960, the world would be celebrating the Year of Africa.

But, just at this point, the geopolitical landscape began to change again. The economic recovery and then expansion of both western Europe and Japan was such that, by the 1960s, the two had become serious economic rivals to the United States. With that, the automatic political control the United States held over its Cold War allies began to decline. In the Soviet Union, the economic upturn played a major role as well. We should not forget that the Soviet zone led the world in economic growth figures in the same period. When Stalin died, the pressures from the cadres and skilled workers for what was then called a "thaw" led to Khrushchev's rise to power and his famous speech at the 20th Party Congress of the Communist Party of the Soviet Union, in which he launched the discussion about Stalin's faults and began to expand political rights within the Soviet system. The thaw, however, diminished the ability of the Soviet Union to control its satellite countries, just as the loss of relative advantage over western Europe and Japan reduced the capacity of the United States to require its camp to act more as satellites than as allies. The world had arrived at a revised geopolitical order: the slow but steady decline both of U.S. hegemony and of its collusive partner, the Soviet Union.

Meanwhile, both the United States and the Soviet Union were forced to back down on their insistence that neutralism was unacceptable. In 1955, at Bandoeng, twenty-nine countries of Asia and Africa met to proclaim the right of the so-called Third World to assert its political autonomy and to put forward its various economic and geopolitical demands. Above all, those in Bandoeng proclaimed the community of interests—the solidarity—of the "South" vis-à-vis the "North." It led, in turn, to the creation of various structures to implement solidarity, most significantly the group of self-proclaimed nonaligned nations.

The process of revision culminated in a worldwide political phenomenon, what may be called the world revolution of 1968 (which actually went from 1966 to 1970). On the surface, the revolution was a series of direct political actions conducted primarily by students and to a lesser extent by workers. There are two notable things about the world revolution of 1968. First of all, it occurred everywhere—in the pan-European world, in the socialist bloc, and in the Third World. Secondly, two underlying themes seemed to recur in all the local uprisings: one was a rejection of U.S. hegemony and a denunciation of the collusion of the Soviet Union in the world order that had been created by the United States (a repudiation of what the Chinese at the time called the two superpowers). The other was a denunciation of the so-called Old Left—the Communist parties, the social-democratic parties, and the movements of national liberation—for having failed to fulfill their promise of transforming the world when they came to power, and for having become more of an obstacle than an aid to further progress. While the originating movements of the world revolution of 1968 faded after a relatively short while, the geocultural impact of these two themes has persisted ever since. Skepticism about the erstwhile national liberation movements has been quite strong in Africa.

This geocultural shift was accompanied by, and to some extent caused by, a downturn in the world-economy that had begun in the 1970s. The enormous world economic expansion of the 1950s and 1960s had reached the limits of effective demand, and suddenly the world-economy had entered a Kondratieff B-phase: declining profits in the former leading industries; delocalization of production from the core zones to the semiperiphery; a turn to speculative financial activities as a source of immediate profit; and a significant rise in unemployment, most notably in the core zones. The downturn in the 1970s took the form of two new phenomena: a steep rise in the price of oil, and stagflation (that is, a combination of production stagnation and monetary inflation). Both had an enormous impact on Africa.

The rise in oil prices was brought about by the revision of policies by the Organization of Petroleum Exporting States (OPEC), an organization that included the major Arab oil-producing states, Iran, Indonesia, Nigeria, Angola, Venezuela, and Ecuador. Their decisions in 1973 and 1979 to adjust output and price so as to increase revenue significantly caused consternation on the world scene. The degree to which the U.S. government actually colluded in this price rise is an open question. Whatever the case, the consequences for the peripheral zones were clear.

The costs of all imports went up because of the rise in the cost of oil, especially given the general inflation of prices. At the same time, countries in the core zone cut back on their import of primary products coming from the peripheral zones because of the stagnation, which led to a decline in overall production (the result both of overproduction and the rise in oil price). This meant that most African countries (and others, of course, as well) found themselves in an economic squeeze and suffered a major maladjustment in their balance of payments. The national budgets, as well as the level of income of the mass of the population, was hurting.

At the same time, the oil price increases had led to swelled incomes of the oil-producing states, which could not spend all their gains immediately and so deposited them in mostly U.S. and German banks. The banks in turn needed to invest their money somewhere. They began to offer loans to the states in budgetary trouble—not only in Africa, to be sure, but in Latin America, Asia, and, let us not forget, countries of the Soviet Bloc. The governments in these regions were happy to accept the loans, which solved some of their immediate difficulties. But loans have a funny way of leading to a demand for repayment. By 1980, accumulated debt was beginning to become so high that many governments found it difficult, even impossible, to continue to service them. Suddenly the world was talking of a debt crisis.

Meanwhile, the decline of the moral legitimacy of the Old Left, which was in power in much of the peripheral zone, combined with the debt crisis led to the virtual abandonment of the ideology of "developmentalism" by the world community. In 1970 everyone had assumed that so-called underdeveloped countries had somehow to use their state machineries to try to "catch up" with the wealthier parts of the world. Indeed, the United Nations had proclaimed the 1970s to be the Decade of Development. But by 1980, a major ideological counteroffensive had begun. Developmentalism itself was now being attacked as the prime obstacle to economic growth. The world began to talk of neoliberalism and then of globalization.

In practice, what this meant is that countries in the peripheral zone were being adjured to abandon any and all forms of protectionism (including that of "infant industries") as well as to downgrade any form of national welfare programs and replace with policies that allowed their border to be open to foreign imports and financial investment. The countries in debt, which included most countries in Africa, were told by the

International Monetary Fund (IMF) that, if they expected to receive any assistance in handling the debt problem, they had to engage in structural adjustment, that is, adhere to the new injunctions of neoliberal globalization as proclaimed by the IMF, the U.S. and British governments, and the so-called Washington Consensus. "There is no alternative" (TINA), said Prime Minister Margaret Thatcher of Great Britain.

In the 1980s and 1990s, most African governments (and other governments in the peripheral zone) felt forced to bend their policies to accommodate the new exigencies. Even governments based on movements with a very strong history of developmentalist rhetoric—such as Frelimo in Mozambique and the African National Congress in South Africa—modified their real policies in this direction. The new policies were supposed to permit the renewal of economic growth in the peripheral zones. However, very few African countries saw a positive result from giving in to these demands. On the contrary, the new policies led quite often to the dismantlement of some of the few economic achievements gained from the previous policies of these same governments or of the policies of the colonial regimes in the post-1945 period.

At this point a worldwide reaction began to occur, which today we call variously the movement for global justice or the altermondialization movement. The movement did not start in Africa, but initially in the Americas and Europe. It was marked by three major moments. First, on January 1, 1994, the very day the North American Free Trade Association (NAFTA) treaty was to go into effect, an obscure group of indigenous people in Chiapas, in the south of Mexico, launched the Zapatista uprising—demanding local autonomy from the Mexican government and calling on worldwide support for their opposition to the neoliberal offensive. While the military aspects of this uprising soon were suspended, the Zapatistas remain a major force in Mexican life.

Meanwhile, the neoliberal offensive continued with the construction of the World Trade Organization (WTO), whose mission was to enforce the ideology of free trade and the presumably unstoppable form of globalization that it was said to represent. To everyone's surprise, at the key WTO meeting in Seattle in 1999, a popular movement arose to oppose this, and the demonstrations were so stormy as to successfully hamper the agenda of the meeting. The WTO has never quite recovered from the event. Furthermore, a pattern of popular demonstrations at such intergovernmental meetings has spread far and wide.

Finally, the growing sentiment of hostility to neoliberalism led to the creation in 2001 of the World Social Forum, which met initially at Porto Alegre, Brazil, and which now meets annually. The 2007 meeting is scheduled to be held in Africa. The World Social Forum brings together movements of every kind that are opposed to neoliberalism and imperialism in all its forms. The meetings themselves proceed in the form of an "open space"—a horizontal assembling of movements from everywhere, as opposed to the kind of vertically integrated international structures of the Old Left.

The spirit of Porto Alegre has infused some of the governments of the Third World with optimism. Specifically, in 2003, at the meeting of the WTO in Cancun, a so-called Group of 20, led by Brazil, India, China, and South Africa, posed clear conditions to the North: "If you want the South to open its frontiers to the North, there has to be real reciprocity. The North has to open its frontiers particularly to the agricultural and industrial products of the South." This, of course, was crucially important to a number of African countries, especially those that have been hurt by the trade barriers in the United States and western Europe. The African countries gave their full support to the G-20. The meeting in Cancun ended in a stalemate, and the WTO stalemate continues still.

One other question remains: what about the economic performance of Africa, in relation to other parts of the periphery (Latin America, the Caribbean, South and Southeast Asia, the Middle East, even east and central Europe). There seems little question that, by and large, Africa has profited the least among these countries during the last thirty or so years of the twentieth century. No simple explanation exists as to why this is so.

Let us start, however, with one general observation about the operations of the capitalist world-economy: during a downturn in the world-economy (and there may be said to have been one in the whole last thirty years of the twentieth century), many kinds of economic activities are shifted from the core zone to various semiperipheral countries, but in a way that is not evenly distributed. There is never enough "economic room," and such relocation always shifts to a few particular areas, which are thus the primary beneficiaries of the world relocation of industrial production. It is quite clear that East and Southeast Asia have been the primary loci of the recent relocation, and have therefore seen the clearest economic advantages from the shifts.

Why it occurred in this zone rather than in some other zone can be found in many factors: the prior levels of social and economic structure, strategic factors, and aggressive state policies, among others. However, it is important to bear in mind that not all countries will see this kind of improved economic situation simultaneously, even if they were to follow identical state policies. It is also important to notice that, in a sort of compensating way, when some new zones "develop" in this way, the national incomes of other countries tend to decline in a complementary way. This is what has happened in much of Africa, but not only there.

Where will Africa be moving in the twenty-first century? It is hard to predict in detail. It depends first of all on the direction the entire world-system will be taking in the twenty-first century. If the world-system is in a structural crisis and the first half of the twenty-first century is an age of transition, as I have argued at length elsewhere (in *Utopistics, or Historical Choices of the Twenty-first Century*, 1998), will the result be a plus or minus for Africa? To begin with, the structural crisis will involve the meeting ground of three quite separate struggles, two of which are continuations of the struggles within the world-system as we know it now, and one of which portends the future.

The first struggle is the economic and geopolitical struggle among the three major loci of accumulation, the so-called Triad of the United States, Western Europe, and East Asia. This struggle has been going on since at least the 1970s and has taken a more acute form since the collapse of the Soviet Union in 1991. To the extent that this struggle is active and unresolved, African countries will gain some extra margin of maneuver (as some of them are in the process of discovering now). Their ability to profit from this margin of maneuver is a function not merely of state policies but of the degree to which economic factors (both natural resources and productive output) are important to any or all three loci of accumulation. This, in turn, depends on what African states do to make themselves significant niches in the world-economy.

The second ongoing struggle in the world-system is between North and South. We need to remember that the North is composed precisely of the three major loci of accumulation. To the extent that producers in the North can limit their infighting to concentrate on their common interests vis-à-vis the South, Africa will face difficulty. But, on the other hand, to the extent that African states can enter into political alliances with other parts of the South, they stand to benefit by new arrangements. This tendency was demonstrated in the support African states gave the G-20 in the WTO negotiations at Cancun in 2003 and subsequently.

Neither of these two struggles is the crucial one. If we are indeed in an age of transition, the result will be, to use the language of the sciences of complexity, a world-system that will be oscillating wildly and lead to a bifurcation (in which at least two quite different outcomes could result) in a new stabilization, a new world-system. Which one it will be is intrinsically impossible to know. On the other hand, all of us, by our actions, will contribute directly to the outcome. This is the struggle between the spirit of Porto Alegre, which is seeking to achieve a new world order that is relatively democratic and relatively egalitarian, and the forces that incarnate the privileged of the present order. The latter may well see that the present order cannot survive, but they will seek to replace it with an order that is equally (or more) hierarchical and polarizing.

The fate of Africa lies primarily in the outcome of this struggle. Africa is as capable as any other region of the world of understanding the alternatives that are before us all, and acting upon them all. But, as in all such situations, the question is always what they will actually put in practice. At that point one should stop talking of Africa and start talking of Africans. Africans are many and do not all share the same interests, the same utopias, the same visions of how to reconstruct the world. There is no reason Africans should be seen as, or act as, a homogeneous mass. The historical choices before us are not defined geographically but rather in terms of what kind of substantively rational order we wish to construct. What one can say is that the present world-system has dealt Africa a bad hand. It is possible, but by no means certain, that the situation for Africans could turn out to be far better in the world-system that emerges at the end of this era of transition.

April 2005

Independence

To Ruth

AND

To the young people of Africa
who are forging their future as they deem wise
and who thereby merit our respect

CONTENTS

"The wind of change is blowing through [Africa], and whether we like it or not this growth of national consciousness is a political fact. We must all accept it as a fact, and our national policies must take account of it."   Prime Minister Harold Macmillan
Speech to Houses of Parliament of the
Union of South Africa
February 3, 1960

"It is not Africa which should be asked whether it belongs to one camp or another; it is rather to the two camps, to the East and to the West, that we must put the question which we consider as fundamental and of paramount importance: Yes or no, are you for the liberation of Africa?"   President Sékou Touré
Address to General Assembly of
the United Nations
November 5, 1959

Dark Africa?
Who nursed the doubtful child
Of civilization
On the wand'ring banks
Of life-giving Nile,
And gave to the teeming nations
Of the West
A Grecian gift!
From the poem, *"Africa Speaks"*
by Michael Dei-Anang

INTRODUCTION

The rapid political developments in Africa in the last five years have made Africa a familiar subject to the reader of newspapers and magazines. The early personal accounts of European travelers, missionaries and administrators have ceded place both to an ever-increasing number of serious monographs by scholars and to surveys and compendia, many of which unfortunately, and perhaps inevitably, become outdated almost as quickly as they are published.

This book is neither an account of travel nor a monograph nor a survey. It is an interpretative essay that seeks to place within an overall perspective the whole range of modern political developments on the African continent. I have hoped to assist the general reader in understanding the day-by-day developments in African countries by enabling him to fit the confusing array of men and events into the framework of general patterns.

For the serious student of African affairs and of political sociology, I have tried to use the empirical analysis of recent African history to throw some light on general propositions. In particular, I have been interested in two central questions in the analysis of society.

First of all, I have been concerned with the ways in which social structures—in this case, colonial administrations—generate within themselves social conflict, and under what conditions this social conflict results in a revolution which overthrows the structure. This question is dealt with primarily in Chapters II–IV on the colonial era.

Secondly, I have been concerned with the ways in which social structures, especially new ones—in this case, the independent African states—hold themselves together, acquire the loyalty of their subjects in a complex economy where the interests of the citizens vary widely. These questions are dealt with in various ways in Chapters V–IX.

Throughout both parts of the book, I have asked the questions: To whom are political allegiances owed? What makes men shift their allegiances from one group to another, from one set of rules to another? How can some men get others to shift their allegiances? In the process of shifting allegiances, what causes resistance and what facilitates the shift? Finally, how can shifts of allegiances be made relatively durable?

These are primarily political questions, then, with which I am concerned. This does not mean that economic factors are unimportant or negligible. This does mean that the focus of this essay will be on the political structures, on the levers of power, including the ideologies of both rulers and dissenters. Purely economic questions such as the natural resources of Africa, the ways in which these resources might most rapidly be developed, and the monetary policies of the new African states will not be considered, except insofar as they reflect or are an integral part of the political process. This is, of course, an extremely difficult line to draw, perhaps an arbitrary one. However, the major concerns of this essay have now been indicated, and the reader will expect that the material to be included has been selected on the basis of its relevance to these major concerns.

This essay, furthermore, in two senses does not pretend to be complete. It will not give the reader much of the story of the developments in any particular African country, and it will give him only to a limited extent the modern political history of the African continent as a whole. This essay attempts only to put forward some hypotheses, to indicate their connections with each other, and to give some suggestive evidence based on African political history. The general statements will usually be illustrated by specific examples, but these examples are not intended to be exhaustive. The essay, in other words, does not provide definitive evidence in favor of its hypotheses. For this, a longer work, based probably on a wider geographical base and certainly requiring much empirical research not yet done, would have to be undertaken.

There are two warnings the reader would do well to bear in mind. First, because the purpose of the essay is twofold—to indicate what is going on in Africa, and to analyze some more general social processes—the statements are of two sorts. There are some which concern a single entity, the African continent, and are necessarily descriptive and historical. This is true, for example, of Chapter I, which tells the pre-European history of Africa, and of part of the discussion of the history of pan-Africanism in modern times. Other statements, probably the majority, use as the unit under discussion the African colony or independent state, of which there are several dozen. These statements are generalizations, true of the large majority. Where there are important exceptions to the rule, they are usually indicated.

This brings us to the second warning. There are some standard exceptions that should be made in advance. Liberia and Ethiopia were at practically no point in the modern era under European colonial rule. Therefore, while certain general statements about the effects of urbanization and modernization apply, neither country knew a colonial administration, and consequently neither saw the rise of a nationalist movement to gain its independence. Many of the generalizations, therefore, do not apply to these so-called "old independent states." Furthermore, Libya obtained its independence in 1950 not because of internal developments but because Italy lost the Second World War, and the victors agreed on Libya's independence as the best way of minimizing each other's role in Libya's future. Many statements, therefore, do not apply to Libya.

Most of the statements in Chapters V–IX apply only to *independent* African nations, but not to the Republic of South Africa,* where a white settler minority rules. As of the writing of this book, it seems likely that the remaining nonindependent states of Africa will become independent within several years. It is my expectation that the problems these new states will face and the manner in which they will face them will not differ substantially from what we have seen heretofore in those African states presently independent.

Lastly, it has been my decision to include within the scope of this book all of Africa, as defined by the physical geographers. The size of the appropriate group about which to generalize has itself been a matter of considerable debate among scholars and politicians. Some write about Tropical Africa from the Sahara to the Limpopo River, thus excluding Arab North Africa and the Republic of South Africa. Others write about Africa South of the Sahara, thus excluding only the North. And some write about Africa. The reasons for my choice for this book will, I trust, become clear to the reader in the arguments of the essay itself.

The interpretation of contemporary history is im-

* Known until July 1, 1961 as the Union of South Africa.

portant for those who wish to advance knowledge in the social sciences because much more extensive and controllable data is available here than from the study of past history. But it is equally important for men who wish to understand their world in order to act upon it. These two tasks are not separable ones. For if knowledge may be distorted when we try to adapt it to the needs of contemporary man, it nevertheless finds its ultimate justification in aiding him rationally to determine the ways to his own betterment. This essay seeks to contribute to both tasks simultaneously.

CARTHAGE

MEDITERRANEAN SEA

SAHARA

• Garamantes

EGYPT

• Tassili

Nile R.

Napata •

RED SEA

Timbuktu •

SONGHAY

• Gao

• Meroë

GHANA

MALI

• Djenné

Niger R.

?

ASHANTI

OYO

DAHOMEY

ETHIOPIA

BENIN

BAMUN

Congo R.

GULF OF GUINEA

ATLANTIC OCEAN

CONGO

AZANIANS

INDIAN OCEAN

• Benametapa

Great
Zimbabwe

Limpopo R.

• Mapungubwe

PRECOLONIAL AFRICA

(Arrows indicate some principal routes
of migration, conquest, and trade)

: I :

AFRICA BEFORE

THE EUROPEANS CAME

Africa has greatness in her past as well as her present. In the past, the history of the world has often been written as though it were the history of Europe, including its precursors and its extensions. Of all the areas of the world, Africa has been the most neglected by historians, who have indeed often denied that there was any history in Africa to study. As late as 1951, a British historian wrote: "Until the very recent penetration by Europe the greater part of the [African] continent was without the wheel, the plough and the transport animal, almost without stone houses or clothes except for skins; without writing and so without history."

Without writing and so without history—this was the theme. Yet it is not true that there was no writing; and even if it were, it would not then follow that there was no history. For history exists wherever man exists, and the history of the peoples of Africa has been one of variety and invention, of skills in art and government. It is a history at least as old as that of Europe, at least as interesting if less known, and some would argue as impressive.

This book is not concerned with all of African history.

It is an interpretation of *modern* African history—how European colonial rule abetted the process of modernization and nurtured nationalism; and how African nations, having regained their independence from Europe, are seeking to further the process of modernization. Yet, in order to appreciate modern Africa adequately, we should start by taking a brief look at Africa before the Europeans came. We do this for two reasons. First, the reader ought to be aware that Africa does indeed have a history, one to which contemporary nationalists make increasing reference, as we shall see. Second, in some ways, the facts of pre-European history partially determine the patterns of modern Africa. The reader may thus find it helpful to know the ancient historical elements that lie behind some aspects of modern African politics. This chapter serves as a rapid survey of Africa's pre-European history.

A history of Africa must start with Egypt. I say "must," although a few years ago many writers would have argued that Egypt was part of a Middle Eastern world, a cradle of Western civilization. But in these last few years, some Africans have sought to reclaim Egypt for Africa and to assert that the ancient Egyptians, builders of temples and of monuments, scientists and religious thinkers, were Negroes. That this question is a matter of scholarly debate is an important reflection of contemporary African history. That Egyptian civilization, be it white or Negro or both, made its influence felt southward into Africa as well as northward into Europe is an important base line for the study of ancient African history.

It perhaps would not matter who the Egyptians were, had such an issue not been made of it during the period of European colonization. As we shall see later, the nonexistence of Negro achievements was fundamental to colonial ideology, which attempted to attribute all signs of human accomplishment to Egyptians, or Hittites, or Phoenicians, or Arabs, or Hamites, and never to Negroes. It was assumed, or implied, or indeed on occasion boldly asserted that Egyptians or Hittites or Phoenicians or Arabs or Hamites were white men, or at least whiter men than the Negroes. We shall return to this issue later in the context of colonialism and nationalism. Suffice it to say now, for the purpose of discussing the African past, that the best evidence of today seems to indicate a very great racial intermingling, in Africa as elsewhere, over the past five thousand years, and that the "Egyptians" or "Hamites" of yesteryear might well find themselves classified as Negroes today, in precisely those countries where such classifications matter. Suffice it further to note that many of the archaeological remains of which we shall speak, at first credited to "Arabs" or "Hamites," have on closer, or less biased, inspection, turned out to be unmistakably Negro-African in origin.

But let us return to Egypt. As the Egyptians turned south, they came upon a people called the Kushites, who seem to have inhabited what is now southern Egypt and the northern part of the Sudan somewhere between 800 B.C. and 300 A.D. Their early center, Napata, gave way in the sixth century B.C. to Meroë. The ruins of Meroë, which are quite extensive, show the flourishing of a Bronze Age. Meroë became a center for the smelting and the manufacture of iron. Our records concerning Meroë are hieroglyphs not yet deciphered, but it is clear that Meroë was a major African center of its time, and that its contributions were not only in the fields of manufacture and trade but as a center for the exchange of ideas, of religious concepts, of technical knowledge.

It may be that Meroë provides the historical link between Egyptian culture and the peoples of the Western Sudan,* which so much legend and harder evidence

* The Western Sudan is not the western half of the Republic of the Sudan, formerly called the Anglo-Egyptian Sudan; it is an area in West Africa on the same latitude as the Sudan. Largely

seems to argue existed. Was the use of iron first brought to Chad and Nigeria from Meroë, or did it come down from Libya? We are not yet sure. We do know that there were important waves of migration westward from the region of Meroë to the Western Sudan. This migration went on over a period of centuries, maybe longer, and established a trans-African route eastward which is still used today by African Moslems, making the pilgrimage of piety to Mecca.

Further west in the Sahara, on the rocks and in the canyons of the Tassili Mountains, paintings have been discovered which show Egyptian-style boats and two-wheeled chariots. And such rock paintings are being discovered straight southward across the Sahara. These naturalistic portraits, painted by ancient Negro peoples, seem to date back beyond 3000 B.C. And in Nigeria we have today many terra-cotta heads of great artistry which date at least to 900 B.C. This is the "Nok" culture.

At the same period of time that Meroë flourished, the city of Carthage in North Africa was born and grew to challenge Rome, and ultimately to be defeated. This story has perhaps been better known than that of Meroë. Carthage seems to have existed since the ninth century B.C. and to have conquered much of the rest of what is today Tunisia about the fifth century B.C.

During the early period, Carthage not only pushed forward into Europe through Spain but made contact through the Libyan desert with Garamantes, in what is today called the Fezzan (southern Libya). It is thought that caravans took thirty days to make the journey, and that the people of Garamantes may themselves have engaged in trade with the Western Sudan.

Carthage was of course conquered by Rome. And Rome proceeded to "Romanize" North Africa, as later

---

grasslands merging into desert, it includes the present-day republics of Mauritania, Mali, Upper Volta, Niger, Chad, and the Northern Region of Nigeria.

Europe would seek to "Westernize" all of Africa.
Christianity, too, spread along with Roman power,
although the Christian missionaries of those days were
not, at least at first, related to the imperial power in
the same way as the Christian missionaries of a later
era.

The collapse of the Roman empire in the West
brought the Vandals to Morocco in the fifth century
A.D. And the slow disintegration of Byzantium permitted the Arab conquest of North Africa in the
seventh century.

The Arab empire in its turn began to splinter, allowing once again the beginnings of autonomous states,
some say the resurgence of anarchy, in North Africa.
During this period of Arab conquest, and even before,
there existed in the Western Sudan the first (as far as
we know today) of its great Negro empires. We know
comparatively little about any earlier period in West
Africa because we have as yet discovered no relevant
written documents. But the great period of the Western
Sudan, the era of its medieval kingdoms, has fortunately had its chroniclers, who wrote mostly in Arabic.
The oldest document is by Wahb Ibn Munabbeh and
was written in 738 A.D. But the two most important
sources are the *Tarikh-es-Sudan*, written around 1655
by Abderrahman es Sadi of Timbuktu, an African of
the Fulani people, and the *Tarikh-es-Fettach*, written
about 1600 by Mahmoud Kati, also a Negro of
Timbuktu. In addition we have the testimony of that
great fourteenth-century Arab traveler, Ibn Battuta,
and a sixteenth-century African Christian convert, Leo
Africanus. It is a serious commentary on European
provincialism and the state of medieval Europe's
knowledge of its world that though the kingdoms of the
Western Sudan began in 400 A.D., Europeans seem to
have remained unaware of their history or even their
existence until 1400, a gap of a thousand years. Once
Europe heard of them, Europeans began to glorify their

wealth and exotic qualities. It is from this period that the perhaps exaggerated legends of Timbuktu originate. The disillusionment of nineteenth-century European travelers with this region is in part a function of the illusion their European ancestors were responsible for creating.

The kingdoms of the Western Sudan—Ghana, Mali, Songhay—were remarkable in the degree to which they were able to establish complex political structures that centralized the government of large areas of West Africa. Political superiority here, as often elsewhere, was based on a technological advantage. The ancient empire of Ghana, which was probably founded about 300 A.D., could conquer its neighbors because it knew the use of iron. But having built an empire by their weapons, the people of Ghana maintained it by trade and tribute. For ancient Ghana lay at an important crossroads, between the salt deposits to the north and the gold deposits to the south. Ghana sought, with increasing success, to dominate both resources and monopolize the trade in them. The empire of Ghana stimulated and maintained the flow of trade at a period when the economy of Western Europe was particularly stagnant, the period known as the "Dark Ages."

Toward the eleventh century, a group of Negro Moslems, living in a monastery at the mouth of the Senegal River, created a purified and disciplined version of Islam. These men were called the Almoravids and, under their impulsion, tribes of veiled nomads and blacks rode north and established a new dynasty in Morocco that has survived until today. The Almoravids were crusading warriors of Islam and in 1054 came south again from Morocco. By 1076, they had conquered the capital of Ghana, thus ending the flourishing trade. The political structure of Ghana collapsed.

Indeed the very cities disappeared and the population was to some extent scattered. In recent years some men have argued that the Akan peoples of present-day

Ghana, a thousand miles to the southeast, are the descendants of the inhabitants of ancient Ghana, who migrated south before advancing hostile peoples.

During the thirteenth century, in approximately the same area, a new empire arose, that of Mali or Melle. Sundiata Keita overthrew the rulers of Ghana, then much in decline, and founded a new dynasty. The emperors of Mali were Moslems, and their reign saw the further spread of Islam in West Africa. Mali was not the only centralizing state in the area. There were many principalities and aspiring empires, and there was a constant back-and-forth of conquest and reconquest. What distinguished Mali was its superior skill in the steady organization of centralizing power. Mali was renowned for the extent of its trade, the success of its warfare, the expanding use of metals in war and industry. It utilized currencies of gold or copper or shells.

When the Emperor Mansa Musa made a pilgrimage to Mecca in 1324, he was said to have been accompanied by 60,000 persons and 12,000 slaves dressed in brocade and pure silk. To dispense the alms expected of the pilgrim, the emperor brought with him eighty loads of gold. It is told that every Friday he stopped his caravan and built a mosque. On his return from Mecca, he brought with him a Spanish architect to build him splendid palaces.

Mali's cities, Timbuktu and Djenné, were the focal centers of a wide network of caravans coming from all points of the horizon. We know, for example, that by 1400 the caravans crossing the Sahara to Mali by one of six routes during one year included over 12,000 camels. If the pilgrimage to Mecca was not a common phenomenon, neither was it a rare one. Especially did the professors of the various Moslem seats of learning travel, and thus it was that Timbuktu exchanged learned men with Cordoba.

The Moslem empire of Mali was challenged in the fifteenth century by the Songhay people, rulers of a

small Moslem state, whose capital was Gao. Songhay
was to become the largest kingdom of them all. At its
apogee, Songhay was perhaps the size of the continental
United States, perhaps five times the size of the Holy
Roman Empire at its largest. It covered all the Western
Sudan from what is today Rio de Oro to Chad. It
reached south as far as the forest line. It could go no
further because its power depended on horses. It extended north well into present-day Algeria and Tunisia.
It covered southwest Libya, almost reaching the
Mediterranean near Benghazi.

Islam deserves at least as much credit as a factor in
this extensive political unification as Christianity does
for the Holy Roman Empire. Founded in the eleventh
century, Songhay was made by Sonni Ali in 1464 the
most powerful kingdom in the Western Sudan. Following him was Songhay's most famous ruler, Askia the
Great, who rose to power in 1493. It was in the regime
of Askia the Great that the boundaries of Songhay
reached their greatest extent. He was responsible for
establishing an administrative network that ensured
control of the wide-flung empire. When he made his
pilgrimage to Mecca, Askia the Great was perhaps less
lavish in alms and retinue than Mansa Musa, but he
included many more scholars, so as to enlarge their
knowledge. The University of Sankoré in Timbuktu
became the center of Muslim learning in Africa, but it
was only one of several universities. The practice of
medicine was much advanced, and doctors performed
some operations that were not known in Europe for
another 250 years. Knowledge of Arabic science and
literature was extensive.

Yet once again, armies from Morocco were to descend
and, this time by the use of muskets, destroy an empire.
In 1591 Songhay was defeated and by 1600 the empire
of Songhay was no more. As has happened often in history, not only were men and political structures destroyed, but books and treasures of learning. Never

again—until perhaps tomorrow?—was an empire like
that of Songhay to arise in the Western Sudan. There
would be smaller efforts in the eighteenth and nineteenth centuries—the Fulani emirates of Northern
Nigeria, the Mandingo conquests of Samory—but
these later attempts were to be circumscribed by a new
factor in West African politics, the armies of colonial
Europe.

As we move south into the forest regions of Africa,
we know less of what happened in history. There are no
Arabic documents going back before the fifteenth century. It is only with the arrival of the Portuguese along
the coast at this time that we have written documents,
and their reliability is limited by the fact that European
travelers in Africa at first restricted themselves to a few
port areas and relied on second-hand reports for information about the interior. Furthermore, forest soil is
often unconducive to the preservation of the objects
which archaeologists later seek to find.

Forests are not as easy to traverse as savanna or even
desert, and the area of governments could not be as
extended as in the Western Sudan. Still, some impressively complex governments were evolved in Ashanti
and Dahomey, Oyo and Benin, Bamun and Congo.
Our knowledge of these kingdoms is due to the fact that
some still exist today or existed until very recently, and
anthropologists have been able to reconstruct their
history. In the last fifty years, the world has come to
know the bronzes of the Yoruba peoples of Western
Nigeria or of Benin, the gold weights of Ashanti, the
masks of the Senufu or Baule.

When we measure the achievements of these societies
—and lack of them among other tribal groups—we
must do it against the background of the fact that since
1444, the only period about which we know anything
much at all, millions of Africans, often the healthiest
among them, have been taken out of Africa by the
slave trade. It is hard to overestimate the havoc—

direct and indirect—this trade caused or how it corrupted area after area of Africa. The Europeans and
the Arabs, by creating and sustaining this trade, were
in part responsible for the decline of higher culture in
tropical Africa which later generations of Europeans
were to deplore.

The other great arena of African achievement was
centered on the eastern coast of Africa, starting from
present-day Kenya down to the Transvaal and extending westward into Southern Rhodesia. And here, once
again thanks to Arabic chronicles, we have written
records. The oldest we know is a record of his travels by
al-Masudi, a native of Baghdad, who in 955 described
his voyage as far as Madagascar. And in 1154, al-Idrisi
wrote for a Norman king a second-hand account of life
on the east coast of Africa, which he compiled by research into existing sources. What they described were
flourishing Iron Age cultures engaged in wide trade
across the Indian Ocean.

The Indian Ocean played a role analogous to that of
the Sahara, permitting the diffusion of technology and
the expansion of trade, so as to provide the economic
and technological base on which to build strong centralized states. Trade with Greece, Alexandria and
Rome probably can be traced at least to the first century A.D., and by the time our first chroniclers wrote,
Arab traders were installed as far south as present-day
Mozambique, as they were in South Asian and Chinese
ports. Thus it was that India was the most important
market and supplier for East Africa, a link that still
exists in altered form today. Indian beads found in
East Africa date back to the eighth century A.D. While
the Indians sold textiles in Africa, Africa exported iron
to India and ivory to China, and gold and tortoise shell
to both. And Africa even sold slaves as early as the
seventh century A.D. to Mesopotamia (for we know of
slave revolts), but slave trading was at that time not
the central focus of trade which it was to become in the

nineteenth century. China's expansion touched Africa even before the arrival of the white men. Chinese mariners certainly landed in East Africa in the fifteenth century, and we have found in Africa Chinese coins and porcelain of the twelfth century.

What kinds of cultures were these that had such far-flung trading partners? Ethiopia is not, properly speaking, one of these cultures, but recent archaeological findings seem to indicate a closer relationship between Ethiopia and these cultures than we previously suspected, so it is perhaps well to remind ourselves of Ethiopia's history. Ethiopia, perhaps more than any other part of Africa, in the eyes of the Western world has been surrounded with legend—beginning with the one that it was founded in 1000 B.C. by King Solomon's son and the Queen of Sheba. Our authentic records go back only to the first century A.D., and it was in the fourth century that Coptic Christianity was introduced. The arrival of Islam in the seventh century cut the Ethiopians off from the coast and caused the kingdom's decline. The restoration of the Solomonian line in 1270 led to a political, cultural and literary revival. It was about this time that the legend of Prester John, that mythical and fabulous Christian king, began to spread in Europe. In the sixteenth century the Portuguese arrived and Jesuit priests followed, to be expelled in the seventeenth century. Ethiopia was not merely a kingdom which by its cohesion survived two thousand years. It was a culture which developed the hillside terracing that contemporary agronomists have rediscovered as indispensable to a rational agriculture in this part of the world.

Terracing and the art of building in dry stone—another Ethiopian achievement—seem to be shared with (to have been exported to?) the other cultures of East and Central Africa. We find it, for example, in the so-called Azanian civilization of Kenya, which is thought to have started between 500 and 700 A.D. As

the tribal legends of many of the West Africans tell
of migrations from the east (Meroë?), so the histories
of East African tribes speak of migration from north to
south (Meroë through Ethiopia?). The Azanians seem
to come to an end about 1500. Why? The fourteenth
century seems to have been a time of invasions from
pastoral nomads, whose impact on the settled agricultural peoples seems to parallel the impact of Moroccan
conquests of Ghana and Songhay. Destructive of the
political systems, the agricultural techniques, and
scorning manual work, they left little of continuing
value in their wake. The Indian Ocean trade that sus-
tained these civilizations was coming into sharp decline
because of European expansion.

Further south, in the present-day Rhodesias and
Mozambique, was Zimbabwe culture. This included
many states built around stone forts. The Portuguese
encountered the Monomotapa, king of Benametapa,
in the sixteenth century, and his kingdom spread from
the hinterland of Mozambique through Rhodesia. But
the earliest-known kingdom may date from 500 A.D.
The Mapungubwe site in the Transvaal seems to have
been settled before 900 A.D., Great Zimbabwe itself in
the thirteenth century.

Great Zimbabwe, now the most famous ruins in
southern Africa, once the center of a controversy about
the role of the Negro in African history, is not too far
from Salisbury, present-day capital of Southern Rhodesia. The two outstanding buildings have been named
—by Europeans—the "Acropolis" and the "temple"
(or "elliptical building"). From a distance the "elliptical
building," on the plain beneath the "Acropolis," takes
on the picture of a solid fortress, with strong battle-
ments. Using local granite, the people of Zimbabwe
constructed a complex building, 300 feet long, 220 feet
broad, whose walls were 20 feet thick and 30 feet tall.
The stepped recesses and covered passages, the gate-
ways and the platforms were all hewed out elaborately,
and inside, all about, were soapstone bird-gods.

We might know more today about what was produced by the gold smelters of Zimbabwe had the British South Africa Company not given a concession to a prospector in 1895 to exploit the ruins. By the time he was stopped in 1902 the copper and gold objects were largely destroyed and melted down. Fortunately, more recently, we have discovered similar objects at Mapungubwe, unravaged by Europeans with a civilizing mission, and we can guess at what we have lost.

The various societies that were the Zimbabwe culture lasted at least a thousand years. They constructed in stone both defensive sites and dams for irrigation. They raised cattle, sowed grain, and traded across the Indian Ocean. Their chiefs enjoyed fine pottery or china, possessed gold ornaments, wore beads from India.

It was a warring culture. Or why would they have needed forts? The societies were highly stratified, with specialized craftsmen and miners, chiefs and priests. There was no system of writing, although Arabic served the coastal areas as Latin did Europe. And Swahili spread as did European vernaculars. Currencies were in use and trade was extensive. Even after the decline of the Zimbabwe kingdoms, there was no anarchy. Later missionaries were to comment on the comparative peace and security that reigned in the interior, at least in those parts less affected by the slave trade.

Yet of course this civilization did decline. These kingdoms had long been fighting off barbarian invaders. The Portuguese intruders, moreover, sacked the coastal cities and thereby sharply reduced the Indian Ocean trade, and this seems to have been a severe blow to the Zimbabwe peoples. The Portuguese with their firearms sallied into the interior, taking sides without too much knowledge (an error to be repeated by others in twentieth-century Africa?), and succeeded in undermining the whole structure. They were too weak to establish a colonial administration, only strong enough to destroy.

With the Portuguese in East Africa and in the Congo,

we enter a new era in African history. It becomes a story in which European skills and values, virtues and villainies play a major role. It is a story of how Africans reacted to their conquest by seeking to learn the secret of their weaknesses in order to reëstablish the autonomous control of their own destiny.

Before we tell this story, we should perhaps rapidly survey the kinds of social structures the Europeans did find when they came to conquer, to trade, and to preach. Every society was not Great Zimbabwe. The range was very wide. And the fact of colonial administration in each case had a somewhat different impact, depending on what was there before. Adequate categories of African tribes are difficult to establish, and for our purposes, less important than an outline of the dimensions along which tribal structures varied.

It is said that the government of tribes is based on kinship. Strictly speaking, this is seldom, perhaps never, true. It comes closest to being true among those small nomadic bands, found, say, among the Bushmen. At the other end of the continuum are those complex empires whose history we have been recounting, where the territorial (rather than ethnic) basis of government is clear. Each tribe, though, even if nomadic, does have an area it considers its own. Some Europeans challenged the veracity of this and sometimes appropriated land that was "unowned." Later, however, anthropologists demonstrated that land was rarely "unowned."

The extent of land, the number of people involved, and the cultural homogeneity of the group within one political community naturally varied. So did the organizing principle of the kinship system. Some systems were patrilineal but many, unlike societies in the Western world, were matrilineal. When more and more land was turned to the production of crops for a money market, the principle of inheritance mattered greatly.

Religious systems varied widely. Some of these systems, as we are only discovering today, attained a very

impressive complexity in the elaboration of their cos-·
mological ideas. The complexity of the religious con-
ceptions was not necessarily related to the complexity
of the political structure. For example, one of the most
celebrated African cosmologies is that of the Dogon
(located in present-day Mali), whose society is without
commandment or police force and maintains a minimum
of social differentiation. The degree to which religious
and political functions were vested in the same man or
group of men differed, although almost everywhere the
chief had some religious role.

The splitting of religious and political functions, like
the degree of social stratification of the tribe, often
derived from patterns of conquest. As we have seen,
the African continent knew great migrations of peoples,
experienced many conquests. When the Europeans
arrived they found many situations comparable to that
of the emirates of Northern Nigeria, where a small
Fulani "aristocracy" had installed themselves as rulers
over Hausa communities. In some areas the degree of
integration was greater than in others. Sometimes the
European colonial administration would side with the
indigenous rulers and sometimes with the others.

Tribes would differ, perhaps most of all, in terms of
the role of the chief. The Asantehene or the Morho
Naba was the apex of a very complicated and extensive
hierarchy of rulers, reaching down through several tiers
to a village chief. They had courts and courtiers. At the
other extreme, there might be nothing but an ill-defined
gerontocracy, a village council with few judicial or
police powers. The chiefs who headed centralized kingdoms had men to assist them. There were wide ranges
in the functions of these men and in the way they were
recruited. Sometimes, as in medieval Europe or Japan,
the subordinate hierarchies were also hereditary.

All of these variations affected the privileges and
powers of the chief. Almost never could an African
chief be said to have absolute power. Sometimes the

constraints on his authority were so severe—when he was seldom allowed to leave his hut, or spoke to his people only through intermediaries—that it could be doubted he had any power at all. Normally decisions were the result of some consensus, though the process of consultation varied. Sometimes there were age groups to protect the interests of the "commoners," or sometimes "secret societies." In many tribes chiefs could be removed—in West Africa the word is "destooled." Later European colonial administrators sometimes destroyed the delicate balance of democratic controls. Succession was often hereditary, but even then, it might be hereditary only in the sense that the successor had to come from a certain lineage, so that there remained a wide range of choice for a new chief.

Africa before the Europeans came? It was neither anarchy nor barbarism, nor unchanged and unchanging villages. It was movement and splendor, conquests and innovations, trade and art. It was above all wide variety and much experimentation. There is no single or simple stereotype we can call "old Africa," against which we can measure how far Africa has evolved today. This is as true of Africa as of medieval Europe, where Roman gens and Scottish clan, Benedictine monk and Druid priest combined to form a varied backdrop against which the Reformation and the Renaissance, the Enlightenment and the Industrial Revolution, all evolved into a movement we have come to call modernization. Neither the multiplicity of European tribes, nor the multiplicity of African tribes, prevents us from seeing certain common features of social change which have occurred in modern times.

It is rewarding neither to denigrate nor to romanticize Africa's past. It can be rewarding to know it.

The Colonial Era

:II:

THE SOCIAL CHANGE

The expansion of Europe was part of the modernization of Europe. In the fifteenth century, the Portuguese first reached West Africa, then South and East Africa, to be followed soon thereafter by other European powers. Along one narrow strip alone, the shoreline of the Gold Coast, forts were established between the fifteenth and eighteenth centuries by Portugal, England, France, Holland, Denmark, Sweden, and Brandenburg.

At first Europeans came mainly to trade and were satisfied with outposts along the shoreline of Africa. This limited interest was reinforced in southern Africa by a geological fact. The coastal strip was very thin. As soon as one went into the interior, the land climbed rapidly above sea level and penetration became more difficult. The degree of evolution of Europe's economy also set limits on the extent of the trade. The raw materials that Europeans most sought—gold and ivory and slaves—were best provided by African intermediaries.

Along with traders came missionaries, and already in 1518 the Portuguese could celebrate in Rome the consecration of the first Negro bishop (at least since the days of early Christianity in North Africa), Henrique of the Congo, the son of the king. The missionaries came not to buy, but to sell. And so they were more inclined to push into the interior than the merchants.

Yet by and large they could not, with success, penetrate areas where they did not have the moral, material, and sometimes military support of other white men. That is why today Christianity is often strongest along the coastline, especially in West Africa.

Then, too, adventurers, soldiers, explorers came. They came to find new worlds, to track down ancient mysteries. And with them often came the flag. The merchants and missionaries also demanded the flag, for their safety, to reinforce their own positions. Still, at the beginning of the nineteenth century, very few parts of Africa were under European rule. The Portuguese colonies—Angola, Mozambique, Guinea, São Tomé e Principe—were already established. The Cape Colony, at the southern tip of Africa, had passed from Dutch to English rule in 1795. Senegal had become a French colony in the eighteenth century, and the Gambia and Sierra Leone became British colonies in the latter half of the eighteenth century. In each case, the area of the colony was much less extensive then than the area with the corresponding name today. The largest portion of the African continent was still self-governing. By 1880 the situation was not too different; only a few other coastal strips, such as the Gaboon, Lagos, the Gold Coast, and Algeria, had become colonial states. Suddenly, for reasons internal to Europe, there started a race to colonize all of Africa. This race was assigned legitimacy by the Congress of Berlin (1884–85), which laid out the ground rules whereby European powers would allow each other to divide up the African pie. By 1900 there was scarcely a corner of Africa that had escaped European rule. Liberia and Ethiopia were the two significant exceptions, and even Ethiopia had suffered an Italian protectorate from 1889–96.

The motivations that led individual Europeans to come to Africa, as settlers, as traders, as teachers, varied widely. There was the lure of adventure, the search for personal freedom, the sense of mission. There was greed and vanity and lust for power. The motives that led European powers to sanction expansion and to establish permanent colonial rule also varied. There was the search for markets and resources, the need for prestige and power, the sense of historic mission (as with some individuals). Whatever it was that brought about colonial rule, it is certain that once a colonial administration was established, something very important happened. For now all the things that men and groups did in Africa, they did within the context of the *colonial situation.*

By the term *colonial situation* we simply mean that someone imposes in a given area a new institution, the colonial administration, governed by outsiders who establish new rules which they enforce with a reasonable degree of success. It means that all those who act in the colony must take some account of these rules, and that indeed an increasing amount of each individual's action is oriented to this set of rules rather than to any other set, for example, the tribal set, to which he formerly paid full heed. The reason for this shift in orientation is very simple. Colonial administration, as opposed to the mere presence of European. traders or missionaries, meant precisely that ultimate power lay with this new government, and that this government tried systematically to inculcate in its subjects a feeling that this new power was legitimate. To a certain extent, this attempt to legitimate colonial rule in Africa was temporarily successful, partly because of the great physical power of the Europeans, partly because the social changes that colonial rule introduced produced changes in the attitudes of Africans, particularly the new elites, toward the colonial government.

What were these changes? There were many economic changes, first of all. In the late nineteenth and early twentieth centuries, the merchants of Liverpool and Bordeaux and Hamburg expanded their operations, and networks of trading houses grew up. The day of the great export-import house in Africa was beginning. Importing Manchester cloth, household wares, bicycles and other appurtenances of Western civilization, these companies became the major, often the only, channels for the export of raw materials. Nor were they satisfied, as were their forebears, with simply acquiring those precious goods that were readily available. They sought to stimulate their production. Southern Africa had the most profitable mineral deposits—gold and diamonds in the Transvaal, copper in Northern Rhodesia, diamonds and tin in the Congo—but there was mining in West Africa as well.*

Great trading networks, mines, *and* administrations needed men, African men, to do the work, at least all but the higher managerial tasks. They needed men, furthermore, who had some of the skills necessary to do the work, and some of the values that would make them willing to do it. And it was difficult at first to find large numbers of such men, particularly for work in the mines or the ports or on engineering projects.

While some African cultures had used sophisticated productive techniques and some were characterized by a market economy, the majority of the population everywhere was engaged in a subsistence economy. Even where African societies were complex kingdoms, the village remained the traditional center of African life. The frame of custom was strong. Money was relatively unimportant (sometimes nonexistent), as the internal economy of the village was communal. In the natural course of events, the villager would not leave his village. The new colonial economy, however, required manpower, and if the needs were to be met, the villagers had to be induced to leave their villages and come to town and mine compound to work. The towns were created because towns were, in Africa as through-

* In the period since World War II, vast new resources have been uncovered, such as oil in the Sahara, iron in Mauritania, and iron in Liberia.

out the world, efficient centers of administration, production and trade, and communications. A modern
economy required urban centers, and these centers
taught men urban, that is modern, values.

One way to induce men to leave villages was to force
them to do so. Slave trading by and large came to an
end in the middle of the nineteenth century, partly as
a result of humanitarian pressures in the Western
world, partly because slavery was no longer economic
in the advanced technologies of the nineteenth century.
Outright slavery was not used within Africa. But forced
labor was.* The usual method was for the colonial administration to give chiefs quotas to fill. Sometimes the
corvées were used on public projects, and sometimes on
the private enterprises of Europeans. As the years went
by, and Africans for various reasons were more willing
to enter the money economy, the recruitment methods
tended more toward persuasion. Indeed, in more recent
years, elaborate recruiting organizations have been
established to advertise the virtues of labor migration.

There were other ways of indirectly forcing men to
migrate to the towns. The appropriation of land by
European farmers, which occurred throughout settler
Africa (French North Africa, Kenya, Southern Rhodesia, the Union of South Africa), led in time, sometimes immediately, to land squeezes among Africans,
especially since Africans had been forced back onto less
productive lands. And a classic remedy for a land
squeeze, as anyone acquainted with recent European
history must remember, is emigration. The appropriation of land by European settlers occurred, however,
only where the climate was sufficiently moderate, the
land sufficiently fertile to make it worth the while of
white farmers. West and Equatorial Africa, for example,
had very few settlers, and in many areas there was

* It still is used in Portuguese Africa, in 1961, and in a variant
form (as punishment for violation of pass laws) in the Republic
of South Africa.

express legislation which forbade the alienation of land to Europeans.

There was another weapon of indirect pressure available to the colonial authorities, that of the head tax. The head tax, in one form or another, was introduced throughout Africa, and imposed often over serious African objection. In a village which lived on its own produce and used no currency, even the smallest tax raised a demand which could not be met within the village. Either the whole village would have to engage itself somehow in the money economy, or as happened more often because it was easier, the village had to ask some of its younger men to sally forth into the towns to earn the money that would enable the village to pay the head tax for all its citizens. Thus, the sentiment of community solidarity of the village, under the pressure of the colonial situation, led to the exporting of its men into a new and often alien world, a process which in its turn would usually lead to a breakdown of this very sentiment of community solidarity.

The colonial administration did not forever have to force men to migrate from the villages. After a while, the town itself lured them. They began to want the things the city has offered since it first was invented: the relative freedom from the pressures of one's neighbors, the opportunities for social advancement, the possibility of participation in a wider range of social activities. And they began to want the things that money could buy: material comforts, a longer and healthier life, contacts with a wider world.

These new values were the result, at least in part, of three major elements of colonial rule. For reasons internal to itself, and deriving from its own needs, colonial administration brought with it order, modern education, and improved transport and communications. Each of these was to play a major role in changing the perspectives of the African.

Order, of course, existed before the European came,

sometimes within very large areas. Often the first result
of European penetration was the breakdown of well-
established order. Still, colonial order was established
more or less in most parts of Africa by 1900, although
parts of Mauritania were officially "pacified" only as
late as 1934. After 1945, of course, the new disorder of
nationalist ferment was to begin throughout the continent.

Colonial order was new in that the colonial power
treated as one unit what had previously not been one,
an area usually a good deal larger than that of a particular tribe. Indeed, as has been observed before, colonial
boundaries quite often ran through the boundaries of
given tribes. European colonial order was also new in
that it introduced new cultural perspectives to the
African, which meant acquaintance with new ideas,
involvement in new groups, the possibility of new
movement.

Colonial order meant, first of all, that in this new
political unit larger than the tribe there was some possibility of safe movement. In some areas this was true for
the first time; in others this new freedom of movement
restored and reinforced a reality which had existed before. The fact of colonial order had a very important
impact on the psychology of the villager and hence on
the structure of control in the African village. The dis-
senter, the misfit, the rebel could now defy the chief
simply by moving out from under his control. He could
"escape" to the city. Needless to say, this often made
it possible to attract to town life precisely those people
with the initiative and imagination to break with tradition, to try new ways, to seek a better fortune outside
the path laid out for them. The best—and the worst—
came to the city, because there was a city to come to.

Order not only affected the chance of the deviant to
live his life in a context that suited him better; it also
affected the lives of whole classes of people in tribal
societies. For example, the tribal warrior—in many

tribes warriors were a separate social group, in some a
full-time occupation—became bereft of any useful function in his group. He could enlist in the army of the
colonial government. But if he did, he was fatally introduced to modern skills and values. In many African
countries where men enlisted, the returned ex-service-
man became not only a major agent of social change in
the village but, except when constantly and carefully
cultivated by the local administration, an early exponent of nationalist ideas.

In some tribes, warfare was linked to a boy's initia-
tion into manhood and his assumption of full responsibility in tribal life. Where the colonial administration
closed off this channel of testing virility and valor,
tribal societies had to invent alternatives. One possibility was to consider a stint in a mine equivalent to
achievements as a warrior. Some might argue that,
especially in the early days of colonial rule, this experience demonstrated far more than earlier tests one's
fitness to survive.

Order within the colony had another consequence. It
became possible for traders to move about or to resume
movement within the colony, where before warring
tribes forbade entry. Quite often in West as in East
Africa, the trading communities were Moslem; they
spread both the relatively modern values that their
commercial activities encouraged as well as Islam,
which, insofar as it was a world religious community,
involved its adherents in currents and ideas broader
and more modern than those of many African tribal
societies. Before the colonial era there were areas where
the expansion of Islam had been stopped by the force
of a strong animist kingdom; colonial rule allowed
Moslem traders (and preachers, for each Moslem is in
a limited sense called upon to be a preacher of his
religion) to enter for the first time.

Just as maintaining order was in the self-interest of
the colonial power, so too was the extension of modern

educational facilities to Africa; it was not a gratuitous gift of benevolent Europe. A modern economy, however limited in scope, needs men to run it, to work its mines, to staff its offices, to drive its vehicles. It needs not any men, but *trained* men. The colonial government needed such men; so did the private trading companies; so did the missions, the schools, and the hospitals. Schools for children are the most economical and effective way of producing them. Therefore schools were started everywhere. The Catholic and Protestant missionaries played an important role in the establishment of these schools, financing and staffing a larger percentage of them in African countries than in European countries. But the colonial governments everywhere established schools as well. In the Moslem areas (North Africa, Northeast Africa, large parts of the interior of West Africa), the colonial authorities often kept the missions out for fear of offending Moslem sensibilities.

Of course, educational facilities were not established exclusively for functional reasons. Ordinarily, there was no simple calculation made of how many people were needed to keep the economy going—although this happened more often than one would think—and therefore how many schools should be opened. There were many Europeans who "believed" in education. Some Christian missionaries saw it as a fundamental aspect of the process of conversion. Some colonial administrators felt they had a "civilizing mission." A passion was aroused for education for its own sake, which sometimes led to the creation of more educated Westernized men than were needed for the pace of economic development; and this caused strains in the structures of various colonies that contributed to the emergence of nationalist movements.

Colonial government also required the improvement and expansion of facilities for transportation and communication within the colony in order to assure efficient administration, the maintenance of order, and the maximization of economic growth and profit. Thus railroad lines were built, roads and airports constructed, telegraph wires installed. Economic rationality was, to be sure, conceived of only within the framework of a single colony, or at best within the framework of the colonies of a single colonial power. Thus we have the resulting mad pattern of today: two roads stopping five miles from each other with no connection because of a boundary line, as between the Congo and Uganda; two railroad lines, parallel to each other and not too distant, running from port to inland on different gauges with no link between them because each was in the territory of a different colonial power, as in Nigeria and Dahomey, or Guinea and Sierra Leone.

The pattern of transport and communications, looked at from an overall African viewpoint, was quixotic. Much later the independent states of Africa would turn their attention to overcoming this obstacle to their closer relations. Furthermore, economic development, even within a single colony, principally served to link a few people in a few centers to the outside world. It did not create an internally integrated economy. Nevertheless, economic improvements were important for their political consequences, for the ways in which they permitted men and ideas to circulate more rapidly.

The railroad brought with it, as it did on the American frontier, new economic bustle, new industries, new horizons. Improved facilities did not merely make possible more circulation but contained a hidden multiplier —they made possible more turnover. African villagers could come and go; they could return to their villages to be replaced by other villagers in the towns. Ever larger numbers of villagers, therefore, were exposed to urban life, even if for a short time only, and permanent residents of the towns could visit their natal villages more often. Thus, modernization spread, moving too fast to be encompassed by the slow pace of colonial economic and political development; and once again, the strains produced would help to account for the sudden outburst of nationalist sentiment that was to come.

The town was not merely the incubator of new values and ideas; it was also a center for the spread of these values and ideas to the villages. But the village bred its own seed of rebellion and modernism as well. The institution of cash crops was as important in the process of social change as mining. Every territory, if it was lucky, had a cash crop, but usually only one. There was wine in Algeria and cotton in the Sudan and Uganda, cocoa in the Gold Coast (Ghana) and coffee in the Ivory Coast, sisal in Tanganyika and tobacco in Southern Rhodesia. Cash crops brought money to the villages. They gave a new importance to the method of inheritance. They also brought problems of land ownership and land alienation; in some areas Europeans virtually appropriated the land.

Cash crops were sometimes introduced by Europeans on plantations, sometimes grown by African planters who were encouraged by colonial governments. Plantations were the common pattern in settler Africa, where active discouragement of African farmers in favor of Europeans sometimes occurred, as in the case of coffee in Kenya. But often in nonsettler Africa, the government would take steps directly to encourage and assist the emergence of a small-holding cash-crop peasantry—as, for example, the Gezira Scheme in the Anglo-Eyptian Sudan and the Office du Niger in French West Africa. Simply preventing alienation of land to Europeans would also serve this end—as for example, in the Gold Coast or the Western Region of Nigeria. Sometimes, as in the Ivory Coast, the African peasants would find themselves in competition with a small group of European planters, the latter having the advantages of forced labor and (by statute) better prices. Such unequal competition was to breed a strong reaction.

The introduction of a cash crop could not help but

change the traditional social structure somewhat. Often it required different work patterns. Usually it meant that there began to grow up a distinction between land on which food was grown, which remained communal land, and land on which cash crops were grown, which tended to shift to a pattern of individual ownership. Matriarchal systems particularly were undermined by cash crops. Insofar as all land was part of a subsistence economy, there was relatively little difference between one plot and another. The young man who, having worked on his father's land, then moves to inherit the land of his mother's brother, which is roughly equivalent, accepts this tradition as just. But if, in a cash-crop economy, the new plot is much poorer or perhaps not even producing the cash crop, he is going to feel aggrieved. And unless the system is changed, he will be reluctant to work hard on his father's plot, which not he, but his cousin, will inherit.

Even where the traditional economy was left intact, however, the rural area was to know change. Colonial administration reached out everywhere and, in order to stabilize its existence, created some organs of local government. The European colonial power might try to establish a rational bureaucratic hierarchy with all officials operating on a state payroll and within a single judicial framework. Efforts in this direction were called direct administration and were often associated with French rule. In fact, of course, complete direct administration never existed. It was too expensive, particularly since it was difficult to find adequate numbers of indigenous personnel who had the necessary skills or to train men rapidly. It would have meant the importation of large numbers of Europeans who were both costly and unavailable. Furthermore, it would have required a very rapid and radical alteration of patterns of government at the village level. The colonial administration was not prepared to deal with such a revolution.

What then of the opposite possibility, "indirect rule,"

leaving in place the traditional system and often the traditional ruler, and operating as much as possible through that system? This style of government has been associated with British colonial rule, and the policies of Lord Lugard in Northern Nigeria and Sir Donald Cameron in Tanganyika. And indeed it has been widespread in British Africa: Zanzibar, the High Commission Territories, Buganda in Uganda, Barotseland in Northern Rhodesia, the Northern Territories of the Gold Coast, the Protectorates of Sierra Leone and the Gambia. Although indirect rule is often thought of as a British monopoly, French policy in Morocco, Belgian policy in Ruanda-Urundi show close parallels.

Indirect rule never meant the complete preservation of traditional authority. It could not, or the entire element of colonial rule would have been eliminated from it. Colonial rule, however circumscribed in its definition, required some limitation on the judicial and political authority of the traditional ruler. Once it became apparent that the chief's authority was no longer ultimate, and that the chief was subject in some areas to the authority of the district administrative officer, the power of the chief was thereby undermined. And the sharp line between direct and indirect rule was thereby blurred. In fact the line was seldom sharp in Africa; all the colonial powers evolved a pragmatic policy which involved, in one way or another, working with or through chiefs but always within the framework of overall colonial rules and values. It meant that wherever and to whatever degree chiefs retained power they did so at the grace of the colonial power.

One important cause of the decline of chieftaincy as an institution was the great ease with which colonial authorities, when they felt it necessary, would remove the incumbent and replace him with another. Sometimes this would be the outcome of the process of overcoming African resistance ("pacification")—death, exile, or retirement for the defeated chief. Sometimes the removal of a chief would be merely an error. An African tribe would occasionally put forward a false chief as a negotiator to safeguard the real one. Whether done deliberately or in error, this kind of replacement at the beginning of the colonial era created in many areas the phenomenon of two chiefs, one having the recognition and support of the colonial authority, one the legitimation of tradition still recognized by the villagers.

But this initial replacement was perhaps less important than the continuing strain on the chief under colonial rule. For whether administration was direct or indirect, colonial rule tended to devolve upon the chief more and more administrative tasks for the colonial authority. The chief was variously expected to enforce colonial law, impress labor, collect taxes. These were not merely administrative tasks; they were unpopular ones. The chief found his role beginning to shift from that of spokesman for his people to that of agent of the colonial administration vis-à-vis his people. The consequence was an increasing frequency of replacement of the chief, either by the colonial authority or, if tradition permitted it, by the African villagers. Occasionally the pace of replacement became so rapid as to lead to the complete breakdown of traditional authority.

Even when such drastic events did not occur, the very process of out-migration to the towns and in-migration of the traders (or of rural laborers in cash-crop areas) meant a steady pressure toward the "territorialization" of the chief's authority—at which point, a demand would grow up for its "democratization," that is, its replacement by an elected village council. Another steady pressure against the traditional authority of the chief was the spread of Christianity, where it did spread. For the Christian villager would refuse to engage in the traditional religious ceremonies of the village, and by extension, would begin to challenge the whole authority of the ruler.

As we have seen, the economic changes, the spread of

education, the immigration to the towns, all led to the growth of a new elite, one not necessarily recruited from among those who had status and authority in the traditional social system. Quite often the opposite was true. This new elite, whether in the town or back in the village, simply was not willing to give the same deference or recognition of authority to the chief as previously. The younger generation had found new sources of reward, new identifications with European and/or modern values, new evaluations of their own achievements.

It was the emergence of this new elite that was the single most important consequence of the social change brought about by colonial rule. Traditional authority, weakened by the assaults of colonial rule (even, ironically, when the latter tried to maintain it, as in indirect rule), was further threatened by the refusal of this new elite to subordinate itself to a system in which it had no place and whose values seemed to it outmoded. This new elite began to react—not merely against traditional rulers, but against the colonial rulers as well.

:III:

THE REACTION

The men of the new elite bred by the colonial administration were "Westernized," that is, they began to
learn and share the values of Western civilization, at
least in part. Furthermore, they began to *want to be*
Westernized. They began to model themselves on the
Europeans with whom they came in contact—in religion, in comportment, in style of life. And European
administrators, particularly in the nonsettler territories
at the beginning of the colonial era, actively encouraged
them in this path. It was flattering and useful for
colonial governments to have an intermediate social
grouping that copied European social patterns.

But once again, social change in Africa outstripped
European expectations. As the new African elite
studied European history in the African schools—for
there was no African history considered worthy of
study—and as they studied in Europe, they became
more and more aware of a great egalitarian movement
occurring within European society itself. The rise of
individualist philosophy in the West, of the doctrine of
the inherent rights of all human beings to liberty and
equality became a familiar story to them—the Reformation and the Renaissance, the Enlightenment, the
French Revolution, the nineteenth-century achievement throughout Europe of wider suffrage, increasing

guarantees against arbitrary government, and the slow emergence of labor and socialist movements designed to extend the gains of bourgeois democracy by creating economic and social conditions that would allow the lower classes to profit fully from the advantages of a free society.

Alongside this current of ideas and institutional change was another development which for a long time ran parallel to it. The end of the Middle Ages was marked by the creation of a new political structure, the nation-state. At first focused around an absolute monarch, the nation-state came increasingly to be built around the concept of a sovereign people. The French and American Revolutions crystallized this convergence of the forces of nationalism and the forces of liberalism. The Napoleonic empire encouraged the spread of these forces, and the various revolutions of 1848 were the culmination of their coalescence. Even after this period, in southern and eastern Europe, liberalism and nationalism went hand in hand. Just as men demanded equal rights as individuals and as classes of individuals, so did they demand equal rights as nations. The right to create and maintain nationhood came to be associated with the fight for freedom, a point of view illustrated by a statement made by Hobhouse in 1911: "National and personal freedom are growths of the same root."

In some ways the Russian revolution was a culmination of these nineteenth-century movements. It was a triumph of European egalitarian ideology. But it also meant the liberation of Russia from the cultural and intellectual hegemony of Western Europe. Russia became an equal, independent participant in the formulation of Western ideology. In freeing itself from the domination of the West, Russia opened the way for colonial intellectuals to break with the West too without rejecting it altogether. It opened the way not only in intellectual terms but in terms of creating a new world power situation which facilitated the long-range process of decolonization.

Before the First World War, even to a large extent before the Second World War, Africa was remote from these events. African problems were not generally analyzed by Europeans in terms of these egalitarian principles. Nor were most Africans specifically aware of these European developments and their implications for Africa. There was one important link, though—the small group of intellectuals that had come into existence in the colonies, particularly those who had been to European universities or others who had traveled in Europe (as, for example, soldiers during the wars). These men had acquired European values; indeed egalitarian principles had been taught to them specifically, to some extent in colonial schools, more emphatically in metropolitan universities.

In addition to lessons on the merits of equality these men also had received training in various occupations and professions leading them to expect advancement in careers which they were not in fact allowed to have. Men trained as engineers could find no employment because it would not do to have an African engineer supervise a white foreman. As Chief Awolowo of Nigeria said as late as 1946: "Only a few parents so far have had the courage to send their sons abroad to study engineering. African engineers did not succeed in getting jobs under the Government or Native Administrations." Men trained as lawyers, especially in the settler territories, knew that they would never become judges. A clerk never, or very rarely, could rise to be head of a government department. And on a simpler level, sergeants could never become lieutenants. At whatever level of skill, Africans had to curb their ambitions because in the colonial situation governments were reluctant, often formally opposed, to making any exceptions in a structure where European ruled African.

And in that intermediate plane where European and African held the same job, the pay scales were widely different, at least until the rise of the nationalist movements after World War II.

Nor was this all. The colonial political structure was an autocracy with the governor at its head, where the citizen had no political rights or very few. It is true that, as time went on, a few municipal or legislative councils were established, in which members were elected (often on a property suffrage); however, they were usually in a minority or did not have significant powers vis-à-vis the administrators. In settler territories, lack of even such minor political devolution to Africans was aggravated by the turning over of power, exclusively or disproportionately, to white settlers.

Thus, the African intellectuals—and more generally, urbanized Africans—were limited in their careers and denied access to political power. Yet the people who demanded the vote and job advancement were precisely those who had broken with the traditional elite and had acquired egalitarian values. They defined this limitation and denial as a frustration, an unjust frustration. What is more, this definition was one which most Europeans, to be consistent with their own values, had to accept as valid.

Africans, then, came to demand equality, and equality not only in the political arena but in all aspects of life: economic equality, educational equality, religious equality, cultural equality. The same theme would arise in many different guises, sometimes fitfully, not always coördinated with demands in other fields, not always accorded acceptance in European circles—even those of the intellectual left. The core of the demand, however, was a political one—equal participation in political decisions that affect all within the community. The question of course arose: which community? Some defined the community as the imperial network; others as the colony.

Demands for political equality in the imperial network meant giving an African exactly the same rights as a European *living in Europe*—voting, access to education and career, equality of pay and living standards. This was the logical consequence of a policy of political assimilation and was particularly favored in French Africa. Early demands of Algerian, Senegalese, Malagasy intellectuals were often phrased in terms of the ultimate objective of becoming part of France, which was moreover officially proclaimed the object of French colonization by many theorists of the empire. Full citizenship was a prime demand. Education, social and economic development were advocated to make the granting of full citizenship possible and meaningful. Assimilation—that is, becoming part of France—meant the renunciation of African culture and adoption of the patterns and ways of life of the metropolitan community.

Ultimately, however, assimilation as a road to political equality came to be rejected in Africa, not because it did not solve the problem theoretically, but because it was so nearly impossible to implement, at least within any reasonable span of time. It was tempting to the intellectuals since they could presumably benefit from it immediately if they had the support of the "liberal" administrators. But the concept that all Africans *as individuals* would be admitted to equal rights in the imperial system was translated very quickly into a formula best summarized by Cecil Rhodes's famous slogan, "Equal rights for all civilized men." Formulated this way, it made admission to political equality a privilege for Africans, contingent on their passing certain tests administered by Europeans, who could thereby control not only admission to these rights but the overall rate of admission. In practice very few were admitted. Africans came to consider the path of assimilation a lure. Even had perfect good will and fairness existed on all sides, it was inevitable that this process be slow, as its accomplishment demanded the complete abandonment of traditional cultures by African peasant masses, whose education and contact with the modern economic world ranged from nonexistent to minor. Moreover, as time went on, African intellectuals began to ask, with some justice, why it should automatically be assumed that it is an unadulterated virtue to accept Western values. We shall examine this contention in detail later on, when we discuss cultural revival.

And so, assimilation having failed, perhaps because (as some say of Christianity) it had never been tried, these intellectuals turned to where others had started, the alternate path to political equality: political separation, that is, national independence. Here the demand was not that individual African be placed alongside individual European in equal status, but that Africans as a group be equal to Europeans as a group, both being organized into sovereign nations.

The classic example of this reversal in attitude is the personal political path of Ferhat Abbas. In 1936, Ferhat Abbas, then advocating assimilation, said: "If I had discovered 'the Algerian nation,' I should have become a nationalist, and should not have blushed for it. . . . I did not find it. I consulted history, the living and the dead. . . . You cannot build on air. We have discarded once and for all the nonsense and the chimeras definitely to align our future with that of the French work in our country. Six million Moslems live on this soil which has been French for a hundred years; they live in hovels, go barefoot, without clothing and often without bread. Out of this hungry mass we shall make a modern society . . . elevate them to human dignity so that they may be worthy of the name of Frenchmen." In 1958 Ferhat Abbas became Premier of the Provisional Government of the Algerian Republic, advocating independence for Algeria.

Obviously, even when national independence was the ultimate goal, it usually was not made the immediate

demand at first. What was called for was the steady
creation of more organs of representative government
with more real powers, the transfer of power from
colonial authority, embodied in the governor, to African
people. The series of demands, each leading to the next,
was like the series that Western Europe witnessed internally with respect to the transfer of authority from
the king to a parliament elected by universal suffrage.

There were many colonies where these demands were
not considered legitimate, either because the colonial
ideology stressed assimilation (French, Portuguese) or
because settler control led to the development of an
antidemocratic ideology (white supremacy in the
Union of South Africa). Sometimes, even when nationalism was proscribed as an ideology by the colonial
adminstration, alternate political outlets were provided
because the ideology of assimilation was to some extent
taken seriously (French North Africa, Senegal). But
there were some cases where no political outlets, or
almost none, were permitted to any group of Africans,
particularly before the end of the Second World War.
This was true, for example, of the Belgian Congo,
French Equatorial Africa, Angola and Mozambique.
This was also true, in varying degrees, of different parts
of English-speaking southern Africa from the Union of
South Africa to Kenya. It is no accident that these
areas saw the greatest flourishing of nativistic, revival-
istic and syncretistic movements, quite often clothed in
religious garb (Kitiwala, Kimbanguism, Alice cult,
Mau Mau). Where no political outlets for grievances
were permitted, at least to the small elite, they or their
followers often turned to pseudotraditional patterns
which were, on the one hand, more familiar and easy to
handle, and on the other hand, could appeal to a legitimation which even colonial rulers accepted to some
extent: religious freedom. In short, political protest did
not always or necessarily take a political form. To see
the nationalist movements in their proper perspective,

it is important to see the rise of political associations in the towns and then in the rural areas as just one element in the steady growth of whole networks of voluntary associations based on the desires and needs of Africans to group together to resolve mutual problems or advance mutual aims within the emerging modern societies of which they were now a part.

The first problem faced by the new urban dweller was not that of achieving equality. It was that of providing some kind of system of social security for himself in this new money-oriented world. It was that of filling the void created when he was cut off from his traditional social ways which had resulted in feelings of uncertainty and loneliness. The urban African was uprooted and hence needed new assurances of economic well-being, new groups of which he could be a part and within which he could re-establish the moral limits of his action. This has been the need and the response of rural migrants to the towns everywhere in the world.

What the family and tribe could not provide because they were disrupted, what the colonial government could not provide because it had not the material means and personnel, nor the confidence of its subjects, urban Africans provided for themselves by creating new organizations. The first to organize were usually the educated. Throughout the continent one of the commonest forms of organization was the alumni association, formed by secondary schools, technical schools, sometimes—if nothing else existed—upper primary schools. It was a natural grouping, one to which colonial authorities could object only with difficulty, one which appealed to the immediate interests of the group who were most apt to have the skills necessary to organize an association. Quite often these associations were disguised trade unions where trade unionism was still forbidden. They grouped together civil servants or schoolteachers or professionals who had common frustrations and common grievances against the colonial

administration. As time went by, many of these groups
would transform themselves into proper trade unions or
become the base for a political party. These groups were
an important means of political action before it was
legal as well as a valuable training ground for later
nationalist activity.

Alumni associations were not the only form such
groupings of the educated took. Westernized Africans
formed social clubs, dancing classes, literary discussion
circles. They formed sports associations in order to play
the European games they had learned in schools and to
associate with each other. Sometimes a group would be
formed on an ethnic basis and would set itself the
explicit task of raising the educational and social level
of its home village; thus the association, as an instrument of modernization, would be brought to the rural
areas, establishing an acceptable role for the educated
in traditional society, from the point of view of both the
educated and the traditionalists.

The educated were not the only ones to form groups,
though they were usually the first. The uneducated
urban dweller—the market woman, the small artisan,
the house servant—rapidly acquired the sophistication
to realize how valuable a technique this was. Friendly
and mutual-benefit societies sprang up everywhere.
Religious groups, ethnic associations, football clubs—
football, or rather soccer, rapidly became the "mass"
sport in African towns—also arose. One key element of
almost all these organizations was that they provided
cash payments to tide the individual over the major
critical turning points of life: birth of a child, marriage,
and most important of all, burial. But this function of
the groups was not merely a financial matter. It was
the means by which the group created an emotional
haven, a new "family" that could support the individual morally, help him to adjust to urban life, teach him
the techniques needed to get along.

The voluntary associations clearly were performing

very important functions, and even the colonial administration saw the virtue of some kinds of associations. Indeed, often the administration took the lead in establishing groups in Africa on the model of organizations in European countries—youth groups, athletic teams, and after the Second World War, even trade unions. But from the point of view of the colonial administration, these associations were useful only to the extent that they served as auxiliaries to the administration. They were useful, that is, if they trained Africans in ways of living that would enable the colony to function better as an administrative or economic unit. They were dangerous if they became a framework within which social protest and political agitation could ferment and become active.

But the very existence of voluntary associations created channels of information other than that of the colonial government; for example, there were links with international voluntary groups. Also, the associations trained people in the skills of organization and of speaking, so necessary in political life. They brought together elements of the population who were otherwise divided. They began, bit by bit, to escape the confines within which the colonial government wished to keep them and became "politicized."

One way this happened was through the creation of autonomous, African counterparts to Western-style groups, such as the *African* scouts, as opposed to the Boy Scouts of given countries, and African trade unions, which broke their links with European groups of which they had formerly been a part. The movement for autonomy grew even among Christian churches, where separatist groups with African hierarchies sometimes were created. Another way in which autonomy was encouraged was not through the creation of Africanized counterparts to European groups but through the establishment of new types of groups, African not only in personnel and name but often in tradition and cul-

tural values as well. The various kinds of groups, both
African and Westernized, appealed to different parts of
the population, channeling different grievances. Their
coördination into a single movement which gave coherent voice to their collective grievances, stressing the
common underlying theme of equality, was to await the
emergence of political leadership.

The earliest openly political organizations were usually offshoots of some of these early associations of the
educated. They expressed limited demands for greater
rights and a measure of self-rule, at least on the municipal level. One of the earliest of such movements was the
African National Congress of the Union of South Africa.
In North Africa, there was the Destour in Tunisia, to be
followed in the 1920's by the Neo-Destour. At the same
time, Messali Hadj founded the Etoile Nord-Africain
among Algerians in Paris. In West Africa at the end of
the First World War, there arose the National Congress
of British West Africa, while in Kenya, in the 1920's,
was founded the Kikuyu Central Association. In the
1930's, a Socialist federation (branch of the French
SFIO), founded in Senegal, served the same purpose,
and in Morocco, the Comité d'Action Marocaine was
founded. It was, however, not until after World War
II that similar groups were started in most other territories.

These early protonationalist groups varied in effectiveness and popular appeal. They did give voice to
grievances. They did assert the right to organize and to
make demands on the colonial government, thus paving
the way for their successors. But by and large, they
were treated lightly by the colonial government, which
usually claimed that they represented no one but themselves—a small urban, highly educated minority. And
in terms of the ability of these movements to mobilize
mass support, there was some truth in this assertion.
But the grievances of the colonial era were real. The
inequalities not only existed; they were built into the

system, and ideologies to justify their maintenance were propagated. Furthermore, the very processes of the colonial system, the expansion of the economy which was at its base, continued to breed, at an ever-expanding rate, the frustrated individuals who would one day revolt.

The Second World War was greatly to accelerate political organization in African societies. For one thing, many Africans served in armies in Asia, Europe, and parts of Africa other than their home territory. And European and American (including American Negro) soldiers served in North, Northeast and West Africa. The increased contact of Africa with the world stirred up new aspirations. Nigerians came into contact in India with Indian nationalists. Gold Coasters or Senegalese or Tunisians saw behavior on the part of European soldiers which they had never encountered before among European settlers or administrators, such as Europeans engaged in manual labor. The defeat and occupation of many of the colonial powers at home made a strong impression. Whatever it was, large numbers of Africans had new perspectives on the possibilities of action. Furthermore, army service and the intensified economic activity which wartime brought to Africa led to an increased training of mechanics, artisans, drivers, nurses, teachers, and others, who then formed a sizable "lower middle class" in each colony. It was this new group who, in the postwar years, would give vent to new grievances—those of colonial frustration generally, combined oftentimes with the particular complaints of ex-servicemen who had not received their due.

Meanwhile, social change in Africa was not occurring in a vacuum. The Second World War resulted in basic shifts in the world power situation. The United States and the Soviet Union became the leaders of two vast power blocs, engaged in a cold war which forced them to seek support in the non-European areas of the world. In Asia, the Japanese conquest of Southeast Asia meant

an ouster of European colonial powers which could not
be undone in the postwar era. England, under a Labor
government, showed the way by gracefully withdrawing
from India, Pakistan, Ceylon and Burma. The Nether-
lands left Indonesia under some pressure, and the
French left Indochina only very reluctantly and very
late. Nevertheless, they all left and the impact of Asian
independence on African developments was not small.
In Ghana the Convention People's Party adopted the
(Indian) Congress cap as their symbol. Ben Bella, one
of the leaders who started the Algerian revolution in
1954, received his military training (and political education?) as a sergeant in the French Army in Indochina.
Many African nationalist leaders throughout East,
Central and South Africa proclaimed themselves
disciples of Gandhi's technique of nonviolent resistance.

Given the changes in the internal structure of African
colonies and the international context, the majority of
African colonial territories, in the fifteen years following
the end of the war, saw the emergence of mass nationalist movements. These movements either transformed
or replaced the protonationalist groupings that had
existed. These movements, sometimes led by younger
intellectuals who had broken with their elders because
the pace of advance was too slow, made use of the
expanded "lower middle class" as the cadres of organization, thus moving out of the confines of an educated
urban elite to organize and educate urban masses in
the slums and peasants in the bush or wadi. Sometimes
the break of mass nationalist movements with urban
educated groups who had previously been the leaders
of protest movements was accompanied by real anger
against these groups for the privileged position that
they had enjoyed under the colonial regime. In West
Africa there was particular resentment against such
groups as the professional men in the Gold Coast
(Ghana), the Creoles in Sierra Leone, the Senegalese
throughout French West Africa. The half-castes and

the West Indians often suffered under such suspicion. The attitude of Africans toward Coloureds in the Union of South Africa was somewhat similar.

Organizing nationalist movements in African territories was not easy, for a nationalist movement is essentially a revolutionary movement. It aims not merely to change the people in power or some of the policies of government, but also to change the system fundamentally; in this case, it aimed to overthrow the colonial government. Revolutionary movements can expect to meet resistance from the powers-that-be. And African nationalist movements did meet such resistance from the colonial governments. In some cases, the changing world situation put outside pressure on the colonial powers to cede their positions, or created situations within the metropolitan country which altered the resolve to stay. But, on the other hand, European settlers or interest groups often could put moral and political pressure on the colonial government, or the retention of a colony became bound up with certain prestige or economic considerations. In any case, it was no easy job to secure independence. It was a struggle, sometimes involving violence, as in Algeria, Ivory Coast, Cameroun, Kenya, Madagascar. It was a struggle in which the colonial government held the reins of force, often had more outside support than their opposition (at least at first), and claimed whatever legitimacy it had been able to gain through the years either directly or via the chiefs.

A nationalist movement, in order to succeed, had to make battle for the minds of men. It had to try to inculcate among the majority of the people resident in a territory a system of values and norms that was often at direct variance with that of the legal government. Above all, it had to make the majority respond to its sanctions rather than to those of the colonial government.

To accomplish this, the nationalist movement had to

do more than just establish a political party. It tried to
create around the political party a whole network of affiliated or linked organizations—youth groups, women's
groups, ex-servicemen's groups, trade unions, farmers'
associations, ethnic associations, friendly societies,
separatist churches. In some cases the nationalist
movement took over existing voluntary associations. In
other cases it created new ones. But in all cases its
purpose was to inculcate large numbers of persons with
new (revolutionary) values and norms. The nationalist
movement sought to corral all the leisure time of the
individual, so that wherever he went, whatever he did,
he would find himself in an environment which reinforced these new beliefs. Thus arose the cry for the
primacy of political values, the politicization of all
activity, at least until independence was won.

The reaction of the colonial government to this
argument was the counterargument of "apoliticism,"
the argument that voluntary organizations should not
be diverted or divided by politics. But talk of diversion
cut both ways, and the nationalist movement asserted
that apolitical leisure activity was a deliberate lure and
diversion created by the colonial government to distract
people from the central issue, the struggle for independence. Thus, one of the key fights came to be the
fight to control the voluntary associations, a fight that
in the long run was won by the nationalist movement.

When this fight was substantially won, when the
party had organized itself throughout a territory, when
the party had given political interpretation to the
manifold grievances of the population, when, therefore,
the majority of the people shifted their passive allegiance from the colonial powers and the traditional
chiefs to the mass nationalist movement, a "time of
troubles" began. Once this happened, the colonial
powers sought to come to terms with the nationalist
movement in order to establish an orderly (that is, as
slow as politically possible) transition. Taking into

account the changing world situation and particularly the emergence of the Bandung spirit, the colonial powers acted with great speed in the nonsettler territories, particularly in West and Equatorial Africa. There seemed no virtue in resisting some transfer of power once the nationalist movement showed itself in relative command of the loyalties of the majority of the population. This was not true in the settler territories (Algeria and southern Africa) where the pressures of the white settler population and the often important economic interests of the colonial power meant both that it was harder to organize the nationalist movement and that a longer "time of troubles" was required once it had begun.

But sooner or later this era came to an end. The colonial powers—first Britain, then France, then Belgium—decided to move ahead, devolving power upon the nationalist movement as a step (sometimes only implicitly) toward full independence. And so for an interim period, the colonial government and the nationalist movement shared power; there was, in short, a dyarchy. How long this existed varied according to the situation in a given territory. Generally speaking, the longer a colonial power waited to begin the transfer of power, the shorter the period of dyarchy was. Compare the French Congo and the Belgian Congo, or British West Africa and French West Africa. And generally speaking, the longer the period of dyarchy, the smoother the transition. This was so not only because more Africans received training to man the administration, but because the political structures that Africans created gave them the sense of control over their own destinies, thus minimizing psychological resentment against the former colonial power.

A long period of shared power also had the effect of moderating the promises that the nationalist movement made to its constituency since the taste of power brought a sobering sense of proportion to the analyses of political decisions. On the other hand, a long transition placed the nationalist movement in an ambivalent position, in which it often lost support precisely because it became more "moderate." The resulting disaffection of intellectuals and young people often changed the nature of the movement.

But the differences between the long and short periods of transition were not too great. We are talking of a variation that ranges from one year or so (say, the Congo) to nine years or so (say, Nigeria). It is an important variation but, in the long perspective of history, it would be unwise to exaggerate its importance.

Eventually, no matter how often the colonial power in a particular colony denied that independence would result from the political changes, independence was gained. And with independence, the nature of the problems facing the governments of African nations—the former nationalist movements which now came to power—changed radically. But before discussing the postindependence era, it would be well to retrace our steps a bit, to review the history of the colonial era in Africa not in terms of the general pattern that was followed everywhere, but rather with emphasis on the differences between colonial powers and differences in developments in various regions.

:IV:

THE DIFFERENT

EUROPEAN LEGACIES

African nationalism did not follow an identical path everywhere for a number of reasons. There were several colonial powers, and they engaged in different practices even within their own territories. Some territories had settlers and others not. Some got their independence early and others late. Some achieved it by violence; some succeeded without violence; a few had their independence handed to them in the wake of others. Arab Africa was in some respects unlike black Africa. The existence of a third grouping (Indians, Coloureds, etc.) sometimes made a difference.

We have seen that although Britain and France had dabbled on the edge of Africa for a long time and even established a few colonies, the period of their greatest imperialist expansion was the last quarter of the nineteenth century. This was the moment of Belgian and German colonization as well. (The Portuguese expanded in those places where they already had been for centuries.) At this point in European history, all these colonizing powers shared one ideological assumption—the supremacy of the values of Western civilization and the moral duty of the West to impose at least some of these values on Africa. There was, in short, a basic element of paternalism which ran through the philosophies of all the colonial powers. But this basic paternalism expressed itself in very different forms, depending on the history and national character of the colonial powers.

From the beginning, there was a sparseness and economy about British colonial policy. The British, of course, had started by using private companies as the mechanism of acquisition, and even later the British would justify the acquisition of a new colony largely on the basis of its economic return. The middle of the nineteenth century saw a political battle in England in which one powerful faction wished to abandon British colonies (including the Gold Coast) on the grounds that they were not worth holding. British colonies were always required to be self-financing, a fact which made it difficult for the colonial administration to pay for basic public works. And since the constitutional structure of Britain itself was one of complex variation, the British saw no difficulty in varying the structure of each of its colonies, according to the immediate needs of the situation. This policy was typical of the famous British pragmatism.

The men who go overseas for an imperial power often are romantics. In British areas these men got more leeway than in other colonies, often because they were the only ones really interested in colonial policy. The romantics among the soldiers teamed up with the romantics among the anthropologists, and it may be said that out of this union emerged the famous policy of "indirect rule," the policy of allowing the powers of traditional rulers to remain intact to the maximum degree consonant with imperial rule. Though Lord Lugard, when he initiated this policy in Northern Nigeria, may have had in mind primarily the fact that he had an inadequate number of soldiers and administrators to govern such a large region directly, the extension of the policy elsewhere and its emergence as an ideology can be traced to the responsive note it touched in British hearts.

Though the British may have felt it their duty to accept the "white man's burden" and bear the responsibility of advancing African interests, they did not assume that Africa one day would be an extension of Britain, or Africans one day British. The bias of the administrator—and more importantly, of the Briton at home—was in favor of the traditional chief in colonial government and not the Oxford-trained lawyer, who was felt to be somehow out of place. In short, British paternalism took the form of pressures to preserve custom, to maintain distance between Britain and Africa, between Briton and African.

The paternalism of France took a very different form. There was a Jacobin tradition in addition to that of aristocratic romance. During the French Revolution (An II Pluviôse), and again in the first flush of the Second Republic, in 1848, France granted full rights of citizenship to the inhabitants of the four communes of Senegal, including the right to send a deputy to the parliament of France. It was a lordly gift, that of human rights, of fraternal participation, in the land of freedom and culture.

Tnere was no preference here for primitive chiefs. ₊he *évolué*, graduate of a French university, denizen of a Paris salon, the African who had thoroughly imbibed French culture was the man to be honored. This is what was meant by "assimilation." In 1946 France would boast that the official grammarian of the Constitutional Convention was an African *agrégé*, Léopold Senghor. Neither distance nor racism here; the cultivated African was a deputy of France.

This Jacobin egalitarianism blended very well with the attempt of the French right wing in the late nineteenth century to restore the country to its former glory. Smarting over the defeat of 1870–71, Jules Ferry led France to seek some compensation in an overseas empire. There was no counting of pennies, no gross economic justification for expansion in this case. Nor did each territory suffice unto itself, economically and administratively. The French tradition of centralization and of consistent logic, applied to the needs of empire building, imposed standardized patterns throughout French colonies; the personnel were interchangeable and the curricula of the schools—all of them in French —were alike.

This, then, is the classic contrast between Africa's two colonial powers, Britain and France: Britain— empirical, commercial, practicing indirect rule, keeping Africans at a distance, verging on racism; France— Cartesian in its logic, seeking glory, practicing direct administration, acting as apostle of fraternity and anti-racism. Anyone who travels in both British and French Africa will see the grain of truth in these generalizations. The flavor of life *is* different; the two colonial powers *have* produced two different cultures. And yet, anyone who travels there well knows the severe limitations of these generalizations.

It is true that the British made a virtue of indirect rule and the French of direct administration. But what Lugard invented for Northern Nigeria and Sir Donald Cameron adapted for Tanganyika, Marshal Lyautey also practiced and preached in Morocco. The French may have ignored many chiefs, but if they were suffi-ciently powerful, as the Moro Naba in Upper Volta or the Lamidos in northern Cameroun, they had a better chance of surviving with customs and powers little changed than many petty chieftains in the coastal areas of British West Africa.

As for "empiricism" versus "Cartesian logic," this comparison smacks more of slogans than of analysis. For if the British permitted much variation, they also established clear patterns for their system of colonial administration, as well as for the political devolution that occurred later. If Cartesian logic led the French to such "strange" steps as granting identical constitutional reforms in 1956 to thirteen African territories, the logic of political wisdom led them to have a different real policy toward each of these thirteen territories. The reality of power did not always match the judicial format.

To contrast motives of money and glory seems even more dubious. For the British were surely proud of their empire, and the French surely profited by theirs. As for "racism" and "fraternity," it may be that French paternalism was based on the exclusive virtue but universal accessibility of French civilization and British paternalism on the equal virtue of all traditions but the unique inaccessibility of British culture. Nevertheless, in practice, there were parallel degrees of political, social and economic discrimination in two settler territories like Kenya and Algeria, and there were parallel ideologies among the settlers. There was also parallel absence of legal discrimination in nonsettler British and French West Africa, though until 1957 the exclusive white clubs of both areas barred Africans as members or as guests.

Having examined some of the differences and similarities between British and French colonial rule, let us now look at the colonial ideologies of the two other major powers whose legacies matter, Belgium and Portugal.

The Congo has a peculiar colonial history. In the late nineteenth-century scramble for Africa, the Congo Free State came into existence. This was a country run by a private corporation presided over by King Leopold of Belgium as a private individual. In the short period of twenty years, the Congo Free State managed to concentrate so many of the horrors of colonialism (vast exploitation by means of forced labor and chopped-off hands) that an international scandal was caused. In the wake of this scandal, the administration was turned over to the Belgian government, who were absolutely determined to wipe out the very memory of the scandal. The Congo became a "model" colony—more hospitals and more primary school education than in any other colony in Africa (except perhaps the Union of South Africa). But to avoid trouble the government would also brook no opposition, allow no one political rights, either settler or African. And in order to be sure that no African would demand them, there would be no elites—much primary education but almost no secondary education, and no university education at all. Nowhere did "papa know better" than in the Congo; nowhere did more sanitary bliss reign.

Only Portuguese paternalism can claim to rival the Belgian variety. Portugal's great colonial era had been the sixteenth century. By the nineteenth and twentieth centuries, Portugal was very tired. And its African colonies were very sleepy—forced labor, a few churches, and an occasional intermarriage (more occasional as the years went by). Neither Angola nor Mozambique was a "model" colony. When Salazar took over Portugal, the rights he denied to Portuguese he was not prepared to extend to Africans. And so a tight lid was kept on, as in the Congo—not because, as in the Congo, it was feared that otherwise matters would explode and call down international wrath once again, but because a tight lid was the normal state of affairs. Belgium and Portugal did share an "assimilationist" bias with France in that each had a system of permitting individual Africans to attain full legal rights by passing a test proving they had surmounted the cultural barrier. But neither Belgium nor Portugal was as close to Britain as France was in terms of permitting some limited political organization by the Africans. This difference would prove to be crucial.

As a result of their special framework of thinking concerning the colonies, the British were the first to begin the process of decolonization. Their attitude could be traced in part to their unhappy experiences in British North America. Having suffered the American Revolution, the British sought to avoid a repetition in Canada and thus began to consider how to devolve powers on the colonists, and how to do it before an explosion occurred. The British tradition of local government plus the fact that the people to whom these powers were at first transferred were largely Englishmen (Canada, Australia, New Zealand) made decolonization a relatively painless procedure.

In the middle of the nineteenth century, legislative bodies on which local people served were created in British colonies in Africa. Thus, the political experience of British West Africans, experience in modern parliamentary government, had a long history and would come to serve this area well. By the same token, in the settler areas of southern Africa, the British also created local legislative bodies, but here the power went in part to white settlers. As these white settlers got more and more autonomy, they eliminated African participation in government, at least until a much later stage of African nationalism. This was the history notably of the Union of South Africa. After the Boer War, the British were generous in their willingness to turn back power to the population of South Africa: the Boers were given coequal rights with the English colonists, but there were suffrage rights and parliamentary representation for Coloureds and Africans as well. When Britain went all the way and granted independence to the Union of South Africa, the dominant white population began to eliminate first the Africans, then the Coloureds, from any political role. Similarly, in Southern Rhodesia the white settlers received substantial autonomy, and in Kenya they received some, for a long time to the detriment of African participation in government.

The British acceptance of the devolution of powers, of the legitimacy of the objective of national independence, led to a situation in which African nationalism could flourish in West Africa and white settler nationalism could flourish in East, Central, and South Africa, until African nationalism caught up with the latter and began to force a rethinking of the political situation, both by the settlers and by the British government. What should be underlined here is that autonomous development, the ultimate acquisition of independence, were always considered reasonable, indeed inevitable, objectives of British colonies in Africa. Once Britain had expanded her previously white Commonwealth after the Second World War to include the Asian dominions of India, Pakistan and Ceylon, there seemed no reason why African countries, first of all the Gold Coast and Nigeria,* should not proceed along this path. Thus, the pace of constitutional development in British nonsettler Africa was rapid and marked by a minimum of violence and antagonism. The rapid transfer of power here was to serve as the model and impetus for it elsewhere in Africa.

The French had experienced no early colonial revolt such as the American Revolution leading to the development of a white Commonwealth whose structure could be extended later to nonwhite nations. The French concept of constitutional advance was to draw colonies closer to France, not push them farther away. The Second World War forced France as well as Britain to reconsider its colonial policy. For one thing, the Free French movement had received early support in black Africa,† and after the war, therefore, the government thought that such loyalty deserved to be rewarded.

* The same logic, at the same time, applied to the Sudan, except that this country, having been a condominium with Egypt, did not remain within the Commonwealth after independence.

† French black Africa is a term that has been used to include what were formerly the eight territories of French West Africa, the four of French Equatorial Africa, and the trust territories of Togo and Cameroun. All fourteen territories are now independent states.

Thus, in 1944, General de Gaulle convened a conference on colonial affairs in Brazzaville calling for great reforms. In his very famous opening speech to this conference, René Pléven, then Minister of Colonies, pledged new institutions and added: "There are populations that we intend to lead, step by step, to a more complete personality, to political enfranchisement, but who do not expect to know an independence other than the independence of France." Consequently, the major constitutional reform of this period was the fact that French African territories were to elect members to all of France's legislative bodies. As constitutional advance in British West Africa from 1946 to 1956 meant allowing more and more Africans to participate in the local legislature and executive, so in French Africa it meant allowing more and more Africans to participate in France's legislature and executive.

The French concept of illegitimacy of independence meant not only that the constitutional patterns were different from the British but also that the organizational patterns were different. African political parties were sometimes mere extensions of metropolitan parties (such as the SFIO in Senegal). But even if they were not, the fact that they had elected members in France's parliamentary bodies meant that, for reasons of parliamentary survival and influence, they had to attach themselves (*apparenter*) to a party in France (an example was the attachment of the RDA* to the French Communist Party, and later, when it broke with the Communist Party, to the center UDSR party). More important even than this political attachment was the fact that various kinds of nonpolitical associations were also organized as branches of French organizations. This was true of everything from boy scouts to war veterans, but it was most significant in the case of trade unions; for a long time all African trade unions

* Rassemblement Démocratique Africain, a party organized in most territories of French black Africa.

were part of the three French federations, the CGT, the CFTC, and the Force Ouvrière, particularly the first.

The end of the Second World War saw French colonies started on a radically different path of development from that of the British colonies (that is, the nonsettler ones). And yet, fifteen years later, they had all arrived at approximately the same point, national independence. What had happened to make the French pattern begin to conform to the British pattern?

There were two principal levers that forced a shift in the French pattern of constitutional development. One was the example of Ghana; the other, the developments in North Africa and Indochina. The French North African states each had a national identity, however limited, that predated French conquest. And although Algeria was juridically the most assimilated of France's African possessions, Tunisia and Morocco were the least. They were technically "protectorates" governed by their own rulers who had signed treaties with France. All of French North Africa had known the beginnings of nationalist ferment before the Second World War. The currents of nationalism in the Arab world had touched them, particularly Morocco. The size of the indigenous elite, the existence of a commercial as well as of a professional middle class, could not fail to have some influence. So when Indochina, in its Asian surroundings, pushed its claims to independence by revolution, and when Libya was handed its independence on a platter because of Italian defeat and cold war rivalries, Tunisia and Morocco became very restive and demanded not more integration into France but real devolution of power. North African trade unionists broke with the French CGT to create their own autonomous structures, thus starting a new pattern.

French black Africa felt these new ideas of autonomism coming from North Africa. They were particularly well received in Togo and Cameroun, which as early as 1946 were able to proclaim openly the objective of independence because of their status as trust territories. The independence of Tunisia and Morocco in 1956, the granting under United Nations pressure of some autonomy to Togo in 1955, the imminent independence of Ghana, and above all the Algerian war that had been going on since 1954, all led to the African demand for the *loi-cadre*,* which was granted in 1956. This law set French black Africa on the path to independence, which most of them obtained in 1960. The French had made the same decision as the British, to come to terms with the new urban elite; and the elite in French Africa had made the same decision as the elite in British Africa, that only independence would meet their demand for political equality. The difference was that the British had long accepted the goal of independence but the French had accepted it only very late and with the greatest difficulty.

These were not the only differences. One thing the British were very eager to export was their particular version of parliamentary government. In the process of turning over power, the British used their influence as a pressure toward the development of a multi-party system. The French did not seem to care. When the French were fighting the nationalist party, they created opposition parties; when they decided to come to terms with the nationalists, they seemed just as happy to have only a single group with which to deal. But as we shall see, after independence the pressures of the social structure toward a one-party state were more important than Britain's effort to encourage multi-party systems.

The fact that the British officially proclaimed the object of independence and the French officially rejected it caused a different attitude during the crucial period of the dyarchy on the question of creating larger polit-

* A law which gave semi-autonomy to the eight territories of French West Africa, the four of French Equatorial Africa, as well as to Madagascar and French Somaliland.

ical federations. The British worked hard and actively toward achieving the constitutional formulae which permitted Nigerian federalism and Ghanaian regionalism. The British also worked for East African unity. The French officially abstained from, unofficially worked against, the achievement of federations in French West and French Equatorial Africa, partly because at critical moments those forces which pushed toward federalism seemed to be pushing toward more rapid independence, which was still anathema to the French. Nevertheless, as we shall see again, the forces pushing toward unitary structures within states (for example, the breakdown of regionalism in Ghana) and toward new ties between independent African states were such as to eclipse the importance of the different attitudes of the British and French during the transition period.

Another difference in heritage was the concept of the role of the civil service. Great Britain has long placed great emphasis on the nonpolitical role of the civil service. Senior civil servants are forbidden to engage in partisan political activity, even as private citizens, in order to reinforce the norm that they impartially serve alternating political masters. The French exclude only the most senior group. Not only are a larger number of positions in a ministry overtly political (*le cabinet privé du ministre*) but most permanent civil servants have the rights of all other citizens in terms of active politics. Indeed, the result is that there are clans of French civil servants "linked" with French political tendencies—a rarer occurrence in Britain. This difference, carried over into Africa, was very important during the colonial period. Since the government was the chief employer of the elite, an African civil servant often had to choose between keeping his job and active association with the nationalist movement. The choice of "apoliticism" did not make the civil servants popular with the future leaders of their country. In French areas there was no such conflict. The French could retaliate against a civil servant who was a nationalist by transferring him, but they could not fire him. The dichotomy between African civil servant and African political leader was therefore never as sharp. But once again, after independence, the conflicts between civil servant and politician deriving from their different interests would far outweigh the importance of the different norms that ex-British and ex-French Africans derived from their colonial heritage. In short, although the British differed from the French in terms of their attitudes toward a multi-party system, the construction of political federations, the nature and role of the civil service, these differences became less important as African nations faced the new imperatives of the postindependence era.

A more significant difference, perhaps, was the cultural heritage. I do not mean here the fact that educated British Africans drink tea and French Africans like *apéritifs*. This is true, and it is striking to the visitor as he moves from country to country; but it represents merely a difference in the thin outer veneer of the styles of life prevalent in various African countries. There is, however, a more important aspect of the difference in European cultural heritage. The French favored assimilation. All schooling was in French from the very first grade of elementary school. African politicians served in French assemblies. The British placed less emphasis on cultural assimilation. Schooling was in English only in later years. Africans in England never were absorbed into English life, as Africans in Paris were absorbed into French life.

The net result was that the French produced a much more *dépaysé* individual. Educated British Africans resumed the wearing of African dress early. It became legitimate for the most formal occasions. Literacy drives were conducted to teach people to read African languages. African intellectuals would often speak African languages among themselves if they had one in com-

mon. French African intellectuals wore European dress
on almost all occasions, and spoke French among themselves—and often their French was much better than
the English of their British African counterparts. This
greater assimilation gave rise to a greater reaction, that
of negritude, the reassertion of the cultural values not
of particular African tribes but of the Negroes as one
large cultural group. As one Nigerian expressed it,
British Africans did not need to invent the concept of
negritude, for they had been practicing it all their lives.
This difference in cultural tone, coming out of different
colonial experience, accentuated by the lack of contact
between Africans in various European colonies during
the colonial period, made a lasting impression on the
new African societies.

Did the fact of having settlers in an African colony
make a permanent difference? Clearly it made a big
difference in the pace and the forms of the struggle for
independence. Settlers meant greater passion, hatred,
violence. Settlers meant searing memories of overt
discrimination. Settlers meant Africans had fewer
opportunities before independence to obtain experience
in posts of responsibility. On the other hand, settlers
also usually meant that more Africans were involved in
the money economy, more went to primary school, and
hence more worked as clerks, typists, and the like.
Most of all, large numbers of settlers meant that the
Africans absorbed more Western values and habits
(compare Africans in the Union of South Africa with
Ghanaians, or even Algerians with Moroccans). How
many of these differences, however, are but mere tran-
sitory differences? It is far too early to tell. In the year
2000 the influence of settlers may seem an insignificant
detail or it may loom large as an explanation of varying
patterns. Its significance will depend in part on how
the transition is made from white domination to
African control in settler areas.

The main factor distinguishing the Belgian or the

Portuguese attitude toward territories from both the British and the French attitudes was their unwillingness to accept not merely the desirability but even the conceptual possibility of independence. When the Belgians suddenly faced rebellion in the Congo, which came in the wake of autonomy and independence for French Equatorial Africa, in turn speeded up by the Algerian war, they evaded the issue by pulling out quickly to avoid a costly colonial war. Because the Belgians had not granted political rights to the Congolese until a very late date, the transition was necessarily abrupt. The Congolese did not have time to develop the kind of strong party structure which enabled Africans in West or North Africa to make similar transitions without difficulty. The effects of this sudden transition may prove long-lasting if the Congolese find it difficult to create sufficient national solidarity to permit continued economic advance.

The length of time involved in the transfer of power was important in determining the makeup and development of the newly created independent governments. Time made possible party organization and administrative experience. The degree of resistance by the colonial power often determined the character of political parties. Too much resistance (Congo) made it difficult to develop a party structure; too little resulted in a weak structure as well. This was the case, for example, of those French African countries—Chad, Gabon—which got their independence as a result of the struggle of the stronger ones. Also, the RDA party structure in Guinea and Mali is tighter than in the Ivory Coast because the French came to terms with the RDA in the Ivory Coast in 1952 and in Guinea and Mali only in 1956. Between 1952 and 1956, the Ivory Coast party did not rebuild its organizational structure, which had been weakened by repression in 1949, partly because it did not need to.

The strength of the traditional African rulers also

determined the course of development of new governments, whether it was strength deriving from precolonial tradition or strength resulting from being favored in the colonial situation (as, for example, those chiefs who used the installation of cash crops to secure for themselves a new, vital role in the money economy). The Istiqlal Party in Morocco could not play the same unifying role (indeed the party itself split in two after independence) as the Neo-Destour Party in Tunisia, in part because of strong traditional rulers, eager to maintain their own supremacy. The strength of traditional rulers in northern Nigeria and Cameroun has meant that the populations of the northern parts of these countries, who are less educated than the southerners, could nevertheless have a vital influence in national politics. Comparable groups in the northern parts of Dahomey, Togo, Ghana, and the Ivory Coast, where the traditional structures were less complex and unified than in the emirates of northern Nigeria and Cameroun, did not have such influence. Ugandan nationalism has proved no faster than Kenyan nationalism, although Africans in Kenya had to contend with settlers, because Uganda is beset with strong traditional rulers who have delayed constitutional advance for fear that it would mean their eclipse. These variations in the strength of traditional rulers may make a long-range difference in the patterns of African nations.

Similarities and differences in African development in a sense depend on the perspective of the observer. Very close up, no two African countries look alike. As the observer recedes into the distance of space or time, the differences too recede. Given the vast expanse of territory, the large number of administrative divisions, and the multiplicity of tribes which Africa knows, one would expect the differences to appear much more striking than they do. If they do not, it is perhaps because the transition to independence from colonial rule has been so compressed in time—almost simultaneous for many African nations.

What is perhaps most important is the degree to which Africans themselves feel their histories are similar. We shall discuss this as part of the vision of pan-Africanism and as part of the process of cultural regeneration. We now turn from the colonial period to see the problems of the new nations after independence, the independence for which they struggled so ably and so hard.

Independence
and After

AFRICA
1 9 6 1

:V:

INTERNAL UNITY:

PARTIES AND HEROES

Independence, as the nationalists had always insisted, makes a lot of difference. It transfers much of the effective power to individuals and structures internal to the country. It gives the governing elite many levers to reclaim still more power from outside agencies. There are, however, many claimants to the exercise of this power, all internal to the country. Unless the power is effectively exercised by a central agency, and unless the rules of the power game are generally accepted by all the competitors, disintegration and secession become not merely possible but probable.

Most African nations do not have long histories as nationalities. Their nationhood has been created in the crucible of a revolutionary struggle against a colonial power. The unity of the nation was forged in the fight against the external enemy. We have sought to explain how it was that colonial governments bred their own dissolution, how nationalism came about as a resolution of many of the basic strains of the colonial situation. The question we must now address ourselves to is the opposite one. It is not how a social conflict can emerge out of a seemingly stable regime but rather how social order can emerge out of a seemingly unstable regime.

The government of a new nation, immediately after independence, is a very unstable thing. For one thing, the existence of an external enemy—the major motivation for unity in the nationalist movement—has largely disappeared. The political mobilization, the subordination of private and sectional claims to the needs of the whole, is inevitably diminished. The country's sense of tension, and of antagonism, is partly abated, partly turned inward. Moreover, there is a sense of disappointment at unfulfilled expectations.

In nationalist activity in Africa there was an implicit promise that the tension resulting from oppression and antagonism, from the restraints of the colonial ruler and from the discipline of the nationalist organization would be temporary. There was a touch of the utopian hope characteristic of every revolution, even when nationalist movements were peaceful and unmilitant, as they were in perhaps half the African states that gained independence. And there were many in all African states who thought that freedom meant the end of social control or the immediate radical redistribution of wealth. The cadres of the nationalist parties may not have had such naïve expectations, but it is understandable that among the peasants or uneducated urban dwellers such illusions existed. Even if these illusions were only momentary, unfulfillment meant a sense of disappointment. Independence was not magic. In country after country in Africa, during the first weeks of independence, the leaders felt the need to make speeches on the theme that independence means hard work and self-reliance.

Even leaving aside simplistic notions, the transfer of power inevitably involves some administrative confusion. In those countries where the transfer was abrupt, as in Guinea, the problem was much greater than in those where the transfer was meticulously planned, as in Ghana or Nigeria. Nonetheless, wherever transfer of

power occurs, it means some changes in personnel and
in formal rules. Temporarily the population feels
unsure of the rules governing behavior, and more particularly, of the limits of possible deviance. Whenever
this happens, people will test the limits, see how far
they can go. And how far they can go depends not only
on the rules, formal and informal, but on the people
who enforce the rules. To the extent that the people in
power are new and inexperienced, they may be either
too rigid or too weak-kneed in their interpretations;
they may either provoke unnecessary antagonism toward the government or allow too much license—or
often do both at once. This commonplace situation is
one of the problems that have been called the "infantile
maladies of independence."

The removal of the prod to unity—that is, colonial
rule—combined with the uncertainty, disillusion, and
hence opposition, created by the new government,
inevitably causes the ethnic, regional, and other particular interests which had temporarily held back their
claims to reassert them. This, of course, is not startling.
The assertion of the rights of private interests to their
share of the community's assets is the daily business of
all governments, not only those in Africa. What is different in new nations is that the government cannot
assume a residual loyalty to the state among the
majority of its citizens.

Loyalty to the state can be measured by the sense of
restraint its citizens feel in pursuing their opposition to
specific policies of the government. If they oppose the
particular government in power but stop at a point
short of destroying the state or seriously weakening it,
they can be said to be loyal. This kind of legitimation
of the state rather than of a particular government is
something that is inculcated in the population over a
period of time. Children are taught it in schools. But
African nations have not yet had time for this. At
present many Africans cannot determine the limits of

opposition, do not understand the distinction between opposition and secession. This is what leaders of African governments mean when they argue that "our oppositions are not constructive." It is not that they tend to be destructive of the government in power; this is the purpose of an opposition. It is that they tend to destroy the state in the process of trying to depose the acting government.

This is particularly true because, in almost every African country, the opposition takes the form of a claim to regionalism—a demand for at least decentralization in a unitary state, federalism in a decentralized state, confederation in a federation, total dissolution of a confederation. Regionalism is understandable because ethnic loyalties can usually find expression in geographical terms. Inevitably, some regions will be richer (less poor) than others, and if the ethnic claim to power combines with relative wealth, the case for secession is strong. Ashanti in Ghana, the Ivory Coast in French West Africa, the Western Region in Nigeria, Gabon in French Equatorial Africa, Katanga in the Congo are all well-known examples. But every African nation, large or small, federal or unitary, has its Katanga. Once the logic of secession is admitted, there is no end except in anarchy. And so every African government knows that its first problem is how to hold the country together when it is threatened by wide disintegration.

The integration of a country can be assured in the long run only if the majority of the citizens begin to accept the state as the legitimate holder of force and authority, the rightful locus of legislation and social decision. President Senghor of Senegal has pointed out that: "In Africa, the Fatherland [*patrie*] is the *Serer* country, the *Malinke* country, the *Sonhrai*, the *Mossi*, the *Baule*, the *Fon* country. The Nation unites Fatherlands in order to transcend them. It is not, like the Fatherland, a natural phenomenon, therefore an expression of the milieu, but a will to construct or rather to reconstruct. . . . In order to achieve its object, the Nation must inspire all its members, all its individuals to seek in it, beyond their Fatherlands, their faith."

If this faith is weak, if citizens tend regularly to question not only the wisdom of the government's acts but its very right to engage in these acts, what can those who are interested in creating a nation do to enhance this acceptance, to diminish this questioning of the very basis of authority? This is not an abstract question; it has been the most urgent question that the government of every newly independent African nation has asked itself. And not surprisingly, most of them have come up with a similar series of answers, suggestions for ways in which they can work to create the bases of stable government.

What are these answers? One problem of new African nations is that they are new. People are not used to them. People cannot tell themselves that the ways of the state are hallowed by tradition, justified by experience. Even a modern rational state depends in part on its tradition (Britain on its unwritten constitution, France on its revolution or revolutions, the United States on its Founding Fathers and their views) to reinforce its legal structure. But tradition is in any case, and anywhere, largely myth. It exists in the minds of men. And if it is not there already, tradition can be created or re-created, revived and installed. And so in countless ways, African nations are today reëmphasizing their links with the past, their historical roots and glories, their cultural achievements, their unique virtues. Thus, Nigeria will invest in archaeological research, Senegal will sponsor a Festival of African Culture, and Morocco will recall the glories of the Almoravid Empire. Every state will build museums and encourage its historians to review and revive its past. We shall discuss this phenomenon in detail when we talk of cultural revival. Let us just note here that one of the immediate results of such emphasis on tradition is that it leads to a greater legitimation of the state.

To build a nation, it is not enough to have a past. One must have a present. To the extent that the various parts of a country are economically interdependent, to the extent that specialization proceeds and division of labor occurs within national boundaries, it becomes difficult, or rather expensive, to "secede." It is no accident that immediately after independence, customs and immigration barriers suddenly become tighter, as for example between Ghana and Togo, or between Guinea and Sierra Leone. There are many reasons for such a development, but one is that it fosters the creation of a *national* economy, which among other things reinforces the sense of nationhood and hence the basic loyalty of the citizens.

Before an African colony achieves independence it is part of an imperial economy. The shift to a national economy after independence is sometimes only a partial one, though the new government may try to intensify it for political rather than economic reasons. The expansion of the road and rail network, the diversification of agriculture, the building of dams and the spread of light industries—all of which have such a high priority in the newly independent African countries—serve many economic functions. They serve as well, however, to make less likely, more difficult, any weakening of the political bonds. The desperate hurry of African leaders for economic development is due not only to the desire for a higher standard of living and the need to fulfill their promises on this front, but also to the sheer political need to hold a unit together. Economic development does this both by showing that the nation works, and by enlarging the penalties of disintegration of the state. The changes in the economy thus affect the psychological attitude of the population toward the state.

Greater functional interdependence, then, leads to

greater integration, because as movements grow up
which pull the state apart they come to see more and
more the disadvantages of their own disruptive processes. The earlier they see this, the steadier will be the
path of government. For functional interdependence
leads to greater integration only if the citizens are aware
of how interdependent they have become. The nation
and its economic network must become "visible." And
whether what is visible is reality or an inflated reality
is rather irrelevant in terms of its effect in enhancing
the loyalty of the citizens; hence, the very great importance of public relations—what is pejoratively
known as propaganda. So everywhere in independent
Africa we see an immediate creation or expansion of
the government information service, of a radio station,
of official newspapers. It is not merely for international
prestige that Nigeria or Tunisia, Mali or Ghana puts
loudspeakers in every village. It is for the sake of informing large numbers of people regularly that the
nation is not merely an invention of remote intellectuals
but something whose structure affects their lives and
economic well-being intimately and increasingly. Perhaps even more than for the sake of informing people,
it is for convincing them.

The legitimation of which we speak, the citizens'
sense of loyalty to the nation, is best tested by the willingness of the average person, in the daily events of life,
to promote the enforcement of the laws, customs and
mores of the state. To some extent it is a question of
their thinking of the state as "we" and not as "they."
If the punishment for deviation must always await the
presence of the policeman, the state will not function
very well. To be sure, formal punishment is important,
and every new African state is eager to ensure that it
has at its disposition an adequate army and police
force which will be entirely loyal to it. However, government control of the army and police force is not
enough. The people must be willing to recognize the

authority of the law enforcement agencies and the government controlling them.

In the colonial situation, African national movements had taught their followers to think of the (colonial) state as "they," not "we." Independence demands a rapid reversal in outlook from opposition to support of the state's authority. This transition is difficult even for the educated and trained cadres of the movement. In Senegal or Guinea or Togo we find the newly independent governments inveighing against bureaucrats who have not learned that "sabotage" is no longer a legitimate tool of argument, that the anarchy which nationalists had demanded before had now become archaic and dangerous. To teach the uneducated majority the meaning of the law, rigorous enforcement with harsh penalties is often instituted. Immediately after independence, there are new and tighter laws governing traffic accidents, theft, murder. The new governments intend to show that they are there and that their laws are to be respected.

But the new governments must also create a climate in which laws are obeyed even in the absence of a regulatory force. The government has to teach people the rules; it has to accustom them to obeying rules. Campaigns are undertaken to induce people to report offenders, no matter how highly placed they are. Ritualized mass activities often are initiated. Americans know the "I Am An American Day" ceremonials which are used to habituate immigrants to American ways. Similar emphasis is being placed on respect for the flag and other national symbols in Africa today, especially among school children. Everywhere in independent Africa programs of "human investment" are being undertaken. The names of the programs may differ in Senegal or the Central African Republic, in Cameroun or Niger, but essentially they all call for the same thing —unpaid labor in the service of the nation. The programs are nowhere compulsory, but everywhere the

social pressure to participate is very heavy. Of course
the economic value of such activity is obvious. It
should also be observed, however, that such "noncom-
pulsory" programs rather forcibly recruit peasants and
uneducated urbanites for a *national* activity, one of
whose objects is to reiterate the norms of the nation
and encourage all the participants to punish the de-
viants by social disapproval of nonparticipation. In
Morocco, in 1957, the road built by voluntary labor
was called "The Road of Unity." Ben Barka, the
Moroccan political leader, said of this road: "It involved transforming these 'volunteers' who divided
their time on the Road between work and civic training
into truly *militant citizens.*"

In speaking of the activities to enhance the integrity
of the new African states we have referred somewhat
loosely to the "nation" as undertaking these activities.
But who exactly is it that does this "enhancing?" To
some extent it is the government, and we have mentioned various governmental activities. But, as we
have seen, the government rests on weak ground because of the shallow loyalty of its citizens. The problem
of establishing the integrity of the state is precisely
that of strengthening the hand of the state machinery,
but the government itself is not necessarily the best
agent for this. The government lacks personnel and
money. Even more important, it lacks the support of
citizens with that diffuse sense of attachment, "loyalty,"
which would encourage them to promote its well-being
without being paid. The dilemma is that the government lacks people with the loyalty to undertake activities which would enhance this very "loyalty" to the
government.

Since the government cannot perform the functions
necessary for increasing its own integrity, the modernizing elite, which is in control of most of the newly independent African nations, looks around for integrating
institutions, mechanisms which are intermediate be-

tween the citizen and the state but national in orientation, mechanisms which can attract the necessary loyalty more rapidly and turn this loyalty to the service of the nation. There are, unfortunately, very few such institutions available in these new nations. Functional organizations (trade unions, students' groups, etc.), while often national in orientation, tend to represent very limited portions of the population, given the degree of economic development in these countries. National churches such as those which served to support nationalism in Europe do not usually exist. The army may occasionally be able to fill this function, but it is generally weak and its usefulness limited. Two major instruments of integration tend to emerge from the nationalist struggle for independence: the nationalist party, and the national hero. The major hope for the modernizing elite lies with these. Let us see first what is expected of these "integrating institutions," and then by what means they try to fulfill these expectations.

For one thing, they must teach the new norms, by example and by precept, by repetition and by sanction. They must teach not only sets of rules and expectations but ways of looking at the world, *national* ways. They must educate people to understand why troops should be sent to the Congo, why diseased cocoa trees must be uprooted, and why government salaries cannot constantly rise. Unless this education is undertaken, it will be difficult to enlist the energies of the population in the service of the nation.

These institutions must somehow make the citizens aware of the nation as an economic entity, of the impact of economic acts on various parts of the country, of the degree to which the peasant relies on the port worker. They have to continue to stimulate the movement of people from the villages to the towns and mines, and, for the individual, they have to serve as a tangible institution on which he can rely for help, for

advice, for consolation. These are large tasks, and the
party and the national hero do not do them alone. But
as one surveys the African scene today, one observes
that where the party and the hero are weak, so are the
processes of modernization and integration of the
nation. For in this transition to a social order in which
the state will be able to rely on the loyalty of a citizenry
born to it and trained in it, the party and the hero can
be seen somewhat as a pair of surgical clamps which
hold the state together while the bonds of affection and
legitimation grow. If one may pursue the analogy,
these bonds may grow even without the clamps, but
without them the process is more arduous and painful,
and the outcome doubtful.

We speak of *the party*, but are there not *parties?* There
are in some countries. Most African nations came to
independence by organizing a nationalist movement
which laid effective claim to power. The standard
pattern was the existence of one major party which
symbolized the struggle for independence, with some
weak, often regionalist, opposition parties. Ghana,
Togo, Sierra Leone, Somalia are examples of this. In
some few cases, as a result of either absorption or suppression, the opposition totally ceased to exist before
independence—notably in the Ivory Coast, the Republic of Mali, Tunisia; or it expired soon after independence—as in Guinea and Upper Volta. Where there was
no one party which commanded overwhelming support
—the Congo, Sudan, Nigeria—or where the nationalist
party split after independence, as in Morocco, there
often was considerable trouble. Where a major segment
of the nationalist movement was systematically excluded from power, as in Cameroun, there was continued civil war. Almost everywhere, the trend after
independence has been in one of two directions: toward
a one-party state with consequent stability (if the
resulting single party grouped the major elements) or

toward a breakdown of the party system with consequent instability and a tendency for the army to play
a growing role (Sudan, Morocco, Congo).

The choice has not been between one-party and
multi-party states; it has been between one-party
states and either anarchy or military regimes or various
combinations of the two. The military regime, beset by
internal troubles, finds it difficult to mobilize energies
for economic development, to keep the intellectuals
satisfied and in line, to allow for participation in
government by any factions other than the small ruling
group. On the contrary, the single-party state—at least
the single-party state where the party structure is well
articulated and really functioning—provides a mechanism whereby the majority of the population can have
some regular, meaningful connection with, and influence upon, the governmental process, and vice versa.

Since "single-party systems" seem to be a standard
feature of the new African nations, it is well to distinguish them from the "single-party systems" in Eastern Europe, for example. The party in Africa, heir of the
nationalist movement, is first of all a mass party, at
least in theory. It seeks to enroll all the citizenry in its
branches, including its women's and youth sections. In
those nations where the party is an effective and real
one, the sections meet on a regular basis, often weekly,
in every village and town ward. Because almost the
whole population belongs to the party, these meetings
resemble "town meetings." The function of the meetings is twofold. They are arenas whereby the government via the party cadres can transmit new ideas, new
projects, new demands for sacrifices—that is, they
function to educate the population, so that government
decisions do not remain dead letters but are really
carried out. But they also serve to communicate the
ideas of the people to the government as well; they are
a direct channel of complaint and suggestion through
which the government can be made sensitive to the

internal realities of the nation and flexible in the means
it uses to achieve its goals. There seems to be considerable evidence that this two-way process is not a sham,
or in any sense based on terror, but that it works fairly
well. Of course it works better in some places than in
others. Tunisia, Mali, Guinea, Tanganyika are models
of single-party states with two-way communication.
Ghana, Togo and the Central African Republic run
close behind. Some party structures place less emphasis
on participation, using more nebulous antennae to
remain sensitive to popular will. In these cases, the
pipe lines transmitting points of view—both upward
and downward—sometimes get clogged. The Ivory
Coast is a prime example of this, and Ivory Coast
leaders often discuss the need to revitalize the party
structure in order to bring it into line with parties of
other countries providing more active communication.

Along with such a structure goes an ideology which
argues that the party incarnates the nation, not because
it is in tune with historical destiny, but because of its
past and present accomplishments. In the past, it
fought for freedom and helped to create a national consciousness. And in the present, it is a mass, not a class,
party. If it is not a class party, it is even less an elite
party. (This is, of course, a fundamental theoretical difference between African parties and Communist parties
in Eastern Europe.) It is a party to which everyone is
encouraged to adhere, and to which the majority do
adhere.

This ideology is the basis of justification for the theory
of parallel authority—the matching of each governmental structure (national, regional, local) with a party
structure, priority always being assigned to the political
over the administrative structure. It is considered the
essence of popular control over government in Ghana
and the Ivory Coast, Niger and Tanganyika, that the
Political Bureau of the party should take precedence
over the Cabinet. The party should run the govern-

ment, not vice versa, because the party, not the government, is the emanation of the people, that is, holds their loyalty and ties them to the state. The party integrates the nation and allows the integration to be accomplished by a method that maximizes the opportunity of every citizen to participate on a regular and meaningful basis in the decision-making process. In practice small elites may still run the show, but they do so to a lesser degree than if there were no party structure.

The party is not alone, however, in performing the integrating function. It shares the stage with its most important adjunct, the national hero. The hero, the leader, is not an isolated phenomenon. He is the leader of the party as well as of the nation. Should he break his ties with the party, he could find it difficult to survive, as we see from the decline of Messali Hadj in Algeria. Nevertheless, his power is not identical with that of the party; he has a drawing power of his own, as a potential arbiter, as a militant fighter, as one who has proved his mettle and will seek the nation's good.

The appearance of national heroes in Africa often makes outside observers uncomfortable, for the latter think of parallel strong men and "dictators" elsewhere. It is important, therefore, to see why the hero looms so large in the new African nations and what function he really fulfills.

Not all "heroes" are alike. Bourguiba of Tunisia and Nkrumah of Ghana, even Abbé Fulbert Youlou in the Congo (Brazzaville) represent one style—flamboyant, triumphant, evangelizing. Sékou Touré of Guinea, Modibo Keita of Mali, even Azikiwe of Nigeria, perhaps Nyerere of Tanganyika represent another style—calculating, militant, analytical. Olympio of Togo, Houphouet-Boigny of the Ivory Coast, even Senghor of Senegal and Ferhat Abbas of Algeria represent a third style—more cautious, sure-footed, quiet. These styles may make a lot of difference in the history of pan-Africanism. They make less difference internally. The

functions of the hero at home are everywhere substantially the same. The methods employed are similar.

The role of the hero is first of all to be a readily
available, easily understood, symbol of the new nation,
someone to incarnate in his person its values and aspirations. But the hero does more than symbolize the
new nation. He legitimizes the state by ordaining obedi-
ence to its norms out of loyalty to his person. This is
what people usually mean when they speak of the
charismatic authority of these leaders.

The problem of integration is essentially one of
getting people to shift loyalty from a structure based
on tradition ("do it because it has always been done
this way") to a new artificial entity, the nation-state,
whose only justification for authority lies in its constitution ("do it because it is the rationally agreed-upon
law"). This is a new basis for authority in Africa, and
as we have seen, the majority is often reluctant to give
it much credence, particularly if there is some immediate economic or prestige advantage for not doing so—
thus "regionalism" based on "tribal," traditionalist loyalties. The charismatic justification for authority ("do
it because I, your leader, say so") can be seen as a way
of transition, an interim measure which gets people to
observe the requirements of the nation out of loyalty
to the leader while they (or their children) learn to do
it for its own sake. In short, the hero helps to bridge
the gap to a modern state. The citizens can feel an
affection for the hero which they may not have at first
for the nation. Insofar as the hero works in tandem
with a party structure, he provides a very powerful
mechanism for integration of the state. Those African
nations which have not thrown up sufficiently "heroic"
leaders clearly suffer by their absence. And since heroes
are largely made, not born, most new African nations
are doing their best to create or reinforce the image of
their hero.

The problem is keeping the special, inflated status

of the hero untarnished. The hero is a human being. He makes mistakes, antagonizes people. He often gets bad press at home as well as in other African countries and beyond Africa. He is particularly under attack by intellectuals, who resent his nonintellectual claims to authority and often his scorn for their pretensions. Actually, the hero himself may be a full-fledged intellectual (Senghor, President of Senegal and poet, Kenyatta of Kenya, an anthropologist), or at least a university graduate (Bourguiba, Nkrumah, Azikiwe, Nyerere). This does not mean that he will not find a majority of the intellectuals opposed to him or chafing under his authority. For as a national hero he represents a nonintellectual outlook. The hero must establish a national myth. The intellectual attacks national myths —though often in the name of other myths, some more local, some more universal.

Under this attack on the hero's status, the new African states have worked out a number of ways of preserving his image so that he may fulfill his function as a mediator between new citizen and new state. The most obvious way is the glorification of the hero. His name must be everywhere. Ghana has its Kwame Nkrumah Circle and the Ivory Coast its Houphouet-Boigny Bridge. Western Nigeria has its statue of Awolowo and Upper Volta its Maurice Yaméogo Stadium. Troubadors sing the praises of Bourguiba, and the late Abbé Boganda is sanctified in the Central African Republic. And there is scarcely a country where the face of the hero does not appear on stamps, where the hero does not regularly conduct triumphal tours of his country in somewhat regal style.

But if in ceremonies the hero becomes more regularly apparent after independence, in actual fact he becomes more removed—both from foreigners and from his own people. He is shielded from soiling his reputation with the day-to-day harsh situations that governments face. He is surrounded by lieutenants and associates who bear the brunt of direct contact with the complainants, who serve as sources of information for the hero and scape-goats for blame. In moving about independent Africa, one can hear the same theme song again and again. "If only the hero knew, he would not permit it. He is good, but the men around him do not understand us."

If all these ways of preserving the leader's authority fail, the hero can resort to "religious" sanctification. "The Abbé Fulbert Youlou, although divested of his sacerdotal functions by the Catholic Church, has con-tinued to wear his cassock always." Houphouet-Boigny would return periodically to the native village of Yamoussoukro to meditate, and Nkrumah would go on "spiritual retreats." The hero often allows an aura of secrecy to build up and rumors to spread about his consulting the imam or the marabout or the fetish priest—any or all of them—without much regard for his own religious affiliation.

The hero and the party, then, work together to keep the nation unified, to hold it tightly together until the majority of the citizens begin to internalize a degree of loyalty to the state which will allow the government to take this loyalty for granted. Are all African states equally controlled by party and hero? No, obviously not. Parties are very strong in about a quarter of the states. These are true mass parties. There are partially effective parties in half the states. The proportion of genuine heroes is about the same.

There is a correlation between the strength of party and hero and the degree of national integration and stability. And, as we shall see, integration and stability make possible economic development and increase the ultimate prospects for a flexible democracy. Before we discuss these questions, let us turn from the problem of how to achieve or maintain internal unity in the newly independent states to the problem of how to achieve larger unities among African states—the whole question of pan-Africanism.

:VI:

LARGER UNITIES:

PAN-AFRICANISM AND

REGIONAL FEDERATIONS

The drive for larger African unity, pan-Africanism, is probably stronger than similar movements elsewhere in the world. It is not strong enough to assure immediate success, perhaps not even ultimate success. But pan-Africanism seems likely to loom large as an active issue in African politics in the near future.

Pan-Africanism is a very loose term and covers several different movements, which it would be well to distinguish. Pan-Africanism may be said to have arisen first as a protest movement of American and West Indian Negroes who were reasserting their links with Africa and the achievements of African civilizations. Its precursors were the early back-to-Africa movements which led to the creation of Liberia and Sierra Leone, movements which reached their high point in the remarkable spread of Garveyism in the United States in the 1920's.

In 1919, during the Versailles Peace Conference in

Paris, the American Negro leader, W. E. B. Du Bois, organized the First Pan-African Congress, presided over by Blaise Diagne, first Negro deputy from Senegal in the French parliament. Du Bois organized four more such congresses between then and 1945, earning the title of "father of pan-Africanism." The Fifth Congress was held in Manchester in October 1945, at the end of the Second World War. Du Bois was chairman. The joint secretaries were George Padmore, West Indian Negro and latter-day theoretician of pan-Africanism, and Kwame Nkrumah. The assistant secretary was Jomo Kenyatta.

The 1945 meeting marked a shift of emphasis in pan-Africanism from a protest movement of Western hemisphere Negroes seeking racial equality, allied with African intellectuals, to a tool of African nationalist movements fighting colonial rule. One of the organizations that grew out of the Manchester meeting was the West African National Secretariat, whose secretary was Nkrumah. It was established in London in 1947. When Nkrumah was called to the Gold Coast in 1948, the Secretariat ceased to function. There were no serious organizational developments from this point until 1957, when the Gold Coast (Ghana) became independent.

Ghana's independence and the first Conference of Independent African States, held in Accra in April 1958, once more changed the character of pan-Africanism. It was still a tool in the African colonial struggle, although now a complication arose. Who would direct and control this movement? Whether independent African nations had some greater right to wield this tool than the nationalist movements in countries not yet independent would become an issue. However, as more and more African countries gained their independence, the central question became rather the unification of sovereign states.

Thus, pan-Africanism has had at least three political

objectives, which to some extent can be seen as occurring in three successive periods. First, it has been a protest movement against racism, largely of American and West Indian Negroes. In this capacity, pan-Africanism still continues. It is an interesting and important story, but we shall not tell it here. Second, pan-Africanism has been a tool in the hands of African nationalist movements struggling for independence. It probably has not been the most important tool in this struggle. It has played some role, but one far less important than internal party organization and, as a rallying force, it has been no more important than territorial nationalism. At some points, it has even caused strains and hence, perhaps, setbacks for particular nationalist movements.

Third and most recently, pan-Africanism has been a movement to establish a supranational entity or entities encompassing various independent African states—at its most hopeful, the United States of Africa. In this last aspect, pan-Africanism has perforce had only a short life, much too short for us to be able to evaluate its achievements properly. Yet in its short history, the pan-African movement has had some important successes and suffered some serious setbacks. Perhaps in reviewing these experiences we shall discern what motivations lie behind pan-Africanism and what structural factors affect its possibilities of success.

Why larger unities? On the surface, this goal seems to make little sense. We have seen how nationalist movements have struggled to create a sense of nation, to establish political and economic institutions within a national framework. Why break down this entity the moment it is set up? Yet large numbers of African politicians cry out against the "balkanization" of Africa, which they say must be overcome. For many people the slogan of the anticolonial revolution was not "independence" but "independence and unity." According to their standards the goal of the nationalist movements has not been achieved by sovereignty; they require African unity as well.

African nationalists feel that in a real sense their struggle is an unfinished business and will continue to be so until unity is achieved. The objective of nationalism was not independence. This was only a means— one of two possible ones, as we have seen—to their real goal: political equality. At one level, independence assures equality in that each nation is sovereign and is legally free to pursue its own national interest. On another level, in the international arena, small and poor nations are scarcely able to compete on equal terms with big powers. Thus there appears an old political theme: in unity there is strength. If we can achieve African unity, it is argued, then we shall really have control over our own society. We shall then be able to remain apart from the quarrels of others; and we shall then be able to obtain assistance from the outside. This, of course, is not an irrational analysis.

The economic case for larger unities, to be sure, is strong. It was used for a long time by colonial governments to justify the establishment of federations of which they approved, such as the Federation of the Rhodesias and Nyasaland. Essentially the argument is that a larger internal market is necessary to stimulate industrial and commercial development, and that a larger geographical area contained within one political framework makes for more rational economic planning. Some claim that economic coöperation is both a justification for pan-African unity and a means through which it can be achieved. Others oppose larger unities because of the economic detriment to their countries (this is true of some relatively richer countries).

Basically, though, pan-Africanism is a political (and, as we shall see, cultural) movement. Economic arguments have proved insufficient to accomplish anything positive. But in the political arena, the quarrels over the pace and method of decolonization since 1957 on the one hand have destroyed some old possibilities of unity and on the other hand have created some new and unexpected channels for unity. In fact, decolonization has caused major political realignments in Africa, largely around the issues of pan-Africanism.

Colonial governments created units larger than the individual territories. Units such as French West Africa or French North Africa, British West Africa or British East Africa existed as institutional structures or at least as well-defined regions with common problems. The degree of administrative unity varied, although usually at least functional organs of coöperation existed, such as the West African Currency Board, East Africa Literature Bureau, the Institut Français d'Afrique Noire. These limited coöperative enterprises at the administrative level were matched by early nationalist groupings that were similarly organized on a regional level. Examples include the early National Congress of British West Africa, the Association des Etudiants Musulmans Nord-Africains, and most impressively, the Rassemblement Démocratique Africain, a French African political movement, at some point or other organized in what are now twelve independent countries. There were structures, then, that brought together political parties, trade unions, youth and students' groups on an interterritorial basis; but before 1957 these did not exist on an all-African basis, nor did they exist outside the framework of the colonial administrative structure, although the nationalist groups chose the widest structure available. The only all-African meeting ground before 1957 had been the pan-African congresses, and these were intermittent, inadequately representative, and without a continuing structure.

Decolonization in Africa, although occurring within a relatively short span of time, seldom occurred simultaneously in different territories, even those in the same area. Thus in British West Africa, Ghana became independent before Nigeria which became independent before Sierra Leone. In French West Africa, Guinea became independent before the Federation of Mali, which became independent before the four states of the Conseil de l'Entente (Ivory Coast, Upper Volta, Niger and Dahomey). Sometimes, as in French West Africa, the very pace of decolonization became a major issue *between* various African countries. The first ones to become independent in a group of territories were reluctant to remain in joint administrative structures with territories that were still colonies. Thus, in 1957, Ghana withdrew from such joint enterprises as the West African Airways Corporation. After Guinea's independence in 1958, she was excluded from the French West African interterritorial structures, which were to disintegrate completely by 1959. The administrative dismantling was sometimes matched by partial collapse of the interterritorial nationalist structures during this period. This was notably true in French black Africa. Between 1958 and 1960, as a result of quarrels over the methods of decolonization, the integrating nationalist structures on the party, trade union and youth levels were all seriously weakened. While Guinea and Mali and the Entente states argued over methods and immediate goals, each was afraid to be associated with interterritorial voluntary structures which might be of a different political tendency than its own. So each pressed its internal groupings to break ties with interterritorial groups of opposite tendencies.

In British East Africa and Central Africa a different type of dismantling of unified structures was occurring. Here interterritorial administrative structures had come into existence against the express wishes of the African population and with the assent of a white settler population. This was notably the case in the establishment of the Federation of the Rhodesias and Nyasaland (Central African Federation) in 1953. This was also largely true of the East African High Commission and its correlative agencies. In both cases, African opposition to unity was based on the fear that a unification of territories would tend to result in the prevalence throughout the larger entity of the policies of the most settler-dominated territory (Southern Rhodesia and Kenya, respectively). Unity in a colonial settler context was seen as a retrogressive step, one that would delay rather than speed up African liberation. In East Africa, African nationalists successfully opposed the creation of a federal structure. In Central Africa, the primary demand of African nationalists since 1953 has been the dissolution of federation.

In spite of their opposition to federation in settler areas, in organizing themselves to pursue their own aims, African nationalists have created the Pan-African Freedom Movement of East and Central Africa (PAFMECA) and have stated quite explicitly their goal of a federal structure for their states, once they have obtained independence and universal suffrage. In 1960, mindful of the experience of West African decolonization and its impact on unity, Julius Nyerere of Tanganyika announced the willingness of his movement to accept a short delay in its then imminent independence in order to enable Kenya and Uganda to receive their independence simultaneously with Tanganyika. His hope was that this would enhance the possibility of creating a single federal state.

A situation similar to that of East and Central Africa may be seen in South Africa. There the three so-called High Commission Territories—Basutoland, Bechuanaland, and Swaziland—which are governed by the United Kingdom Colonial Office, had resisted incorporation into the Union of South Africa, an issue which had been discussed since 1907. In South-West Africa, a former mandate which the Republic of South Africa has refused to place under United Nations trusteeship, African nationalists call for the recognition of the trust status of the territory as a step toward ultimate independence. Here again, as in East and Central Africa, Africans are against unity insofar as it means subjection to white-settler rule. The economic arguments put forward are scorned. The political reality is primary. On the African organizational level, however, a different picture is seen. The African nationalist organizations of both South-West Africa and the Republic of South Africa find themselves together since 1959 in the South Africa United Front. There is very close collaboration between the Basutoland nationalist groups and those in the Republic.

The picture on the northeastern Horn of Africa is somewhat different, but it also stresses the significance of the timing of independence. In this region live the Somali people, who during the colonial era were found in five areas: Italian Somaliland, British Somaliland, the southern half of French Somaliland, the Ogaden district in eastern Ethiopia, and the northeast corner of Kenya. There has long been a pan-Somali movement to unite this people. The largest single group is found in Somalia, which was Italian Somaliland, an Italian trust territory which long in advance was promised its independence in 1960 by the United Nations. When the date of independence approached, the United Kingdom responded to pressure in British Somaliland by granting this territory independence four days before Somalia, with the express expectation that the two would merge, which they did.

Still another variant occurred in North Africa, the Maghreb. Here Tunisia and Morocco received their independence in 1956, while Algeria was still fighting for hers. The long struggle of Algeria strengthened the moves for Maghreb unity, as various attempts were made by independent Tunisia and Morocco to assist Algeria. At an early point in the struggle, Tunisia's Bourguiba proposed to France that Tunisia (and Morocco) should retrocede some of their sovereign powers to a new French-North African confederation, provided that Algeria first was allowed to enter on an equal basis into a North African federation. Here is the same simultaneity principle advocated by Nyerere in East Africa, applied to somewhat different circumstances. This move failed, and in 1958 the governments of Tunisia and Morocco, and the Provisional Government of the Algerian Republic proclaimed a confederal structure, which was not seriously implemented because of the continuing French rule over Algeria. This was a clear case of utilizing unity as a weapon in the fight for independence.

The vagaries of the decolonization process, insofar as they have affected the possibilities of African unity, have not been entirely fortuitous. Colonial governments were not entirely indifferent to these questions. On the contrary, it can be argued that France was systematically, although not outspokenly, hostile, the British to a limited degree favorable, and the Belgians veered sharply between extremes.

Between 1956 and 1960, as French black African territories went from colonial status to autonomy to independence, the French seldom threw their support to elements favorable to larger political unities. The reason was very simple. Those who most strongly advocated unity were also those who most strongly pushed the advances toward independence. French repudiation of the goal of independence led to deep suspicion of the goal of unity. This was true of their attitude toward the moves made in this period to establish strong federal executives in French West Africa and French Equatorial Africa. The same was true of their attitude toward the reunification of both Togo and Cameroun with their British trust counterparts. It was true, as well, of their view of the pan-Somali movement in French Somaliland. And of course the French would never sympathize with moves for North African unity because these moves were predicated on the assumption of Algerian independence from France.

The British position was less clear-cut. In the early colonial era, they too sought to divide and conquer. But once they came to terms with the nationalist movement in a particular area, they looked with favor on achieving larger unities, chiefly on the grounds that larger entities showed more potential for stability and economic development. We have already mentioned the case of British Somaliland. There, having long opposed pan-Somali tendencies, the British surprised everyone, including the Somalis, by timing British Somaliland's independence to coincide with that of Somalia. In Nigeria, the British bore much responsibility for the rise of regionalism. But once having decided to go forward to independence, the British, between 1956 and 1960, were one of the important forces working toward the establishment of the strongest possible federal state for an independent Nigeria. In the settler territories of East and Central Africa, the Colonial Office was historically a stalwart supporter of moves toward federation, imposing its point of view on the Africans and to some extent even on the settlers. Nevertheless, by 1960 British support had somewhat abated as a result of the persistent African opposition. At this stage, having once again decided to go forward to independence (with universal suffrage), the British sought means of preserving the federal link (tainted by its association with white-settler domination) between the future independent African states. The work of the Monckton Commission in Central Africa and the Raisman Commission in East Africa are illustrations.

The factor that has made for the greatest difference between the British and the French attitudes toward larger unities in Africa has been the British willingness to acknowledge the legitimacy of the goal of independence. This has enabled the British, during the transition period, to look ahead to the postindependence period and plan their policy accordingly. They have

thus always been able to take a more relaxed view of
African unity than the French.

The Belgian policy has been quite different from both
the French and the British. The Belgians had always
ruled the Congo as a unitary state with some administrative decentralization. When they decided to grant
the Congo its independence, they were eager to retain
this unitary character. They feared that separatist
movements would destroy the strong economy of the
Congo in which they intended to remain involved.*
Shortly after independence, when it appeared that
Belgium's continuing political and economic relationship with the Congo was threatened by the strong supporters of the unitary state, the Belgian government
veered to a strong support of separatist, indeed secessionist, elements.

The policies of the colonial powers in relation to
larger African unities can be seen to reflect their views
of their own interests. That Britain, France and Belgium analyzed these interests differently does not de-
tract from the reality of this motivation. Even insofar
as colonial powers were favorable to unity, it was a
unity within the family, so to speak. When it came to
moves for pan-African unity that cut across the traditional colonial divisions, even the more sanguine British
hesitated occasionally. Yet, of course, African unity
will have real meaning only in the degree to which the
new entities will cut across divisions of European language and demarcations of European colonial spheres.

What concrete achievements can be pointed to as evidence of the reality of pan-African aspirations? There
were, first of all, the Conferences of Independent African States, in Accra in 1958, in Addis Ababa in 1960.
These were among the several successors to the Pan-

---

* However, during this period, 1959–60, the *French* government, characteristically, gave tacit encouragement to the
Bakongo separatists led by Joseph Kasavubu.

African Congresses. Up to now these assemblies have been largely resolution-passing bodies, but they have been able to secure the adherence of all the independent states.* The one permanent structure to grow out of these Conferences was the African bloc at the United Nations which, by regular meetings of the permanent representatives of the African states, forged an impressive unity between 1958 and 1960. With the admission of sixteen more African nations in the 1960 session of the United Nations and the divisive explosion of the Congo, this unity at least temporarily disappeared.

Parallel with these Conferences of Independent African States have been the meetings of the All-African People's Conferences (AAPC), another of the successors to the Pan-African Congresses.† The AAPC groups include nationalist political parties and trade-union federations of both independent and not-yet-independent African countries. Hitherto the major concern of the AAPC has been the liberation of the remaining colonial Africa. The first meeting was held in Accra in 1958, followed by one in Tunis in 1959, and a third in Cairo in 1961. The AAPC has set up a continuing machinery, a secretariat whose headquarters is Accra. The first secretary general was George Padmore, Trinidadian and close collaborator of Nkrumah, with whom he was joint secretary of the 1945 Manchester Pan-African Congress. When Padmore died in 1959, he was succeeded by Abdoulaye Diallo, Guinea's resident minister in Ghana and former trade-union leader in French West Africa.

It is important to note the close links, through personnel and ideology, between the Conferences of Independent African States and the All-African People's

* Except the Union of South Africa, which was actually invited to the 1958 Accra Conference but refused to come because the colonial powers were not invited also.

† The third major successor, the Congresses of Black Men of Culture, we shall discuss in Chapter VII.

Conferences. The latter have been the nongovernmental parallel to the intergovernmental body,* and have had a certain flexibility of maneuver, structure, and even language from which the exigencies of government protocol restrain the former. It is also important to note that both these structures have joined together black sub-Saharan Africa and Arab North Africa. This has been not peripheral but central to the conception. Indeed, thus far, these structures have been better at bringing together black and Arab Africa than at bringing together French-speaking and English-speaking Africa. The structures thus far have not been able to involve some of the significant groups in French-speaking black Africa, despite the fact that the North African participants are largely French-speaking. This was because, as we explained earlier, some of the French Africans have resisted greater African unity.

Many of the forces behind the AAPC have attempted to create an All-African Trade Union Federation (AATUF) as a concrete method of furthering African unity. Here there has been an added complication: Some African trade unions today are members of the International Confederation of Free Trade Unions (ICFTU), a non-Communist body.† One of the force behind AATUF has been the Union Générale de Travailleurs de l'Afrique Noire (UGTAN), an interterritorial group whose base was in former French West Africa.‡ UGTAN achieved internal unity in 1957 by

* The same double structure of intergovernment meetings on the one hand and interparty, inter-trade-union and interstudent organization meetings on the other hand has been used on a smaller geographic scale in North Africa.

† A few less important unions belong to the International Federation of Christian Trade Unions; also a very few belong to the Communist-dominated World Federation of Trade Unions. Finally, there are a large number affiliated with none of these internationals.

‡ The headquarters were in Conakry, Guinea, and the president of UGTAN was Sékou Touré, President of the Republic of Guinea, who started his political career as a trade-union leader

getting all the constituent members to break ties with internationals—"positive neutrality" on the trade-union scene. UGTAN leaders and others have thought that such international nonaffiliation should be the basis of the projected AATUF. Some trade unions affiliated with the ICFTU, notably those of Tunisia and Kenya, have argued that they do not wish to cut their ties with the ICFTU. This quarrel has made the realization of AATUF difficult. But here again it should be noted that all the preparatory meetings for AATUF have included both North and sub-Saharan Africans, both French-speaking and English-speaking black Africans, and the divisions over international affiliations have crosscut the geographical and language differences. Similar efforts in the field of youth and students' groups have been even more tentative.

On the intergovernmental level, the chances for unity, as we have seen, were affected by the decolonization process. We have mentioned the real, if partial, success of the pan-Somali movement, as well as the more limited results of efforts to create a unified North Africa. There has also been the reunification of Cameroun with the southern half of the British Cameroons, as well as the earlier federation of Eritrea with Ethiopia.

In French black Africa, we have shown, decolonization worked against unity. This was particularly evident in the attempt to create a federation of French West Africa. Though originally there were eight territories, an attempt to create a structure called the Federation of Mali could rally only four, of which two failed to ratify the constitution, and the remaining two, after a year and a half of coexistence, broke apart in August 1960. One move intended to counter the Federation of Mali was the Conseil de l'Entente, a loose confederation of sovereign states. The Conseil de l'Entente was as much a move designed to prevent unity (of the federal Mali variety) as one to promote unity. Another attempt in former French Equatorial

Africa to found a federal Union des Républiques d'Afrique Centrale (URAC)—similar in conception to Mali
—foundered before it was ever ratified. As for plans
to establish unities that transcended colonial spheres,
the proposal of the Abbé Boganda for a United States
of Latin Africa (to group Cameroun, Congo, Angola
and the four states of former French Equatorial Africa)
and the plans of the Senegalese for Senegambia (to
incorporate the tiny British colony of the Gambia into
Senegal or, at one point, into the Federation of Mali)
never got beyond the talking stage.

On the other hand, out of the destruction of French
West African unity caused by the process of decolonization came the construction of one political unity that
does transcend colonial language barriers, the Ghana-
Guinea Union in 1959.* Ghana and Guinea do not
have contiguous frontiers, and the Union has no structure beyond the fact that the two countries exchange
not ambassadors but resident ministers, who have the
right to attend the cabinet meetings of the partner.
The Union has neither common institutions, common
language, nor common currency. And yet it would be
rash to discount it. For the Union has brought together
two dynamic countries which, despite many common
attitudes, had almost no contact until the very time
of the Union. The Union may be thought to be nothing
but a very strong alliance, which is all it amounts to
in terms of structure. But its significance lies in the fact
that it symbolizes the possibility of transcending the
"language barrier" and, by this very fact alone, is a
force of attraction for pan-Africanists throughout Africa.

Ghana and Guinea both separately and together are
major pressures toward African unity. Their force lies
in their internal strength and dynamism, their vigorous positions on international affairs, their neutralism,
their constant efforts to promote liberation in colonial

* To which the *Republic* of Mali adhered in 1960, making it
the Union of African States.

territories and to support, financially and otherwise, pan-Africanist elements. The North Africans represent another such pressure, not always a united one. Presenting an image of themselves as Africans first, Arabs second, they are working very hard to see that African unity includes them, although they may conceive of this unity as a coalition of regional frameworks (such as North Africa, West Africa, East and Central Africa, etc.).

The United Arab Republic (UAR) is often credited with being a major force in pan-Africanism. Actually, despite money expended both in propaganda and in assistance to various nationalist movements in their anticolonial struggles, and despite the fact that at various points some nationalist leaders (for example those of Algeria, Cameroun, Uganda) have had bureaus in Cairo, the UAR has played only a minor role. The reason is that their image of themselves, as well as that which other Africans have of them, is of a country primarily interested in Arab unity and only secondarily concerned with all-African unity.

It is more significant to ask what are the present and future roles of Nigeria and the Ivory Coast. Nigeria, Africa's largest country in population, enjoys the prestige and power of its size and the fact that in itself it represents an achievement in terms of African unity. Thus far, the need to maintain the balance of internal unity has kept it from playing the downstage role of Ghana in the pan-African movement. However, the very fact that Nigeria considers Ghana's role an exaggerated one may push her to advocate pan-African doctrines even more strongly. The Ivory Coast, by contrast, has shown itself cool to larger unities which would impinge on her own autonomy and development. Unable to fight pan-Africanist forces alone, the Ivory Coast has taken the lead in creating the Entente, as well as a coöperative arrangement of a larger group of French-speaking states (Abidjan, Brazzaville, and Yaoundé Conferences of 1960-61).

The Congo crisis temporarily divided most of the half of Africa which was independent in 1960 into two camps: the strong pan-Africanists who attended the Casablanca Conference, and the advocates of a milder form of unity who attended the Brazzaville Conference. This crystallization into separate units is only momentary, however. As East, Central and South Africa attain independent governments based on universal suffrage, the crosscutting alliances should begin to make the realization of African unity a reality.

It is clear from this discussion that not all Africans and not all African states are equally pan-African in their enthusiasm. What should be noted is that there is some correlation (not a perfect one) in each African state between those elements who are modernizing and centralizing and those who are oriented to pan-Africanism. The strength of the pan-African drive can be attributed precisely to the fact that it is the weapon of the modernizers—those throughout Africa who are most radical in their nationalism, most vigorous in their demands for equality, most conscious of the primacy of political solutions to the problems of Africa. Pan-Africanism may one day be divorced from modernization in Africa. It is not so today. To the extent, then, that pan-Africanism fails, modernization too is set back.

:V I I:

CULTURAL REVIVAL

In the colonial era, whether the system of administration was direct or indirect, whether assimilation was or was not a specifically developed policy in the educational and judicial spheres, the Europeans in Africa—administrators or traders, missionaries or educators—shared one basic assumption: the superiority of Western cultural values to those they found in African countries. Moreover, they usually assumed that they had, in one form or another, what the French liked to call a "civilizing mission," which always meant a Westernizing mission and quite often meant a Christianizing mission. This was no passing mood. It was the fundamental ideological justification of the whole colonial enterprise. And it was a justification which Europeans sought to have the African educated elite accept.

To some degree, this policy of cultural denigration of African society was successful. The African intellectuals did at first reject their own culture—not only its religion and its technology, but its dress and its music, and most important, its link with the past. These intellectuals very largely accepted the notion that Africa had no history, that the future lay in adopting a Western style of life.

We have seen how the nationalist movement, for various reasons, ultimately rejected the alternative of assimilation as a means of achieving political equality and went on to demand political independence. In the political sphere, the choice, once clarified, was a simple one. Either total assimilation or total separation would assure equality. Nothing in between would do. But in cultural questions, the problem was the opposite, how both to assimilate and preserve, how both to be universal and to be oneself, how to modernize without being Western.

For its own organizational purposes, the nationalist movement began to find much virtue in cultural revival. In seeking to turn a protonationalist movement that was limited to an educated urban group into a mass nationalist movement that could appeal to peasant masses who were still strongly traditional in outlook, nationalist leaders began to rediscover and praise the heroes of ancient Africa once more. They would choose most particularly the heroes who had resisted the colonial powers, especially those whose empires had been expanding at the moment of European contact. Thus the West African Mandingo chief Samory and the Zulu king Chaka, the Mad Mullah of Somalia and Abd-el-Kader of Algeria, all treated in colonial textbooks as barbarians, as cruel warriors whose conquest or defeat was the beginning of progress, came to be seen once again as noble victims of colonial rapacity. An objective analysis of their role is not to the point. The point is that the nationalist movement began to reject the colonial interpretation of recent events. Many nationalist leaders sought to trace their own lines of descent (some spurious) from these earlier kings and heroes. Jomo Kenyatta, working under the British anthropologist Malinowski in the 1930's, shocked the colonial world with his ethnographic survey of the Kikuyu, *Facing Mount Kenya*, by making it an open defense of many Kikuyu customs, including female circumcision. He wrote: "The missionaries who attack the *irua* of girls are more to be pitied than condemned, for

most of their information is derived from Gikuyu converts who have been taught by these same Christians
to regard the custom of female circumcision as something savage and barbaric, worthy only of heathens who
live in perpetual sin under the influence of the Devil."
Up to that time, no African intellectual had dared
openly to question the illegitimacy of such traditional
practices.

Yet a nationalist movement must be cautious. Seeking to find themes that will draw it mass support,
seeking the enlistment of traditional attitudes and
grievances on behalf of a modern cause, the nationalist
movement risks losing more than it gains—and on two
fronts. At home, as we have seen, the traditional rulers
were quite often closely bound up with the colonial administration. Traditional themes could be used against,
as much as in favor of, uprooted urban intellectuals.
Furthermore, nationalists had to consider international
public opinion, which played such an important role in
the timing and ease of transition. At the critical moment of the "time of troubles," and still more so during
the dyarchy, the nationalist movement hesitated to
risk alienating the outside world. Compare the Mau
Mau rebellion with the Algerian rebellion. Mau Mau
repelled large segments of British and world opinion.
Even Kenyan nationalist leaders tried to remain un-
associated with it (at least at the time). This was one
reason—of course not the only one—why Mau Mau
could be crushed. The Algerians, even when they used
means of violence which met with reprobation in the
outside world, did so in a Western tradition to which
they pointed as justification. Presenting a resolutely
modernist image, and toning down terrorist tactics under international pressure, the Algerians were able to
use international sympathy as a major tool in their
struggle.

The colonial situation, then, placed many limitations
on cultural revival, both by the direct pressure of the

administration and the indirect one of international opinion. Independence would lift these restraints. Indeed, the demands of national integration would press directly for more cultural revival, which in turn would create new dilemmas for the new states. But before we consider these dilemmas, let us see what are the forms and expressions of African cultural revival: in the writing of history, in philosophy and religion, in linguistic matters, in literature and the arts, and even in political and economic theory.

The primary fact to note about the revival of African history is the uphill battle that had to be fought to demonstrate the very existence of the thing to be studied. A cardinal premise of colonial rule had been that "Africa has no history." In the schools of the colonial era, the African history that was taught was the history of the colonial era. French African schoolchildren used a notorious textbook that began "Our ancestors the Gauls." Neither European nor any other universities had chairs for African history or men specializing in African history. A certain historical past was accredited at most to North Africa, but that area was treated as part of the Mediterranean world, and the importance of the Arab part of its history quite often minimized. As for black Africa, since it was believed there were no written records and since Africans were thought incapable of higher cultural achievement, it was considered inconceivable to apply the term history to the story of unchanging savage cultures.

But as we have seen in Chapter I, the history of Africa shows diversity and change, development and progress, like the histories of other continents. And since our knowledge of this history, though greatly enlarged in very recent years, has been acquired gradually over at least a century, how was it that Europeans maintained the image of an Africa without history? They did so by systematically refusing to believe that the archaeological finds, the works of art uncovered,

the travelers' tales of ancient empires were the products of a black civilization. Indeed, a European in 1895
doubted the African origin of some ruins in Rhodesia:
"It is a well-accepted fact that the negroid brain never
could be capable of taking the initiative in work of such
intricate nature."

All sorts of people—the "whiter" the better—got
credit for these works. There were, as we have seen,
the ubiquitous Hamites who seemed to be everywhere
and were at least not Bantus. There were "Hittites"
and "Phoenicians," Arabs in East Africa, Jews and
Berbers in West Africa, and even the ancient Greeks or
the Portuguese later on. Not all of this was fiction,
but much of it was. It has been proved, for example,
that ancient Greek ships were technically incapable of
reaching West Africa, given their construction and the
tides. In any case, serious scholarly proof was seldom
attempted. On the contrary, many persons seemed to
reach out deliberately for improbable explanations of
obvious situations so as to maintain the myths in
which they so profoundly believed. Even some anthropologists, who could have been expected to be
more sympathetic to the reality of African achievement,
tended rather to search for primitive purity—which
seemed by implication to deny any higher achievement.

Since the Second World War, there has been a new
way of looking at African history. First there were a
number of European, American and Soviet scholars
(archaeologists, historians, anthropologists, art historians, even ethnobotanists) who began to make important new discoveries that helped to create an understandable pattern of the migratory movements and of
the rise and fall of African empires. But it was the
emergence of African scholarship about Africa that did
most to create a significant change in atmosphere. The
way was prepared by an older generation of amateur
African scholars—ministers, schoolmasters, lawyers—
whose research, if not always of the highest quality,

was inspired by a feeling that the themes they were treating were important and had been neglected. Their work has been taken up now by African historians, sociologists and anthropologists of full professional status, especially those in West Africa—men like Nigeria's K. O. Dike and S. O. Biobaku, Ghana's K. A. Busia and Nana Nketsia, Senegal's Cheikh Anta Diop and Ly Abdoulaye, and Joseph Ki Zerbo of Upper Volta.

The revival of history was important for the anti-colonial revolution, not only to create a justification for nationalism in terms of the past but to destroy the myth of European virtue that enchained so many of the educated group. It began to break down the effectiveness of the myth of white superiority in the colony, even among the European colonials, and in the metropolitan country. Thus it built up African confidence as it lessened European. After independence the rewriting of history became central to the evolution of the new nation.

We have already remarked that one of the problems of national integration is that most African nations have only a short past as nationalities, and that this means that the concept of loyalty to the nation has no roots in tradition. Conscious efforts have been made by African governments to review educational curricula at all levels in order to reorient the history that is taught. Many countries have built museums before libraries. Historical journals have been started for the educated elite, and children's books are being written on African historical themes.

It is for the intellectual particularly that this re-awakening historical sense seems to be important. He who was most conscious of being cut off from his cultural heritage now turns to it with a vengeance and a fascination. His concern is not merely the practical one of discovering themes which will somehow create a national consciousness among the peasantry. It is the classic concern of the intellectual who finds himself somehow out of the mainstream of his society's attitudes and ways of life, and seeks a way of personal reintegration into the community. Precisely insofar as the intellectuals have found some difficulty in achieving political power in the new African nations, precisely insofar as they have been uncomfortable in the shadow of a heroic leader, they have turned to their specialty—cultural nationalism, the interweaving of new and old myths.

It is interesting to see what subjects they have concentrated on. One, obviously, is the period of colonial conquest. There have been works to underline the economic interests involved in colonial "pacification," the profits extracted by cruelty. Or there have been works trying to demonstrate that African empires such as the Ashanti or Zulu were at important points of consolidation and expansion when forcibly stopped and partially destroyed by European forces; that is, that important African achievements went unrealized because of colonial penetration. This kind of historical focus is understandable and will continue for a long time. The documents are reasonably ample and the material scarcely has been touched. Aspects of history that usually have been avoided thus far are the more recent colonial period and the nationalist movements. The material in these fields is perhaps *too* recent. In any case, the authors are often too involved in this very history, and find the subjects too delicate. There are some exceptions, like *The Sudan Question*, by Mekki Abbas. And there are, of course, the growing number of autobiographies by leading African politicians that are, to some extent, short histories of the nationalist movements of their countries (for example, the autobiographies of Bourguiba, Nkrumah, Awolowo).

The historical problem that has evoked the greatest interest in Africa is one which is much less often the focus of Western European history. This is the question of origins, the problem of looking into the far past and trying to see where Africans as a whole, or a given African people, originated. In Chapter I we reviewed some of the facts known at the present time. What we emphasize here is the nature of the interest and the reasons for it.

On analysis, it is not so surprising to find that Africans place great emphasis on this question of origins. First of all, to discuss origins, one has to turn to a remote past, shrouded in mystery because of lack of documents. The very remoteness in time of the subject matter emphasizes the historical existence of the group under study, their presence in the world *over a long period of time.* Second, as one pushes back in time, the disparity in technology between a given African society and any other society is less than at present; indeed, the comparison may well be to the advantage of the African society. Third, it may be possible to demonstrate not merely the nonsuperiority of Western civilization but, conversely, the superiority of African civilization, if one pushes the analysis sufficiently far back.

So far much of this writing on origins has been about West African peoples, perhaps because nationalism had an earlier start there. In East, Central and South Africa, which are faced with claims of white settlers to the rights of permanent inhabitants, Africans emphasize how long they have been in the area rather than where they came from at some earlier period. It may be that once independent African states exist in this area, they too may begin to explore their origins.

In West Africa, two peoples particularly have been the focus of historical interest: the Akan and the Yoruba. The Akan peoples include most of the major tribes of the southern half of the Gold Coast. In 1926 the Rev. W. T. Balmer suggested that these peoples derived from the inhabitants of the ancient empire of Ghana. He argued that after the destruction of the empire these people migrated southeast a thousand miles to their present habitat. The claim was based partly on tribal legends which indicated such a migration. The Rev. Mr. Balmer's idea might have lapsed into obscurity had it not been picked up, amplified and reinvigorated after World War II by Gold Coast nationalist politicians, particularly Dr. J. B. Danquah. This claim of descent became so important a theme of Gold Coast politics that it overrode all factional differences, and Ghana was selected in 1957 as the name of the newly independent nation. Scholars are still arguing over the validity of the claim, but the name of Ghana will remain.* As for the Yorubas, the first suggestion that they migrated from Egypt, again partly based on tribal legends, was made in the nineteenth century by an African Anglican bishop. In this case, too, the claim was picked up and emphasized in the post-World War II period, and the Nigerian Western Regional government invested special funds in furthering the study. The Yoruba claim has had a strong Christian bias, and there has been some attempt to show parallels between Yoruba customs and those of the ancient Hebrews.

Perhaps the most ambitious attempt to reconstruct African history has been the numerous writings of Cheikh Anta Diop. Diop has a theory that there is a basic global division of peoples into two kinds: the Southerners (or Negro-Africans), and the Aryans (a category covering all Caucasians, including Semites, Mongoloids and American Indians). Each grouping has a cultural outlook based on response to climate, the difference between them being that the Aryans have had a harsher climate.

The Aryans have developed patriarchal systems characterized by the suppression of women and a propensity

---

* Another ancient empire, Mali, gave its name to a new nation, formerly the French Sudan, but in this case Mali was presumed to have occupied somewhat the same territory.

for war. Also associated with such societies are materialist religion, sin and guilt, xenophobia, the tragic drama, the city-state, individualism and pessimism. Southerners, on the other hand, are matriarchal. The women are free and the people peaceful; there is a Dionysian approach to life, religious idealism and no concept of sin. With a matriarchal society come xenophilia, the tale as the literary form, the territorial state, social collectivism, and optimism.

According to Diop's theory, the ancient Egyptians, who were Negroes, are the ancestors of the Southerners. This bold hypothesis, which is not presented without supporting data, has the interesting effect of inverting Western cultural assumptions.* For, Diop argues, if the ancient Egyptians were Negroes, then European civilization is but a derivation of African achievement. He writes: "It is impossible to insist on everything the world—in particular, the Hellenic world—owes the Egyptian world. The Greeks did nothing but take up and sometimes, to a degree, develop Egyptian inventions, all the while despoiling them, because of their materialist tendencies, of the idealistic religious shell which surrounded them." Thus, even Western technology is traced to its Egyptian (Negro) origins.

Not all African scholarship is this sweeping in its claims. But another aspect of African culture has received special attention in recent years: its philosophy and religion. Perhaps the greatest contribution in these fields has been made by a non-African Catholic priest, Father Tempels. Father Tempels, in his book *The Bantu Philosophy*, based on long research through African informants, analyzed the cosmological ideas of the Bantu people. He discovered them to be highly complex, and fundamentally monogamous in spirit. He discovered that one could talk of a Bantu ontology, a

---

* The hypothesis is not original with Diop. Other scholars, such as W. E. B. Du Bois, had earlier presented the argument that the ancient Egyptians were Negroes.

Bantu psychology, a Bantu ethic, and concluded that
these "discoveries" made it necessary to revise basic
European attitudes toward the African. Father Tempels
ended his book by offering an apology for those Europeans who had previously disdained African thought.
The book was written in 1944–45 and contributed to the
new spirit of the postwar period.

Similar work by the French anthropologist Marcel
Griaule among the Dogon of the western Sudan further
undermined assumptions of African primitivity. In this
same region the works of an African sage of this century,
Tierno Bokar, have been presented to the intellectual
public by his disciple, Amadou Ba Hampaté, who was
named the first director of the research institute of the
Republic of Mali. African Catholic priests (and some
Protestants) have tried to review Christian rituals and
their relation to African customs and have sought new
syntheses that would allow the universal principles of
Christianity to take on a specifically African form.
African philosophy and theology, drawing upon the
traditions known to African soil, have become living
and creative disciplines.

This revival of history and philosophy has been part
of a wider movement known as negritude, the earliest
spokesmen of which were poets. Two very significant
facts should be noted about negritude. First, the word
is French and for a long time the movement has been
dominated by the French-speaking African world, perhaps because of their greater revolt against previous
assimilationist tendencies. Second, the word was invented not by an African but by a West Indian Negro,
Aimé Césaire of Martinique, and then picked up by
Léopold Senghor, a poet who is now the President of
Senegal.

Organizationally, the proponents of negritude in 1947
founded a magazine, *Présence Africaine*, edited by a
Senegalese, Alioune Diop, and published in Paris.*

* An English edition was started in 1958.

The intellectual ferment that grew out of this magazine
led its participants to convene the first World Congress
of Black Men of Culture in Paris in 1956, and another
in Rome in 1959. The lines of admission to these Congresses have not been absolutely clear. Congresses of
the Negro world, they have included inhabitants of
black Africa and Negroes from the United States, the
Caribbean, and Brazil. However, they also have included Malagasies, who are of Malaysian stock, but
whose island, Madagascar, is considered part of the
African continent and whose present political history
has been closely tied to that of black Africa. And
North African (Arab) intellectuals have tried to maintain a special relationship with these Congresses. The
first Congress created an international African Society
of Culture, whose explicit model was the European
Society of Culture.

The definition of negritude, and the determination of
the scope of "African culture," has not been a simple
matter; indeed it has been the central point of debate
among these intellectuals. There have been two main
trends within this movement. One point of view has
been that negritude is a matter of form, of some innate
emotional quality of the Negro soul which binds Negroes the world over. Senghor has been a leading exponent of this point of view, characterizing the Negro in
terms of intuitiveness and sensitivity, qualities thought
to be derived from the Negro's tropical agricultural
existence but now hereditary. He has said: "That
which constitutes the Negritude of a poem is less the
theme than the style, the emotional fervor which gives
life to the words, which converts the words into speech."
Cheikh Anta Diop's theories make a similar assumption
of some special quality in African culture. This is why
both these men have preferred to speak of Negro-
African rather than of African culture.

Another point of view is that negritude is a quality of
revolt which derives from the political and cultural

oppression the Negro has known. Jean-Paul Sartre adopted this viewpoint in his famous essay, "Black Orpheus," in which he described contemporary Negro literature as the only revolutionary literature in the contemporary world. This is also the viewpoint of Jacques Rabemananjara, Malagasy poet, politician, and major contributor to *Présence Africaine*, who has said: "Now who forges these arms of salvation? It is not the Negro as a Negro; it is the Negro as one frustrated, it is the Negro as one humiliated in the depths of his soul, it is the Negro as one mutilated in his dignity as a human being. . . . I do not know further how belonging to Negritude has ever dictated to its poets an esthetic attitude."*

Clearly the second point of view is more compatible with a pan-African political unity that would include North Africa than the former approach. Clearly, too, it is more in line with the dominant trends of Western thought. The division between these two outlooks, however, is by no means sharp; negritude, African cultural nationalism, is still garnering its forces and feeling its way. But this division, which arose out of the ambiguities of the movement for African independence (movement against racism, movement against colonialism, movement for supranational unity), may mean that what we have called the third legatee of the Pan-African Congresses may someday move away from the other two, more directly political, legatees (the Conferences of Independent African States and the All-African People's Conferences). For the moment, this is not so.

These theoretical differences about the nature of negritude have not been without their immediate implications, even in what might seem so remote a field as political and economic theory. For a long time Afri-

* The South African author Ezekiel Mphalehle represents a third group, which is deeply suspicious of possible "racist" implications of negritude.

can nationalism has had as one of its subthemes the establishment in the new nations of an "African socialism." The adjective "African" is significant, for it has been argued that, in the process of technological advance and economic development, there is no reason to adopt Western economic structures, either capitalist or state socialist, when the traditional African communal ownership of land offers the base for a coöperative socialist economy with a peculiarly African stamp. This emphasis on the coöperative in the economic structure, made most explicit by Mamadou Dia, economist and Prime Minister of Senegal, has been matched in the field of political structure by the contention of Guinea's Sékou Touré that Africa's traditional political structure—what he calls "communocracy"—can be the basis of a peculiarly African form of democracy. Julius Nyerere of Tanganyika, arguing the same point, has called the African "communitary" in his thinking. In these theories of Dia, Touré and Nyerere can be found a middle road between those who see an almost physiological uniqueness about African culture and those who view it purely in universal terms. These economic and social theories have been arguments for universal values within the forms of traditional African institutions, for being modern without being Western.

The cultural revival of Africa presents no simple, clear pattern. Revival always implies a selection of the past, a selection that is made not only in terms of the exigencies of the present but of the plans for the future. We revive the past, but which past? Biobaku writes of the origin of the Yoruba and Cheikh Anta Diop of the origin of the Negro-African, while Algerians speak of "we Africans." Each may have a different image of Africa; certainly each enterprise, each locution will have a definite bearing on the future structure of African society.

If cultural revival has caused much pain, it is in part because it both abets and hurts the process of

modernization. Adopting the techniques of another
culture, when that culture has been dominant politically
until only recently, is a very hard thing for a people to
accept. The psychological stance is one of weakness,
of lack of self-confidence. The danger is that if one feels
weak, one finds any change threatening and therefore
rejects all change. Mau Mau was a momentary instance
of this attitude. The reassertion of the values of African
culture, the creation of an African cultural unity, can
instill a sense of security in Africa such that it will be
able to adopt technological changes from outside Africa,
principally the Western world, without fear that these
adoptions will destroy the African character, the "African personality," of the independent nations.

But the revival of tradition means also the strengthening of the traditional elite. The two cannot be sep-
arated entirely. Having fought the traditional elite in
the colonial era, the modernizing intellectual elite is
in no mood to cede power after independence. Yet to
build the unity of a nation, to give it the psychological
strength to be modern, the modernizing elite must in
part reassert tradition and reinforce some traditional
institutions. In this new alliance, whereby the traditional elite is absorbed into the party structures, the
question of the future remains: who will control whom?
This is particularly the question at the village level.
What seem like monolithic parties from the outside
are often the scenes of subtle, or not so subtle, struggles
inside, between those forces who stand against change
and those who stand for modernization. Both present
themselves as the exponents of an African way. But
the party structure is an uneasy meeting ground, and
the future developments remain uncertain.

:VIII:

AFRICA

AND THE WORLD

Having emerged from colonial rule, Africa is determined to be subject to no one but itself. And Africa is determined somehow to be distinctively different, distinctively African. The depth of its sensitivity to outside control, the suspicion of outside links, should not be misinterpreted, however. It is not a rejection of the world. It is an embracement of it. For African nationalists held, as one of their cardinal criticisms of colonial rule, that it maintained Africans in a cocoon, that the colonial administration hindered contacts with, even knowledge about, areas and peoples outside the particular network. Independence was accompanied by a strong desire to taste the forbidden fruit, to visit and enter into relations with all those parts of the world somehow previously withheld from Africans. Yet, paradoxically, Africans feel they can guarantee this continued contact with the whole world best by emphasizing the autonomy, even the apartness, of Africa. They see pan-Africanism not as the creation of a super-nationalism but as a means of contributing to the spirit and reality of world coöperation.

The coöperation of Africa with the rest of the world

takes many forms. The form that is still dominant in most cases, despite decolonization, is the link with the former metropolitan power. In some cases, this is a strong link, formed by institutions and affective ties. In others, it is a reluctant link, made necessary by economy and language. And even where there has been a sharp and bitter break, as in Guinea or the Congo, there continue to be important ties.

These links can take the form of formal structures: the Commonwealth of Nations, or the "renovated" Community, for example. Ghana, Nigeria, Sierra Leone are in the Commonwealth; Senegal, Gabon, Madagascar are in the Community. But the Sudan, a former British colony,* is not a Commonwealth member. Tunisia, Mali, the Ivory Coast, Togo, among others, are not in the Community. Libya and Somalia are not politically linked to Italy, nor the Congo to Belgium. The peculiarities of the political evolution of each colony, particularly during the period of decolonization, explain which remain in these structures and which do not.

Participation in these structures involves meetings of chiefs of governments or their ministers on an irregular basis, normally some reciprocal privileges for citizens (sometimes the right to dual citizenship), sometimes juridical structures. To symbolize the special relationship, Commonwealth states recognize the Queen of England as the "head of the Commonwealth," and Community states the President of France as "head of the Community.' These states exchange not ambassadors but "high commissioners" for the Commonwealth, and "high representatives" for the Community.† The details of the relationship are worked out separately for any given pair, for these structures have

---

* Technically speaking, it was an Anglo-Egyptian Condominium. But during much of this time, Egypt was under British rule.

† Similarly, Ghana, Guinea, and Mali, because of their union, exchange not ambassadors but resident ministers.

turned out to be highly pragmatic legal entities. The ties between these structures are not very different from the ties of treaty and diplomatic recognition that African states which have chosen full independence maintain with the former colonial power. There is a wide spectrum of possibilities for interweaving the two countries, by means of which former colonial powers retain certain privileges in return for making certain concessions, often economic.

The link that may last the longest, and is perhaps the most real today, is that of language and, to a lesser extent, of culture. For all African independent states have retained their colonial language as the language of the elite. Even where Arabic has been reintroduced in North Africa, these states have retained the colonial language as either an official or second language (French in Morocco and Tunisia, English in Egypt and the Sudan, Italian in Libya). Even the primary schools in many African independent states utilize the colonial language, certainly the secondary schools and the universities. With the enormous expansion of educational institutions after independence, and the equally great shortage of teachers, the new African nations have had to rely heavily on recruiting teachers from the former colonial powers. Thus, even when relations were most exacerbated between France and Morocco, Tunisia, or Guinea, a special diplomatic effort was always made on both sides to keep the flow of teachers open.

A similar flow in the reverse direction, the flow of African students to the universities of the former colonial power, is also kept open. In most cases the majority of students from a given African nation studying abroad —in almost all cases at least the plurality—are in the metropolitan universities. Given the paucity of African institutions of higher learning, this means that at the present time a large percentage of all university graduates studied in the former colonial country, and that a smaller but still substantial part of the annual output of university graduates continue to have studied there. This cannot help but mean a continuing cultural link with the former colonial power.

The continuing cultural influence of the former metropole is a hard thing to measure. We have already outlined in Chapter IV the legacies of the different colonial administrations. Despite the reaction against these European cultural influences, despite African cultural revival and pan-Africanism, the stamp of the colonial cultural heritage is still strong and is perpetuated among the intellectuals by the continuing flow of students to metropolitan universities. It is perpetuated too by the channels of communication. Politicians and intellectuals in former French areas still tend to read *Le Monde, L'Express, France-Observateur;* and in former British areas, they read *The Times*, the *Guardian*, the *New Statesman and Nation*, and *The Economist*. This is especially true because there are almost no African papers or journals in the independent states that give reasonable coverage of international happenings.* Because of the use of these European channels of information, a Dahomean today may still be more aware of the nuances of politics in Vietnam—the link of the old French Empire—than of those of his neighbor Nigeria. This situation may not last. If the political impulses of pan-Africanism are reinforced by newspapers and cultural exchanges that cross language barriers—which is happening increasingly—then the corresponding cultural ties among African states should increase and those with the former colonial powers should weaken.

The economic links that bind former colonies to Europe are presently even more important than the cultural links, although they may turn out to be less enduring. In a majority of cases, African independent nations remain in either the sterling or the franc monetary zones. They are, however, in the process of developing their own national banks, and there are a

* *Afrique-Action*, published in Tunis since 1960, is an exception.

variety of special arrangements with the former colonial powers concerning the control of currency transactions.

There are also continuing reciprocal customs concessions. Furthermore, for the former colonies of France, Belgium and Italy, there is the possibility of remaining within the orbit of the European Economic Community, which thus gives them certain trade advantages over their African neighbors.* Perhaps most fundamentally of all, trade and investment channels still remain largely in the old colonial rut. There are few African independent states, the majority, or at least plurality, of whose exports and imports are not with the former colonial power. The strength of established business connections, the difficulties and expense of reconversion of all kinds of machinery and durable goods help to maintain this pattern. The relationship between colonial power and independent state is also reinforced by the fact that, in a number of cases, the former colonial power continues for political reasons to purchase some primary products at above the world price.

Closely allied to the continuing trade and investment ties are the ties of technical assistance and the supply of skilled personnel. African nations after independence have needed more, not fewer, outside technicians to help them run their much-expanded administration and economy. Most newly independent nations show an immediate rise in the absolute number, if not the percentage, of non-Africans in the senior government service. In many cases, there is even a rise in the absolute number of the nationals of the former colonial power (more Frenchmen in service in Tunisia, more Englishmen in Ghana). Furthermore, both the British and French governments have evolved special schemes whereby their civil servants and military officers may be seconded to work for determinate periods with inde-

* Ghana and Nigeria are worried, for example, by the competitive advantage of the Ivory Coast and Cameroun in the sale of cocoa to Germany because of the EEC arrangements.

pendent African governments (former colonies) without loss of pay or seniority in the metropolitan country.

Although there may be as many Europeans in African independent nations today as there were before independence, or more, the turnover has often been very large. They are different Europeans. Sometimes as many as 80 percent have served in the independent African country only since independence. Former officials have left because they could not accept the new political climate or because they were asked to leave. Others have gone because of exceptionally generous offers of severance often made at the moment of independence. In many cases these offers allowed officials in their middle years to obtain large grants as compensation, but only if they left immediately. As a compromise between the demands of Africanization and justice to the overseas civil servant, these provisions have often misfired, fulfilling neither goal adequately. Still it is important to realize that a significant proportion of senior civil servants in African independent nations today come from the former colonial power, although the number and percentage will decline as accelerated programs of university education produce sufficient graduates.

It can be seen that, even with independence, the relation of former African colony to former European colonial power still retains some of the flavor of province and metropole. The strength of this bond, nevertheless, is uncertain. It is under severe attack by the more militant pan-Africanists as "neo-colonialism." There is no question that, even among those Africans who wish to maintain their special relationship with the former colonial power, there is a deeply felt desire to establish ties with other nations and to lessen the dependence—economic, political, and even cultural—on one power. African nations are taking a number of specific steps to make this possible.

African independent nations are reaching out to establish new ties with both the United States and the Soviet Union. In the case of the United States, these contacts often are not new. The United States established diplomatic relations with the Sultanate of Morocco in the eighteenth century, and much of the early diplomatic history of the United States revolves around dealings with North Africa, with what were at that time called the Barbary States. In the mid-nineteenth century, it was the efforts of the American Colonization Society that led to the establishment of the Republic of Liberia as a haven for liberated slaves. Many Africans, therefore, at least in the past, have considered Liberia an American colony for which the United States bears a special responsibility. Henry Stanley, journalist and explorer of the Congo, though British by birth went to Africa on behalf of an American newspaper. Partly as a result of his activities, the United States was involved in turning the Congo over to King Leopold at the Congress of Berlin. The United States was one of the signatories of the Berlin Convention that partitioned Africa (as, indeed, was Russia).

American missionaries have been in Africa, especially the central and southern parts, from the mid-nineteenth century. American Negro evangelists played some role in the rise of African separatist movements, most notably in the uprising of John Chilembwe in Nyasaland in 1915. And it is the American Negro Du Bois, who is called the "father of pan-Africanism." In the twentieth century, American business has entered into the African market, particularly the mining industries of the Union of South Africa, Northern Rhodesia and Liberia (as well as rubber in Liberia).

African students have been coming to American universities since the mid-nineteenth century. Many of the leading nationalist leaders of English-speaking African states have studied in the United States, including two heads of state: Kwame Nkrumah, President of Ghana, and Nnamdi Azikiwe, Governor-General of

Nigeria. One of the attractions of the United States for some African students has been that it is not an African colonial power and, despite race prejudice within the country, has had a reputation for anticolonialism on the international scene.

American contacts have been primarily with English-speaking Africa. First of all, there was no language problem. Furthermore, among the various colonial authorities, the British placed the fewest barriers in the way of contact between Americans and Africans. However, the Belgian Congo was officially a free trade area, and this meant that both businessmen and missionaries were allowed access. In Portuguese Africa, there were some missionaries. Perhaps the least contact was with French Africa, where even American consulates were discouraged, and from which no students ever went to the United States.

The reputation of the United States in Africa during the colonial era was a mixed one. It was composed of two central images: a tradition of anticolonialism, because the United States produced the first nationalist anticolonial revolution; a tradition of racism and lynching, which received wide coverage in whatever press existed in Africa. The balance of the two was considered somewhat more favorable in English-speaking Africa than in French Africa, perhaps because of the closer contact, which allowed the individual behavior of Americans (the informal, democratic mores) to be added to the scale. The period of decolonization after World War II saw a sharpening of this favorable image in the minds of Africans. There were also many improvements in race relations in the United States during this period. On the other hand, the anticolonial image was tarnished by United States hesitation to push the colonial powers on decolonization because of the Cold War (most notably, the North African and South African issues at the United Nations).

Nevertheless, one of the first steps of newly independent African states has been to initiate or intensify relations with the United States. In the case of French black Africa, this contact amounts to a discovery of a previously little-known quantity. The new contacts sought are primarily economic and educational. African states, attempting to industrialize, are seeking capital from the United States government (the Volta River Project in Ghana) and, in some cases, from private investors as well (Fria in Guinea).* These nations are also trying to send more students to the United States and, in some cases, to obtain for African universities and secondary schools American personnel and technical assistance.

This reaching out by African nations for international contacts applies to Western Europe generally as well as to the United States. In the case of former French colonies, this means contact with England; for former British colonies, contact with France. In all cases, contact with West Germany has been extensive, particularly in terms of commerce and investment. The story of new contact with the Western world also must include a special word about Israel. Beginning in 1956, the state of Israel made a special effort to establish links with the newly independent states of black Africa, even those which are predominantly Moslem. In this attempt it has been somewhat successful since it combines three features particularly attractive to the new African nations: it is a small power and therefore poses little threat; it has available large numbers of skilled technicians, whom it can lend to the African states; it has a socialist ideology, and two unusual structures, the kibbutz and the Histadrut, which Africans think may have some relevance to their needs. Israel's success has been limited by the fact that she has been unwilling openly to oppose France on the Algerian issue. This reluctance, which derives from Israel's military

* Both the Volta River Project and Fria involve aid or investment from other than American sources as well.

need for French arms, has meant that Israel continues to be thought of as a European rather than as an Asian country, with all the psychological limitations such a denotation implies.

If, during the colonial era, contact of Africans with Americans was limited, it was infinitely more so with the Soviet Union. Historically, the ties between Russia and Africa were few,* and no colonial power gave any encouragement at all to African contact with a Communist state. There were occasional, relatively rare, instances before World War II of African students in Europe going to the USSR. After the Second World War, however, contacts with the Soviet Union began to increase, particularly those of French Africa, through the intermediary of international Communist-dominated nongovernmental groups (World Federation of Trade Unions, World Peace Movement, World Federation of Democratic Youth, etc.). Even so, part of the compromise of the dyarchy was to eliminate, or at least cut down, these contacts. Therefore, it is only with independence that real contact has been established, and even that has happened slowly. Nevertheless, the desire of the African states not merely to have contact with, but to receive economic aid and technical assistance from, the Soviet Union is genuine and growing and probably will become a normal feature of African political life.

In some ways, the Soviet Union is to Africans, particularly black Africans, simply another part of the Western world. It is China, not the USSR, that fascinates. China is not a white nation. It is more militant than the USSR on colonial questions. It is a poorer country, and its efforts at economic development are more relevant to Africa's problems, the Africans think. Above all, China has been a colony of the West, or at least a semi-colony. When Mao Tse-tung received an Algerian

* There were some ties, resuscitated recently, between the Russian Orthodox Church and the Coptic Church in Ethiopia.

delegation, he is reported to have said: "The Europeans and Americans despise you and they despise us. There are only 10 million of you and there are 600 million of us. But the bond that unites us is that we have both been humiliated, and this is a stronger bond than numbers." This bond has meant little as a concrete political or economic reality so far, but increasing links are to be expected. The work of the Afro-Asian Solidarity Council, in which the Chinese are very active, is the prelude of this increasing contact.

Africans also are seeking increasing contact with "the underdeveloped world," with Asia and Latin America. Japan is establishing commercial links with Africa. India, Ceylon and Indonesia are establishing political links, as are Cuba, Brazil and Mexico.

The very diversity of these new contacts testifies to the desire not to be enclosed in any limited Eurafrican framework, such as the proposed schemes that would bind Europe and Africa into a close economic community. For Eurafrica symbolizes neo-colonialism, and the rejection of neo-colonialism is what is meant by African neutralism. Neutralism is the determination to judge other countries by how they help solve African problems, the determination to be tied too closely to no one, and somewhat to everyone. Neutralism is indeed very closely linked with pan-Africanism. It is a means toward pan-Africanism. It is one of the ideological justifications for it since it is argued that a divided Africa will soon fall prey to a cold war polarization, whereas a united Africa will be strong enough to enforce its uniqueness and own interests. Neutralism serves African interests because it maximizes the possibilities of political maneuvers and the possibilities of economic assistance.

Neutralism is more than a doctrine that governs the foreign relations of African independent states. It affects the very nature of the political and economic doctrines that inspire the structures of the new nations.

We already have mentioned the fact that most African states speak of their goal as the establishment of socialism. The books they have read are either from the Marxist tradition or from the Catholic social tradition centering around Emmanuel Mounier's doctrine of "personalism" and the contemporary work of Father Lebret. The books they write, however, and the speeches they make, refer not to socialism but to "African socialism." The concept of "African socialism" is part of Africa's cultural revival, mentioned previously in Chapter VII, but we look at it here because of its implications for Africa's international relations.

African socialism is a doctrine defined in various ways by contemporary African thinkers. What they all have in common is the tendency to emphasize the point that African socialism is somehow distinctively African, rooted in African tradition, and therefore not intrinsically related to socialism anywhere else. The idea is usually expressed thus: Africans can learn much from the Soviet, Chinese, Scandinavian, British, Israeli, and Yugoslav varieties of socialism, but should adapt these techniques to African realities, using as a basis traditional African communal practices. Some few intellectuals oppose the adjective "African," arguing that socialism is a system of universal applicability. Usually these persons are referring to the Communist model. It is important to note that these few intellectuals are opposed systematically by the persons in power in all the African independent states. This is precisely because "African socialism" is set up as the alternative to "socialism," since the latter implies some sort of subordination to a non-African, largely European, doctrine and movement.

In particular, "African socialism" rejects the doctrine of the class struggle as inapplicable to the African situation since, it is argued, there are no classes in Africa. This argument is based on the fact that there are very few individual property owners who engage in business enterprise, also on the fact that there are very few persons in the liberal professions. The overwhelming proportion of the population are peasants. And, it is further contended, the small percentage of urbanites have not yet acquired a "bourgeois mentality." The evidence of this is their continued willingness to recognize obligations deriving from the extended kinship system, and the relative absence of class-based snobbery.

While observers may argue with the contention that one cannot speak of classes in a modern African nation —this is less true in some countries than in others— the contention serves some useful purposes. It underlines the priority of the national (political) struggle over any economic considerations. It is part of the ideological armory used by the nationalist party to help integrate the nation. For if there are no classes in Africa, then there is no reason to justify internal divisions. There is also no reason to justify an elite as opposed to a mass party. If there is only one class, the "class of the dispossessed," then the country as a whole, or Africa as a whole, has a claim against the more developed areas of the world. If Africa is already a classless society, then the corpus of Marxist analysis about the inevitable necessity of a further social revolution is denied, and the relevance of Communist doctrine to African problems becomes remote. Finally, as Sékou Touré has argued: "If we can demonstrate that without the class struggle a profound revolution is possible, we shall thus have begun the integration of Africa into the world of universal thought, to which she will have brought a new experience in the domain of political science and human action." Here we see how African neutralism leads us back to African cultural revival, each being the proud assertion of African uniqueness.

It is for these reasons that Communism, as a world movement, has had a smaller impact on Africa than on any other continent. Historically, there have been official Communist parties only in Morocco, Algeria, Tunisia, Egypt, and the Union of South Africa.* It is no accident that these countries (except Egypt) are the settler extremities of Africa. For in French North Africa and in the Union of South Africa it was largely persons of European descent who formed the cadres and the membership of the Communist parties. This reinforced the impression that Communism was external European doctrine.

The struggle to create unified nationalist movements in African countries was not merely a matter of overcoming procolonial groupings among the population. It also involved breaking with the Communist movements. This was particularly true in the French areas where, between 1950 and 1957, the major political party in French black Africa, the trade unions in French North Africa, and the trade unions in French West Africa broke their links with Communist movements as a means of asserting their autonomy. Since independence, this rejection has been reasserted many times. Even those countries most vigorously reaching out for contacts with the Soviet Union and China on a governmental level are very restrictive internally with Communist movements. The UAR continues to keep leading Communists in jail. Guinea and Mali have refused to allow the Parti Africain de l'Indépendence, a Marxist-Leninist party, to operate within its borders. Sékou Touré has also declared that Communists are not welcome as members of the governing Parti Démocratique de Guinée. Indeed, the stronger and more neutralist the party in power in Africa, the more effective have been the barriers to the formation of Communist parties because the doctrine of African neutral-

* These parties are presently outlawed everywhere except in Tunisia. The Communist party of the Sudan has never been legal. A party was formed in Somalia in 1956 (but not officially recognized) and in Madagascar in 1958.

ism has shown itself essentially hostile to subordination to a European ideology.

The population of Africa is very small in proportion to the rest of the world. Yet Africa plays a role in world politics out of proportion to its size. Its importance is partly a function of its turbulence, but even more a function of its vigorous autonomism, its intense desire to eliminate all vestiges of foreign control, however disguised. This desire for autonomy is not unique, but it is found in Africa in a very concentrated form.

:IX:

PROSPECTS

FOR DEMOCRACY

In the ten years following World War II, there were perhaps two major views of the African political scene held by outsiders and to a considerable extent by Africans themselves. One view held that Africans were incapable or not yet capable of exercising responsible self-rule and creating modern, democratic societies. Originally, this was a majority point of view but it has rapidly declined in acceptance until only a small group of impenitent white settlers still cling to it. A second view was that the nationalist anticolonial revolution would lead to the establishment of parliamentary democracies of a Western style, dominated by a small but growing middle class, reasonably devoted to the defense of civil liberties. This view was particularly popular amongst Western "liberals" who supported African nationalism. This view was shared, however, by Marxist analysts, with the difference that the latter often saw the development of a bourgeois democracy as an essentially unstable transitional stage on the road to communist society. Most African nationalists would have proferred the same analysis of what would occur after independence.

Yet by 1960 not only had both points of view been belied but there were few persons left, certainly few Africans left, who could be found to put forward these arguments. Indeed, what had happened was that African nationalists had begun to proclaim as valid the kinds of institutions which were in fact coming into existence in the newly independent states of Africa. They were no longer ashamed of the fact that these institutions bore only an outward resemblance to the Western parliamentary system. On the contrary, they now proclaimed these institutions as a peculiarly African contribution to the theory of *democratic* society.

It is important to appreciate that African nationalists make a clear distinction in their own minds between parliamentary institutions and "democracy." This is a distinction not unknown to Western political thought. It has been rediscovered by contemporary African statesmen, who almost unanimously are building their state structures on a model they might admit was neither liberal nor individualistic but which they would insist was "democratic."

We have previously noted the tendency of independent African states to have a single-party political system, or at least a single-dominant-party one. We have analyzed how the need of a new nation to maintain its territory and enhance the loyalty of its citizens accounts for this tendency. We have furthermore discussed the special role of the national hero in this transitional phase of African history. It is not surprising, then, that Africans create ideological justifications for the structures they find necessary to resolve their primary problems.

Multi-party systems have often been considered indispensable to a democratic society on the theory that freedom involves the possibility of choice between alternative groups, each being a separate set of men with a particular program, presumably different from that of any other group. Heroes have always been suspect

in the eyes of supporters of democracy on the theory
that they resemble absolute monarchs in potentially
being able to impose their will arbitrarily (or by il-
legitimate emotional appeals) on the majority of the
population. Single parties and heroes have often been
assumed to lead to dictatorships whereby a small group
of men effectively dominate the society.

What in fact is the situation after independence?
What are the possibilities for dissent and free discussion? What degree of protection does the individual
citizen have against the arbitrary decisions of those in
power? To what degree is decision-making a collective
process, or rather are decisions based on consensus or
imposed rule? The situation obviously varies from state
to state and from one point in time to another. Nevertheless, we can detect a general pattern which holds for
most independent African states within a certain range
of variance.

Most independent African states have one form or
another of preventive detention acts.* These acts are
quite often the direct inheritance of the colonial situation, and are now used in behalf of those against whom
they were originally directed. Most states (for example,
Sudan, Upper Volta, Niger, Ghana, Gabon) not only
have these acts; they use them. The justifications the
governments usually offer is that the persons detained
are "unconstructively in the opposition," that is, they
are engaged in activities tending toward the disintegration of the nation, sometimes actual secession. Emergency powers allowing special restrictions, also have
been voted for governments. This is most notably true
of Cameroun, where a civil war continued after independence because, with the coöperation of the French,

---

* This is in fact true of many states throughout the world. Even
the so-called traditional democracies have such acts in times of
emergency: for example, in the United States, the Japanese
Relocation Act in World War II; in France, the special powers
voted to the French government during the Algerian War.

the core of the original nationalist movement was excluded from power.

In many cases, preventive detention has seemed inadequate to governments, and they therefore have resorted to deportations. The deportations might be of high-level political leaders born in other countries, as in the case of the 1958 expulsions from the Republic of Mali, Upper Volta, Guinea, Niger, or in Chad in 1960. Sometimes these would be of middle-level opposition leaders who were "foreigners" (Ghana in 1957) or even locally born (Ivory Coast in 1959). But there has been another kind of "deportation" as well, the encouraged departure of a whole segment of the population: the Guinean diamond seekers from Sierra Leone, the Dahomean and Togolese civil servants from the Ivory Coast and Niger. In the case of the Dahomeans in the Ivory Coast, the expulsion was the result of popular riots, to which the government acceded. In the case of Sierra Leone, it was a government-initiated move to crack down on illicit diamond mining.

There has been considerable manipulation with the electoral laws aimed at eliminating small opposition parties from seats in legislative bodies. Under the British colonial regime, most legislative bodies were elected on a single-member constituency regime. Under the French regime, a portion of the constituencies were single-member. This made it more difficult at first for the nationalist party to win seats, as there were always rural areas in which the party was weak and the seat could be a fief of the local traditional ruler who was friendly to the colonial administration.

In the time of the dyarchy, many of the African states began to adopt systems of multi-member constituencies. This was particularly true in French Africa. One of the arguments advanced was that only in this way was it possible for the nationalist party to overcome tribal commitments. In multi-member constituencies, a party could present candidates simultaneously from several tribes. Furthermore, during the dyarchy, it was often the policy to elect a few Europeans on the nationalist ticket. Single-member constituencies would have been inappropriate for this purpose. Of course, multi-member constituencies could be run either on a majority vote (winner takes all) or proportional basis, which assures minority representation. There was a strong tendency toward the majority vote system.

As time went on, the number of constituencies was successively reduced, the number of legislators to be elected in each being increased. By the 1959 elections in French Africa, for example, most states had reduced the number of constituencies to four and six, Mauritania to only two. This practically assured the majority party all the seats. There were some few states where the opposition party was particularly strong in one region, and could win one constituency, however large it was made. Thereupon, to eliminate this group, a final step was taken in 1961 in Dahomey, Togo, and Gabon: in each case the whole nation became a single constituency. One vote of the voter elected a list, including the president of the republic and all the members of parliament.

These obvious manipulations are necessary to eliminate opposition groups. Once they are eliminated, however, multi-member constituencies remain as an aid to the process of national integration. However, it probably is useful also to have a number of constituencies in order to provide intermediate points of regional attachment between the individual and the state. A mild version of regionalism may serve to relieve the pressures of local demands.

If manipulation of the electoral laws is insufficient to assure the one-party state, other mechanisms are available. African governments have outlawed parties, or refused recognition* to parties newly created, for

---

* Under most African legal systems, political parties must register with the government, and can only operate once their legality is recognized. This arrangement is a heritage of the colonial administration.

example, in Morocco, Sudan, the UAR, Senegal, Mauritania, Upper Volta, Niger, Mali, Cameroun, the Central African Republic. Another way of eliminating opposition members from parliament is by simple expulsion. The justification may be preventive detention, or charges of falsified election procedures, or the outlawing of the party to which the parliamentarian belongs. There have been instances of such expulsion in Chad, Niger, Togo, Ghana, the Central African Republic.

To achieve some of these objectives, African governments have tended to treat lightly the question of the independence of the judiciary. Sometimes they have openly demanded that political considerations take priority for judges over legal considerations. Sometimes the legislatures simply by statute have overridden unfavorable judicial decisions. Governments have felt free to alter constitutional provisions that created obstacles to immediate goals, and with their overwhelming majorities in the legislative bodies, they have had no trouble acquiring the extra vote necessary for constitutional amendment. The concern for substantive as against procedural justice has been made central by the new African governments. The protections of form and due process are feared by these governments because a system which places great emphasis on these protections works on the assumption that the individual exercises certain restraints in his actions toward the state. We have seen previously that this is not yet true, and that African governments are working hard to achieve this kind of national integration. It should not be surprising, therefore, that until this sense of self-restraint permeates the citizenry, the government should be reluctant to allow the liberties of due process their full play.

Another form of restriction in the one-party state is that related to voluntary associations. There has been considerable pressure to keep them in line with the position of the party. When these groups have deviated sharply, they have been pressured, either by purges inspired by the party, or by withdrawal of financial and other aid by the government. Instances include the trade unions in Tunisia and Senegal, the women's organizations in Ghana, the youth councils in Senegal and Niger, the students' organizations in Guinea, Mali, and the Ivory Coast.

We see, then, that the newly independent African states are not models of liberalism. It is important to note, from the examples given above, that this non-democratic tendency is a very general phenomenon. It is not limited to states with a particular colonial tradition. It has nothing to do with the attitudes of the government toward pan-Africanism or the East-West issue. It is almost universal since it results from the similar needs of national unity and economic development that all these countries face. The one important exception thus far has been Nigeria. In Nigeria, there are three regions, each with a dominant party. Were those regions independent states, there is little reason to suppose each would not have evolved along the lines of its neighbors. Because they are in a federal structure without any effective national party in existence, no group has been able to engage in electoral manipulation, expulsions, deportations, and detentions—at least not to the extent of other states. Because no one has a clear majority at the federal level, each party can protect its friends in the other regions. Whether this situation will last indefinitely remains to be seen.

Although African independent states are not liberal in their practices, they are by no means totalitarian. The citizens do not live in terror of a secret police. Political debate is a commonplace of African life. Opposition to government policies exists, is heard, is even listened to. Policies change; the composition of governments changes. There is an enormous amount of give and take in almost every independent African state.

How is it possible at one and the same time not to have liberal political structures in the African states and yet to have many of the presumed consequences of liberal political structures? One explanation is that the intensive political concern which African nationalist movements created as part of the struggle for independence has bequeathed an atmosphere in which popular participation in political matters is still considered the normal thing. At national elections, it is quite common to have turnouts of 80 to 90 percent. Nationalist movements cannot simply at will turn on and off this enthusiasm for mass involvement in the political arena, even if they want to. And indeed, as we have seen, they do not want to. For popular participation is one of the tools the party uses to achieve national integration. In those states where the party structure is best articulated, mass membership in the party means that party meetings at the village level resemble "town meetings." This is of course an ideal situation, and in many African countries, this ideal is not achieved.

Mass participation in itself would not be significant were there not a climate in which free discussion is encouraged. Such a climate does exist today in most of the new states, insofar as such discussion is kept within the framework of the party structure. This is a limitation, to be sure, but not one that eliminates the reality of debate. There is no single-party structure in African independent states where the observer cannot identify factions and tendencies which argue with each other to some extent over issues. The parliamentary structures, even if one party has all the seats, are not entirely docile. Debate is spirited, and the voice of the backbencher is often heard. Indeed, there are instances where the open revolt of government backbenchers (Ghana, Gabon) have forced the government to change its views.

It must be remembered that these single-party structures are not integrated organisms but integrating or-

ganisms. That is, they are carefully built coalitions, in
need of constant nurture, whose primary aim is to keep
the country together. The principal method of maintaining party unity, indispensable to national unity, is
the constant balancing of interests. The allocation of
seats in the legislature, or expenditures of the public
works department, are the result of hard bargaining
and careful calculation, which bear comparison with the
interplay of special interests in Western parliaments.
The image of a small elite imposing their will, through
the party structure, on an inert mass fails to take account of the real dispersion of power that still exists in
every African country.

The national hero is not a dictator who reigns by
whim and fiat. He tends to be the spokesman of, probably the dominating figure in, a national political bureau of a political party. He is the chairman of the
inner policy debates, which go on constantly. He is the
mediator of the various political factions, the different
ethnic and religious groups. He is, as Africans tend to
call their chiefs, "the grandfather." He is exalted, to be
sure, because his glorification serves the purpose of
helping to create a nation. He is exalted, too, because
he then can become a symbol of African achievement
in the wider world, the proof that African states can
produce statesmen and heroes to match those of the
rest of the world. But his independence of action tends
to be very rigidly constrained by the party of which
he is the leader, and the nation which he must bind
together.

The possibilities of discussion within the party and
the limitations on the power of the leader are not guaranteed by legal protection for the opposition or the
institutions of a multi-party system. They are not,
however, without any cultural support. There are two
major underpinnings for this continued democratic atmosphere. One is the African tradition of government.
While this is less true in Arab Africa than in black

Africa, the traditional structures of government in Africa are built on the principles of debate and consensus, with the chief as mediator and transmitter of the will of his councilors. The tradition requires too that the councilors be drawn from the various segments of the community. In most cases, succession to the throne is not automatic but involves a choice by the councilors, and often by the people, of one candidate from among a large group of eligible persons. There is a remarkable similarity between these familiar traditional ways and the formulas that in fact govern the newly independent national governments.

It is not only African tradition that protects dissent and discussion in Africa today. There are also more modern factors which contribute to this result. One is the continued turmoil and movement of the African political scene. Nationalist struggle has been succeeded by pan-Africanism to assure constant change, political maneuver, realignment. The arteries of political activity have scarcely been permitted to harden anywhere. Such constant agitation requires an atmosphere in which ideas can be constantly debated, in which the angers of the moment are not allowed to become permanent enmities; it requires that each government keep in reserve men to implement new policies. At least thus far it has been so.

Furthermore, the ceaseless onrush of political happenings has meant that inter-African structures and contacts have continued to be significant in the political life of any given African country. Ideas have constantly flowed across frontiers—dissenting ideas. And because pan-Africanism has been so strong a sentiment, men and parties have constantly intervened in the affairs of other African states to protect those who shared their point of view. What has guaranteed the give and take of African politics to some extent has been the fact that no African state has lived within itself but each has been very much a part of a wider African movement. To the degree that inter-African exchange has been characteristic of a given state, the free interchange of ideas within that state has been possible.

The assessment of the degree of democracy in African states must be based on an appreciation of the alternatives that exist. The choice is not between a one-party system and a multi-party parliamentary system. The structural prerequisites for the latter do not yet exist to a sufficient degree in Africa. The effective choice for the newly independent states is between a one-party (or one-dominant-party) system, which allows for some real popular participation in, and control over, the government, or anarchy, which means that power reverts 'to local princelings and patrons, remote from the intellectual contact and stimulation which infuses the modernizing elite of the national structures.

The one-party system in the African context is often a significant step toward the liberal state, not a first step away from it. For the purpose of the one-party system is to create a national state sufficiently well-rooted in the loyalties of its citizens so that the distinction between state and government will begin to emerge. Without this basic loyalty, the relative stability of the state cannot be assumed, and governments will continue to refuse to tolerate opposition that is not contained within their own party, for fear that such opposition will lead to the dismantlement of the state. This fear is not wholly without foundation.

The national orientation of the mass of citizens is not the sole prerequisite for the creation of institutions that can guarantee the rights of opposition, even outside the party. African states, as we have seen, are determined to raise their economic level by industrializing and by mechanizing their agriculture. The point of economic development is to achieve greater equality with the rest of the world, as well as to further the integration of the nation. A developed economy creates a new pattern of social strata. Occupational and income groupings become more nearly balanced. The disproportion of a situation where 95 percent of the population are peasant farmers disappears. As this new stratification develops, the interest groupings of citizens become defined largely in terms of these economic and occupational roles. But these groupings tend to be nationwide rather than regional in scope, which the present groupings based on ethnic considerations usually are. As interests become nationwide, opposition will cease to lead to territorial secession, since territorial secession will then usually be irrelevant to the political objectives of the opposition.

Dissent and discussion in African states today are guaranteed in part by African tradition, in part by the continued political turmoil. These are not long-term guarantees, since tradition is being weakened and turmoil may cease. The one-party systems may begin to stagnate without any internal structural protection for the opposition (independent judiciary, free press, etc.). This is clearly a danger of the future. Yet these structural guarantees will not be acceptable as long as they threaten the preservation of the state. The building up of loyalty to the nation, combined with the economic differentiation that development will bring, plus the resulting creation of nationwide interest groups will create a situation in which the institution of structural guarantees will no longer threaten the preservation of the state.

It does not follow, however, that these structural guarantees will thereupon be instituted. The emergence of long-range institutional guarantees of a democratic society is by no means automatic. However, it is not really possible at all before the prerequisites are fulfilled. The problem therefore is twofold: how to fulfill the prerequisites as rapidly as possible, and how to do so in such a way as to maximize the possibility that the authoritarian regimes of the present will not stagnate and harden but will develop further toward the increase of personal freedom within the state.

All those steps which promote national unity are therefore steps in this direction. Pressure for formal constitutional guarantees and outward conformity to parliamentary norms, if premature, may only lead to the breakdown of these institutions, as has occurred in a number of Asian countries, and consequent disillusion with the usefulness of such institutions *at any time*. On the other hand, entry of the opposition into the government and the machinery of the governing party not only serves the interests of unity, but usually, though not always, helps to maintain within the dominant party openness of discussion and the necessary pressures for arriving at a consensus that takes into account all interests.

Rapid economic development too moves in this direction, and rapid economic development is tied to national integration, simultaneously as cause and consequence. Those processes that aid national integration—strengthening the party structure, creating inter-African unities, or obtaining international aid from a variety of sources—all help the states pass through the transitional postindependence phase as rapidly as possible.

Since among the factors which preserve the present flow of ideas and discussion in Africa today are the inter-African links, it follows that insofar as these links expand or take more concrete political form, the climate remains attuned to liberal norms and formal guarantees of dissent. Thus, the movement for African unity, both by improving the prospects of economic development and by widening the channels of communication and sources of ideas, strengthens democratic mores in Africa.

What is true of inter-African links is true of wider international links. Increased familiarity and contact with the vast panorama of variant conditions and political structures on the world scene should make for subtler and more tolerant analyses of problems and their solutions. Given the strong sense of African autonomism, reinforced as it continues to be by pan-African trends, increased contacts not only with the United States and the Soviet Union, but with Europe, Asia, and Latin America are moves toward the creation of an interwoven mosaic, which encourages flexibility of tactics and ideas, and serves to moderate the extremism of all. The transitional era of African life coincides with a transitional era of the world polity in which the polarized structure of international politics is being attenuated. Of course, world tensions may increase, despite the decolonization process, in which case the internal structure of African states will become tighter instead of more flexible.

The one-party structure is an interim system of African states which they are maintaining for the present. And with the one-party structure goes, as we have seen, the continued politicization of the voluntary associations on the African scene, the continued domination of trade unions, youth groups, women's associations, etc., by the mass political party. Yet, with an eye to the future, the separate existence of these functional groups, no matter how dependent currently on the party, cannot but serve the end of political diversification. Youth and trade union structures may be required to subordinate their special interests today to the national views of the party. But by maintaining and extending their separate structures, they may, when the moment is ripe, serve as the bases of separate political groupings, even parties. Many African trade unionists, therefore, prefer to restrain their demands today, the better to be in position to put them forward tomorrow. Also, the wider links which these groups have, through inter-African and international trade union (or youth or women's) organizations, serve to strengthen their own positions internally vis-à-vis the party structure, as well as allow these groups to be the initiators of ideas and methods other than those taught within the state.

All of this patient contact and rapid integration and economic growth may not pay off in terms of the institutionalization of devices that protect and stimulate dissent unless the currents of intellectual life are strong and original. Here too, pan-Africanism can have a healthy influence, as can the multiplication of sources of intellectual stimulation (an opinion press, universities, seminars which bring together politicians and intellectuals). The serious intellectual discussion of African and human problems by Africans, among themselves and with others, is a key to political evolution, and is by no means incompatible with the present trends toward one-party states, cultural revival, and pan-Africanism.

A democratic society, in Africa as elsewhere, depends on a certain climate of opinion. This climate of opinion can only be maintained in the long run if it is supported by the norms of the society, reinforced by appropriate structural protections, defended in turn by significant strata of the population who have a positive interest in, and relatively little fear of, dissent. The independent African states are moving in this direction in ways not unlike those which other states used in comparable periods of their nation-building.

Africa has greatness in her past as well as her present. And probably in her future too.

APPENDIX

INDENT STATES (1961)

Country	Capital	Population	Area (sq. mi.)	Year of Independence
Cameroun	Yaoundé	4,028,000	183,381	1960
Central African Republic	Bangui	1,177,000	241,700	1960
Chad	Fort Lamy	2,600,000	495,368	1960
Congo	Brazzaville	795,000	134,750	1960
Congo	Leopoldville	13,658,185	905,380	1960
Dahomey	Porto-Novo	1,725,000	43,630	1960
Ethiopia	Addis Ababa	16,000,000	457,265	11th century B.C
Gabon	Libreville	420,709	102,317	1960
Ghana	Accra	6,690,730	91,843	1957
Guinea	Conakry	2,800,000	95,000	1958
Ivory Coast	Abidjan	3,100,000	127,500	1960
Liberia	Monrovia	2,000,000	43,000	1847
Libya	Benghazi and Tripoli	1,091,830	685,000	1950
Malagasy Rep.	Tananarive	5,191,085	227,900	1960
Mali (Republic)	Bamako	4,300,000	464,752	1960
Mauritania	Nouakchott	624,000	470,000	1960
Morocco	Rabat	10,330,000	171,305	1956
Niger	Niamey	2,555,000	458,875	1960
Nigeria	Lagos	32,202,000	322,588	1960
Republic of South Africa	Pretoria	14,673,000	472,359	1910
Senegal	Dakar	2,550,000	78,000	1960
Sierra Leone	Freetown	2,260,000	27.925	1961
Somalia	Mogadiscio	1,980,000	246,000	1960
Sudan	Khartoum	11,390,000	967,500	1956
Tanganyika	Dar es Salaam	8,788,466	363,000	1961
Togo	Lomé	1,161,314	21,850	1960
Tunisia	Tunis	3,830,000	48,194	1956
United Arab Republic (Egypt)	Cairo	25,000,000	386,198	1922
Upper Volta	Ouagadougou	3,531,571	105,811	1960

NONINDEPENDENT TERRITORIES (1961)

Country	Capital	Population	Area (sq. mi.)
GREAT BRITAIN			
Basutoland	Maseru	658,000	11,716
Bechuanaland	Mafeking	37,000	275,000
Gambia	Bathurst	289,000	4,003
Kenya	Nairobi	6,351,000	224,960
Mauritius	Port Louis	613,888	720
*Northern Rhodesia	Lusaka	2,300,100	288,130
*Nyasaland	Zomba	2,770,000	49,177
*Southern Rhodesia	Salisbury	2,900,000	153,333
Swaziland	Mbabane	260,000	6,704
Uganda	Entebbe	5,770,000	93,981
Zanzibar	Zanzibar	304,000	640

* These three territories together form the Federation of the Rhodesias and Nyasaland, whose capital is Salisbury.

Country	Capital	Population	Area (sq. mi.)
FRANCE			
Algeria	Algiers	10,265,000	80,920
Comoro Islands	Dzaudzi	165,613	838
French Somaliland	Djibouti	69,000	8,494
Reunion	Saint Denis	310,000	969
PORTUGAL			
Angola (and Cabinda)	Luanda	4,392,000	481,350
Cape Verde Islands	Praia	192,000	1,557
Mozambique	Lourenço Marques	6,244,000	302,250
Portuguese Guinea	Bissau	559,000	13,944
São Tomé e Principe	São Tomé	60,159	372
SPAIN			
Ifni	Sidi Ifni	42,000	932
Spanish Sahara	Aiún	7,749	102,680
Fernando Po and Río Muni	Santa Isabel	215,000	10,828
REPUBLIC OF SOUTH AFRICA			
South-West Africa	Windhoek	539,000	317,725
BELGIUM			
Ruanda-Urundi	Usumbura	4,700,000	20,916

BIBLIOGRAPHICAL NOTE

The library of books about Africa is a very fast-growing one. I shall try here to indicate only a few books which the reader might easily turn to if he wishes fuller detail on some of the themes covered in this book.

Basil Davidson has attempted to reconstruct all of precolonial African history in *The Lost Cities of Africa*. E. W. Bovill has written an account of the medieval Sudanic empires and the trans-Sahara trade in *The Golden Trade of the Moors*. J. D. Fage has put together a series of historical maps in *An Atlas of African History*. There are also two textbooks recently written which summarize more recent history: J. D. Fage, *An Introduction to the History of West Africa;* and Zoe Marsh and G. W. Kingsworth, *An Introduction to the History of East Africa.*

A survey of African cosmologies is available in D. Forde, ed., *African Worlds*. Surveys of the traditional political systems of African tribes include E. E. Evans-Pritchard and M. Fortes, eds., *African Political Systems;* J. Middleton and D. Tait, eds., *Tribes Without Rulers;* I. Schapera, *Government and Politics in Tribal Societies*.

Overall surveys of Africa appear in growing number. Those that are considered most scholarly and comprehensive are R. L. Buell, *The Native Problem in Africa*, 2 vol., written in 1928; Lord Hailey, *An African Survey Revised 1956;* and G. H. T. Kimble, *Tropical Africa*, 2 vol., written in 1960. Two overviews of the rise of nationalism and the process of decolonization are T. Hodgkin, *Nationalism in Colonial Africa*, and R. Emerson, *From Empire to Nation: The Rise to Self-Assertion of Asian and African Peoples.*

For those who wish to pursue this subject more closely, the following monographs can be recommended. On the changing role of the traditional chief, see K. A. Busia, *The Position of the Chief in the Modern Political System of Ashanti,* and L. Fallers, *Bantu Bureaucracy.* On a religious separatist movement, see G. Shepperson and T. Price, *Independent African.* On the emergence of a labor movement in urban and mine areas, see A. L. Epstein, *Politics in an Urban African Community,* and S. el-din Fawzi, *The Labour Movement in the Sudan, 1946–1955.* On the growth of a nationalist movement, see D. Apter, *The Gold Coast in Transition,* and J. S. Coleman, *Nigeria: Background to Nationalism.* Two useful histories of South African developments are E. Roux, *Time Longer Than Rope,* and G. Carter, *The Politics of Inequality.* For those who read French, the various works of Ch.-André Julien on North Africa and of Georges Balandier on black Africa will be most helpful.

A survey of recent political developments in sub-Saharan Africa is available in the chapter by J. S. Coleman found in G. Almond and J. S. Coleman, eds., *The Politics of the Developing Areas.* A rapid description of major economic schemes in Africa is found in W. A. Hance, *African Economic Development.*

The journals of the African cultural renaissance include *Présence Africaine* (Paris), now available in English, and *Black Orpheus* (Ibadan, Nigeria). An interpretative analysis of these developments is found in Janheinz Jahn, *Muntu: An Outline of Neo-African Culture.* How African leaders view their own country or continent can be seen in the following works: *Awo, The Autobiography of Obafemi Awolowo; Ghana, The Autobiography of Kwame Nkrumah;* G. A. Nasser, *Egypt's Liberation;* L.-S. Senghor, *African Socialism;* Sékou Touré, *Towards Full Reafricanisation.* A view of pan-

Africanism from the inside is available in G. Padmore, *Pan-Africanism or Communism?* Chief H. O. Davies discusses future developments in *Nigeria: The Prospects for Democracy.*

This list is only meant to be suggestive of a few titles that will take the general reader further into the subject. Particularly in the section on monographs, this list is necessarily arbitrary and there are other books available of equal interest.

ACKNOWLEDGMENTS

Acknowledgments should really start with those who have contributed most to the author's understanding. In my case, this is a group of people—friends and acquaintances—who have been part of the process of social change, the rise of nationalism, the building of new nations described in this book. What I learned most from them, from wherever they have come, has been the similarity of themes—the frustrations and hopes, the uncertainties and self-assurance—which they all, in varying degrees, display. I am grateful that they enriched my world and my appreciation of my own culture by allowing me closer access to theirs.

My friends and colleagues, Professors A. Etzioni, T. K. Hopkins, and R. Schachter, read the manuscript and gave me valuable advice, but, as usual, bear none of the blame.

INDEX

Unity

To Thomas

Gentleman and scholar,
Mallam and friend,

Who respects Africa's past
and therefore has a reasoned
confidence in its future

"The myth must be judged as a means of acting on the present; any attempt to discuss how far it can be taken literally is devoid of sense."

GEORGES SOREL

"To achieve the possible is not failure but success, however inadequate the success may prove in the end."

JOSEPH SCHUMPETER

CONTENTS

THE PROBLEMS OF A MOVEMENT

UNITY AND MODERNIZATION— ACHIEVEMENTS AND PERSPECTIVES

PREFACE

This book is a sequel to my previous book, *Africa: The Politics of Independence,* written in 1961. It is an interpretation of the major political developments in Africa between 1957 and 1965 from the perspective of a major social movement on the continent, the movement toward African unity. It is the thesis of this book that this movement represented the strongest indigenous political force on the continent during this period, though not a force strong enough to achieve all the objectives it set itself.

Such a perspective is of course not the only one from which one can analyze the social change that has occurred in contemporary Africa. But the movement toward unity has been the most significant single African attempt to affect in an important way the rate and direction of social change, and thus it merits our close attention. I believe that a good deal of the internal developments of individual African states during this period cannot be adequately understood unless one takes into account the existence and the actions of this all-African social movement. Nor do I believe one can adequately appreciate the relationships of non-African states and movements to particular African events unless one is aware how these relationships have been affected by, and have affected, this social movement.

As for the time period involved, I think the text will justify it as a logical unit, representing one great phase in the history of this social movement. Since I wrote this book in early 1966, the narrative perforce stops there. But I believe that December 1965, or perhaps February 1966, marks an appropriate terminal point, as the argument of the book will attempt to demonstrate.

There are particular problems to doing research on contemporary social processes, especially large-scale ones. There are special difficulties in gaining access to some of the data, since secrecy is a necessary ingredient of the policies of many of the actors. This is compensated to an uncertain degree by the ability of the researcher to interview people involved and thus perhaps acquire information that is unrecorded elsewhere. There are difficulties too in the narration of events. The action described is still very much current and there are legitimate demands on the scholar to be prudent and compassionate. I may not always have responded to those demands to the degree that was expected of me, and if that be so, I regret it.

I have been working on this book in one way or another for three years, and I was able to make three different trips to Africa during the period 1963–1965. The rest of the time I spent for the most part in New York, which is one important center of African activity, principally because of the United Nations. In the course of this work, I had to prevail on the courtesy and kindness of African friends and acquaintances too numerous to mention. I thank them all for the varying degrees of confidence they placed in me in a situation in which it was most understandable that some were reticent and a few suspicious. I thank also those non-Africans who have aided me and were in a position to aid me because of their sympathetic and perspicacious awareness of the African scene.

I was able to make the trips to Africa because of successive grants from the Faculty of International Affairs of Columbia University, the Council for Research in the Social Sciences of Columbia University, and the U.S. Office of Education. I thank them all and absolve them from any responsibility for what I have written. The hospitality of Africans is proverbial, but I must single out for appreciation the Institute of African Studies of the University of Ghana and the Institute of Public Administration of the University College, Dar es Salaam. My family and I imposed on their personnel in numerous ways for the relatively long periods I used these two institutions as a base of operations, and our lives would not have been as pleasant nor my research as fruitful without their assistance.

When I completed the manuscript, three men agreed to read it, in whole or in part, to give me the benefit of their knowledge and perspectives and to save me from the errors I did not wish to commit. They were T. K. Hopkins, J. T. Nye, Jr., and B. Verhaegen. Their pertinent and pointed suggestions assisted me and reassured me, and I believe improved the book. I appreciate their efforts as a scholarly courtesy and an act of friendship.

: I :

THE ORIGINS

OF A THEME

The starting point of much of social analysis is the observation of an anomaly. In Africa today one of the most persistent themes of political discourse is African unity, which is put forward both as an ideal and as an objective. In the abstract, unity is an innocent concept that precludes dissent. But in its concrete manifestation—the desire to create, reinforce, or increase the unity of a specific social group—it is far more controversial.

The anomaly we observe is a very simple one. Virtually every African spokesman—politician, civil servant, or intellectual, of whatever political persuasion—states today that he is in favor of African unity and that he is actively seeking, in his own way, its realization. Yet most non-Africans tend to treat the subject of African unity with skepticism if not derision, basing their argument usually not on the undesirability of unity but on its impracticality. This argument in turn tends to make Africans irritated if not indignant, and the discussion becomes a subject of some sensitivity.

Why should this be so? When a statement of political aspirations, especially one formulated in so general a manner, is greeted by different publics in such different and even opposite ways, it may indicate that beneath the surface question of the feasibility of the objective, there lies a deeper schism. There may, for instance, be different opinions of the general competence of those who hold the aspirations. It may also indicate that the very expression of the idea has significant social consequences which some wish to advance and others to retard.

It is to this anomaly that we address ourselves. There exists today a movement for African unity whose origins, strength, and history we shall discuss. What is the *raison d'être* of this movement? Why has it attracted at least nominal adherence among nearly all those it deeply concerns, but at most nominal adherence on the part of outsiders? What have been the forces at play in the implementation of the aspiration toward unity in the period 1957–1965? To answer such questions, we must start by looking at the origins of the movement toward African unity in its particular historical context. It is only then that we can treat analytically the subthemes and the roles of the participants.

In modern times, Africa's contact with the outside world was at first principally through the slave trade. The slave trade came to an end in the nineteenth century, but at that very time Europe expanded its conquests and almost all of Africa became colonial territories. The relationship of black man to white man, both in Africa and in the Western Hemisphere, became unmistakably that of social inferior to superior. And as usual, those who benefited from this social fact created an ideological schema to justify and thus to sustain it. The schema was racism, and its tenets spread far and wide among the oppressors and the oppressed.

The arguments of racism were that Africans, black men, suffered from inherent social backwardness, probably rooted in their biological make-up and certainly entrenched in their cultural history. Africans were presumed to be deficient in technological inventiveness and competence. ("They never invented the wheel.") They were presumed to be less rational than Westerners and more emotional. (Lévy-Bruhl spoke of the "prelogical mind.") And these deficiencies were presumed to make it impossible for Africans to function adequately in the modern world of a rational economy and bureaucratic government. Africans, they said, had no historical achievements to their credit—no records, no monuments. They had created no high culture, no world religion, no great empires. There were no alphabets, no literature, no music. The racists even occasionally pointed by contrast to India, China, Persia, and other colonial or semicolonial nations. These latter at least had a glorious past, if a less splendid present. But Africa had virtually nothing. The peoples of Africa were said to be the bottom of the world's totem pole. They had what Richard Wright called, borrowing a phrase of Nietzsche's, a "frog perspective."

That these arguments were sociological and psychological nonsense, based on a distortion of historical fact, has been shown over and over again, and particularly since 1945. Nonetheless these ideas were the working frame of reference of white men in Africa, and elsewhere, for a very long time. And they are far from entirely extinct even today.

The writing of scientific history, of course, was in its infancy when such theories held fullest sway. Today there are libraries of books to refute these simplistic ideas. Nonetheless in the late nineteenth and early twentieth centuries, there were few who could command the data to refute the dominant orthodoxy. It is no accident then that as men began to want to grapple seriously with the dismantling of the world-wide apparatus of racial oppression, they directed much of their effort to the search for history, a different history—especially of Africa—from the one taught so cavalierly in the schools of the world.

This was no easy task. What were a handful of spokesmen for the outcasts against the weight of white opinion which proclaimed its thought universal and which was part of a social system that had the military and political power to support its analyses? Especially when these spokesmen were only part-time scholars, often with limited formal intellectual training. They were the professional men and politicians who, in Africa and in the Western Hemisphere, began to organize the movements for the assertion of African (or Afro-American) rights.

This social situation accounts in part for the fact that the revival of interest in African history focused at first largely on ancient history (the empires of the Western Sudan, and beyond that, ancient Egypt) rather than on recent (that is, nineteenth century) history. At first, Africans (and Afro-Americans) spoke less of the accomplishments of the conquering nation-builders like Shaka of the Zulus or Samory of the Mandingos than of Sundiata Keita of Mali or Askia of Songhai. The former were those who had recently resisted European conquest and were thus the target of full-scale attack as savages, while the latter were leaders of a remoter past in whose denigration the white man had relatively less interest. This intellectual emphasis on the remote past had important social consequences, for it turned the revival of interest in African history and culture into pan-African channels. Had the earliest modern African historians concentrated on the nation-builders of the nineteenth century, they might have created a nationality literature somewhat like that of the nineteenth-century European romantic historians. Instead, the new intellectuals of the nascent African elite were turned toward pan-Africanism.

Of course, the concentration on the glorious past was not the only factor that helped to create the intellectual aura of pan-African sentiment. There was the fact that for the Negroes of the Western Hemisphere, thrown together in a common fate and usually ignorant of their precise descent, Africa as a whole was the inevitable motherland. There was the fact that the workings of colonial administration brought together Africans of very many different areas—through territorial educational structures, the routine transfers of African civil servants, and the common interest in the metropole, the home country of the empire. To be sure the links among Africans were contained within the particular colonial mold (*British*

West Africa, *French* black Africa,etc.). But in the self-image of Africans, their interterritorial organizations were pan-African, even if in fact they did not cross the imperial boundary lines.

Thus new ideas, which were considered by their proponents to be liberating ideas, began to circulate and to take hold among politically conscious Africans. And around these ideas, a few sought to create a movement. A movement is amorphous, both to its participants and to its analysts. Its contours not only are not clear but, in the nature of things, change as new peripheral elements make their weight felt. The details of the history of a movement are perhaps of less interest than an outline of its meanderings. Each turning leaves a residue in the emotions and even the tactics of later generations. For our purpose, it will be most useful to trace these meanderings, to see how the world social situation determined their path and how they in turn helped to transform the world social situation.

Pan-Africanism was born, in the words of Diallo Telli, in the emotional atmosphere of "complete alienation, physical exploitation, and spiritual torment." When Henry Sylvester-Williams of Trinidad convened a Pan-African Conference in 1900, he did this largely to mobilize solidarity for Africans threatened in various ways by depredations of colonizers in various parts of the continent. The conference was held in the wake not only of the Boer War and of Rhodes's expansion into Central Africa, but of the enactment of Jim Crow laws in the southern United States. At the time, racism was a respectable doctrine, popular even in the universities. These black men met together, to defend their rights, protest their humanity, and exhibit their fraternity. To this new sentiment of racial self-assertion and solidarity they applied the term "pan-African," and proclaimed with W. E. B. DuBois at this conference that "the problem of the twentieth century is the problem of the color line."

This sense of racial solidarity began soon thereafter to take organizational forms. In the United States, there was the Niagara Movement of 1905, followed by the creation of the

National Association for the Advancement of Colored People in 1910. In South Africa, the African National Congress was founded in 1910. In West Africa, the first contacts were made which led to the convening in 1920 of the National Congress of British West Africa. In Senegal, Africans assumed a leading role in the politics of the commune of Dakar, and the first African deputy was elected in 1914.

In all of these cases, the social composition of the new organizations was the same. They were made up of relatively well-educated, relatively well-off African (or Afro-American) professional and business men. All of their programs were dedicated to achieving equal rights and increased educational opportunities, and to the assertion of the validity of the African cultural heritage—an assertion which was, however, not very much reflected in the daily lives of the participants. Their program was the program of Western liberalism. Its demands seem almost timid today. Its boldness for its time consisted in the elementary dignity with which they put forward their limited demands. As DuBois himself said in *The World and Africa*, their plans "had in them nothing spectacular nor revolutionary." Nor did they press them with very great vigor. They could not, for their organizations had no mass following, and even very little resonance.

In 1917, the Russian Revolution occurred. There came into power in a major European country a group of men whose doctrine was in one sense the very apogee of the liberal egalitarian ideals to which these African (and Afro-American) intellectuals had dedicated themselves, but which also included the concept of class as a crucial variable in the analysis and the prognosis.

Protest based on race had to come to terms with protest based on class, especially since the latter seemed relatively more successful, certainly intellectually more sure of itself, and commanded more mass support. The intellectual impact was slow rather than sudden. In time, Marxist hypotheses came to permeate the thinking of African (and Afro-Amer-

ican) intellectuals, who began to see colonial and racial oppression as based on economic considerations.

Ironically, this slow assimilation of class analysis served to
integrate these African (and Afro-American) intellectuals into
the white world. In Richard Wright's pungent description (in
White Man, Listen): "The fear inspired by white domination
breeds a tendency . . . to make Asians and Africans act, pretend. And this same almost unconscious tendency to pretension
will spur them to pretend to accept an ideology in which they
do not believe. They accept it in order to climb out of their
prisons. Many a black boy in America has seized upon the
rungs of the Red ladder to climb out of his Black Belt. And
well he may, if there are no other ways out of it. Hence, ideology here becomes a means toward a social intimacy."

This latent function of ideology helps to explain why that
generation of African (and Afro-American) intellectuals was
never truly radical even when they were most vocal in their
avowed adherence to what was then the world's revolutionary
ideology. They did not take up the ideology for its own sake
but for another end which they confused with the first. But,
as we shall see, when the choice came, they were faithful to
their own specific needs.

There were two quite separate lessons symbolized by the
Russian Revolution (though perhaps not by it alone). One
was a way of analyzing the world. The other was a way of
changing it—by organized, militant, mass action. It was possible to absorb one lesson without absorbing the other. Most
of the intellectual leaders of African and pan-African movements of this time really learned only the first lesson. They
were in this sense armchair revolutionaries. The leader of the
black world who learned the second lesson best was, paradoxically, one of the few who rejected the theories of Communism outright—Marcus Garvey. For all his failures, he had
a profound impact on the African world. He organized a mass
movement around the theme of black nationalism. He understood the possibilities of anticolonial solidarity. In 1920 he

gave to Eamon de Valera and the cause of Irish freedom the moral support of his movement. In 1922 he petitioned the League of Nations for the redress of black grievances via the Persian delegation. But above all he represented a taking in hand by black men of their own destiny.

Garvey's ideas were echoed in the far corners of Africa—in French-speaking as well as English-speaking areas. His writings were read, and banned. He inspired such enterprises as the African Orthodox Church in Uganda. His insistence on self-help and defiance was in line with another current that had been coursing through Africa for some years—the "Ethiopian" movement, or the emergence of separatist Christian churches, which emphasized the need for exclusively black personnel in the church hierarchy. Garveyism and separatism had one basic theme in common—the desirability of black control over their own institutions, the need to reinforce the solidarity of the black community against the white world. In a sense this was too vulgar and unsophisticated for the intellectuals, most of whom never ceased to look with disdain, fear, and even repugnance on assertive, black-oriented, action-oriented mass movements. Whether in the Western Hemisphere or Africa, these intellectuals concentrated on the weapons of the mind and of the word.

There were two main circuits of discourse for African (and Afro-American) intellectuals in the period between the two world wars. One, the more famous one, was centered around the leadership of W. E. B. DuBois. Dr. DuBois had been active in the Pan-African Conference of 1900. After the First World War, he convened in 1919 in Paris a Pan-African Congress with the aim of influencing those who were drafting the peace treaties. This first congress was followed by a second in 1921 in London, Paris, and Brussels, a third in 1923 in London and Lisbon, and a fourth in New York in 1927. All these congresses were dominated by Western Hemisphere Negroes and the organizers had a difficult time establishing rapport with the major African groups, such as the National Congress of British West Africa. Although these congresses petered out, partly because the impact of the Depression on American Negroes cut off financial support, the circuit survived in various activities centered in England in the 1930s. In 1935 a number of former participants in the congresses plus a Gold Coast group that had been created in 1934 to protest certain colonial legislation formed the International African Friends of Africa. In 1937 virtually the same group formed the International African Service Bureau, which merged in 1944 with a number of African groups, largely in England, into the Pan-African Federation. It was this group which convened the Fifth Pan-African Congress in Manchester in 1945 and called on Dr. DuBois to preside over it.

Among this group, a flame was preserved, and an intellectual tradition—one that was influenced by Marxism but never subordinate to it. This group was concerned primarily with the world-wide rights of black men. Increasingly, however, it concentrated on purely African problems, first land rights, later political emancipation in general. It always saw the relevance of the wider struggle of the colonial peoples[1] and the need for alliance with progressive white forces, but remained nonetheless primarily a black pan-African movement.

The second major circuit of discourse was located in the French literary world, especially among the surrealists. Here in the midst of European civilization was a group of harsh critics who sought to answer the distortions of a rationalized, industrial society by an appeal to the senses, to a renewal of so-called primitive vision. Denouncing bourgeois capitalist society, denouncing racism, denouncing the ethnocentrism of Europe, they could not fail to find a sympathetic audience, indeed disciples, among the African and Caribbean intellectuals in Paris and in the French world, men such as Léon Damas, Etienne Léro, and later, Aimé Césaire. The group of Caribbean students who in 1932 founded the journal *Légitime Défense* accepted surrealism "unreservedly" as its basis. This

---

[1] At the Second Pan-African Congress, for example, there were fraternal delegates from Annam, India, Morocco, and the Philippines. Note that Morocco was in the same category as the three Asian states.

journal stood against the cultural assimilation that had for so
long dominated the intellectual atmosphere of the French-
speaking black world. This group, like the French surrealists
themselves, were men of the left, close to the Communist
movement, with which they shared opposition both to racism
and to bourgeois society. But, as in the case of the DuBois
circuit, their primary preoccupation was an assertion of black
values, of the legitimacy of African culture.

The two circuits were not entirely separate. They were
linked by a perhaps unexpected group, the American authors
of the Negro Renaissance—Claude MacKay, Langston Hughes,
Countee Cullen. Produced by the new American Negro intellectual world so deeply influenced by DuBois, they followed
the path of American white authors attracted to Paris in the
1920s. They shared the discontent with the bourgeois world.
They sought human freedom in artistic freedom and in throw-
ing off the constraints of traditional forms. In this period,
American Negro, Caribbean, and French African writers rediscovered Africa together.

Slowly an intellectual attitude was evolving, the elaboration
of which was the major achievement of these intellectuals in
the years between the wars. But it yielded no immediate results. The one black mass movement of this era, Garveyism,
was impervious to their ideas. Garveyism had few real ideas
of its own and so was rather easily crushed. Some of the pan-
African intellectuals tried to find an organizational base in
the world Communist movement. George Padmore was active
in the Black Bureau of the Profintern, the trade-union adjunct
of the Comintern. Some Africans in South Africa joined or
collaborated with the Communist Party (heavily white), as,
for a time, did the Algerian leader, Messali Hadj and his
Etoile Nord-Africain. But they encountered what Padmore
called the "eroding influence of doctrinaire Marxism," including the curious Soviet pressure to support black states within
the United States and the Union of South Africa, and thus
they took their distance from the Communist movement.

For all these reasons, as the Second World War approached,

the results of their efforts were meager. A French colonial administrator, Henri Labouret, could write in 1937: "At the present time, the pan-Negro movement born in the New World scarcely seems to menace the white hegemonies in Africa. It is clearly premature." Still, Labouret had the prescience to use the word "premature."

In the period following the Second World War, from 1945 to 1957, the pan-African movement became far more visible to the rest of the world, and indeed to Africa itself. But no new ideas emerged during this time. In 1945, as we have mentioned, the Fifth Pan-African Congress was convened in Manchester and presided over by DuBois. The delegates still came overwhelmingly from the English-speaking world, but for the first time Africans—men such as Kwame Nkrumah, I. T. A. Wallace-Johnson, and Jomo Kenyatta—were at least as prominent in the leadership as Western Hemisphere Negroes. Antiimperialism and anticolonialism became the major themes of the Congress, and, also for the first time, national independence was openly asserted to be the only valid solution to Africa's political aspirations. A resolution on North Africa's struggle for independence was specifically included, which is the first sign of a "continental" orientation of the movement. The delegates espoused socialist or "Marxist socialist" ideas. One of the reasons for the choice of date and site of the meeting was to enable African delegates going to the founding meeting of the World Federation of Trade Unions in London to proceed on to the pan-African meeting.

When, however, the meeting was over, there was no clear structure within which to continue and implement the ideas of the Conference. The only formal structure to be established was West African rather than pan-African, the West African National Secretariat formed by Nkrumah in London in 1946. It was at this time that Nkrumah was discussing with his colleagues ways and means of creating a "Union of African Socialist Republics." The Secretariat was relatively inactive, though it held one conference in London. But when Nkrumah succeeded in getting the British to concede internal self-government in the Gold Coast, he convened, in Kumasi in December 1953, a West African Nationalist Conference which was attended by a Nigerian delegation headed by Nnamdi Azikiwe and a few delegates from Liberia and Sierra Leone.

Meanwhile, however, the Paris circuit continued on its largely separate way, although there was some slight contact between Nkrumah and various French West African leaders such as Houphouet-Boigny, Senghor, and Apithy in 1946. And, for the time being, pan-Africanism for the French Africans remained a cultural ideal. The reasons were obvious. French colonial policy ruled out political devolution of power as unthinkable. French cultural policy created far greater pressure on African (and Caribbean) intellectuals than did British, and consequently evoked a greater reaction. Thus the French-speaking black intellectuals in Paris evolved the now famous doctrine of negritude, in the elaboration of which Aimé Césaire of Martinique and Léopold Senghor of Senegal collaborated. The journal *Présence Africaine,* founded by Alioune Diop, became the focal point of this movement. The tradition of contact with the French intellectual world was maintained by the participation in a *Comité de Patronage* of the journal of such figures as Sartre, Gide, Camus, and Mounier. The tradition of contact with the American Negro literary world was maintained by the close collaboration with such later exiles as Richard Wright. The tradition of contact with the Communist world was also maintained, notably by the membership in the French Communist Party of Aimé Césaire, who was for many years elected a member of the French National Assembly from Martinique on the Communist Party's ticket.

In 1955, however, *Présence Africaine* discreetly dropped its European *Comité de Patronage.* The following year Aimé Césaire sent the famous *Letter to Maurice Thorez,* published by *Présence Africaine,* in which he resigned from the French Communist Party. He explained: "One fact of primary importance to me is this: that we, men of color, in this precise moment of historical evolution, have, in our consciousness, taken possession of the whole domain of our particularity and that we are ready at all levels and in all matters to assume the responsibilities which devolve from this new consciousness. . . . What I want is that Marxism and Communism be placed at the service of black peoples and not black peoples at the service of Marxism and Communism."

In September 1956 *Présence Africaine* convened in Paris the first World Congress of Black Writers and Artists, which was able to get significant participation from the English-speaking black world even though it was an outgrowth of the Paris pan-African circuit. The gap was beginning to close between the two linguistic-social worlds into which black men had been divided. Alioune Diop, editor of *Présence Africaine,* summed up most aptly in his opening address the key proposition which was to pervade and justify this most important cultural event in the history of the pan-African movement. "It is important to point out here that all of us, whether we believe in God or are atheists, whether Christians, Moslems, or Communists, have in common the feeling of being frustrated by Western culture." To which Césaire added: "There are two ways to lose oneself: by segregation within the walls of the particular or by dilution in the 'universal.' My conception of the universal is that of a universal rich with the particular, rich with all the particulars, a deepening and a coexistence of the particulars."

Conferences, however important for the formation and articulation of ideas, were now no longer enough. The mainstream of world political development was pulling Africa along. Nationalist movements were taking root everywhere. For English-speaking Africa the independence of the Indian subcontinent, and for French-speaking Africa the struggle in Indochina were formative experiences which transformed the realm of the politically possible. Bandung in April 1955 was the assertion of strength and identity vis-à-vis Europe. It transformed the sense of solidarity among the colonized into the Afro-Asian concept which would play a role for ten years to come. And in Africa specifically it brought together black and North Africa, English-speaking and French-speaking Africa for the first time in a significant international political arena.

This then is the background to a movement, the origins of a theme. But what exactly was this theme? It was that African development could only be the consequence of African strength, and that strength would come both from unity of action and from a recognition of the total worthiness of African culture, the total possibility of African achievement.

It is useful to analyze the relationship of this theme, and hence of this movement, to the themes and organizations of the European left. Insofar as pan-Africanism (and kindred movements of the Third World) represented a protest against the groups that dominated Africa and the rest of the world, its proponents sympathized with and were in turn supported in varying degrees by that other main group of protesters, the European left (from Communists to Social Democrats to Radicals). To the European left, the grievances of the pan-Africanists were but a variation on their own themes—indeed perhaps a minor variation. Insofar, however, as pan-Africanism represented a rejection of European leadership, even in the intellectual spheres, then the European left itself was under attack—perhaps even more so than the right, which after all was less swept up in universalist pretensions.

This ambivalent relationship between pan-Africanists and the European left was present from the beginning and remains to this day. Of the spokesmen for the European left, the one who came nearest to appreciating the problem as seen from the perspective of Africa (or of the Third World) was perhaps Lenin. The Russian Revolution itself, after all, represented a rejection of orthodox Marxist strategy, conceived in Western Europe, as inapplicable to the Russian situation. And in the Report of the Commission on National and Colonial Questions at the Second Congress of the Communist International in July 1920, Lenin accepted the concept of "oppressed nations and oppressing nations" and the possibility of collaboration between the Communist movement and "nationalist-

revolutionary" movements. But in practice it was always difficult to make the distinction between such revolutionary movements and reformist movements, and European socialists, of
whatever variety, always were uncomfortable with theoretical
analyses based on ethnic-racial rather than class interests.

We will return again to the question of this ambivalent relationship between the radicalism based on class and that based
on national or group oppression. This question not only com-
plicates the alignment of forces in the international arena (in
our day, the degree to which it is possible for Communist
countries and countries of the Third World to consider themselves in the same camp), but it came to complicate the relationships within the pan-African movement itself.

: II :

MOVEMENT

VERSUS ALLIANCE

The declarations and themes of a group of intellectuals do not
constitute a social movement. Only with the upsurge of African nationalism was there for the first time a mass base for
such a movement. In many ways 1956–1957 marked a turning
point, because these years saw some major victories and consequent signs of new boldness among nationalist movements.
In 1956 the Sudan, Morocco, and Tunisia gained their independence and Egypt asserted hers in the Suez War. In 1957
Ghana became the first "black" African state to obtain independence from colonial rule. That same year, in French Africa,
the interterritorial Rassemblement Démocratique Africain
(RDA) held its Third Congress, which proclaimed itself
the Congress of Black Africa, and for the first time a major
political organization of French black Africans asserted the
"right to independence." Even in the more repressed, politically quieter areas Africans dared to raise the new issues. In
1956, in the Belgian Congo, a number of intellectuals grouped
around the journal *Conscience Africaine* asked for independence in thirty years. It was a very moderate demand, but
nationalistic nonetheless.

At this point the tenor of nationalism in black Africa was at least as much pan-African as it was territorial. The nationalists were imminently to achieve concrete power—within territorial limits. Pan-Africanism thus could no longer be merely the denunciation of racial indignity, the revalorization of African achievements. It now would have to come to terms with a very specific political problem—the merger of separate political units into a larger one. Facing this problem, pan-Africanism now became transformed into a new movement, the movement toward African unity.

It is a characteristic of a movement to pull into its orbit a far larger number of people than those fully committed to its goals. There is always a peripheral group for whom the larger objectives and accompanying ideology are merely tactical weapons designed to secure simple goals. In the early stages of a movement when the momentum is forward and responsibilities few, it is easy to be unaware of the differences between the core and the periphery. Even the participants scarcely notice the distinctions. But as a movement begins to acquire elaborate organizational structures (*a fortiori* when these are sovereign states), the tension between the core and the periphery becomes more evident. Part of the periphery may begin to dissociate itself actively from the movement, perhaps still proclaiming their fidelity to its ideals. However, as long as the movement seems to have mass appeal, because it still responds to social demands of a large group for access to power, privilege, or material reward, few are willing to renounce the movement altogether. But many are willing to reinterpret its meaning and its implications for political action.

We have spoken before of the ambivalence of the relations between the European left and the pan-African movement, the strain between an analysis based on class and one centered on race. But the core of the pan-African movement has always sought to resolve the antinomy by creating some more subtle schema that would incorporate both and perhaps even translate one set of concepts into the other. The periphery of the movement, however, was always more attracted by race analysis. They wanted entry into the world community as equals but did not seek to transform the nature of this world community, nor the nation-state system that was one of its essential elements.

If you will, this is the difference between those who were social revolutionaries and those who were not. Both spoke in the name of unity. But they meant different things by it. For the core, unity was the unity of people, the theme of a revolutionary *movement*, a key rallying point and a key prerequisite to the achievement of its goals. Its intentions were to transform Africa and thereby the world. For the periphery, unity was the ultimate point of an alliance of nation-states whose object was to strengthen the participants in the world power game, to advance them but not to transform them.

Social movements do not emerge because a few men are inspired by a new set of ideals. They represent a demand for change by an entire social stratum convinced that its interests will be served by change. The demands are usually radical when compared with the value system of the established order, and they are usually justified by an ideology which argues that the desired object is for the common good. The argument is often buttressed by assertions that the change is historically inevitable. Such has been the case with the movement for African unity.

Since World War II, and particularly in the period 1957–1965, the unity movement has incarnated the demands of the most radical segments of the modern African managerial classes. These were the men who believed their own and their country's future lay in a rapid development of the economy into a modern industrial system. For the attainment of this goal, they recognized two preconditions in sequence. First of all, the development of their economy to a point approaching parity with the West would require a basic alteration in the world system of exchange, a redistribution of resources, and a major shift in the terms of trade. To achieve such an alteration, they would need the kind of political strength to be found in a state large enough to support the economic disciplines concomitant with industrialization and to prevent outside interference with such disciplines.

Though all of the elites in Africa claimed to advocate economic development, a number of groups found sufficient immediate profit in various economic changes which, while providing the elites with expanded consumption incomes, did little to break the over-all economic dependence of African economies on outside forces. For them, African unity meant an alliance among the governing groups to share in the immediately available portion of the pie allocated to their countries in the existing world market. The revolutionary elements in the elite wished, however, to challenge the world allocation itself. In this sense they were radical, for they questioned the values of the dominant world system, in the name of an ideology which asserted that change would benefit the African masses by creating both a wealthier and a more egalitarian society.

Because they used the same slogan and occupied the same political terrain, the proponents of movement and the proponents of alliance were able to work together up to a point, were perhaps condemned to work together, found it mutually useful to work together. As in all social movements, the core hoped to use the periphery, the periphery to tame the core. This is the drama and the vulnerability of a movement. It is also its inner dynamic, the tension that enables it to proceed. The core consisted of those who were most stably committed to achieving a revolutionary transformation of Africa by means of unity, and who were satisfied with nothing less. The periphery tended to take a more instrumental view of the movement. The periphery was concerned with achieving and maintaining power within African independent states. Unity was useful insofar as it served these ends. There were, of course, many who moved back and forth between the core and the periphery, so that the composition of the core seemed to fluctuate over the years.

It is this story we wish to tell, analyzed from the inside. This work is then at one and the same time contemporary history and a case study of the operation of a social movement. It speaks to what has been most urgent in Africa's recent politics. But it speaks as well to our understanding of a key process in the modern world and in the modernization of the world.

The Political Struggle:
1957–1965

〰〰〰〰〰〰〰〰〰

:III:

BRIGHT HOPE:

THE DOWNWARD SWEEP

OF AFRICAN LIBERATION

The period from March 6, 1957, the date of Ghana's independence, to June 30, 1960, which marked the independence of Congo (L),[1] was one of optimism and glory for Africa. By the end of 1960 most of West and Equatorial Africa had won its independence. So had North Africa, except for Algeria, where a war was being fought. East and Central Africa were well on their way. And Africans grew confident that southern Africa would follow in this path in a mere few years. This was a period of bright hope—for African independence and for African unity. It was toward the end of this period, on February 3, 1960, that the Prime Minister of the United Kingdom, Harold Macmillan, told the Houses of Parliament of the Union of South Africa that a "wind of change" was sweeping Africa. Almost everyone believed it.

When Ghana became independent, the nations of the world sent high dignitaries to celebrate this "first" black African

[1] In this book, we shall use Congo (L) to indicate the former Belgian Congo, whose capital is Leopoldville, and Congo (B) to indicate the former French Congo, whose capital is Brazzaville. Both countries call themselves, since independence, "the Congo." On July 1, 1966, the name of Leopoldville was changed to Kinshasa; and thus, Congo (K).

state to be liberated from colonial rule. Tunisia even sent its head of government, Habib Bourguiba. The host government invited nationalist leaders from all over the continent of Africa. The celebrations probably brought together the largest and most representative sample of African leaders up to that date. It is here that the idea of a meeting of independent African states was first evoked, and notably in the conversations between Kwame Nkrumah and Bourguiba.

The transition and continuity of the movement for unity was most romantically symbolized by Dr. DuBois in a public letter to Nkrumah. DuBois said: "I hereby put into your hands, Mr. Prime Minister, my empty but still significant title of President of the Pan-African Congress to be bestowed on my duly-elected successor who will preside over a Pan-African Congress due, I trust, to meet soon and for the first time on African soil, at the call of the independent state of Ghana." On April 18, 1957, the government of Ghana invited the governments of the eight other independent African states to come to Accra for a conference.

Soon thereafter, African ambassadors in London began to meet to plan for such a conference and they created a joint secretariat to conduct their work. All the independent African states were invited, even the Union of South Africa. The latter refused to attend unless other "responsible powers" on the African continent, meaning the colonial powers, were invited. The matter was dropped and this was the last time South Africa was invited by other African states to participate in an African conference at any level. The Conference of Independent African States (CIAS) was convened for April 15, 1958.

While the preparations for this meeting were proceeding, another one of a slightly different sort was held. From December 26, 1957, to January 1, 1958, the first meeting of the Afro-Asian Peoples' Solidarity Conference (AAPSC) took place in Cairo. This organization, which one of its delegates called the "peoples' Bandung," brought together nongovernmental organizations from both Africa and Asia (including Asian republics of the U.S.S.R.). Delegates from some nineteen

African states came, the majority from nonindependent countries. In many cases, these were leading political personalities.
The function of the AAPSC on the African scene will be discussed later. Here it is important to note the special attention
paid by this conference to two problems of African liberation:
Algeria and South Africa. The Conference decided to establish
a permanent secretariat in Cairo. This Afro-Asian precedent—
an intergovernmental conference (Bandung) followed by,
paralleled by, and yet distinct from a peoples' conference
(Cairo)—would be adopted later on the African scene.

The distinction between independent governments and nationalist movements in colonial states had to be faced immediately. The independent African states felt they had to restrict
their conference to themselves. The self-consciousness of responsible authority weighed upon them from the beginning.
But in order to permit the voice of nonindependent Africa to
be heard the independent states decided to admit representatives of the nationalist groups in these countries, more or less
as petitioners, modeled on the precedent of the United Nations. Most notably, at Accra there were representatives of
the Front de Libération Nationale (FLN) of Algeria, Juvento
of Togo, and the Union des Populations du Cameroun (UPC),
which resulted in strong special resolutions on the colonial
situation in these three countries.

The principle that would henceforth prevail in African conferences was that nationalist movements in nonindependent
countries would not be considered the political equals of sovereign states. Representatives of nonindependent states might
at best be observers, if they enjoyed power in a partially self-
governing state. Otherwise they would be appellants. African
decisions would rest primarily with the independent states,
to the exclusion of that portion of Africa not enjoying full
sovereignty. The nature of the world system of sovereign states
seemed obviously to require this, but in accepting this exigency
the revolutionary movement had made a first and quite important concession. Once made, many consequences would
flow naturally from it.

Two significant political decisions emerged from the Accra meeting. One was the recognition of the FLN as the legitimate representative of Algeria. This placed the independent African states in direct opposition to France on the key issue of her African concern. The second was the decision to constitute the African ambassadors to the United Nations as an "informal permanent machinery" which would come to be known as the "African Group" with its own bylaws and secretariat.

The Algerian question, more than any other, constantly put pressure on independent states to substitute revolutionary values for those of recognized international law. One instance was to be seen in the conference of North African nationalist parties convened in Tangier on April 27–30, right after Accra. There the representatives of each of the principal nationalist parties of Algeria, Morocco, and Tunisia decided on a federal form of unity of the three states, although Algeria was still a French colony. They established the Consultative Assembly of the Arab Maghreb, composed of delegates from the National Assemblies of Tunisia and Morocco, and the National Council of the Algerian Revolution (and this before the FLN had even created a government-in-exile). Similarly, when the African Group was convened in May in New York, the question of the political equality of a nationalist movement of a nonindependent country was reopened. Because of the special importance of Algeria, and because the FLN maintained a permanent mission at the U.N. that operated inside the corridors by being attached to various friendly missions, the African Group decided on the compromise that the FLN delegation would participate in its meetings but would speak only on Algerian questions. Although this was merely a small breach of juridical correctness, it indicated the pressure that a social movement could exert on the international norms that often effectively constrain such movements.

Algeria was the one African state engaged in a full-scale war of independence at that time. For this reason, it preoccupied the African Group. One of the decisions of the Accra Conference was to undertake joint diplomatic missions (three groups each, with delegates from three countries) to visit Scandinavia, Central America, and South America, to canvas for support among the "neutrals" for the Algerian resolution in the forthcoming U.N. session. These missions were relatively successful, and the U.N. resolution for the first time acknowledged the existence of a "war."

The second concern of the African Group from the outset was the effect of the world economic structure on their own development. In May in Geneva, African diplomats engaged in united action at the debate in the Economic and Social Council (ECOSOC) of the U.N. over the creation of the U.N. Economic Commission for Africa (ECA). ECA was an old idea. It had been first formally recommended by a U.N. group of experts in 1951. The colonial powers had been unenthusiastic, since they had their own organ of cooperation, the Commission for Technical Cooperation in Africa South of the Sahara (usually abbreviated CCTA, following the French nomenclature), which had been established in 1950 and which was not subject to potentially embarrassing control by the United Nations. But at the Twelfth General Assembly of the U.N., on November 26, 1957, the world atmosphere had sufficiently changed so that a recommendation that ECOSOC establish ECA was passed unanimously (except for the abstention of Belgium).

At ECOSOC, however, there was a clear tug of war between the African states and the colonial powers as to the scope of the proposed commission, and the conference was faced with two drafts, one prepared by the United Kingdom (the colonial power relatively most prepared to cooperate with the Africans) and one prepared jointly by the African states (excluding South Africa, of course).

Both texts agreed in some respects. There was no question that all independent African states would be included. It is perhaps surprising that none of the colonial powers sought to exclude North Africa. But here, as at the Accra Conference, the sheer question of numbers (there were only three independent "black" African states at this time) undoubtedly played its part. Another factor may have been that the attempt many years earlier to establish a U.N. Economic Commission for the Middle East had been abortive because of the refusal of the Arab states to countenance the membership of Israel; hence, the various North African states were in 1958 affiliated to no regional economic commission. Nor was there any question yet of excluding the colonial powers, although the resolution provided that "states which cease to have any territorial responsibilities in Africa shall cease to be members of the Commission." South Africa was included but declined to participate "for the present." In its communication to the Secretary-General of the U.N., the South African government raised questions both about the inclusion of North African countries and also the possible overlapping with CCTA.

The differences in the two texts lay in the issues of voting rights for associate members and whether or not the U.S. and the U.S.S.R. would be members. On the first issue, the African states did not want the vote given to delegations from colonial territories, who composed the category of potential associate members. The United Kingdom, which was the only colonial government at this time willing to enroll its colonies as associate members, pleaded for their full vote. The African states won on this issue. They lost, however, on the other. The African states (except Liberia) sought to include the two major world powers on the Commission in order to underscore their nonalignment. The Western powers were anxious to exclude the U.S.S.R.; the U.S. was willing to sacrifice its own membership toward this end. It is ironic that the Western powers thereby established a principle of exclusive "African" membership which the Africans would later also use to exclude the colonial powers from ECA.

The second difference in the two texts centered around the desire of the African Group to include "social development" in the scope of reference of the Commission. This seemingly innocuous phrase, finally adopted in a compromise form, gave rise to great controversy in which the Africans were supported notably by Brazil, Indonesia, Mexico, and Yugoslavia.

The U.S. and the U.K. led the opposition. Although no doubt the perception was dim on both sides, the debate reflected a sense of the long-run implications of the movement toward African unity. The Africans were asserting that their demands were very broad and far-reaching. The Western powers were indicating their reluctance to accept the legitimacy of such broad demands as "social" seemed to imply. This tension was a portent of Western hesitations about African unity, an idea which the West supported only as long as it in no way actively threatened Western interests.

Meanwhile, nationalist movements in nonindependent states began to see how they might use the unity movement to aid their cause. Among the observers to the April Accra meeting of the CIAS were a number of prominent East African politicians, including Nyerere of Tanganyika, Murumbi of Kenya, and Muhsin of Zanzibar. In the discussions that were held on preparations for a follow-up peoples' conference, the idea of a special regional structure for East and Central Africa, an area of immediate major struggle for independence, was revived. There had been several abortive attempts to convene such a meeting. The last one had been called by Kenneth Kaunda of Northern Rhodesia but had been frustrated by colonial immigration officials. However, on September 17, 1958, in Mwanza, Tanganyika, representatives of nationalist movements of five territories were able to meet, and they formed the Pan-African Freedom Movement of East and Central Africa (PAFMECA).[2]

This seemed just another link in the expanding chain of pan-African structures. Its very name indicates the ideological sympathy. But it raised an issue that would grow in importance—the relation of regional unity movements to a pan-African movement. No one was quite aware of this yet. After all, the Kumasi conference convened by Nkrumah in 1953 had itself established a National Congress of West Africa, a regional structure which, however, never came to life.

[2] In fact, at this time Central African participation consisted of one Nyasaland delegate. PAFMECA was essentially an East African organization until 1960.

Events in French Africa took a different turn. On October 28, 1958, French Africa voted in the constitutional Referendum which had grown out of the settlers' revolt in Algeria in May and the consequent return to power of Charles de Gaulle. Guinea under Sékou Touré voted "no," thus opting for independence. It was then refused admission to the association with France provided for in Title XIII of the new French Constitution. Guinea immediately became a rallying point of revolutionary ardor in Africa. Many intellectuals from other parts of Africa, especially French-speaking Africa, flocked there to help maintain the independence of this new, bold, and very struggling state.

Guinea's appearance on the African scene had two important consequences. One was that its mere existence, combined with the continued pressure of the Algerian FLN, contributed heavily to the decolonization of all French black Africa in the subsequent two years. The impact this had on the movement toward unity we shall discuss later.

The second major impact of Guinea's independence was on the other independent African states. When Diallo Telli came to New York to obtain Guinea's admission to the U.N., an admission opposed by France but granted nonetheless two months later, he convened the African Group. He told them that they were his brothers, that before he came to the Afro-Asian group he came to them. He said that his instructions were that he was to be at their disposal, that Guinea was not Guinea but Africa. This was a new language at the United Nations, one which would transform the African Group in the coming two years from a group that scarcely mattered to a central caucus of the world body. Whereas in 1958 Western diplomats considered the Afro-Asian group an instrument that pushed the moderate Africans further than they intended, by 1960 these same diplomats wished the Afro-Asian caucus had its old authority and could thereby restrain the African Group.

Guinea's independence also led to what is to date undoubtedly the most spectacular gesture on the pan-African scene —the Ghana-Guinea Union, announced on November 23, 1958.

The joint communiqué stated: "Inspired by the example of the thirteen American colonies, the tendencies of the countries of Europe, Asia, and the Middle East to organize in a rational manner, we have agreed to constitute our two States as a nucleus of a Union of West African States." Actually very little institutional change followed, even when the Ghana-Guinea Union later expanded to include Mali. (The Union was eventually dissolved with the creation of the Organization of African Unity in 1963.) But to concentrate on its lack of concrete achievement is to ignore the important consequences of the Union for the movement. For one thing, it helped to sustain Guinea politically and materially at a moment of great difficulty, thus helping Guinea to play the role referred to above. Secondly, and perhaps more importantly, it was the first major break-through in the language barrier of African politics. From this time on, although linguistically based alliances never disappeared, the lines were primarily ideological. Not least of the consequences was the impact on Ghana. For the link with Guinea ultimately led to Ghana's surmounting its initial basically regionalist and linguistic focus, a focus of which it was in fact scarcely aware.

The true successor to the Pan-African Congresses was not the Conference of Independent African States but the All-African Peoples' Conference (AAPC), whose first meeting was held on December 5–13, 1958. Though the Preparatory Committee had been composed only of representatives from the eight independent African states, delegates came from twenty-eight African countries, most of them still colonies. None represented a government as such. Rather they had come in the name of two kinds of groups: political parties or movements, and trade unions. Tom Mboya of Kenya was elected chairman, partly to emphasize the participation of other than West and North Africans and partly to pay tribute to the active Kenyan struggle for independence. The achievement of independence was clearly the primary problem facing the delegates. Mboya said: "The problem is not to know if we want independence, but how to get it." In principle, the organizers had hoped to attract all of Africa's nationalist movements. They did rather well, but the governing political parties in the French Community states which had just become autonomous did not come, except for that of Senegal. The resolutions were not very radical, considering that the atmosphere of a peoples' conference was expected to be less prudent than a conference of sovereign states. They did mention for the first time a "Commonwealth of Free African States" as an objective, but they also found regional federations to be a "first step" toward this, provided they did not prejudice "the ultimate objective of a Pan-African Commonwealth."

One of the central issues of the meeting was the legitimacy and desirability of using violence. It was agreed that there were and would continue to be colonial situations in which it must be used. This would remain the position of most African leaders and movements throughout future developments. Algeria once again came in for special attention, and full support was given to the recently proclaimed Gouvernement Provisoire de la République Algérienne (GPRA). For Cameroon, where the UPC maquis was fighting, the Conference demanded full amnesty and U.N.-supervised elections. This was a crucial issue with great consequences for all of Africa, as we shall see. The Conference called for the establishment of various all-African organizations, such as trade unions and youth groups. This too would be of extreme importance. It also called for setting up a Bureau of Liberatory Movements. Finally, the Conference decided to set up a permanent secretariat with headquarters in Accra. The first secretary-general was George Padmore, now a Ghanaian by adoption. When he died the following year he was succeeded by Guinea's Resident Minister in Ghana, Abdoulaye Diallo.

The impact of this and subsequent AAPC meetings on political awareness in Africa is difficult to measure, but nonetheless very real. The AAPC brought many African nationalist leaders into contact for the first time with others who had already won independence for their countries or were in active and violent struggle for it. The head of the Congolese delegation was Patrice Lumumba. The meeting he and two other delegates held in Leopoldville to report on the Conference was, for example, one of the precipitating factors that sparked the riots of January 4, 1959, which in turn set in motion the process that was to lead the Congo (L) through an exceptionally rapid decolonization.

There were now two fronts of action. One was in the field, so to speak. Nationalist movements throughout colonial Africa were pressing for the independence of their countries. The second front was at the United Nations, where the independent African states were pursuing with unexpected vigor their collective demands. One result was that the United Nations held in February 1959 a special resumed session to deal with the French Trust Territory of Cameroon. This territory was moving toward independence under nationalist pressure. However, the major nationalist party, the UPC, had been outlawed in 1955 and its leaders were heading an insurrection. The French were working with other elements led by Ahmadou Ahidjo, later to become the first president. The basic issue was that the UPC, through its exiled President Félix Moumié, was demanding that the United Nations not give its blessing to independence until U.N.-supervised elections, in which the UPC could participate, were held. There had been a precedent for this in the case of French Togoland.

In the fall of 1958 the General Assembly had adopted a compromise resolution introduced by the Indians, which was accepted by all sides. It was that the Trusteeship Council send one of its visiting missions, a normal procedure, to Cameroon, and that there be a special resumed session to hear the report of the mission and to decide about elections on the basis of it. The mission was composed of Haiti, India, New Zealand, and the United States. Since India was at that time the leader of the anticolonial bloc in the U.N. and since India had attacked France on this very issue, the Africans regarded India as their representative on the mission. Their shock was unbounded when the commission turned in an incredibly strong report, saying that the Ahidjo government was representative beyond a doubt and that there should *not* be elections. Unlike the usual mission report, there were no criticisms of the trust regime. The Indian delegate who went to Cameroon conveniently was absent from the resumed session. Thus, having the unexpectedly total support of both India and the United States (which considered the UPC to be pro-Communist), France anticipated no opposition to its program. However, Guinea, Ghana, and Tunisia pressed very hard to have the African Group proclaim their own position on this question separately from the Afro-Asian Group. The other six states in the African Group were initially reluctant. Ahidjo spoke to them, pledging his loyalty to the African Group after Cameroon achieved independence. Nonetheless, seven members of the African Group introduced an amendment to the report, calling for elections. On the final vote, the two other members of the African Group, Liberia and Ethiopia, switched their votes on the amendment to "for" and abstention, respectively, out of solidarity.

A new cohesion and a new militance were emerging among the Africans in the United Nations arena, despite the fact, or perhaps because of the fact, that most Asian delegations were unwilling to go along with this African militance on decolonization. On this issue, the Africans found themselves isolated with the Soviet bloc in the United Nations for the first time (with the exception of a Soviet amendment in the previous session on target dates for independence in Africa).

While solidarity was being forged at the United Nations, there were clearly some weak links, and in the ebullient atmosphere of West Africa it was hoped to force the pace. Liberia became the target of diplomatic maneuvering in Africa. Ghana and Guinea had made formal their union at a meeting in Conakry on May 1, 1959.[8] The leaders of the two countries met with President Tubman of Liberia at Sanniquellie (Liberia)

[8] It should be noted that whereas in the November 1958 declaration it was said that the Ghana-Guinea Union was a nucleus of a Union of West African States, by May the charter provided that it was to be the nucleus of a Union of Independent African States. The geographical scope was now resolutely continental.

on July 19. Despite the fact that a new organization was set up on paper, to be called the Community of Independent African States (which never thereafter functioned in any way), the Sanniquellie declaration was a check on the momentum that was building up for the sentiment of unity. It became clear that more than a little verbal pressure would be necessary to induce conservative, established regimes (of which Liberia was a model) to abet the essentially unsettling process of erecting new structures with supranational powers. This lesson would become more and more clear as the years went by and would push at least part of the core of the movement toward more militant action vis-à-vis the conservative elements.

Still, Liberia made some concessions to the temper of the times. The three powers agreed that they would "consider" the recognition of the Algerian GPRA at the special session of the CIAS convened the very next month at Monrovia. This meeting of foreign ministers, the secretariat of which was provided by the African Group at the U.N., was being held at the request of the GPRA, which wanted the meeting in order to gain further material and diplomatic support. The Algerian revolutionaries had decided to make African backing a major element in their own struggle and they began to orient themselves toward an African, rather than a purely Arab, identity in a way that has not been reversed since. The GPRA had not hitherto been recognized by a black African state. But Ghana just prior to the meeting, and Guinea during the meeting, accorded *de facto* recognition. Liberia, as the host government, agreed after initial resistance to hoist the Algerian flag "as a courtesy." The Conference unanimously decided to call for international recognition of the GPRA, but it would be another year before Liberia in fact accorded recognition. Nonetheless, bit by bit, African governments were willing to do more and more on questions concerning liberation.

Although the Conference was specifically called to discuss Algeria, Félix Moumié of the UPC came hoping to get the African states to seek the reopening of the Cameroon issue at the U.N. Despite the fact that they reaffirmed their position in favor of "free elections under United Nations supervision before independence," the resolution was very prudent in its wording. Guinea continued to give full support to the UPC, but the imminent independence of a Cameroon that would be governed by Ahidjo gave pause to the other governments that might otherwise have supported the UPC.

If one takes the Sanniquellie and Monrovia meetings together, one sees the outlines of the *de facto* compromise between the core and the periphery of the movement. The relative caution about institutional advances in African unity (the Sanniquellie concept of a Community of Independent African States) and the recognition, if sometimes an uncomfortable one, of existing African authorities in independent states, however conservative (attitude toward Cameroon at Monrovia), were compensated for by relative militance on issues of anti-colonial liberation (call for recognition of GPRA). This compromise was essentially a victory of the periphery of the movement, and was to be repeated on many subsequent occasions. The revolutionary core made the compromise, and would do so again later, because of the urgent priority it gave to liberation issues. The compromise, even then, did not go uncriticized among the ranks of the core elements. Already at this stage, the revolutionary core was finding its freedom of action greatly constrained by the fact that some of its leading spokesmen were also leaders of sovereign states, and thus conformed more and more to the traditional political practices of sovereign states.

Even in the presumably more radical atmosphere of the All-Africa Peoples' Conference, where governments as such were not represented, when it held its second meeting in Tunis in January 1960 the avant-garde elements were obliged to accept compromise positions. Although the most conservative elements excluded themselves totally from the AAPC, generally speaking the AAPC sought to include everyone. Consequently, it paid the price of having many in its ranks who wished to modify its avant-garde posture. Anthony Enahoro, representing the Action Group of Nigeria, criticized the continued support of the UPC even after the independence of Cameroon and succeeded thereby in getting a relatively tame resolution on Cameroon.

The issue of pan-African trade-unionism, decided upon in principle at the first AAPC, was to be a thorny one, which we shall discuss in detail later. But the famous question of "disaffiliation" (from international trade-union structures) had by now been raised and this Conference was seized by it. The East African elements, led by Tom Mboya, chairman of the first AAPC but more or less suspended from this position and personally absent at Tunis, stood at the time strongly against disaffiliation. Instead of calling for disaffiliation, the AAPC evaded the issue. Ghanaian proposals for political union were not adopted.

The most revolutionary proposal was that of the Algerians and Moroccans for an "international corps of volunteers" to go to the aid of the Algerians (in the manner of the International Brigade in Spain). The proposal for such a corps was adopted. But although its use was to be strictly limited to Algeria, President Bourguiba of Tunisia denounced the proposal as propaganda and indicated that such a corps would not be permitted on Tunisian soil. This illustrates what was to become a major factor in the strategy of liberation. The independent border states of a country fighting a colonial revolution have had more power to affect tactics than any pan-African structure, however strong. And border states have been prudent, since they pay the price of imprudence most immediately. The self-interest of the sovereign African states led inevitably to moderating revolutionary action. Thus when the Conference proclaimed the "irrevocable character of the movement towards African independence, liberty, and unity," there was no assurance that for everyone present it meant the same kind of independence, liberty, and unity.

The concept of alliance as a substitute for a movement now began to take concrete form. The view that all independent states in Africa (except South Africa), whatever their political orientation, were members of the family, became a firm principle of all-African interstate meetings. In June of 1960 the second Conference of Independent African States was convened, as planned, at Addis Ababa. The most significant difference was the presence of Cameroon, now an independent state under Ahidjo.[4] The UPC was denied audience. The other states now had to sit beside a government whose credentials they had actively questioned a short time before. The Cameroon UPC reacted immediately. Analyzing the meeting in its journal, it said: "The situation is thus perfectly clear: in the months and years to come, we shall see the birth of governments which are called independent but are clearly directed by the imperialists. From then on, African solidarity will be more and more a sentiment in the service of imperialism, if as at Addis Ababa the truly independent governments seek unity at any price."

To be sure, the admission of Cameroon was slightly counterbalanced by the admission of the GPRA to full status in the CIAS, despite the fact that Ethiopia had not yet recognized the GPRA[5] and that Ahidjo's Cameroon actively opposed its seating. The Conference also invited as full participants five states whose date of independence had been announced for later that year: Congo (L), the Malagasy Republic, the Federation of Mali, Nigeria, and Somalia. But the Malagasy Republic, the Federation of Mali, and the Congo (L) did not come, the latter because it was in the midst of its first internal crisis, a relatively minor one that occurred just before independence over the choice of the president and prime minister. The CIAS discussed at Addis Ababa the advisability of sending a Conciliation Commission to Leopoldville. This was the first time such a proposal, which would recur often, was offered. In fact, it would not be necessary to send a Conciliation Commission,

[4] Togo, also now independent, was invited but did not come, presumably because of missed plane connections. In fact, it was the beginning of the isolationist policy that President Sylvanus Olympio would pursue in Africa until his assassination.

[5] The Emperor did, however, agree at this time to offer his mediation between the GPRA and France, which amounted to a semirecognition.

since at that very moment a solution to the dispute was found through the joint efforts in Leopoldville of the missions of Ghana and Israel.

The concept of political union as a legitimate objective of common interest now met active opposition from a leading African state. The Ghanaian delegation's formal demand for union was met by the vocal opposition of the Nigerian delegation, which stated: "President Tubman's idea of the association of states is . . . more acceptable for it is as yet premature to form a Union of States under one sovereignty." The issue had become polarized. The pressure for "practical" inter-African economic cooperation as a priority was being felt. Picking up on an idea found in a resolution of the Tunis AAPC, the CIAS at Addis Ababa called for the establishment of two inter-African banks, one for development and one for commerce. The former would in fact eventually be established, albeit in a compromise form.

Finally, the CIAS viewed the decolonization of southern Africa as virtually assured, requiring only firm pressure from the African independent states. Though the use of violence was not thereby eschewed it was certainly played down, and reliance was placed on appeals to liberal elements in the Western world. Regarding South Africa, the CIAS decided on a twofold action. First, it called for the severance of diplomatic relations and a transportation boycott, and asked the Arab states to cease oil shipments to South Africa and the African states that were members of the Commonwealth to work for the exclusion of South Africa. Secondly, the CIAS decided to engage in litigation before the International Court of Justice against the Union of South Africa for violation of the League of Nations mandate in South-West Africa. Though this action would be brought formally only by Ethiopia and Liberia as signatories to the Covenant of the League of Nations, the project would be jointly financed with an executive committee made up of representatives from four nations to decide tactics. It is important here to appreciate the strategy of liberation that this implied. Such court proceedings were known to be long and laborious.[6] The real justification was that a successful judgment might place significant pressure upon the United Kingdom and the United States to bring about major political change in South Africa.

The sum of three years of political struggle underlay the decisions of the Conference of Independent African States at Addis Ababa. Was African unity to be the focal point tha⁺ would rally revolutionary movements and states, or was it to be an alliance of the independent states? As we have noted, at Addis Ababa the state of Cameroon, the legitimacy of whose government the other independent states had challenged so vigorously a year earlier, was admitted. Even Guinea, considered at that time the most consistently revolutionary state, sat at the same table. Was this meeting of states to pursue the steps toward rapid political unification? Clearly not. What was to be the stance of the CIAS toward the problem of liberation? Although the GPRA was admitted to membership and a boycott of South Africa proposed, the basic collective tactic adopted was one of diplomatic pressure on the colonial powers. In all cases, those who accepted the limitations of the system of sovereign nation-states prevailed over those who challenged these limitations in the name of a new African order. If the revolutionary core did not press harder, it was partly because it could not and partly because it was confident that time was on its side. What no one expected was the crisis in the Congo.

* In fact they lasted six years and eventually were unsuccessful.

:IV:

HOPE DIMMED:

THE FIRST CONGO CRISIS

AND ITS AFTERMATH

A week after the close of the Conference of Independent African States in June 1960, the Congo was granted its independence. Within two weeks, the events occurred that were to lead to a continuing disorder there. The Congo crisis is a turning point of some importance, the nature of which it is well to underline, for it transformed the political life of the African continent.

In the first place, the successful sweep of African liberation down the continent was halted, although this was not immediately seen in 1960, the so-called "Year of Africa." Some eighteen states gained their independence then (as did several more in the next few years). But, essentially as a consequence of Congolese developments, a hard core of resistance to African advances was consolidated. It comprised Portuguese Africa, Rhodesia, and South Africa, and was far stronger after 1960 than before.

Secondly, the Congo crisis along with the continuing Algerian war, was to reveal—and intensify—the fissures beneath the apparent solidarity of African independent states. The many new independent states of 1960, most of them former

French colonies, were not absorbed into the African Group at the U.N. and its parent CIAS. Rather, new (and divided) structures came into existence, and it would take three years for them to disappear.

Thirdly, as of this point and in the wake of the Congo crisis, the United States actively entered the African political scene. Before that time, it had been a minor bystander, scarcely more important than the U.S.S.R., and active only as a counterbalance to potential long-range Soviet influence. The U.S. had the reputation of mild anticolonialism and sympathy for African aspirations. But after 1960, the United States came bit by bit to play a role as large as, often far larger than, that of the former colonial powers. And it was no longer certain that Africans would find a more sympathetic viewpoint in the U.S. than in Europe. This was as true on the question of African unity as on other questions.

Still these changes in the general situation did not come overnight. When the Congo issue was first placed before the United Nations in July 1960, the only African member of the Security Council was Tunisia. Tunisia agreed to act as the agent of the African Group, whose work had just been commended and whose existence was reaffirmed at the Addis Ababa CIAS. The collective African point of view, as mediated by Mongi Slim, Tunisia's delegate, was very influential at this point. When, in the following month, relations between the Lumumba government and the United Nations forces seriously deteriorated, it was to the collective African powers that Lumumba turned to reinforce his hand. He toured various African countries and called for a summit conference to be held in Leopoldville.

Finally, a "preparatory conference" at ministerial level was in fact held from August 25 to 31 in Leopoldville. The countries that came were for the most part those that had been at the last CIAS at Addis Ababa.[1] The various former French states that had just obtained their independence did not at-

[1] They were Cameroon, Congo (L), Ethiopia, Ghana, GPRA, Guinea, Liberia, Mali, Morocco, Somalia, Sudan, Togo, Tunisia, and the U.A.R.

tend, although invited, despite the special appeal of Bourguiba. Lumumba had hoped to get the group to endorse his idea of direct African military aid to the Congo, but aside from Guinea and to a certain extent the GPRA the response was cautious. The assembled delegates did reaffirm support for the unity of the Congo and did recommend that a conference of heads of state be convened before the opening of the U.N. General Assembly. But the meeting was a letdown for Lumumba and presaged his imminent fall from power. Already at this point it was evident that the African states were divided into three (somewhat fluid) camps—what the Western world would tendentiously call the "revolutionaries," the "moderates" (who did not attend this Leopoldville meeting), and the "neutrals." This conference was the swan song of the original African Group.

When Lumumba was deposed by Kasavubu in September, Lumumba contested the legality of the action. Since Kasavubu was in fact given support both by the United Nations Command and, from October on, by those elements of the Congolese army controlled by Mobutu, Kasavubu held *de facto* control of the capital. Nonetheless, Lumumba still claimed that his was the legal government, and some of his supporters, led by Antoine Gizenga, established *de facto* control over the northeast of the country by November of that year. The Gizenga government functioned from Stanleyville. Even before this, the United Nations General Assembly was faced with the legal-political problem of which of the two rival Congolese delegations it should seat. And the African states that were members of the U.N. had to cast a ballot. This forced a choice, and revealed a split which was to dominate African politics for the next three years. Some supported Lumumba and some Kasavubu (and one or two secretly, or not so secretly, Tshombe). Two (or three) Congos led to two (or three) Africas. The African Group of the United Nations, though it continued to exist in desultory form, was unable to contain this division and could not function effectively.

The newly independent French African states were the first

to create a formal bloc. In October 1960 President Houphouet-Boigny of the Ivory Coast convened a meeting in Abidjan of former French black African states to discuss a common position at the U.N. on three principal questions: the Congo, Algeria, and the admission to the U.N. of Mauritania.[2] No doubt such a meeting was the logical continuation of the old French Community structure, *mutatis mutandis*, and was under discussion for some time. But the imminent key vote on the seating of the Congolese delegation gave it urgency. Suspicious of the political motives of the conveners, Guinea refused to come, and Mali sent only an observer.[3] President Olympio of Togo also refused to come, stating that unless Morocco and Tunisia were invited, one could not usefully discuss Algeria. The Malagasy Republic declined to attend for the opposite reason, that Algeria was on the agenda at all, since "Algeria is an internal French concern." The Abidjan meeting decided to back Kasavubu (who sent an observer to the meeting), to take a restrained position on Algeria at the U.N.,[4] and to give full support to Mauritania's prospective candidacy for U.N. membership. At the next meeting, in December in Brazzaville, the so-called "Brazzaville Group" came into formal existence and would be later named the Union Africaine et Malgache (UAM).[5]

The consolidation of one bloc led to the consolidation of others. In November Nkrumah visited Mali and the two countries established in principle a "joint Parliament." This was followed shortly thereafter by a Guinea-Mali meeting in which it was agreed to exchange resident ministers, a formula already

[2] Mauritania's admission became an issue because the Moroccan government claimed that Mauritania was part of Morocco and that the newly independent state was a French puppet.

[3] Since August, when the Federation of Mali broke up, and all relations ceased between Senegal and (the Republic of) Mali, the Ivory Coast was the major exit to the sea for the Malian economy, and Mali did not wish to offend too strongly the Ivory Coast.

[4] The votes of these states were responsible for blocking, at the 1960 session, the U.N.'s intervention in this question.

[5] The Malagasy Republic attended the Brazzaville meeting and remained subsequently a faithful member of the Group.

utilized in the Ghana-Guinea Union. And in late December at Conakry the Ghana-Guinea-Mali Union, which was later to be called the Union of African States (UAS), was established. Of course, all three states supported the Lumumba delegation at the U.N. Their declaration of December 24, 1960, further stated: "The three Heads of State deplored the attitude taken by certain African Heads of State whose recent stand is likely to jeopardize the unity of Africa and strengthen neo-colonialism. They condemn all forms of African regroupment based on languages of the colonial Powers. They therefore appeal to these Heads of State to follow a higher and more healthy conception of African unity."

The emergence of two blocs placed the still nonindependent states of British East and Central Africa in a delicate position. At the very same time as the Abidjan meeting, PAFMECA was meeting at Mbale, Uganda. Tom Mboya presided, and Abdoulaye Diallo of Guinea, the secretary of the AAPC, attended. Since it was a meeting of nonindependent states that did not have to vote in the United Nations, they were not forced to choose sides in the Congo. Nonetheless the representatives volunteered their support without reservation to the Lumumba government as the legitimate one. Regarding their own problems, this meeting endorsed the idea of a federation of East (or East and Central) African states, once they all attained independence. This idea had been launched by Julius Nyerere when he attended as an observer the Addis Ababa meeting of the CIAS in June. On the other hand, the meeting called for the "immediate destruction" of the Central African Federation dominated by white settler elements.

Most of the African states that had troops in the United Nations Command in the Congo voted at the U.N. against seating the Kasavubu delegation. When they lost this vote, they became increasingly discomforted with being the military bulwark of a policy that they largely repudiated. The continued crisis led to the request of King Mohammed V of Morocco for a conference in Casablanca primarily to discuss the Congo. This conference took place on January 3–7, 1961, and was attended by the heads of state of Morocco, the U.A.R., Ghana, Guinea, Mali, the GPRA, the Foreign Minister of Libya, and an observer from Ceylon. The grouping was a somewhat mixed one. For the King of Morocco, the conference helped him steal the thunder from his left opposition by adopting a strong pro-Lumumba stance.[6] For the U.A.R., joining the Casablanca group represented its first commitment to a deep involvement in pan-African affairs. Tunisia did not come (to the regret of some participants), in part because it was beginning to differentiate its position sharply from its old allies in the African Group, and partly because its relations with the host country, Morocco, were upset as a result of Tunisia's recognition of Mauritania.[7] This had a very long-range consequence in that it made for a real de-emphasis in all three North African countries of Maghreb unity in favor of trans-African allegiances.

While all the participants at this conference supported Lumumba, there was a division of tactics vis-à-vis the U.N. Guinea and Mali had withdrawn their troops from the Congo because they rejected the use made of these troops by the United Nations Command. Morocco shared this view and the U.A.R. leaned in the same direction. They argued that Ghana's reluctance to follow suit was jeopardizing the solid support African troops could give directly to the Lumumba regime installed in Stanleyville. Ghana argued that, on the contrary, removal of African troops only left the field open to the opponents of Lumumba and that, behind a façade of militance, this suggestion was in fact a major concession. Morocco's support was suspect in that the Moroccan commander, General Kettani, was the adviser to Mobutu at the time of the depo-

[6] It also did the same to another opposition group, the Istiqlal, by rallying support on the Mauritanian issue about which the Istiqlal took the most vigorous position.

[7] Ghana had in fact also recognized Mauritania shortly before the conference. There is some uncertainty as to the Tunisian invitation. Nkrumah states in his book *Africa Must Unite* that the Tunisians were invited. Others say they were not. An official invitation list has never been made public.

sition of Lumumba and was thought to have worked closely with Americans and Belgians. In fact, Nkrumah convinced Nasser of his point of view.[8] The conference decided to give the U.N. a "last chance," failing which troops would be withdrawn. It also established a continuing structure, in which however Libya (and Ceylon) declined to participate.

Shortly after the Casablanca meeting, on January 17, Kasavubu turned Lumumba over to Tshombe and he was murdered.[9] And in a real sense this vitiated for the time being the strength of the revolutionary forces which the Casablanca powers represented, albeit as only a moderate version thereof. With the removal of Lumumba from the scene, followed a few days later by the inauguration of President Kennedy,[10] United States and United Nations policy in the Congo markedly changed and began to work toward the reconciliation of the Leopoldville (Kasavubu) and Stanleyville (Gizenga-Lumumbist) forces, under the leadership of the former, and at the expense of Tshombe. One key element in this reconciliation was the resolution of the U.N. Security Council, introduced by Ceylon, Liberia, and the U.A.R., and adopted on February 21, giving authority to the U.N. Command for the "use of force, if necessary, as a last resort." It was necessary, and it was eventually used against Tshombe. The new alignment of forces was in fact consummated in August 1961, with the installation of Cyrille Adoula as Prime Minister of the Congo, elected by a reunited Parliament and ending, for the moment, the Leopoldville-Stanleyville duality.

With this change in policy, a change consequent upon the

[8] Nasser, in turn, induced Nkrumah to sign the statement denouncing Israel "as an instrument in the service of imperialism and neo-colonialism, not only in the Middle East, but also in Africa and in Asia."

[9] It is worth bearing in mind that three months earlier, Félix Moumié, President of the UPC of Cameroon, was poisoned in Geneva. His death considerably weakened the opposition in this key former French African country and removed from the scene one of Africa's most active revolutionaries.

[10] Although Lumumba's death preceded the Inauguration, it was not officially confirmed until February 13.

effective defeat of the Lumumbist forces in the Congo, a slow effort began toward bridging the gap between the differing blocs in Africa. But the wounds went deep because they resulted from important differences in perspective and objective. Within countries, these differences were often clearer and more permanent than among countries.

Right next door to the Congo, in Angola, the war of independence began—or rather, there were two starts. On February 4, 1961, the Movimento Popular para Libertação da Angola (MPLA) started an uprising in the capital, Luanda. It was crushed and many of the leaders imprisoned. The failure of the Luanda uprising represented a serious setback for the MPLA, which had headquarters at the time in Conakry, Guinea, and which shared many of the options of the Casablanca group. On March 1, the União de Populações da Angola (UPA), led by Holden Roberto, began a rural guerrilla war which at first had more staying power than the MPLA insurrection. With a base in the Congo, and arms initially put at its disposition by the Congolese and the Tunisians, the UPA gained control for a while of northern Angola. From this double beginning of the war, the MPLA and UPA uprisings, the divisions in Angolan nationalism, whose roots in fact go back a number of years, would take its place beside those of the Congo and would be linked with the Congo as a divisive issue in Africa.

While the Congo crisis ultimately resulted in slowing down the pace of African liberation, its immediate effect in British Africa was undoubtedly to hasten, beyond all original plans, the process which led to the independence of the four East African states, particularly Kenya, as well as the breakup of the Central African Federation and the consequent independence of Malawi and Zambia. The British were aware that, given the considerable disorder in the Congo, long delays in progress toward independence in these countries could only lead to their radicalization. As it was, Congolese developments were responsible for a new level of political consciousness and a pan-African orientation that broke out of the

British mold. In the light of this new policy, it is understandable that it was at this moment in history—March 1961—that Britain decided to divest the Commonwealth of South African membership.[11]

The tide was thus turning—toward the middle of the stream. But its direction was by no means sure. Congolese leaders of the Leopoldville (Kasavubu) and Elisabethville (Tshombe) wings had met in March in a round-table conference in Tananarive convened by President Tsiranana of the Malagasy Republic. The conference had called for a Congolese confederation, which would have virtually consecrated the Katangese secession. The third meeting of the All-African Peoples' Conference in Cairo, March 25–31, provided some counterpoint to this maneuver (which was formally undone two months later at a subsequent round-table conference in the Congo). The mood of compromise of the Second (Tunis) AAPC was less in evidence at the Third (Cairo) meeting, partly because certain groups had eliminated themselves from attending, but mainly because of the Congo. The Secretary-General, Abdoulaye Diallo, set the tone in his opening address: "Today there are two forces existing in the Congo; forces which represent the imperialist interests, and forces which represent the interests of the Congolese people. The former are led by Messrs. Kasavubu, Tshombe, and their cohorts; the latter, or in other words ours, are led by Mr. Gizenga, who has the sympathy of all the people and the support of the immense majority of the population." The resolution on the Congo was very strong, and did not hesitate to attack even a Casablanca power. "The Conference denounces the role played by General Kettani in the degradation of the situation in the Congo

---

[11] Technically, when South Africa became a republic, it declined to reapply for membership in the Commonwealth. It did so because it knew it would be vetoed by African members. Particularly influential was a statement by Julius Nyerere of the not-yet-independent Tanganyika, that his country would not seek membership in the Commonwealth were South Africa a member. The need for "reapplication," however, was a British invention.

and demands the dismissal of Dag Hammarskjöld equally responsible[12] for the murder of Lumumba." Lumumba was proclaimed the "hero of Africa."

The AAPC had become the meeting ground of three groups: African nationalists in nonindependent countries, whose revolutionary ardor was often tactical and hence temporary; leaders of the so-called revolutionary African states, whose militancy was often tempered by the exigencies of diplomacy and the reality of world economic pressures; African radical-nationalist opposition movements in independent states, which states were considered by these opposition movements as clients or "puppets" of the West. This latter group (which included the UPC, the Sawaba of Niger led by Djibo Bakary, the Moroccan Union Nationale des Forces Populaires [UNFP] represented by Mehdi Ben Barka) was perhaps the most genuinely and the most persistently militant. It also had the least real power. Therefore, while this third group often dominated the conferences and gave the tone to the resolutions, it was the second group (the governments) that dominated the structure and held the purse strings. Theirs would be the fatal conflict within the AAPC. For, although the third AAPC formally decided that a fourth meeting would be held in February 1962 in Bamako, Mali, the meeting in Cairo was in fact the last one ever held. The Casablanca governments were content to let the AAPC disappear quietly in their attempts to come to terms with the other African governments.

The Cairo meeting did leave an important intellectual legacy, however. It attempted the one serious, collectively agreed upon definition of neo-colonialism, the key concept in the armory of the revolutionary core of the movement for African unity.[13] Neo-colonialism is defined as "the survival of the colonial system in spite of formal recognition of political independence in emerging countries." It is against the hydra-

[12] Others mentioned as responsible in a prior clause are Kasavubu, Mobutu, Tshombe, Kalonji.
[13] Nkrumah, in 1965, published a volume entitled *Neo-Colonialism: The Last Stage of Imperialism*. The full statement on neo-colonialism of the Cairo meeting appears in Appendix B.

headed enemy that neo-colonialism was considered to represent that the movement struggled. The manifestations of neo-colonialism were principally economic but could be found in all spheres of life. Furthermore, those who attacked neo-colonialism drew sharp lines among Africans, as President Modibo Keita of Mali made clear in a speech later in 1961. "[Neo-colonialism] is when an 'independent' country is indirectly administered by its former colonial power, by the intermediary of traitors which she has helped to place in power. . . ."

The concept of unity and its full implications were becoming clearer, as time went on, to the revolutionary core. They now began to feel that unity was not an end in itself but was desirable only insofar as it would destroy neo-colonialism, designated by Nkrumah the "greatest threat to African countries that have newly won their independence or those approaching this status." In 1965 the Ghanaian journal *The Spark* said in an editorial: "The central issue is that of unity—not unity for the sake of unity, not unity expressed merely in piously worded resolutions forgotten as soon as they are adopted, but anti-imperialist unity, unity for world peace, unity for liberation and for economic independence and advance—WITH A SINGLE POLITICAL DIRECTION."

The search for an organizational framework within which to express and propagate these theses would be the chief problem for the revolutionary core from this point on. The Union of African States, formally launched in Accra the next month, would never serve this function despite its listing as one of its aims "to work jointly to achieve the complete liquidation of imperialism, colonialism and neo-colonialism in Africa and the building up of African unity." The problem was never solved because of the commitments of that part of the core composed of sovereign states, which tended to constrain those parts of the core which were not legal governments.

In May 1961 there were two meetings which symbolized two approaches to resolving differences over African unity. The first was the Monrovia Conference, which grouped twenty

African countries: the twelve members of the UAM plus Ethiopia, Liberia, Libya, Nigeria, Sierra Leone, Somalia, Togo, and Tunisia. The Conference had intended to include all the independent states, but the Casablanca nations did not come, nor did the Sudan out of solidarity for Morocco's opposition to an invitation to Mauritania. Congo (L) had not been invited, in order to avoid a quarrel, between the Casablanca group and some others, about its credentials, since there were still two factions that claimed to be the legitimate central government of the Congo.

Monrovia was the first of a series of attempts to consolidate the defeat of the Lumumbist elements in the Congo by creating a pan-African structure that would build very firmly on the principle of noninterference in the internal affairs of sovereign states. It represented the search for an alliance of African states. The origins of this particular meeting are confused. At the beginning of 1961 President Houphouet-Boigny addressed letters to the heads of all African states outside the Brazzaville Group asking for a conference where the points of view of all states would be heard on the Congo, Algeria, and economic and cultural cooperation, but where all participants would accept the principle of noninterference. President Senghor of Senegal had a similar idea, but because of the relative diplomatic isolation of Senegal at this time he asked President Olympio of Togo, the most "neutral" neutral, so to speak, to take the lead. Prime Minister Balewa of Nigeria launched the idea, at the same time, of a conference of independent sub-Saharan African states.[14] Finally, as a result of much negotiation, a conference was convened for May 8 in Monrovia under the sponsorship of seven heads of state: Cameroon, Guinea, Ivory Coast, Liberia, Mali, Nigeria, and Togo—representatives of all the different camps.

Holding an all-African interstate conference was, however, quite premature. The Congo did not yet have the Adoula

[14] During the whole period from 1960 to 1963, Nigeria was the one state that openly seemed to prefer excluding Arab Africa from pan-African meetings. This reflected to some extent a series of Nigerian internal concerns.

government. The GPRA was not yet engaged in formal negotiations with the French. The more militant powers feared
their voices would be drowned out and their causes jeop-
ardized. At the Accra meeting of the UAS in April, the three
states had sought a postponement of the proposed Monrovia
meeting. This led to considerable ill-feeling, and the Monrovia Group came into existence as a counterbalance to the
Casablanca Group.[15] The viewpoint of the former is best
summarized in its own resolution on unity: "The unity that is
aimed to be achieved at the moment is not the political integration of sovereign African states, but unity of aspirations
and of action considered from the point of view of African
social solidarity and political identity."

Quite different was the tone a few weeks later when the
trade-unions of Africa met, from May 25 to 30, for the oft-
postponed Casablanca meeting to set up an all-African trade-
union organization. There the chairman of the Preparatory
Secretariat, Mahjoub Ben Seddik of Morocco, stated in his
Report of Doctrine and Orientation that "the true liberation
of Africa cannot be achieved without its profound transformation." Almost all the African trade unions came to this conference, but many declined to participate in the All-African
Trade Union Federation (AATUF) which emerged from it.
The issue that divided the delegates was that of international
affiliations. The militant elements stood for a complete organizational break with the Western world, represented in the
trade-union field principally by the International Confederation of Free Trade Unions (ICFTU). This position, based on
the view that the ICFTU was a major instrument of neo-
colonialism, was opposed by some important trade-union cen-

[15] A. K. Barden, Director of the Bureau of African Affairs of Ghana,
summarized his view of the differences in September 1962 as follows:
"The first Casablanca platform is the logical development of the spirit
and decisions of the First Accra Conference of Independent African
States. The second Monrovia platform is largely the handwork of imperialism in its desperate attempt to defend its position against the on-
slaught prepared (and launched) on it by the First Accra Conference
of Independent African States. Imperialism has succeeded in creating
for its use a front of Independent African States."

ters, notably in Tunisia, Kenya, and Nigeria. AATUF could
have had a pan-African structure from the start had it been
willing to compromise on the question of affiliation.[16] But for
most of the organizers of AATUF, trade-union unity was desirable only because it was a weapon toward revolutionary
political ends, and a compromise on disaffiliation would have
nullified these ends.

A number of events occurred in the second half of 1961, the
consequences of which were to narrow differences in the
foreign-policy positions of the African states.

In July Tunisia called for negotiations with France over
the evacuation of the Bizerte base. When France declined, the
Tunisians blockaded the base. This led to a violent clash,
which in turn led to a break in diplomatic relations. The case
was brought twice before the U.N. Security Council and
Tunisia's now very militant stand received the support not
only of the Casablanca states but even of some of the Brazzaville states and Nigeria.

On August 2 the reunited Congolese Parliament, by a near-
unanimous vote, chose Cyrille Adoula as the Prime Minister
of the central government and Gizenga as Vice-Premier. There
was now only one central government, supported by the Lumumbists but not led by them. The new government received
the blessings of the Casablanca powers when they arranged
for an invitation to the Congo to attend the Belgrade Conference of Non-Aligned States, September 1–6. Adoula came with
Gizenga, and both addressed the Conference. Adoula thus acquired a certain moral legitimacy, in addition to his juridical
legitimacy, from the revolutionary forces. The Belgrade Conference was also noteworthy in that the African attendance
included not only the Casablanca Group, but Ethiopia, Sudan,
Somalia, and Tunisia as well. Nigeria declined to attend because of the initial opposition by an African power, presumably Ghana, to its being invited. Togo and Upper Volta also
declined invitations.

[16] It did in fact make a limited compromise offering a ten-month delay
for disaffiliation.

In August the Nigerian government convened the All-Nigerian Peoples' Conference, which took a rather militant line on foreign affairs. The most significant outgrowth was the subsequent decision to abrogate the much-criticized Anglo-Nigerian Defence Agreement on January 21, 1962.

In November 1961 political difficulties erupted in Guinea. On December 11 the Guinean government denounced a plot to overthrow it fomented by France and an unnamed East European embassy. The Soviet Ambassador was asked to leave a few days later. This changed the image of Guinea's foreign policy, especially among the Brazzaville Group.

Though the states were coming closer on foreign-policy issues, they were not yet quite close enough. On January 3–14, 1962, in Dakar a trade-union conference was held which established a rival structure to AATUF called the African Trade Unions Confederation (ATUC), which permitted member unions to continue their international affiliations. Thus the divisions among states were paralleled by a division on the trade-union level. On January 25–30, in Lagos, the Monrovia powers met again. All twenty-eight independent states were invited. The Casablanca powers refused to attend, because Nigeria, prompted by the objections of the Brazzaville Group, declined to invite the GPRA.[17] As a result, Tunisia also declined to come and Sudan and Libya withdrew.[18] The Conference proceeded without them (and thus without any North African representation), to establish a formal structure called the Inter-African and Malagasy States Organization (IAMO).

IAMO made clear that it in no way symbolized revolution. The then Governor-General of Nigeria, Nnamdi Azikiwe,

[17] It would have been a serious step backward had *all* the African states met without the GPRA, since the latter had already been given full status at the second CIAS in Addis Ababa in June 1960.

[18] Tanganyika, which had become independent on December 9, 1961, at first attended the meeting of Foreign Ministers. However, it did not come to the heads of state and government meeting, using as a pretext the political crisis which erupted just then at home when the Prime Minister, Julius Nyerere, resigned. Tanganyika was following the long-standing reluctance shown by PAFMECA to be caught between the Casablanca and the Monrovia powers.

opened the Conference with this analysis: "From a general observation, it would appear that there is not much to choose between the respective accords reached by the member-states of the Casablanca conference and those of the Monrovia conference. . . . But there is one basic difference. . . . It is the conspicuous absence of a specific declaration on the part of the Casablanca States of their inflexible belief in the fundamental principles enunciated at Monrovia regarding the inalienable rights of African States, as at present constituted, to legal equality . . . to self-determination . . . to safety from interference in their internal affairs through subversive activities engineered by supposedly friendly states. . . ."[19] The issue of "subversion" now became, and remained, a focal issue among African independent states. It was crucial less as a reality than as a symbol of the basic debate about unity as movement versus unity as alliance.

Nonetheless there were other voices urging that this debate be resolved essentially by ignoring it. At the Lagos meeting Emperor Haile Selassie said of the blocs in Africa: "Ethiopia considers herself a member of one group only—the African group." This presaged very active Ethiopian diplomacy along these lines from this point on. President Houphouet-Boigny of the Ivory Coast also called for an end to divisions. This call led to an elaborate exchange of state visits among West African states in 1962, in each instance between a Casablanca power and a Monrovia power. Whereas the projected February 1962 meeting of the AAPC in Mali was not held, largely because the Guinea[20] and Mali governments had now become reluctant to press forward with such a revolutionary, and hence divisive, activity, PAFMECA held a large meeting in Addis Ababa that month. Not only were Ethiopia and Somalia included for the first time, but the organization was expanded to include the various southern African movements of na-

[19] Five months later, in June, the Foreign Minister of Nigeria, Jaja Wachuku, was openly to accuse the Ghana High Commission of being a "center of subversion."
[20] It should be recalled that the secretary-general, who controlled the administrative machinery, was a Guinean.

tional liberation.[21] This structure took on the appearance of a mediating force between Casablanca and Monrovia.[22]

Signs of practical *political* cooperation among all African states began to appear, albeit on what were perhaps minor fronts. At the Seventeenth Session of the CCTA held in Abidjan on February 10–16, 1962, the conference decided to expel South Africa and Portugal, reduce Great Britain, Belgium, and France to the status of "associate members," drop "south of the Sahara" from the title, and elect the first African secretary-general, Mamoudou Touré of Mauritania. The CCTA, which had been founded originally as an instrument for technical cooperation among colonial powers in Africa, now was beginning to escape European control. Similarly, at the Fourth Session of the U.N. Economic Commission for Africa, February 19–March 3 in Addis Ababa, the conference recommended[23] that Portugal, Spain,[24] and South Africa be deprived of membership and Britain and France be reduced to associate membership. A similar move the year before had failed because of the opposition of the Brazzaville states. Furthermore, at this meeting of the ECA the principle of the creation of an African Development Bank was adopted and a Committee of Nine was established to work out the details. (The nine were Cameroon, Ethiopia, Guinea, Liberia, Mali, Nigeria, Sudan, Tanganyika, and Tunisia—politically, geographically, and linguistically a balanced group.)

European concessions also helped to improve the atmos-

[21] The name was changed accordingly to add the word "Southern" and the initials became PAFMECSA.

[22] Even those in PAFMECSA who felt sympathy for one side or the other avoided doing so publicly for fear of perpetuating the division. For example, in August 1962, at the Annual Conference of the Uganda People's Congress, sentiment ran at first in favor of joining Casablanca, but the ultimate decision was to refrain in order to help bring about unity.

[23] ECA could not *decide*, because decision on membership resided with the Economic and Social Council of the U.N., which delayed accepting this recommendation for a long time.

[24] At the Fifth Session of the ECA the African states relented on Spain, when she made some gestures on decolonization, including the submission of reports to the appropriate U.N. committee.

phere in Africa, to calm it, and thus to make reconciliation among African states easier. In March Central African constitutional talks began in London, which led within two years to the total dissolution of the Federation of the Rhodesias and Nyasaland, a great triumph for African liberation. On March 19 the GPRA and France finally reached an accord in Evian that would grant independence to Algeria in July. The Algerian obstacle had been removed. The quickness of its impact could be measured by the broadcast of President Sékou Touré immediately afterward: "Guinea changes its stance toward France." Guinea now became one of the most active diplomatic agents of reconciliation.

Along with Ethiopia and Guinea the third active diplomatic agent of reconciliation was Tunisia. At the Second CIAS in 1960 it had been decided to hold the Third CIAS in Tunisia in 1962. Though the CIAS had been virtually forgotten by 1962, Tunisia decided it might be opportune to try to convene at least a meeting of foreign ministers in Tunis. But this projected meeting was not given encouragement at the Lagos meeting in January, which recommended its postponement, and a first attempt to call it for April 9–15 failed. The issue of the GPRA's invitation to any all-African meeting still existed in early March, when the decision to postpone the meeting was taken. Nigeria was uncertain about a North African site.[25] At least two more tentative dates were discussed, but the meeting was never held.

West African divisions were being smoothed over. In April 1962 President Hamani Diori of Niger visited Ghana and received assurances that the offices in Accra of the Niger opposition, the Sawaba party led by Djibo Bakary, would be closed.

[25] In July 1962 Presidents Bourguiba and Nkrumah exchanged correspondence pledging themselves to work for an all-Africa structure and against one based on "black African solidarity." This opposition to racial separation in African political structures was a constant concern of Bourguiba. Three years later, on a state visit to the Ivory Coast, Bourguiba said: "[the] link of linguistic community which crisscrosses Africa is more significant than climatic lines."

Diori made a similar visit to Guinea in June.[26] From April 26 to 30 in Conakry, Guinea, the founding meeting of the Pan-African Youth Movement was held. Unlike the Casablanca meeting, where AATUF was founded, or the various meetings of the AAPC the organizers were careful to invite the pro-government youth groups of the Brazzaville countries, rather than sometimes resorting to exile opposition groups. Though this conference had grown out of the AAPC structure, it now took on a rather inoffensive tone.

Despite the growing attempts to minimize disunity in Africa, the UAM was nonetheless strengthening its own structure. At its second conference of heads of state in Bangui on March 25–27 it decided to establish a joint secretariat for its U.N. delegations. Between the second and third sessions (Libreville, September 10–13), the very active then Secretary-General of UAM, Albert Tevoedjré, canvassed the three ex-Belgian colonies as prospective members of the UAM, which would thus become a "French-speaking" family. This led to the early admission of Rwanda, whose fairly conservative foreign policy and internal social revolution had led it to feel somewhat isolated amongst its immediate neighbors. On the other hand, shortly after Libreville Mauritania announced that it would not press its UAM-backed candidacy for a seat on the Security Council (Mauritania's candidacy, of course, was strongly opposed by Morocco), so as to permit an African united front in the struggle against the "injustice" of the distribution of seats.[27] In fact, African joint initiative at the coming session

[26] The assassination of a Sawaba leader in Bamako, Mali, on May 19 ended prospects, however, of serious negotiations between Djibo and Diori which might have permanently eliminated this issue that divided West African states. Nonetheless, when at a press conference in Accra in October 1962, Djibo announced the establishment of an "Association of Freedom Fighters," grouping opposition movements in independent states, his proposal was disavowed by Ghana's Ambassador to the Ivory Coast and the issue was dropped.

[27] The "injustice" was the consequence of the fact that the six non-permanent seats on the Security Council were then divided according to a gentleman's agreement drawn up long before there was any substantial number of African member states.

of the U.N. led to the eventual adoption of the first amendment ever added to the U.N. Charter, expanding the number of seats on the Security Council and the Economic and Social Council. In November 1962 the Regional Conference of the Food and Agriculture Organization could not be held in Tunis because the Secretary-General would not exclude South Africa at the demand of the twenty-two other African nations present, which thereupon refused to attend.

It was, however, events in the Congo which provided the crucial final touch. In late December of 1962 the U.N. Command finally occupied Katanga. The last major obstacle to African reconciliation was removed. The ending of the Katanga secession had been one of the principal demands of the Casablanca powers and the Lumumbists in the Congo. Though by now Adoula had ousted the Lumumbists from his national government, the fall of Tshombe in Katanga counterbalanced this. Finally, on March 11, 1963, the Ghana government suspended its demand that the Security Council pursue its investigation of the death of Lumumba.[28] The way was now paved for a conference of all Africa. If the UAM states still had any hesitations, the new French policy begun in 1963 of progressive reduction of military aid and budget subsidies reinforced their sense of need to be part of an all-African structure.

The compromise solution in the Congo created great pressure on the revolutionary core of the movement toward African

[28] Ghana's willingness to go along with a compromise solution on the African scene at this point was in part, paradoxically, the consequence of the attempt to assassinate President Nkrumah at Kulungugu on August 2, 1962. Although the long-run impact of the attempted assassination was to strengthen the revolutionary elements in the Convention People's Party, the immediate impact was to throw a cloud of suspicion on many of these revolutionary elements because they had been associated in one way or another with Tawia Adamafio, the principal accused in the affair. One other result was to restore to the cabinet on March 17, 1963, Kojo Botsio as Foreign Minister. Botsio had earlier been purged as a result of attacks on his financial integrity. Botsio had always placed great emphasis on serving first the diplomatic ends of the state of Ghana and secondly the revolutionary goals of the movement toward African unity.

unity to accept a similar compromise solution for Africa as a whole. The real debate at this point was not between the core and the periphery. It was within the core itself, and was more or less between those who were in positions of governmental responsibility and those who were not (or not quite). The former group tended to argue that colonialism was a greater enemy than reactionary regimes in Africa, and that priority must be given the problems of liberation of southern Africa, which implied for them that a single structure englobing all states was essential. To establish such a structure, certain compromises had realistically to be made. The theme of this group was that an analysis that there were two Africas, a "revolutionary" and a "reactionary" Africa, served the interests of the outside world, that fundamentally all African states stood for the same thing. If some countries were more timid than others, they would be brought along by the solidarity of the group. This view is of course, the view that ultimately prevailed within the core.

The tone of the minority was quite different. A pamphlet of the Cameroon UPC dated May 30, 1962, entitled "African Unity or Neo-Colonialism?" stated that "There is an Africa of the peoples and one of the servants. . . . The road of true African unity is not that of the fusion of the groups of Brazzaville, Monrovia, Lagos, and Casablanca. That would be a confusion which would profit only neo-colonialism and imperialism and which would induce African leaders to relegate to the background the fundamental problem of the struggle against neo-colonialism in order to amuse themselves with economic and social hocus-pocus." And in February 1963 Djibo Bakary, leader of the Sawaba party of Niger, wrote an editorial on "Revolutionary Unity" in the Algerian journal *Révolution Africaine* in which he issued a warning that became famous in Africa: "Finally, in no way must African unity become a sort of trade-union of men in power who will seek to support one another to resist popular currents."

Despite these arguments of revolutionary opposition movements, the desire to consolidate stability in the Congo after the fall of Tshombe and the parallel desire to consolidate African cooperation in the United Nations by abolishing the two separate competing pan-African organizations—Casablanca and Monrovia—was so strong that even the assassination of Olympio could not stop the emergence of the new single structure, despite the emotion this event stirred among Africa's governments. On January 13, 1963, Sylvanus Olympio had been shot by a group of military rebels in an otherwise bloodless coup. This was the first murder of a head of state in the course of a *coup d'état* in modern Africa's history, and no African president appreciated the precedent. Although Ghana and Senegal recognized the new regime almost immediately and Dahomey recognized it *de facto,* many other governments reacted most violently and negatively, refusing, they felt, to reward murder by recognition. Guinea declared eight days of national mourning and called for an international investigation. The coup was denounced as well by Liberia, the Ivory Coast, Nigeria, and Tanganyika. Nigeria convened a meeting of IAMO in Lagos on January 24–26. Internal divisions among the Monrovia powers led to the weak compromise of sending an inquiry commission to Togo (which was received by the new government) and leaving the question of recognition up to each government. (Seven more accorded recognition in the next few months.) Ultimately, the dust merely settled. What should be noted about the Togolese affair is, first, that the division of opinion cut across Casablanca-Monrovia lines (showing the thinness of the links among both groups[29]). And secondly, and more important, no one used Togo as an excuse not to convene the all-Africa meeting (although Guinea and others successfully insisted that Togo not be invited).

The time for structural unity had thus arrived. From May 22 to 25, 1963, in Addis Ababa, thirty heads of state and government of Africa, the largest such assemblage in the history

---

[29] If the Lagos meeting of January 24–26 suggested lack of coordination among IAMO, the Casablanca powers were unable to hold at all a projected meeting at Marrakech, Morocco, on May 8 when President Ben Bella of Algeria flatly refused to come.

of the modern world, met in a summit conference and, "determined to safeguard and consolidate the hard-won independence as well as the sovereignty and territorial integrity of our States, and to fight against neo-colonialism in all its forms," signed the Charter of the Organization of African Unity (OAU).

:V:

HOPE REKINDLED:

THE BIRTH OF THE <u>OAU</u>

In the euphoria of the aftermath, the meeting in Addis Ababa
was hailed as a miracle. What was the miracle? What was
the surprise? In reality there was none. Rather there was a
compromise, which is usually how large groups of states set
up international organizations. Here it was a compromise between a weakened core and a self-confident periphery. It was
to some extent the Monrovia formula succeeding at last on the
third try. The Casablanca powers and Tunisia were heavily
committed to aiding the liberation movements of southern
Africa. Very few of the Monrovia powers offered more than
moral support. Most of the latter and some of the former were
deeply concerned about internal security[1] and the maintenance of economic assistance from the Western world. The
Charter of the OAU accommodated both sets of objectives.
On the one hand, it consecrated the principle of noninterference (strengthened by private assurances from some of

---

[1] For example, President Houphouet-Boigny of the Ivory Coast said in
his address to the Conference: "The moment has come to condemn
collectively and publicly political assassination as a means of coming to
power. The Conference must take a clear stand on this matter or else
Africa will fall into so-called revolutions."

the African states in question),[2] and created a confederal structure that placed strong emphasis on practical socioeconomic
cooperation. The latter was in itself reassuring to Western
powers, promising greater economic rationality without the
threat of a political structure strong enough to attempt to
transform world economic relationships. On the other hand,
it committed the OAU to considering "the imperious and urgent necessity of co-ordinating and intensifying their efforts
to accelerate the unconditional attainment of national independence by all African territories still under foreign domination." Toward this end they established a Coordinating
Committee[3] to harmonize assistance from the African states
and to manage a special fund for this purpose to which all
OAU member states would contribute. They pledged themselves further to "receive [on their territory] nationalists from
liberation movements in order to give them training in all
sectors" and to promote "the transit of all material aid." President Ben Bella of Algeria, who took the lead in fighting for
the creation of this committee, made his now-famous exhor-
tation: "So let us all agree to die a little or even completely
so that the peoples still under colonial domination may be
free and African unity may not be a vain word."

The meeting, however, avoided the issue of regionalism,
which was what made the compromise both possible and
tenuous. The Charter did not mention regional groups. One
resolution committed the OAU "to explore the effects of regional economic groupings on the African economy." The general understanding at Addis Ababa was that while regional

[2] They argued this was not a total abandonment of past commitments.
President Modibo Keita of Mali, for example, explained what had happened to a conference of his party cadres in the following manner:
"Your delegation also had the opportunity to give its views on the
problem of patriots in exile in other African countries, who were called
by some other delegations subversive elements. We courageously recalled
the fundamental position of our party, that African unity requires national unity, and we urged consequently various Heads of State to
facilitate the return home of the opposition living abroad."

[3] This Committee became known variously as the Committee of Nine,
or the African Liberation Committee.

groupings might be admissible, even desirable (at least to some), blocs were not. Since the OAU represented a bringing together of the Casablanca and Monrovia powers, these two separate structures had to disappear. So did the UAS. So, in fact, did PAFMECSA.[4] But what about prospective federations? Some member-states were already federal in structure —Nigeria and Cameroon, for example. East African Federation seemed a very definite prospect at this time. Indeed, it would be very shortly after the Addis Ababa meeting, and under its impact, that the leaders of Kenya, Uganda, and Tanganyika would announce on June 5 that they expected to federate by the end of the year.[5] And other regions, such as North Africa, talked of similar hopes in slightly vaguer terms. Very few states seemed opposed in principle to these federations, except Ghana. (President Nkrumah asserted that "regional groupings of any kind are a serious threat to the unity of Africa.") Indeed, regional federations were often mentioned at the time as a positive aspect of prospective inter-African cooperation.

Some regional groupings seemed less innocuous than others. It was the UAM that was the sticking point. This was a grouping with a clear political role, yet a grouping that fell short of being a federation. It also fell short of being regional, most notably as a result of the inclusion of the Malagasy Republic. At Addis Ababa there was a covert agreement not to mention the UAM. Yet immediately thereafter it was to become an explosive issue. When the UAM announced that its regular semiannual meeting of heads of state would be held in Cotonou, Dahomey, on July 27–30, 1963, President Touré of Guinea denounced the proposed meeting as an "insolent recrudescence" and the UAM as incompatible with the OAU. Nigeria was openly critical too.[6] President Maga of Dahomey,

---

[4] Although originally nongovernmental, PAFMECSA had in February 1962 at Addis Ababa decided that "in the case of an independent state only the government shall be eligible for membership." Hence, at this point, it was at least in part an intergovernmental regional bloc.

[5] In fact, this federation never came into existence.

[6] Although Nigeria and the UAM held broadly similar views on African questions, they had a history of minor quarrels. In 1961 they

on the contrary, stated at the July session of the UAM that "far from being eclipsed, as some people have thought, by the charter of the OAU, [the UAM] is on the contrary one of its best guarantees. With the Maghreb and the East African Federation the UAM will constitute the framework of a new Africa." Nevertheless there was considerable debate even inside the UAM as to its future. As a gesture to the OAU, the UAM did abolish its collective representation at the U.N., since this was acknowledged to be purely political. On the other hand, the UAM admitted Togo as a fourteenth member at this session. Though some leaders spoke of a "progressive fusion" of the UAM and the OAU and others of their "harmonization," none seemed ready to end the organization outright. This continued presence of the Brazzaville Group as a bloc was reinforced and given meaning by the signing in Yaoundé, Cameroon, on July 20, 1963, of the Convention of Association between the six members of the European Economic Community on the one hand and the eighteen African independent states, fourteen of which were then members of the UAM, on the other.

Nonetheless, despite the controversy over the UAM, the first summer of the OAU's existence was a time of relatively vigorous united anticolonial activity against Portugal and South Africa. The African states began a coordinated international campaign to oust these two states from world bodies. The Addis Ababa meeting had authorized four foreign ministers (from Liberia, Tunisia, Malagasy Republic, and Sierra Leone) to raise issues at the Security Council concerning both Portugal and South Africa on behalf of all the OAU members. This was done for the first time in late July, and resolutions were passed in the Security Council, one calling for Portugal to recognize the right of self-determination and independence of her colonies and another calling for an arms embargo on South Africa.

---

fought openly at the U.N. over the issue of the validity of the U.N. plebiscite in the northern half of the British Cameroons, which resulted in the latter's attachment to Nigeria. Later, the UAM countries at first opposed Nigeria's desire to negotiate an association with the European Economic Community.

On June 5, 1963, thirty-two African states had walked out of the meeting of the International Labor Organization (ILO) because South Africa did not honor a Nigerian-sponsored resolution at a previous meeting asking her not to attend.[7] This led to a decision of the Executive Board of ILO to take three practical measures toward the exclusion of South Africa, which was confirmed by ECOSOC in late July. Similarly, at the International Conference on Education in Geneva on July 4, the African states withdrew when Portugal refused to heed a resolution demanding its exclusion in the name of humanity. On July 16 South Africa suspended its membership in the Economic Commission for Africa until the African states changed their attitude, and a few days later ECOSOC voted to expel Portugal from ECA. On August 28 the African states demanded the exclusion of Portugal and South Africa from the U.N. Conference on Tourism. On September 23 a meeting of the Regional Committee for Africa of the World Health Organization broke up because of African protests at the presence of Portugal and South Africa. In October the African states demanded the exclusion of South Africa from the Olympic games. On December 5 the Food and Agriculture Organization (FAO) adopted a motion to refrain from inviting South Africa to any regional meeting of the FAO.[8]

[7] The Africans were joined in their walkout by five Arab states, Israel, and the Communist bloc.

[8] The effort was to be a continuing one. In 1964 South Africa withdrew from the ILO and the FAO. The South African Olympic Committee informed the International Olympic Committee that it couldn't comply with their conditions for participation in the Olympic games. The African Conference of the International Telecommunications Union at Geneva was adjourned *sine die* on October 19, 1964, when Western delegates walked out after the conference voted to exclude Portugal and South Africa. In May 1965 in Geneva the World Health Organization approved a constitutional amendment permitting the expulsion of South Africa. In July 1965 the Executive Committee of the International Civil Aeronautics Organization voted to recommend the temporary or permanent exclusion of South Africa. In October 1965 the Executive Committee of UNESCO continued an earlier decision of May to exclude Portugal from international conferences it held. In December 1965 the U.N. General Assembly withheld recognition of the credentials of the South African delegation, a tactic which previously had only been used in the case of the Hungarian delegation in 1956.

The other major summer activity was the establishment of the African Liberation Committee (ALC), as called for in the Addis Ababa resolutions. The ALC was initially composed of Algeria, Congo (L), Ethiopia, Guinea, Nigeria, Senegal, Tanganyika, Uganda, and the U.A.R. Tanganyika was the chairman in the person of Oscar Kambona, and the headquarters were in Dar es Salaam.[9] The Committee's role will be discussed in detail later.

Here it is important to note that the first decision of far-reaching importance was on Angola. The split between the two principal movements, the UPA and the MPLA, had become encrusted and the divisions between the two movements had come to be viewed as parallel to the divisions of Monrovia and Casablanca, or between Kasavubu-Adoula and Lumumba-Gizenga in the neighboring Congo. The UPA had formed a common front with smaller parties and had proclaimed on April 5, 1962, a Govêrno Revolucionário de Angôla em Exilo (GRAE), ostensibly patterned on the Algerian model. In the midst of the first meeting of the ALC in Dar es Salaam in June 1963, Premier Adoula of the Congo (L) announced the formal recognition of the GRAE, the first such recognition by any independent state. Since the Congo (L) was a member of the ALC and the principal independent border state of Angola, this amounted to forcing the Committee's hand. The ALC decided to send a special conciliation commission to Leopoldville to try to bring the MPLA and the UPA together. The MPLA was itself in a moment of internal crisis and badly split, reflecting the disorientation of African radical-nationalist movements in the period following the Congolese setback (and to some extent reflecting the feedback of pressures resulting from the ideological split between China and the U.S.S.R.). Thus the GRAE was strong in its relative military success and in the total backing of the Adoula government in the Congo (L), and the MPLA was at a nadir. The conciliation commit-

---

[9] The ALC Secretariat came to be composed of a Secretary-General from Tanganyika and two Assistant Secretary-Generals from Nigeria and the U.A.R.

tee thereupon recommended unanimously (including Guinea and Algeria, two states which had been historically sympathetic to the MPLA) that the GRAE be formally recognized by all African states. This was accepted at the following meeting of the Council of Ministers at Dakar on August 2–11, and such recognition was accorded within the year by virtually all African states, with the important exceptions of Ghana and Congo (B).

Thus, in Angola as in the Congo, the African consensus had favored what the Western world considered the moderate elements.[10] This tone of relative restraint by the former Casablanca powers was evident in other ways as well. It could be found in the extensive diplomatic cooperation between Ghana and Nigeria in the year following Addis Ababa. While this meant that Nigeria would support Ghana's proposal at the meeting of the Defense Commission, from October 29 to November 2 in Accra, for the establishment of a "small permanent military headquarters" of the OAU (a proposal which did not carry, nonetheless), it meant in return that little was heard from Ghana during this period about active support for opposition movements in independent countries. The collaboration carried over into the United Nations in the fall of 1963, when Ghana took the lead in establishing secret negotiations between the African states and Portugal, over the vehement objections of nationalist movements from Portuguese Africa

[10] That these ideological considerations played a role is clear from the parallel case of Portuguese Guinea. The same conciliation commission was charged with resolving the same kind of difference in this small West African territory. There were two main movements, the Partido Africano da Independência da Guiné e Cabo Verde (PAIGC) and the Frente de Libertação de la Independência Nacional da Guiné (FLING). The PAIGC was formally allied with the MPLA. FLING was considered parallel to UPA. There was one important difference. The PAIGC was clearly the major military force. Since the commission gave as its principal argument for the exclusive recognition of the GRAE its pre-eminence in fighting (and not its ideological stance), the same logic should have applied to favoring PAIGC. At the Council of Ministers in Dakar, Senegal was nonetheless able to prevent a parallel exclusive recognition of PAIGC, despite the committee's call for such recognition. PAIGC was not considered "moderate."

which were themselves excluded from the talks. The talks were eventually broken off.

At this point the Algerian government most nearly spoke for the revolutionary core. But it was suddenly immobilized by the outbreak of the Algero-Moroccan war which erupted over a border dispute in October. In one sense this war resulted in a great victory for the OAU. For it was by African mediation, that of Mali and Ethiopia,[11] that a cease-fire was brought about at a meeting in Bamako, Mali, on October 29–30, to be enforced by Ethiopian and Malian observers. In addition to a cease-fire the four heads of state present at Bamako requested an extraordinary session of the Council of Ministers of the OAU "with a view to setting up an *ad hoc* commission of arbitration" to ascertain responsibilities and examine the substantive border problems. This meeting was held on November 15–18 in Addis Ababa and a seven-nation commission was established, composed of Ethiopia, Ivory Coast, Mali, Nigeria, Senegal, Sudan, and Tanganyika. The commission met during the following several years and succeeded in quieting the issue without in fact resolving the points of contention. That Africa's first war between independent states could be so quickly contained, and within the framework of the OAU, was a remarkable achievement and testified to the effectiveness of the covenant. But it was an achievement of restoring a *status quo ante,* a victory for the proponents of unity as alliance. In the meantime Algeria's efforts on behalf of unity as movement were effectively diverted for a while.

Despite this quiescence of the former Casablanca powers and the relative calm in the unliberated territories, there were rumblings in a number of the other independent states. Indeed there were so many events in these states, in the nine months following Addis Ababa, that they began to amount to a countertrend to the growing conservatism of the African

[11] Mali and Ethiopia were agreed upon after offers from many others to mediate, including the League of Arab States. Algeria was very insistent on African mediation. Morocco was cool to this idea, but finally conceded the point.

scene. In mid-August of 1963 in an unexpected and sensitive place, Congo (B), there was a revolution which ousted Abbé Fulbert Youlou, the friend of Tshombe, and replaced him with a revolutionary regime which became more militant as time went on.[12] In October the government was overthrown in Dahomey, and the government's policy shifted, at least for a while, from one in which Dahomey had been the strongest supporter of the maintenance of the UAM at the Cotonou meeting in July to one in which Dahomey virtually suspended all links with such countries as the Ivory Coast. According to the governments in power, there were abortive attempts at coups, similar in tone, in the Ivory Coast (late August) and Senegal (December 1).

East Africa was as volatile as French Africa. On January 12, 1964, the Sultan of newly independent Zanzibar was overthrown in a profound social revolution. There were immediate reverberations throughout East Africa. On January 20 an army mutiny broke out in Tanganyika, but with none of the social content of the Zanzibari revolution. Nonetheless the government's existence was seriously menaced. On January 23 there were similar army mutinies in Uganda and Kenya. On January 24 the Tanganyika government, followed by Uganda and Kenya, requested British troops to help restore order. On January 28 the government of Tanganyika requested an extraordinary session of the Council of Ministers of the OAU to consider "the grave situation arising from many revolts . . . in East Africa." [13] This meeting was held on February 12–15 in Dar es Salaam, Tanganyika.

President Nyerere, in opening the OAU meeting, explained why he convened it:

[12] One very important consequence of the change of government in the Congo (B) was that the MPLA, formally ousted from Congo (L) territory, found a base of operations and a strong support. Congo (B) borders the enclave of Cabinda which is part of Angola, and MPLA ability to start military operations in Cabinda meant it could begin to reassert itself on the African scene.

[13] That same day the government of Tanganyika also announced the formation of the commission on a "democratic one-party state," whose creation had been previously promised.

The presence of British troops in Tanganyika is a fact which is too easily exploited by those who wish to divide Africa or to dominate Africa. Already it is clear that there are some people who will seize upon this opportunity to play upon natural fears of neo-colonialism in the hope of sowing seeds of suspicion between the different African States. For this reason alone the meeting in Dar es Salaam would have been worthwhile. . . .

But there are other factors behind Tanganyika's decision to ask for an All-African discussion of our current circumstances. For Africa, Tanganyika is a "border-state." By virtue of that fact the headquarters of the Liberation Committee of the OAU is situated in our capital. In addition we have many Freedom Fighters from Mozambique and Southern Africa organizing their affairs in this country. . . . It is obvious to us that a state of affairs in Tanganyika which might interfere with the effectiveness, or even the psychological comfort, of these Freedom Movements is the concern of the whole of Africa. And although there is nothing to hide in Tanganyika, the situation is obviously exploitable. I am told that Portugal has already complained that Britain has not used the presence of her troops to tell them what is going on here.

The Council endorsed "the decision of the Government of Tanganyika to have the British troops withdrawn and replaced by Africans." [14] On March 20, 1964, the Nigerian government sent a battalion to Tanganyika and the British troops left immediately thereafter. The rapid political changes in East Africa came to a climax on April 27, when Tanganyika and Zanzibar announced their merger in a United Republic, the joint name of which would later come to be Tanzania.

[14] Some suggested a permanent African military force for use in such situations. One of those strongly opposed to this suggestion was the Foreign Minister of Congo (B), Charles Ganao, who said: "We Congolese are especially unfavorable to it since if this force had existed last August, Fulbert Youlou could have appealed for it and thus have entrenched his dictatorship."

Adding to the widespread sense of general African instability was the civil war in Rwanda and the clashes on the
Somalo-Ethiopian border. Both outbreaks posed issues in which
none of the other states in the OAU was very anxious to become overly involved. In Rwanda the majority Hutus had
overthrown the ruling minority Tutsis with Belgian aid in
1959, and the government was consequently not at all revolutionary on the pan-African scene. But internally the Tutsis represented a formerly privileged group. Civil fighting broke out
there anew in December 1963. A group of five hundred Tutsi
guerrillas had come from Burundi, a neighboring parallel state
in which, however, the old Tutsi hierarchy still exercised
power. The Tutsi guerrillas almost succeeded in taking power
but failed. The consequence was a wide-scale slaughter of
Tutsis. On January 28, 1964, the Premier of Burundi appealed
to the OAU to intervene to "put an end to provocations by
Rwanda." The U.N. received a similar request. The secretary-
generals of both organizations appealed for peaceful settlement, but neither organization took direct action.

The border disputes between Somalia on the one hand and
Ethiopia and Kenya on the other were similarly of long standing. Somalia called for the incorporation of the Ogaden in
Ethiopia and the Northern Frontier District in Kenya (along
with French Somaliland) into a greater Somalia on the grounds
of ethnic relationship. Somalia's demands have long created
a problem for the movement for African unity. Since most
African states are ethnically very variegated, most find their
stability in asserting the validity of present borders and reject
any attempt to recarve borders on the grounds of ethnic
nationality. Somalia is the prime exponent of the opposite view,
representing the exceptional case of a country which is virtually homogeneous *and* has large ethnically related groups
outside its borders. Somalia has seldom been granted more
than an embarrassed hearing in all-African meetings. For the
proponents of unity as alliance wish to assert the inviolability
of borders. And the proponents of unity as movement, while

conceding the possibility of change, are dubious that a claim
to ethnic nationality is revolutionary as such.

As a result of the frustration of Somalia at its isolation in
Africa and the impatience of a proud and militarily strong
Ethiopia over guerrilla sniping, border incidents have occurred a number of times since 1960, the year of Somalia's
independence. The most serious, however, took place at this
very time of general African turmoil, and on February 8, 1964,
Ethiopia asked for an OAU session to resolve the affair. On
February 10 Somalia did the same. It was decided that the
meeting in Dar es Salaam on February 12 would include this
dispute as the second item on its agenda. The Council called
for an immediate cease-fire (as well as for an end to pro-
vocative actions and propaganda between Somalia and Kenya)
and bilateral negotiations. On March 28 such negotiations were
entered into in Khartoum, with the Sudanese government as
mediator. The situation was kept in check. The OAU could
add this to its list of successful mediations, although essentially Somalia felt frustrated over the maintenance of the
status quo.

The Dar es Salaam meeting was to have impact not only
in the country itself, soon to be called Tanzania (where the
government felt it had to strengthen itself internally if it was
to be an adequate base for liberation movements), but also
across the continent in French-speaking Africa. It was only
two days after the close of the Dar es Salaam Council of Ministers meeting, at which African states had given indirect approval to the use that the East African states had made of
British troops, that a military coup was attempted in Gabon
on February 17, 1964. The coup had in fact succeeded when,
on the following day, French paratroopers landed, ostensibly
at the request of the vice-president of the overthrown government, and restored President Mba to power. The French had
not intervened in the coups in Togo, Congo (B), or Dahomey,
although in the case of Congo (B), President Youlou, at a
moment when he still occupied more real authority than the

vice-president of Gabon, had appealed for troops on the basis of the same kind of military accords that were invoked as a justification in Gabon. Yet the French had said "no" to Youlou. What was different in Gabon?

It was true that the Gabon military coup was not preceded by popular demonstrations as in Congo (B) and Dahomey, and thus it could be looked upon as purely a palace coup. It is true also that Gabon is economically more significant than the other three countries. But what seemed to be most important was the consideration that the Gabon coup was getting to be one too many and there might now be a quick series throughout the UAM states, all moving their government toward a somewhat more revolutionary position on African affairs and cumulatively creating a powerful reinforcement for the revolutionary core of the movement.

In any case, the French action was openly applauded by six UAM states (Central African Republic, Chad, Ivory Coast, Malagasy Republic, Niger, and Upper Volta). Dahomey made only a mild demurral. Nevertheless one would normally have expected a vigorous reaction from outside the UAM to what amounted to direct military interference by the former colonial power. It was what had happened in East Africa that prevented this. For while the political nuances of the East African mutinies were substantially different from those of the Gabon coup, the juridical situation was very similar. Once again the revolutionary core found itself hoist on a petard of legalism. The result was that France went virtually uncriticized [15] in Africa. The issue was not even discussed at the Lagos meeting of the Council of Ministers of the OAU, held one week later from February 24 to 29, and the revolutionary movement in French-speaking Africa was sharply stopped for the time being. The shock of the Gabon affair did, however, help to convince the leaders of the UAM that they had best tread softly for the present. In Dakar on March 7–10, 1964, the heads of

[15] It is true that rather weak statements against the French intervention were made by the Mali and Algerian governments, and in Ghana the Bureau of African Affairs issued a condemnation.

state of the UAM decided to dissolve the UAM over the ener-
getic protests of Presidents Tsiranana of the Malagasy Republic and Grunitsky of Togo, and replace it with a non-
political structure, the Union Africaine et Malgache de Coopération Economique (UAMCE). President Ould Daddah
of Mauritania said: "The political domain ought to be left
to the OAU."

The OAU meeting at Lagos was most significant for its failure to take note of the French intervention in Gabon, which
was in fact even praised by a number of members of the OAU.
Aside from this it took two significant decisions. Because of
the Rwanda crisis, the issue of refugees was posed and the
OAU set up a ten-nation commission to look into the matter.[16]
The problem of refugees turned out to be an important and
thorny one, still in the process of adjudication as of mid-1966.
Ordinary refugees in large numbers from unliberated states
and even those from independent states posed largely technical and relatively few political problems. It was the issues
concerning high-level political refugees, especially those from
independent states, which would create such a knotty discussion and indeed become a central problem for the OAU
during 1965.

The other question discussed at Lagos was also a precursor
of much 1965 activity—Southern Rhodesia. Here we have the
first call of the OAU to Britain to "prevent effectively the
threat of unilateral independence or subtle assumption of
power by the minority settler regime," and to convene a constitutional conference to decide on independence on the basis
of "one man, one vote." This was accompanied by the first
threat to "reconsider . . . diplomatic and other relations with
Britain should the British government ignore the . . . recommendations."

But it was neither refugees nor Rhodesia that chiefly preoccupied Africa (and hence the OAU) in 1964. It was once

---

[16] The Commission on the Problem of Refugees in Africa was composed of Burundi, Cameroon, Congo (L), Ghana, Nigeria, Rwanda,
Senegal, Sudan, Tanganyika, and Uganda.

again the Congo. We have seen how the Congo crisis was the central issue around which Africa had divided into two main blocs—Casablanca and Monrovia. And we have seen how the "resolution" of the Congo crisis—the formation of the Adoula government and the U.N. occupation of Katanga —made possible the compromise of Addis Ababa. We have seen too how·just at a moment when almost all the governments of independent Africa were willing to bask in the indolent pleasure of such an alliance, border disputes, civil wars, and *coups d'état* seemed to erupt everywhere, and African governmental efforts were turned toward containing these outbursts rather than toward the liberation of southern Africa. It was, then, in a climate of increasing instability throughout Africa that the unresolved social and political issues of the Congo led to renewed internal disorder. The impact of the renewed Congo crisis on the over-all African scene would once again be immediate and telling.

On September 29, 1963, President Kasavubu dissolved the Congolese Parliament. This act was the final negation of the spirit of the Congolese compromise of August 1961 which brought Adoula to power. The following day, "nationalist-Lumumbist parties" met in Leopoldville, condemned the dissolution of Parliament, and formed a coordinating body—the Conseil National de Libération (CNL). In the beginning of October the leaders of CNL emigrated to Brazzaville, which had become, since the revolution in Congo (B) of August 1963, a sympathetic haven. We now know that disorders began in Kwilu province even before this, but it was only at the end of 1963 that it was widely reported that guerrillas were operating under the leadership of Pierre Mulele. In the first half of 1964 rebel activity erupted in other parts of the Congo and steadily gained strength. Beginning in February 1964 U.N. planes gave logistical support to the Congolese army fighting the rebels. By April the CNL, claiming control over the various rebel units, issued a declaration which accused the United States and Belgium of launching a deliberate aggression against the Congo by their military aid to the Adoula government.

They added that "certain African countries have lent them-selves to our enemies and betrayed African solidarity. . . ." [17]

The continued military success of the CNL coincided with the approach of June 30, 1964, an important date in the Congo for two reasons. First, it marked the expiration of the man-date of Parliament, a date prior to which elections were sup-posed to have been held. Secondly, it marked the date of the final withdrawal of United Nations troops, a withdrawal that had already once been postponed for six months under strong U.S. pressure and which would mean the end of a major mili-tary underpinning of the Congolese government. [18] Further-more, Tshombe, in voluntary exile, had not been inactive. On June 10 he made a surprise visit to Mali at the invitation of the ruling party, which seemed to give him some tacit accept-ance in circles where he had been considered totally *non grata* up to that time. [19] While the Malians later denounced Tshombe for having deceived them, his reception there caused some disarray on all sides.

At this point, the authorities in Leopoldville were faced with two problems: the continuing success of the rebels; and the potential threat of a new secession by Katanga, once the U.N.

[17] Specifically, the charges were as follows: "Some Nigerians are camou-flaged as soldiers of the [Congolese National Army] and are killing Con-golese in Kwilu in order to alienate our national sovereignty menaced by the enemies of Africans. Forgetting that after the Congo their country will have its turn. To Tunisia, African brother country, as to certain interested countries of Europe, such as Italy and West Germany, the National Liberation Council gives a last warning on their responsi-bility in the Congolese affair.

"As to Northern Rhodesia led by an African nationalist, a country to which Adoula has just made certain commitments, the CNL asks its support for Congolese unity and not encouragement to a man recognized as bloody and a slave to powers known to be enemies of Africa in general and the Congo in particular." The Nigerian government formally denied these charges, and this denial was widely accepted.

[18] In June 1964 the Belgian government pledged to replace the U.N. in furnishing pilots and maintenance personnel for transport airplanes.

[19] Tshombe had long prepared this attempt to improve his public re-lations among radical-nationalists. On January 30, 1964, he had tried to absolve himself of responsibility for the death of Lumumba by charging that Kasavubu, Adoula, Bomboko, and the Belgians had sent a dying Lumumba to him.

troops left, since Tshombe's former *gendarmerie* and some mercenary officers were sitting in wait in Angola. President Kasavubu decided to deal with this double menace by a simple tactic, that of calling on Tshombe to become Prime Minister. Thus the grant of power to Tshombe on the national level both ended the threat of secession and brought new strength to the struggle to end the rebellion by acquiring the services of Tshombe's ex-gendarmes plus the mercenaries Kasavubu knew Tshombe would be willing to use.[20] What had happened, however, was that the Compromise of 1961, the coalition of the Kasavubu-Adoula-Mobutu forces with the Lumumbists against Tshombe, had now been formally replaced by a coalition of these forces with Tshombe against the Lumumbists. The first coalition in the Congo had made possible the inter-African compromise of Addis Ababa in 1963. The new coalition in the Congo undid this compromise, and therefore threatened the very foundation of the OAU.

[20] This was all quite self-conscious. On October 13, 1965, President Kasavubu, addressing the Congolese Parliament, destituted Tshombe and said: "The former forces of secession had not been completely disarmed and in a neighboring country [Angola] were set up as a veritable army composed of Congolese and foreigners. . . . To assure [their] reintegration, a political gesture was alone possible; and this political gesture could be made only by one man [Tshombe], he who had the power to order these forces to rejoin the ranks of the regular army. . . . At present, the mission which in the name of the Country I confided to him in the month of July 1964 is finished. I tender him my thanks for having brought to a successful conclusion, in circumstances that often made it difficult, the tasks which I asked of him."

:VI:

HOPE DIMMED AGAIN:

THE SECOND CONGO CRISIS

AND RHODESIA

It was because the Congo crisis had been temporarily shelved and because they gave priority to the liberation of southern Africa that the revolutionary core of the movement toward African unity had been willing to accept the compromise of the OAU, a compromise which on the face of it seemed to constrain their activities and inhibit the achievement of their objectives. The balance sheet of the first year of existence of the OAU was unclear, but up to this point the revolutionary core could not argue that the OAU represented the primary obstacle. The next eighteen months were to put the OAU to a severe test. The second Congo crisis was to lead to a renewed open confirmation within the OAU of the two competing outlooks of African independent governments. And the Rhodesian crisis was to demonstrate the limitations of the OAU as an instrument of liberation.

The Congo issue was not long in coming to a head, once Tshombe was installed as Prime Minister on July 10, 1964. On July 17–21 the Assembly of Heads of State and Government of the OAU was scheduled to hold its first Ordinary Session in Cairo. The immediate problem was that Tshombe wculd attend, to sit with all the African leaders who had not merely condemned him but had pictured him as the incarnation of treachery to Africa. A reaction built up quickly, especially among those states that had been most vociferous in their opposition to Tshombe.[1] His accession to power in the Congo was so startling to *all* the African states that it was possible to persuade the Council of Ministers of the OAU that met in Cairo, just prior to the meeting of the heads of state, to recommend (with no negative votes) that a telegram be sent to President Kasavubu asking that he not include Prime Minister Tshombe in his delegation. The Congo (L) government, feeling somewhat weak in this situation, reacted merely by not participating in the conference. By the time the heads of state met, some were ready to protest against this interference in the internal affairs of a member country. Most notable was President Tsiranana of the Malagasy Republic, who argued: "We all deplored the death of Patrice Lumumba, but that doesn't give us the right to interfere in Congolese affairs. While we are about it, search your hearts. Have we not all signed an execution warrant against one of our compatriots? We are not all angels and if Mr. Tshombe goes to hell, there shall be others among us who shall go with him."

The exclusion of Tshombe was of course an important event, arguing as it did against the concept of unity as alliance and in favor of unity as movement. For it amounted to the OAU members' making a judgment on the moral worth of a fellow member. There had, of course, been a precedent, the exclusion of Togo from Addis Ababa, supported by many of those who

[1] The strongest statement was, unexpectedly, from King Hassan II of Morocco, who said: "The United Nations asked our country to send contingents to aid [the Congo] to ensure its independence. . . . I must ask the question: Why did we go to the Congo? . . . As for us, we said to our troops: You are going to be killed and to kill men who have done you no harm; you are not going to be killed for your country or your flag, but you are going to fight for a sacred cause and because a certain number of Congolese have decided to secede from their fatherland and to remain under the tutelage of foreigners. How can you imagine that as a representative of our national conscience, I can be seated at a conference table or at a banquet at the same time as a representative of this state of rebellion and secession?"

now opposed the exclusion of Tshombe. On August 23, 1963, the UPC of Cameroon had sent a letter to the OAU requesting that an inquiry commission be sent to the Cameroon, basing the request on the Preamble to the Charter. This request was ignored. After the Cairo OAU meeting, the request was repeated, this time citing as precedent the refusal to seat Tshombe. It was nonetheless still ignored. The exclusion of Tshombe was, furthermore, as we shall see, a very temporary victory for the forces of movement.

Having excluded Tshombe from the Cairo meeting, the delegates proceeded to concern themselves with a series of organizational matters: the choice of the headquarters site at Addis Ababa; the choice of the Secretary-General, Diallo Telli of Guinea; establishment of two new permanent commissions; reinforcement of various previous decisions concerning action on Rhodesia, South Africa, and the Portuguese territories. They adopted the Protocol of the Commission of Mediation, Conciliation, and Arbitration which had been provided for in the Charter.

For the first time, too, the heads of state debated at length the Ghana proposal for "union government in Africa." The idea received a serious hearing, if little real support. President Nkrumah argued the case: "[The neo-colonialists and their agents] became [after Addis Ababa] particularly active and vocal in preaching the new and dangerous doctrine of the 'step-by-step' course towards unity. If we take one step at a time when they are in a position to take six steps for every single one of ours, our weakness will, of course, be emphasized and exaggerated for their benefit. One step now, two steps later, then all will be fine in Africa for imperialism and neocolonialism. To say that a Union Government for Africa is premature is to sacrifice Africa on the altar of neo-colonialism."

Most of the heads of state, however, agreed with President Nyerere who argued against Nkrumah: "To rule out step-by-step progress in a march to unity is to rule out unity itself." Nonetheless, the meeting decided to refer Ghana's proposals to the Specialized Commissions so that these commissions could present their studies at the next session of the heads of state. While many external observers cited this debate on union government as the sign of a fundamental cleavage in the OAU, some internal observers made the opposite analysis, asserting the usefulness of the debate for the objective of union. For example, the editor of *Jeune Afrique*,[2] Bechir Ben Yahmed, commented on the meeting in this fashion: ". . . The very fact of persistently putting forward an objective so grandiose forces some steps toward unity which perhaps would not otherwise have been taken. It is in this sense that between the objective proclaimed by Nkrumah and those sought by the majority of members of the OAU, there is a happy complementarity." In any case, the question would not be dropped in the year following Cairo.

At first, the OAU action on Tshombe seemed to matter. It marked an important diplomatic defeat for Tshombe, and it was matched by a similar internal political defeat when his half-hearted attempt to secure the political surrender of the rebel forces was unsuccessful. Furthermore, he continued to receive military setbacks until August, when he began systematically to recruit mercenaries, many of them South African whites, backed up by strong material assistance from the outside, especially the United States. The importation of mercenaries and the deteriorating relations of the Congo (L) with its neighbors, especially Congo (B) and Burundi, led a number of African states to demand an extraordinary session of the Council of Ministers, which was held in Addis Ababa on September 5–10, 1964, despite last-minute attempts of the Congo (L) government to have it postponed.[3] The meeting adopted a strong resolution, by a wide majority (27–0–6), appealing to the Congo (L) to "stop immediately the recruitment

[2] *Jeune Afrique*, a Tunisian weekly on African affairs, is probably the most widely read African journal of opinion among African elites, especially, of course, in French-speaking countries.

[3] The government presumably hoped to complete important military thrusts before any such meeting was held, and thus to present the OAU with a *fait accompli*.

of mercenaries and to expel as soon as possible all mercenaries of whatever origin," and called for "national reconciliation." Furthermore, it established, under Prime Minister Kenyatta of Kenya, an *ad hoc* ten-member Commission,[4] whose terms of reference were twofold: to restore normal relations between Congo (L) and its two neighbors, Congo (B) and Burundi, and "to help and encourage the efforts of the Government of the Democratic Republic of the Congo in the restoration of national reconciliation."

By this latter clause, the OAU asserted that national reconciliation within a member country, at least if it were the Congo (L) with its particular history, was a legitimate concern of the organization. Although the resolution did not term the rebels "patriots," and although it did not call for "immediate and unconditional withdrawal" of mercenaries, the Congo (L) was not happy with it, and showed this by abstaining in the vote.[5] Nonetheless, the meeting marked the first major diplomatic victory for Tshombe in Africa. For he attended this meeting, albeit in his capacity as Foreign Minister, and no objection was made to his presence. On the contrary, it was the representatives of the CNL who were not heard—partly because there was already an open split in CNL ranks.[6] But it was also because the OAU, by virtue of being an intergovernmental structure, was imprisoned by juridical considerations, as had been the CIAS in 1959 and 1960 when the issue of Cameroon's representation came before it. Unlike 1960, when the Lumumbists could claim the mantle of legality under international law and Tshombe was the rebel, the situation now was reversed. It is true that the CNL contested Tshombe's legality. In the middle of the meeting, on September 5, the CNL in fact formally proclaimed the constitution of the Peo-

[4] The other members, besides Kenya, were Cameroon, Ethiopia, Ghana, Guinea, Nigeria, Somalia, Tunisia, U.A.R., and Upper Volta.

[5] The other countries that abstained were Liberia, Nigeria, Senegal, Sierra Leone, and Togo.

[6] The representative of the CNL at this meeting was Egide Bocheley-Davidson, whose wing of the CNL had previously "expelled" Christophe Gbenye, while Gbenye was, precisely during the meeting, named by his faction to head the provisional government.

ples' Republic of the Congo, with a provisional government located in Stanleyville. Despite this, no African government, then or later, was ready to withdraw legal recognition from the Leopoldville regime.

The *ad hoc* commission pursued its task energetically, under the impulse of Kenyatta and with the active support of the OAU's Secretary-General, Diallo Telli. It met on September 18 in Nairobi. The commission decided to send a special five-nation delegation to President Johnson, since "It is the feeling of the Ad Hoc Committee that without the withdrawal of all foreign military intervention in the Congo the Ad Hoc Commission cannot find the right atmosphere which fits the high mission of reconciliation entrusted to its members." The Congo (L) protested this move and President Johnson refused to meet the delegation.[7]

The increasing frustration of the OAU, its inability to affect the Congo situation, was vented at the Cairo Conference of Non-Aligned Nations, held from October 5 to 10, 1964. Originally all OAU members had been invited to attend, and most of them came.[8] On October 4, repeating the previous Cairo OAU formula, the foreign ministers asked Kasavubu to come to the meeting without Tshombe. This time, Tshombe simply showed up and was promptly placed in gilded confinement. The Congo (L) government retaliated by surrounding the U.A.R. and Algerian embassies in Leopoldville. The heads of the twenty-eight African delegations present unanimously stated that Tshombe's attendance was inappropriate as long as the Ad Hoc Commission had not satisfactorily fulfilled its mandate. They further warned that the action of surrounding the embassies in Leopoldville endangered the relations of the Congo (L) with the rest of Africa. The next day the U.A.R. and Algerian embassy staffs were allowed to exit freely, and the following day Tshombe flew home. It was an elaborate

[7] The State Department Press Officer stated at this time: ". . . We could not agree to discuss our aid to the Congo without participation of the Congo government, at whose request our aid is given."

[8] The absentees were only the Central African Republic, Gabon, Ivory Coast, Malagasy Republic, Niger, Rwanda, and Upper Volta.

symbolic game, but one which did not affect the reality of power in the Congo, where the mercenaries were steadily advancing.

The balance of forces in the Congo was now threatened by developments in a neighboring country. At the end of October 1964 the military regime in the Sudan was overthrown by a broad coalition of forces. The immediate result was to place in power for the first time in the Sudan, which bordered the Lumumbist-controlled areas of the Congo, a regime which was more sympathetic to the Lumumbists than to the Leopoldville authorities. This made possible a simple route for the passage of arms aid. Before this new situation had time to take effect, Stanleyville was menaced. On October 29 Gbenye made an open appeal to Algeria, Ghana, Guinea, Mali, and the U.A.R. for recognition and assistance, an appeal which was not directly answered. Radio Stanleyville further announced that "the Belgians and the Americans in Stanleyville have been placed under home confinement." From this point on the situation deteriorated. The Stanleyville regime held its hostages against a cessation of hostilities. President Kenyatta appealed both for the cessation of hostilities and assurances of safety for the foreign civilian population. On November 23 in Nairobi discussions were held between the U.S. Ambassador, William Attwood, and the Foreign Minister of the Stanleyville regime, Thomas Kanza, under the auspices of Kenyatta and Diallo Telli. On November 24, while the discussions were taking place, Belgian paratroops, conveyed in United States planes, landed in Stanleyville and turned over control to the Leopoldville authorities.[9] In the process both Congolese and foreign lives were lost.

African states responded to military intervention by diplomatic moves. At the United Nations a resolution was introduced in the Security Council condemning the Belgian-American intervention in Stanleyville, signed by eighteen African

---

[9] This aspect of the invasion was particularly resented. In the bitter U.N. debate that followed, Tanzania's Foreign Minister, Oscar Kambona, referred to this action as "the Pearl Harbor of Africa."

states (out of thirty-five members of the OAU). They were Algeria, Burundi, Central African Republic, Congo (B), Dahomey, Ethiopia, Ghana, Guinea, Kenya, Malawi, Mali, Mauritania, Somalia, Sudan, Tanzania, U.A.R., Uganda, and Zambia. If one compares this list to the split in Africa at the time of the first Congo crisis, it may be seen that African states had evolved in a "Lumumbist" direction. Now, in addition to the former Casablanca powers, the signatories included four UAM states (including Congo [B] and Dahomey, which had had revolutions), several former "neutrals" (Ethiopia, Somalia, Sudan), plus all the East and Central African states that had since gained independence (and were previously in PAFMECSA).

Because of the split among African states at the U.N., the OAU held an extraordinary session of the Council of Ministers in New York on December 16–21, 1964. The debate was heated. The Foreign Minister of Congo (B), Charles Ganao, is reported to have said: ". . . If in the name of African unity one seeks hereafter to hold back the African revolutionary movement, and if, to assure a so-called respectable façade for the OAU, we must silence all differences of view when vital interests are at stake, then I say as do others: let the OAU split up." The final resolution that was passed called upon the Security Council "to condemn the recent foreign interventions," and "to recommend an African Solution to the Congo problem." This resolution received twenty votes (the eighteen countries that had signed the Security Council resolution plus Chad and Sierra Leone). The others abstained, were absent, or refused to participate in the vote (Congo [L]). The end result of this activity was a rather weak resolution adopted by the U.N. on December 30 which merely "deplored" recent events in the Congo and "encouraged" the OAU to pursue its efforts to achieve national reconciliation.

The Ad Hoc Commission continued to try to play a role in the matter, but Tshombe's *de facto* military victory was leading to increased African diplomatic support.[10] At the Nairobi

[10] A move by Ghana at the January meeting of the Scientific, Technical, and Research Committee of the OAU in Lagos not to seat the representative of Congo (L) was defeated 17–3.

meeting of the Council of Ministers from February 26 to March 9, 1965, the debate was again heated, but the only resolution adopted was to refer the issue to the next meeting of the heads of state in Accra. Those who supported Tshombe failed to obtain the formal dissolution of the Ad Hoc Commission, but in fact it ceased to function. On the key issue of whether the Council would hear formally representatives of the former Stanleyville regime, only thirteen countries voted in favor of the resolution.[11] In effect, the issue was now allowed to die.

The position of the revolutionary core, who had hoped to proceed from the compromise of Addis Ababa to further advances, was now under severe attack. Though Tshombe had lost every preliminary diplomatic battle in the OAU, he had, with extensive outside help, won on the field in the Congo. This led to a major confrontation of strength over the orientation of the OAU. As the second Congo crisis revitalized the spirit of combativity of the former Casablanca powers, it saw a resurgence of the UAM group in counterposition. In March 1964 the UAM had disappeared under the pressure of the OAU and the weight of its own internal rivalries. Some countries, like the Ivory Coast, now openly regretted the "haste" with which the UAM had been dissolved. On February 10–12, 1965, at Nouakchott, Mauritania, the former members of the UAM created the Organization Commune Africaine et Malgache (OCAM).

The official communiqué of OCAM left no doubt that the Congo was the central concern of the conference[12] and asserted that "the malaise from which the OAU is suffering arises essentially from the non-respect of its Charter." Although many heads of state spoke of the menace of Communist China to Africa, the communiqué attacked not China but a fellow-OAU member, Ghana. "They strongly condemn the action of

[11] They were Algeria, Burundi, Congo (B), Ghana, Guinea, Kenya, Mali, Somalia, Sudan, Uganda, U.A.R., Tanzania, Zambia. Seven voted against and fourteen abstained.
[12] This was reinforced by the presence in the corridors of a Belgian diplomat and a delegation from Congo (L), whose representatives were initially rebuffed by the reluctant host Mauritanian authorities.

certain States, notably Ghana, which offer a welcome to the agents of subversion and organize training camps on their territory." This was the opening volley of a year-long campaign by OCAM against Ghana, the country whose government was considered by these states to be, at this point, the leading element of the revolutionary core.

From this time on, the issues of subversion in independent Africa, civil war in the Congo, and the creation of a union government in Africa, became closely intertwined. The Nouakchott group continued to show its aggressiveness at the Nairobi Council of Ministers meeting. We have already discussed the inability to obtain a majority in the Council for any further action concerning Congo (L). OCAM states also attacked the Secretariat because it had taken a too active role in the OAU attempts to secure "national reconciliation" in the Congo. In the atmosphere of Nairobi the proposal of the Defense Commission of the OAU, which had met in Freetown from February 2 to 5, for the creation of an African peace force toward which each state would earmark contingents for operations as determined by the OAU, failed to get a majority vote at the Council of Ministers. To this OCAM offensive, certain states decided to react. The old trio of the presidents of Ghana, Guinea, and Mali, joined by President Ben Bella of Algeria met in Bamako, Mali, on March 14.[18] No official statement has ever been made, but on his return to Algiers Ben Bella said that the four presidents had arrived at "a common attitude toward the maneuvers which are cropping up in Africa, inspired by imperialism and colonialism." And President Nkrumah in his speech to his National Assembly stated that he could "assure our brothers who met at Nouakchott that it is not from Ghana that they should expect a subversion of their regimes and threats to their sovereignty."

OCAM now challenged the viability of the OAU if some member-states persisted in revolutionary objectives. The OCAM states had first threatened in February a boycott of the

---

[18] This meeting was followed by a two-day meeting of Guinea, Mali, and Algeria in Conakry, Guinea, March 15–16.

forthcoming Accra OAU heads of state meeting. The threat became vociferous after the unsuccessful attempt to assassinate President Hamani Diori of Niger on April 13. The Niger government charged that the assassin was a member of the illegal opposition Sawaba party headed by Bakary Djibo, that this party received support and encouragement from Ghana, and that the assassin was trained in China and Ghana. The Ghana government denied that it was in any way whatever involved in the assassination attempt or in any other subversive activities against Niger. Nonetheless, a coordinated diplomatic campaign against Ghana was undertaken by certain OCAM states. The most important step was the visit on April 27 of Presidents Diori and Yaméogo (of Upper Volta) to Prime Minister Balewa of Nigeria in Lagos.

All the states that conceived of the OAU primarily as an alliance were not necessarily in accord on the tactics to follow. It is well to comprehend the differences in the positions of the OCAM states, particularly the Ivory Coast, Upper Volta, and Niger on the one hand, and Nigeria and some others on the other. The OCAM group seemed ready to risk breaking up the machinery of the OAU in order to isolate, even quarantine, Ghana and perhaps some other states.[14] They seemed to place the threat to their immediate internal security so high, either directly or through further revolution in the Congo, that the alliance of African states against the external world seemed a secondary consideration. The Nigerian government shared many of the grievances of the French-speaking trio, especially concerning the fact that certain of their citizens who were being judicially pursued in Nigeria held important posts in Ghana.[15] Nonetheless, the Nigerian government saw the structure of the OAU as a restraint on pre-

[14] This is somewhat parallel to the attempt of these same states to isolate, or quarantine, Guinea in 1958–1960.

[15] The most prominent of these was S. G. Ikoku, Secretary-General of the Action Group (Nigeria), who was at this time a senior lecturer in the Kwame Nkrumah Ideological Institute at Winneba, and a member of the editorial staff of *The Spark,* a journal of the Bureau of African Affairs of Ghana.

cisely the kind of subversive activities they too felt the Ghana government indulged in. Hence they were anxious not only to maintain the OAU but to strengthen its ability to control "interference" of one state in the affairs of another. They feared the generally unsettling consequences of a breakup of the OAU precisely on the internal stability of independent African states, including their own. Thus, although the general outlooks on world affairs of the Ivory Coast and her allies and Nigeria and hers were the same, the tactical approaches were quite different as a consequence of different analyses of the role the OAU had played and could play in the pursuit of their policy objectives. Hence Prime Minister Balewa of Nigeria proposed that instead of boycotting the Accra meeting, there should be convened an extraordinary meeting of the Council of Ministers in Lagos to discuss the accusations of the three states against Ghana.

The position of the revolutionary core was a difficult one at this point. For they too were split in their tactical appreciation of the situation. Some felt that the OAU served primarily as a restraint on revolutionary activity. Hence they were not too worried about the possibility of a boycott or even of the breakup of the OAU which might clarify the conflict and thereby advance it. Others felt that such a breakup would limit the possibilities of a structural advance on the pan-African front (which would have revolutionary implications) and that the OAU had served historically as a mechanism of pressure on some African governments to take more militant positions in world affairs than they would otherwise have done. This latter point of view prevailed and was particularly reflected in the diplomatic activities of the Ghana government in the coming six months. Ghana's diplomats exerted themselves to palliate every openly expressed fear and complaint of other members of the OAU in order to eliminate any excuse for boycotting the Accra meeting.[16]

---

[16] Some thought the Ghanaian diplomats overexerted themselves. For example, the Algerian trade-union newspaper wrote:

. . . The Conference of Foreign Ministers of the Organization of

There were thus at this time four points of view in Africa: the view of the part of the core that saw the OAU as an obstacle to revolutionary ends; the view of the part of the core that saw it as an instrument; the view of the part of the periphery that saw the OAU as embodying an alliance, one of whose functions was to inhibit revolutionary ends; the view of those who feared that the OAU legitimated, however partially, revolutionary forces. Those elements of the revolutionary core that were skeptical of the OAU did not renounce their activities. On the contrary, they sought to have other agencies which could at least complement the OAU. Since the AAPC no longer existed, they turned to the Afro-Asian Peoples' Solidarity Conference which held its fourth session from May 9 to 16, 1965, in Winneba, Ghana.

As at previous meetings, the AAPSC served principally as a meeting ground of Asian Communist governments and movements and African radical-nationalist governments and movements. And as at previous meetings, the latter were composed of three separate groups: the movements of national liberation in nonindependent countries, movements in "progressive" independent states, and opposition movements in other independent states, such as Sawaba (Niger), UPC (Cameroon), Parti Africain de l'Indépendance (Senegal), and the UNFP (Morocco). The dominant tone of the meeting was created by a coalition of representatives of African independent governments (Algeria, Ghana, Guinea, Mali, Tanzania, U.A.R.),

---

African Unity which was held in Lagos from June 10–14, 1965, by wanting to satisfy everyone, was in reality nothing but a reward to the neo-colonialist assault.

It is true that the conference kept Accra as the site of the OAU summit meeting but, in the name of "tolerance, mutual understanding and solidarity," Ghana was asked to make amends, to get on its knees, and to promise not to annoy any more that great African, Moise Tshombe, the man of Union Minière.

We must say that what imperialism was looking for was the breakup, pure and simple, of the OAU. It should be noted that in this respect progressive Africa did not fall into the trap and that Ghanaian diplomacy went to the limit of "tolerance, mutual understanding and solidarity." One even wondered if Ghanaian diplomacy did not go too far.

plus the representative of the UNFP, Mehdi Ben Barka. This group held in check the various dissensions (China-U.S.S.R., India-Pakistan, Malaysia-Indonesia, rival movements of national liberation in southern Africa, rival opposition movements in independent African countries).

On the African scene there were two major consequences of this meeting of the AAPSC. One was the resolution in favor of continental union government, which is the first time that the AAPSC or any organization in which Communist movements played a role committed itself formally to this objective. This was an important ideological concession and reflected the strength of the movement toward African unity in the eyes of both the U.S.S.R. and Chinese Communist parties. The other major consequence of the meeting was the reaffirmation by certain African independent governments of the legitimacy of revolutionary objectives. Mehdi Ben Barka analyzed the problem well in an article which appeared the following month in *L'Etincelle,* a journal published in Ghana: "The popular organizations in power in [progressive States such as the U.A.R., Algeria, Guinea, Ghana, Mali, and Tanzania] as well as the movements of national liberation understand in effect that the struggle against imperialism is a long fight which must be pursued even under conditions of peaceful coexistence with the States on the African continent which were artificially created by neo-colonialism. It has therefore become necessary to bring this long-term strategy into line with a policy to be pursued within the OAU which includes countries still in the process of liberating themselves from political or economic dependence or from both."

The Winneba meeting was therefore a riposte to the OCAM offensive. President Houphouet-Boigny decided to pursue his diplomatic campaign even further by convening in Abidjan, Ivory Coast, on May 26, 1965, an extraordinary meeting of OCAM. This call was somewhat irregular, as it should have come from the current president of OCAM, President Ould Daddah of Mauritania, who was reluctant to convene the meeting. As it was, five states did not show up: Mauritania, Cameroon, Congo (B), the Central African Republic, and Rwanda. The first three had done so out of open disapproval of the purposes of the meeting. The principal activity of the meeting was the decision to support the admission of Congo (L) to OCAM. Tshombe arrived for the closing session, thus climaxing his military victory in the Congo with a political blessing from at least part of Africa. OCAM further pledged itself to aid the Congo (L) in every way, although it specified that military aid had not been requested. As for Ghana, the states present pledged themselves formally not to participate in the Accra meeting because of Ghana's alleged complicity in the attempt to assassinate Diori. They would, however, come to Lagos, a concession not to Ghana but to Nigeria. The price of OCAM's admitting Congo (L) was the withdrawal of Mauritania (on June 24), a loss the group was apparently ready to sustain.

The Lagos meeting finally took place on June 10–13, although the necessary two-thirds consent had been acquired only two days before the scheduled opening. The meeting was presented with the joint dossier of Ivory Coast, Niger, and Upper Volta, in which Ghana was directly accused of aiding Djibo Bakary and the Sawaba in the assassination attempt as well as aiding subversion in general. A special committee of five nations (Ethiopia, Gambia, Mali, Nigeria, and Tunisia) was established to hear the charges and the reply, and came up with a compromise proposal which was unanimously adopted. It reaffirmed the venue of the Accra meeting, noted the assurances Ghana was willing to give that it would "send away from its territory before the next Conference all those persons whose presence is considered undesirable" and "forbid the formation of political groups whose aims are to oppose any member State of the OAU." The resolution further noted that Ghana had invited Diallo Telli and the Chairman of the Council of Ministers, Foreign Minister Joseph Murumbi of Kenya, to visit Ghana "to ascertain the measures which are being taken towards the success of the Conference." While the resolution did not guarantee that there would be no boycott, it was a considerable diplomatic victory for Ghana and blunted the OCAM offensive.

The issue of "subversion" was virtually impossible to resolve within the ambiguity of the political compromise that led to the creation of the OAU. For the proponents of unity as alliance, the second principle of the OAU Charter, "noninterference in the internal affairs of States," which all signatories were bound to uphold, was clear and straightforward. It required that independent African states refrain from active support for opposition movements in other states, aside from [bare] asylum, and even the right to asylum was occasionally questioned. The proponents of unity as movement were equally indignant about interference by outsiders. But for them the significant unit was Africa as a whole. Within Africa, all were brothers and one could aid brothers. Outside interference was action by non-African powers in African independent States—or the continuation of colonial rule. The revolutionary core felt that African "client states" were abetting such outside interference. Each side had a sense of legitimate outrage at the hypocrisy of the other. As it was, two other issues came along to divert the attention of the OAU members from the issue of subversion: Rhodesia and the Afro-Asian Conference.

Ever since the meeting at Addis Ababa in May 1963, the OAU had operated on a dual strategy for the liberation of southern Africa; on the one hand, the inevitability of the need for force in Portuguese Africa and South Africa; on the other, the possibility of peaceful constitutional advance in Southern Rhodesia as a result of pressure on the United Kingdom, particularly from African members of the Commonwealth. This approach was now to be put to a major test. Rhodesia of course had been a standard issue at African meetings for many years· and the subject of resolutions at various OAU conferences, including the second ordinary session at Lagos in early 1964, at which the Council "again [called] upon the Government of the United Kingdom to meet its responsibilities and invited it . . . to convene a new constitutional conference for the purpose of preparing a Constitution founded on universal suffrage of all inhabitants of the territory." It is the "again" that is most significant. At the meeting of Commonwealth Prime Ministers held in London from June 17 to 25 the major issue of contention was Rhodesia (and also the abortive proposal of a peace mission to Vietnam). With much effort the African leaders obtained the following promise from Britain: "If, the discussions [with the government of Rhodesia] did not develop satisfactorily . . . in a reasonably speedy time, the British Government, having regard to the principle enunciated by the Commonwealth Secretary of unimpeded progress towards majority rule, would be ready to consider promoting such a [constitutional] conference in order to ensure Rhodesia's progress to independence on a basis acceptable to the people of Rhodesia as a whole." At that point the issue was not pressed any further by the African members, except for Tanzania, which dissociated itself from this section of the Commonwealth communiqué because it was unable to get "assurances that the negotiations taking place between the British and Rhodesian governments are aimed at achieving independence on the basis of majority rule." On the Rhodesia issue, Tanzania replaced Ghana as the leading nation in the revolutionary core. From this point until the unilateral declaration of independence by the Government of Rhodesia on November 11 the OAU persisted in its tactic of pressure on the British government, along with vain attempts to force unity upon the two African nationalist movements in Rhodesia.

The other issue that absorbed African attention at this time was the proposed Afro-Asian Conference, an issue which reflected confusion in the ranks of the revolutionary core. This "second Bandung" had been decided upon at a meeting in Jakarta from April 10 to 16, 1964, at which twenty-one nations were present, including the following African states: Algeria, Ethiopia, Ghana, Guinea, Morocco, Tanganyika, and the U.A.R. It was decided that the venue would be chosen by the

OAU, which accepted the offer to act as host tendered by Algeria at the Cairo meeting of the OAU in July 1964. Eventually, the date, after some postponements, was fixed for June 29, 1965. For the revolutionary core, holding the Afro-Asian Conference was a delicate operation since, unlike the AAPSC, the sponsors could deal only with governments. Thus, all the OAU members were invited, including the OCAM states. Thus, too, the proposed invitations to the U.S.S.R. and Malaysia promised to be a central issue of contention. Ten days before the opening of the Conference, President Ben Bella was overthrown by the Algerian army and replaced by a Revolutionary Council of twenty-five headed by Colonel Houari Boumediene. This event was to have grave consequences for the whole concept of Afro-Asianism on the world scene. As a result of the confusion in Algeria the conference was postponed to October, at which time, because of various developments during the interim, principally in Asia, and the unwillingness of China to lend herself to an occasion that might now have an unrevolutionary atmosphere, the conference was postponed *sine die*. It is, however, the particular impact of the abortive conference on Africa that concerns us here.

One major reason for the postponement of the Afro-Asian Conference in June was the extreme reluctance of African governments, especially Ghana, Guinea, Mali, Tanzania, and the U.A.R., to attend the meeting and thereby give recognition and thus approval to the new Algerian regime. In many revolutionary circles in Africa it was argued that the destitution of Ben Bella was part of the same process that returned Tshombe to power. This argument was made despite the prompt and total support of China for the new Algerian regime and despite the regime's protestations that nothing had changed except a man. This meant that Algeria's diplomatic activity for the next few months concentrated heavily on an attempt to restore its revolutionary reputation in Africa. However, the focus of this activity was on the successful holding of the Afro-Asian Conference, which ultimately was in fact not held. Furthermore this activity brought the Algerian regime into a dispute from July to October with Ghana over the alleged conflict in dates of the proposed Accra and Algiers meetings.[17] In short, the summer of 1965 saw a welter of somewhat confused diplomatic activity in Africa. Thus, when the Accra meeting was in fact opened in October, it was widely felt that the victory for the OAU consisted in its having been held at all. Diallo Telli, the Secretary-General, said: "Africa each year awaits its miracle and each year the miracle is accomplished."

The threatened boycott by the OCAM states of the OAU meeting was an issue up to the last moment. Eight days before the October 13 opening of the Accra meeting of heads of state, President Nkrumah met Presidents Houphouet-Boigny (Ivory Coast), Diori (Niger), and Yaméogo (Upper Volta) in Bamako, Mali, under the chairmanship of President Modibo Keita of Mali. Here Nkrumah made the extreme concession of agreeing to deport from Ghana all political refugees and their families opposed to the governments of Ivory Coast, Upper Volta, and Niger, such deportation being final. Despite this, on October 18 the latter three states plus Dahomey and Togo met in Ouagadougou, Upper Volta, and decided that because of the "unfriendly policy of the Ghana government towards them," they would not go to Accra, "for reasons of security, certainly, but also of dignity." In addition to those five governments, no representative came from Chad, Gabon, and the Malagasy Republic. In short, the majority of the OCAM countries, all of those that had been at Abidjan in May except Senegal, were absent from Accra. The meeting went on without them. Nonetheless, partly as a concession to the absentees, a resolution against subversion was adopted and the meeting did agree to the proposal of these OCAM states that all future meetings of heads of state be held in Addis Ababa.

Although the over-all impact of the OCAM offensive had

[17] The conflict arose because, in July, Ghana requested that the member-states of the OAU approve a postponement of the opening of the Accra meeting from September 1 to October 15, for material reasons. Algeria felt this brought the Accra meeting too close to the Algiers one, thus threatening attendance at the latter. Algeria wanted a further postponement of the Accra meeting, which was eventually not agreed to.

been contained by the extensiveness of Ghanaian concessions, the campaign had succeeded in tying down the energies of the more militant states during this period and ending the diplomatic pressure against the Leopoldville government. As an OAU issue, the Congo crisis was spectacularly resolved when President Kasavubu destituted Tshombe just before the Accra meeting. Kasavubu thereupon agreed to come to the meeting at Accra after assurances were given that the Congo issue would be dropped from the agenda, to which it had been referred by the Nairobi meeting of the Council of Ministers in February-March. The composition of the new Congolese government, the statements of Kasavubu, and the voting pattern of the Congo (L) delegation at Accra were interpreted widely as an "opening to the left." It presaged the possible return to the 1961 Congo compromise of a Kasavubu-Lumumbist alliance against Tshombe in place of the 1964 formula of a Kasavubu-Tshombe alliance against the Lumumbists. It is ironic that just as Kasavubu deposed Tshombe because he had served his purpose (ending the military rebellion) but now hindered full acceptance into African circles, so after Accra, on November 25, General Mobutu ousted Kasavubu and assumed the presidency, now that Kasavubu had served his immediate purpose (that of getting the Congo issue dropped by the OAU) but was subsequently threatening to endanger the army by removing mercenaries.

If the net result of the internal African struggle regarding the Congo was a defeat at this stage for the revolutionary core, the balance sheet was not so different on the liberation front. It is true that some progress had been made in Portuguese Africa and that the second meeting in Dar es Salaam, October 3–8, of the Conferência dos Organizações Nacionalistas das Colonias Portuguesas (CONCP)—which grouped PAIGC (Guinea), MPLA (Angola), FRELIMO (Mozambique), and CLSTP (São Tomé) and which decided to coordinate the military action in the three territories where there was active rebellion—gave new promise of action. But the Angolan revolution was bogged down because of internal divisions among the nationalists, South African repression was impressive, and the Rhodesian situation showed no signs of yielding to African demands. In this atmosphere of nonaccomplishment, President Nyerere, whose minister was the chairman of the African Liberation Committee, gave an interview to *Jeune Afrique* just before Accra in which he stated: "I have been one of the defenders of [the African Liberation Committee][18] but it is a fact, which I recognize, that this committee has failed in its task. And the Organization of African Unity must restudy the question." [19] The restudy was made, but no essential changes in structure or strategy resulted.

If there was any sense of accomplishment at Accra, it was principally in the field of strengthening the organization itself. When the Secretary-General, Diallo Telli, made his report to the meeting, he noted that "the problems arising from the institutional complexity of the Organization have been uppermost in my mind." He spoke with the knowledge of how much the Secretariat had accomplished in two years in the attempt to rationalize the structure of inter-African institutions and to bring them under the political control of the OAU. One major achievement had been the total incorporation of the CCTA and its associated structure, the Scientific Council for Africa, as the "nucleus" of the Scientific, Technical, and Research Commission of the OAU. The OAU also absorbed the Commission of African Jurists as a specialized commission of the OAU. It succeeded in fusing UNESCO's Conference of African Ministers of Education with the Educational and Cultural Commission of the OAU, and ILO's Conference of African Ministers of Labor with OAU's Economic and Social Commis-

[18] President Nyerere refers to his defense the previous year at Cairo against President Nkrumah's criticisms of the Committee.

[19] This viewpoint was seconded by Diallo Telli, who stated: "It must be recognized that despite the laudable efforts made by the Co-ordinating Committee for the Liberation of Africa, its results are not as positive today as might have been predicted at the time of its establishment in May 1963."

sion. The OAU was seeking to obtain similar close accords with the various other specialized agencies of the U.N.[20] The exact relationship of the OAU to the ECA was less clear, the ECA remaining a separate structure with the same membership as the Economic and Social Commission of the OAU, but deriving its funds from the U.N. The OAU defined its view of the distinction at the first meeting of this Economic and Social Commission when it said that it "is basically a policy-making and executive body, while the role of the Economic Commission for Africa is generally limited to technical and advisory functions." The OAU established an accord with the U.N. on November 15, 1965. This accord provided for reciprocal consultations and the exchange of observers. Finally, in principle, the Secretariat had begun steps to bring various pan-African organizations (trade unions, youth, etc.) under the sponsorship of the OAU.

This remarkable reshaping of the organizational map of Africa could be seen as a solid implantation of the OAU as a permanent entity. It gave rise to some doubts among spokesmen of the revolutionary core. For example, shortly after Accra, *The Spark* wrote an editorial in which it said: "The [OAU] Secretary-General's Report revealed that there has been the proliferation of Commissions and Agencies of the OAU which parallel the United Nations Commissions and Agencies almost directly. This has led to the growth of the attitude that the Organization of African Unity exists to be a regional organization of the United Nations. . . . The Organization of African Unity is not only a Governmental body, with its Secretary-General and its specialized commissions operating like those of the United Nations. The OAU is the organization of the mass of the people, mobilizing them for action in a way that the United Nations never can and is not intended to do. It is necessary to demand an immediate change of emphasis. In Africa the OAU is the highest form of anti-

---

[20] For example, the OAU Secretary-General had urged the World Health Organization to establish a single office for the whole of Africa to facilitate coordination.

imperialist struggle; it draws its power not only from the support of Governments but from the grass roots of the mass organizations of the people." Thus was posed once again the problem of the appropriate strategy for the movement toward African unity, for it was clear that a majority of the member-states of the OAU did not agree that it was an "organization of the mass of the people."

Alongside the report of organizational accomplishment at Accra was the proposal of the Ghana government for structural reform, the proposal to create an Executive Council of the OAU with a chairman elected by the heads of state responsible for implementing decisions of the OAU. Though this was the third successive year in which Nkrumah had spoken of union government, much had matured in the year since the Cairo conference of July 1964. The second Congo crisis had brought division to the OAU but it also brought evolution of thinking. Whereas Cairo saw a debate between Nkrumah and Nyerere, at Accra President Nkrumah could cite for his cause these words of President Nyerere: "For Africa the lesson of our East African experience is that although economic cooperation can go a long way without political integration, there comes a point when movement must be either forward or backward—forward into political decision or backward into reduced economic cooperation." Although not all members were yet convinced, the key vote on Ethiopia's motion to set up a seven-nation committee to study the proposal received a surprisingly high vote, albeit on a limited motion. Eighteen members voted for it and only five against.[21] Although the motion failed for want of a two-thirds majority,[22] it could no longer be said that the proposal for union government was

[21] The eighteen in favor were Algeria, Burundi, Congo (B), Congo (L), Ethiopia, Ghana, Guinea, Kenya, Libya, Malawi, Mali, Mauritania, Sierra Leone, Sudan, Tanzania, Uganda, U.A.R., Zambia. The five against were: Cameroon, Central African Republic, Liberia, Nigeria, Senegal.

[22] The heads of state also did not adopt the proposal of the Council of Ministers for the creation of an African peace force, a proposal that had been first adopted by the Defense Commission in February but rejected at the earlier Council of Ministers meeting in Nairobi in February-March.

not getting a serious hearing in Africa. The issue was referred to the next session of the heads of state.

The balance sheet of the Accra meeting and the OAU as a whole at this point is uneven. President Ould Daddah commented on the meeting with this formula: "Addis Ababa was the birth, Cairo the organization, and Accra the test. But in the end a salutary test, and one from which the OAU emerges reinforced." President Boumediene of Algeria was less poetic. Asked to judge the situation and the future of OAU after Accra, he said: "There has been since [Addis Ababa] a certain decline of African solidarity. . . . We must avoid at any price the danger of this trade union [of heads of state], which would hold back the necessary evolution of our peoples." His journal, *Révolution Africaine*, called Accra an "undoubted setback" for African unity. S. G. Ikoku, writing in *L'Etincelle* on January 20, 1966, was even stronger:

> We must be honest with ourselves. The OAU as it is presently constituted will never allow us to achieve African political union. And because it cannot evolve in this direction, the OAU will tend to degenerate into an organism protecting the existing regimes in various African countries. This explains why imperialism, which opposes the idea of an African political union will not go so far as to break up the OAU. The OAU is rapidly becoming a suitable agency to arrest the revolutionary *élan* of Africa.

The Rhodesian issue, more than any other, was the one that would test the efficacy of the compromise of Addis Ababa. It was understandable that the OAU's role was indecisive during the second Congo crisis, since the Congo issue had long been the one that most deeply split independent African states, in large part as a consequence of the enormous role non-African states played in Congolese affairs. But if the revolutionary core was willing to accept the OAU with all its inherent restraints on its activities, it was in order to facilitate the liberation of southern Africa. Rhodesia was the first great issue and one on which all African states and parties agreed as to the objective and indeed even its urgency. The white government of Southern Rhodesia had delayed the unilateral declaration of independence until after the Accra meeting. Hence the resolution of the Accra meeting continued to emphasize Britain's "sole responsibility for the present situation," and appointed a committee composed of Kenya, Nigeria, Tanzania, U.A.R., and Zambia "to ensure the effective implementation of the resolution."

Rhodesia proclaimed its independence unilaterally on November 11, 1965. The British government responded by a series of measures which amounted to an economic boycott. An extraordinary meeting of the OAU's Council of Ministers was held in Addis Ababa on December 3–5, 1965. It called on its five-nation committee "to invite military advisors from member states in order to study and plan the use of force to assist the people of Zimbabwe." It further resolved "that if the United Kingdom does not crush the rebellion and restore law and order, and thereby prepare the way for majority rule in Southern Rhodesia by December 15, 1965, the Member States of the OAU shall sever diplomatic relations on that date with the United Kingdom." The rebellion was not crushed by December 15 and only ten of thirty-eight members of the OAU carried out the resolution. Those who broke relations were Algeria, Congo (B), Ghana, Guinea, Mali, Mauritania, Sudan, Tanzania, and the U.A.R.[23] The result was less than brilliant and somewhat discouraging to the revolutionary core. The comment of President Sékou Touré of Guinea was: "The Rhodesian affair has created a cleavage between free and truly sovereign Africa and Africa in the service of foreign interests." President Nyerere of Tanzania called the failure of the majority of the states to carry out the resolution a "death blow" to the OAU.

The Rhodesia fiasco of 1965 was in no sense, nonetheless, a failure to be ascribed to the OAU. To demand success in this

[23] Somalia, which associated itself with this gesture, had already broken diplomatic relations with the United Kingdom over a different issue.

matter was to demand of that frail organization a strength it could not yet have achieved. The failure indicated rather the unworkability of the compromise of Addis Ababa. The revolutionary core had not gotten its part of the bargain. The story went on from there, but it necessarily would become a somewhat different story with a somewhat new cast of characters. The ouster of Nkrumah on February 24, 1966, marked the end of this first phase of the political struggle. The movement toward African unity, as it developed from 1957 to 1965, succeeded in clarifying the issues at stake, not least of all to itself. It accomplished much, but the weapons at its command were limited.

Revolutions are not casual affairs, but the outcome of hard struggle, great awareness, and serious organization. African independent states were one possible (perhaps not the best) instrument of such a social movement. In any case, this period revealed sharp differences among African states, dramatically evident in the two Congo crises and the Rhodesian crisis. These differences were not differences over the stated common objective of unity. They were differences over the meaning of unity, its rationale, and its import. These differences were not formal but ideological.

The Problems
of a Movement

ᚹᚹᚹᚹᚹᚹᚹᚹ

:VII:

REGIONAL UNITY

AND AFRICAN UNITY

The geographical limits of a unity movement are historically accidental and arbitrary in the sense that they do not derive inevitably from the stated objectives of the movement. We have seen already that pan-Africanism, originally an idea which spoke for the unity of black men, became transmuted into African unity, which speaks in terms of continental unity. The basic economic and political arguments for unity remain the same. If some of the cultural justifications seem stronger for black African unity, there are arguments drawn from colonial history or contemporary geopolitics that argue for continental unity. In a sense, these justifications are all open to cogent objections. However, the most important thing for the analyst to note is simply what limits are in fact being spoken of in terms of unity.

In Africa, much of the sentiment for unity has in the past focused more on smaller regions than on the whole of Africa. North Africa, West Africa, East Africa have all been suggested as the areas to unite, or to unite first. And such regional unity has often been spoken of as African unity, a terminological confusion that is a true reflection of the fluidity of the concept in the minds of its advocates. Even Nkrumah, later considered one of the foremost advocates of *all*-African unity, at one time showed the same uncertainty. He wrote in 1962: "Twenty years ago my ideas on African unity, important as I considered them even at that time, were limited to West African unity. Today . . . I see the wider horizon of the immense possibilities open to Africans—the only guarantee, in fact, for survival—in a total continental political union of Africa."[1]

However, as the political struggle for unity developed, the concept of regional unity became increasingly distinct from that of continental unity and there came to be a major debate about the relation between the two—between those who saw regional unity as a desirable and even necessary steppingstone and those who saw it as a distraction from, even an obstacle to, African unity. That is, there were those who thought the two goals were complementary and those who thought they were mutually exclusive.

This argument derived from the difference between those who believed in unity as alliance and those who believed in unity as movement. But for those who saw unity as an alliance, because of the very nature of the concept, there was no firm or continued commitment to one set of geographical limits against another. It was a matter of the tactics of the day. In any case, the wisdom of alliance was never to commit oneself beyond recall. Thus, a double commitment, to regional and to African unity (or in the case of Arab Africa, to Arab and to African unity as well as perhaps to a regional unity), was not only feasible; it was desirable. It was less that the two unities were complementary than that the issue of choice could be

---

[1] Habib Niang, a theorist of Nkrumahism, expounding it in 1965, defended this shift in focus on the basis of the concept of optimality. "When in 1947 Kwame Nkrumah proposed to M. Houphouet-Boigny the creation of one common political party for all the West African colonies, French and English, to struggle for the liberation of this region, he considered West Africa as an optimal zone. Today, the exigencies of technology and the national liberation struggle give the optimal zone a continental dimension."

temporarily avoided. Such an attitude was recurrent through-out the political struggle for unity in Africa.

But there was an argument as well within the camp of those who were committed to unity as movement. If unity was an objective because of its revolutionary content, then it required a long-term commitment, because it would take time to create the ideological adherence of a large enough number of people to realize the goals. Hence, while the choice might be somewhat arbitrary as to which geographic limits will best serve as the framework for the revolutionary change envisaged, the choice should be nonetheless binding, once made, since it could not be altered with ease lest the ardor of the supporters be dissipated.

In the late colonial era, it was understandable that African nationalist movements thought of unity in terms of the colonial context. That is to say, in a struggle for independence from a specific colonial power, the relevant unity was the unity of those fighting the same immediate battle. Thus it meant the unity of those under the same colonial power and even more narrowly the unity of those within a single colonial region. The unity, however loose, of nationalist movements reflected, therefore, colonial administrative groupings: French North Africa, French West Africa, and French Equatorial Africa (or sometimes the latter two combined as French black Africa); British West Africa, the High Commission Territories, British East Africa, and British Central Africa (or sometimes the latter two combined as East and Central Africa); Portuguese Africa. For each of these cases there have been coordinating structures of nationalist parties and sometimes of other groups (trade unions, youth, students, women).

Unity of action was a natural response to the immediate political needs of the separate movements. As such, it was not looked upon too happily by the colonial powers or the white settlers against whom it was directed. There was, however, some ambivalence in the attitudes of the colonial powers (and of the white settlers). The regions in question were in most instances contiguous units which had been grouped together by the colonial power for rational economic and administrative reasons. There were advantages to maintaining these regions, not only in the colonial present but—especially for the British who were willing to plan ahead—in the postcolonial future.

Thus, from the beginning, there has been ambiguity about whose interests were served by regional unity, and this ambiguity has been reflected in the instability of the nationalist movements' position on the issue of regional unity. There have in fact been only three serious *movements* toward regional unity and each is now defunct as a movement. The three were centered in French North Africa, French West Africa, and British East Africa. It would perhaps be well to consider each in turn to see if we can discern the reasons for the rise and fall of these regional movements.

Of the three, French North Africa is perhaps relatively the most integrated region. The cultural similarities of these contiguous countries—which go far back into their history and which were accentuated by a period of common French colonial rules (and French settlement) as well as by their collective differences from Europe, from black Africa and even from the Arab Middle East—mark them as a unit even today. They have had a collective name, the Arab Maghreb, and many of their modern elites have been closely linked together since at least 1927, the year that saw the founding in France of the Association des Etudiants Musulmans d'Afrique du Nord.

As their political struggles developed in the period after World War II, the various organizations of Algeria, Morocco, and Tunisia—the parties, the trade unions, the students—created formal links with one another. They tended to coordinate their policy on the international front, as indicated by the creation in Cairo in 1948 of the Comité de Libération du Maghreb Arabe, or later by the common decision of the trade unions to adhere to the ICFTU.

But North African unity became most serious as a theme

not when all three countries were colonies nor when all three were independent, but precisely during the in-between period. In March 1956 both Morocco and Tunisia gained full independence from France. Shortly thereafter a meeting between Bourguiba of Tunisia, Mohammed V of Morocco, and the leaders of the Algerian FLN was planned. It was to be held in Tunis on October 22 but was made impossible by the kidnapping by the French of Ben Bella and the other Algerian leaders en route to the meeting. Despite this, talk of unity grew until it reached a climax at a meeting on April 27–30, 1958, at Tangiers, of representatives of the three nationalist parties—FLN (Algeria), Istiqlal (Morocco), and Néo-Destour (Tunisia). The resolution of this conference insisted that North African unity required first the independence of Algeria, and it decided that, as a major next move, the FLN should create a provisional government after consultation with the Tunisian and Moroccan governments. This was the crux of the meeting —the total commitment of Morocco and Tunisia, as independent states, to fight for Algeria's independence.

The six-man permanent secretariat that was established did in fact meet three times that same year, and on September 19 the Gouvernement Provisoire de la République Algérienne (GPRA) was officially announced. But the proposed interstate Consultative Assembly never was convened. From then on, the momentum seemed broken. What had happened? For one thing, in December 1958 the All-African Peoples' Conference met, and the Algerians in particular decided to place great stress on an African orientation, hoping thereby to create diversionary fronts for their own struggle with France. For another, the Moroccan Istiqlal split in two and it was impossible to maintain a simple alliance of the three states at the level of political parties. And also De Gaulle had just returned to power and the process of slow preparation for decolonization began. The movement for Maghreb unity as symbolized by the Tangier meeting had obtained its major immediate goal— aid to the liberation of Algeria—and seemed thereupon to be devoid of any further revolutionary content. There would be

of course in the future, after the independence of Algeria, new
steps toward economic coordination, but this was unity as
alliance, not as movement.[2] Insofar as North African revolutionaries wanted to transform world society, they needed a
larger arena in which to operate than the Maghreb alone.
This arena came increasingly to be the African continent.

In French black Africa, unity of action was assumed from
1946 on by the creation in Bamako, Mali, of the Rassemblement Démocratique Africain (RDA), which grouped at its
height political parties from twelve territories.[3] But unity as
a postindependence concept became an issue only when the
French government in 1956 adopted the so-called *loi cadre*
which devolved political authority on the separate territories
of French black Africa, and not on the interterritorial structures of the two federations: French West Africa and French
Equatorial Africa. It was this move which Senghor denounced
as "balkanization." And in the period 1956–1958, unity became
the central political issue of French black Africa, meaning the
unity of each of the two federations, particularly the federation
of French West Africa.

It was at the Third Interterritorial Congress of the RDA
at Bamako, on September 2–5, 1957, that the political struggle
was sharpest. At this meeting, called the "Congress of Black
Africa," attended not only by the delegates of the RDA parties
but by observers from the interterritorial structures of trade-
union, youth, and student groups as well as of other smaller interterritorial parties, the great majority stood for giving power
to the federal governments. The spokesman for this point of
view was Sékou Touré of Guinea. The leader of the minority

[2] When the Maghreb Ministers of Economic Affairs met in November
1964 it was under the auspices of a technical body, the U.N. Economic
Commission for Africa.
[3] Only Mauritania and Togo of the fourteen French black African territories never had a section of the RDA. Even those groups not adhering
to the RDA felt the need for interterritorial coordination. This was most
notably so in the creation of the Indépendants d'Outre-Mer, later transmuted successively into the Convention Africaine and the Parti du
Regroupement Africain, and also the creation of the Mouvement Socialiste
Africain.

against it was Félix Houphouet-Boigny, President of the RDA. The French saw in the pressure for unity a pressure for independence which they were not yet prepared to concede. In the end the Congress maintained unanimity by agreeing to an ambiguous formula calling for the "democratization of the federal executives." When this "democratization" was to occur was unspecified. In fact, Houphouet-Boigny's point of view later prevailed. The unity of the party was temporarily preserved by sacrificing the key immediate demand of the movement for unity. And so the momentum of this movement was broken.

When in fact French Africa voted in the Referendum of September 28, 1958, on the issue of the maintenance of the French Community, only Guinea, the leader in the move for unity and independence, voted "no" and thus went forward to separate independence. From then on, Guinea was drawn into a larger movement for African unity, continental in scope rather than limited to French West Africa. And ex-French West Africa as an entity, despite the common history and schooling of the elites, despite the common struggle against colonial rule, could no longer command the allegiance of any revolutionary group.

East Africa's movement for unity was the shortest, most intense, and most unexpected of the three. It was unexpected because, despite once again the common background and schooling of the modern elites and the common anticolonial struggle, the drive for East African unity had been initially identified with a move of white settlers, particularly in Kenya, to assert their dominance in the region.

Yet when, as a result of Mau Mau, the British government showed signs (at the 1960 Lancaster House Conference) that it now believed that Kenya might eventually become an independent state based on majority rule, East African nationalists began to consider seriously the idea of federation. It became respectable as an idea when Julius Nyerere in June 1960 offered to delay Tanganyika's independence so that the three East African territories could go forward together to independence and federation. As in North and West Africa, the desire for federation led to increased coordination between political parties (in PAFMECA) and trade unions. As in North Africa, the movement reached its climax at a point when two of the countries were independent and the third was not. The third was Kenya, which was, like Algeria in North Africa, the most difficult to decolonize because it had the greatest concentration of white settlers.

On June 5, 1963, Nyerere (of Tanganyika), Obote (of Uganda), and Kenyatta (of Kenya) met in Nairobi, agreed to form a federal government of East Africa, and said quite baldly: "The three Governments having agreed to establish a federation this year expect the British Government to grant Kenya independence immediately." The declaration had the desired result of inducing the British to decide on a clear and early date for Kenya's independence. On July 2 the British government announced that Kenya would obtain its independence on December 12 and added that the British government fully supported initiatives toward federation. The expectation was that the federation would be created before the end of the same year.

However, the federation never came into being. By late August 1963 negotiations between the three states broke down over distribution of powers and rewards in the prospective structure. By 1964 the idea had been effectively abandoned by its strongest advocate, Tanganyika, which turned its attention to domestic problems. Insofar as it was concerned with external affairs at this point, it became involved in *all*-African engagements. In August 1964 President Kenyatta of Kenya said in a speech that the independence of his country had been obtained by its "ingenuity" [4] in talking about federation.

The three movements for regional unity were similar in several respects. They all represented militant demands in the immediate political context. They all led to the rise of

[4] The speech was in Swahili. The first translation used the word "trick," but the Kenya government then corrected the translation to read "ingenuity." Nyerere soon thereafter asserted his full conviction of the sincerity of the 1963 declaration.

close coordination not only between political parties but between other popular organizations in the region. They all reached their climax just before total independence, and served as effective rallying points of pressure on the colonial power. They all collapsed quite quickly thereafter as movements. The revolutionary core then transferred its energies to a wider African scene. The advocates of unity as alliance became then the champions of regional economic cooperation as a "practical" measure and as a defense against the revolutionary core.[5] Thus, insofar as the movement toward unity sought the objective of independence, the regional context was not only possible; it was probably the most effective in terms of mobilizing pressure against the colonial power. But insofar as the movement toward unity turned to longer-term revolutionary ambitions—that of transforming the relationship of its countries and peoples to the rest of the world through economic development and international power—then the regional units were too small to be meaningful, whereas an all-African focus seemed to be worth the investment of energy.

The most significant regional political grouping on the African continent in the recent past has, however, not been the consequence of a movement toward unity but the result of desire to block it—because the movement toward unity seemed to have too revolutionary implications. It is the grouping of French-speaking Africa in its successive forms as the UAM and as OCAM.

To understand the origins of this grouping, we must refer back to the movement for French West African unity. The Referendum of September 28, 1958, had ended that chapter in African history. Houphouet-Boigny, of the Ivory Coast RDA, who had led the opposition to this movement, understood his victory. Sékou Touré, of the Guinea RDA, who led the struggle for this movement appreciated that such regional unity

[5] The case of the Sudan and the movement for unity with Egypt shows some parallels to these other three cases. The movement also reached a climax just before independence, in 1955, and served as pressure on the British. It too was abandoned after independence although the "pro-union" party had formed the government.

was no longer feasible. He transferred his energies to the larger African scene, and on November 23 signed with Nkrumah the agreement to establish the Ghana-Guinea Union, seen, let us recall, as the nucleus of a United States of Africa.

There was, however, a middle group in the RDA that had sided with Sékou Touré at the Third RDA Congress at Bamako in 1957 but had voted "yes" in the Referendum in 1958. The leadership of the middle group was under Modibo Keita and the Soudan[6] RDA. This group was committed to one last try at achieving French West African unity. This led to the proposal to establish the Federation of Mali, which was endorsed on January 17, 1959, by representatives of the governments of Senegal, Soudan, Upper Volta, and Dahomey. In fact this was a very heterogeneous grouping and did not last long. The leaders of Upper Volta and Dahomey were far from committed to the radical implications of the Federation, and under pressure from the Ivory Coast decided soon thereafter not to ratify the accord. The government of Senegal headed by President Senghor was committed to unity not as a revolutionary movement,[7] but because the Senegalese economy was structured to service the larger area that was French West Africa and it feared the economic implications of separation. Only the Soudan leadership saw federation as a mechanism of transforming society, not only their own but Senegal's as well, which latter pretension was to be the difficulty.

What indeed happened is that after Upper Volta and Dahomey withdrew from the picture, Senegal and Soudan decided to go ahead anyway with a bipartite federation. The Federation of Mali did in fact take the lead in negotiating "international sovereignty" from France in 1960, thereby forcing the Ivory Coast and all the other French African territories to do the same. In this sense, the Federation was the fulfillment of the movement for regional unity, performing its ap-

[6] The territory then called the Soudan is now called the Republic of Mali, and is not to be confused with the Republic of the Sudan, formerly the Anglo-Egyptian Sudan.

[7] This was essentially the reason why the Senegalese party headed by Senghor had never been in the interterritorial RDA.

pointed task. The Senegalese withdrew two months after independence, essentially because they feared Soudanese "subversion" of their system. The Soudanese were then left with nothing but the shell and renamed their country the Republic of Mali as a souvenir to lost battles well fought.

The Federation of Mali had one other consequence besides hastening the pace of independence. On May 29, 1959, in order to help compensate Upper Volta and Dahomey for the economic gains they forwent in renouncing the Federation of Mali, the Ivory Coast formed with them and Niger the Conseil de l'Entente, a loose confederal structure, an alliance which enshrined opposition to political union, and which despite various difficulties has continued to survive as the nucleus of the structured opposition to political union in Africa.

The picture in French Equatorial Africa served as a footnote to that in French West Africa. At the Bamako RDA Congress in 1957 the major ally of Houphouet-Boigny was Léon Mba of the Gabon RDA. Gabon had the same relationship to French Equatorial Africa that the Ivory Coast had to French West Africa. They were both wealthy territories taxed for the benefit of the others but not receiving the compensating advantage of having the capital of the federation located in their territory. Just before the independence in mid-1960, the three other territories in French Equatorial Africa—Central African Republic, Chad, and Congo (B)—decided on May 14–17 to form a Union of Central African Republics which, like the then still extant Federation of Mali, would go forward to independence as a federated state. But very slight pressure from the Ivory Coast on Chad and Congo (B) sufficed to end the Union even before it was launched.

Thus by September 1960 almost all the former states of French black Africa had become separate independent states[8] and were admitted to the United Nations. It was at this point that the split between Kasavubu and Lumumba occurred in

[8] The exceptions were Mauritania, which, however, received independence on November 28, 1960, and French Somaliland, Reunion Island, and the Comoro Islands.

the Congo. We have already discussed how this situation (as well as the Algerian issue at the U.N.) forced the various African states to make a public choice. In this situation, given the history of developments in French black Africa which we have described, it was natural that President Houphouet-Boigny took the lead in convening the Abidjan conference in October, which led to the Brazzaville meeting of December and the establishment of the UAM.[9]

The UAM was in spirit the extension of the Conseil de l'Entente. The Conseil de l'Entente had been established in counterpoise to the movement for West African unity as symbolized by the Federation of Mali, as an alliance which could contain a revolutionary movement. The UAM in its turn was established—in counterpoise to the movement for African unity, which would be symbolized by the UAS and the Casablanca Group—as an alliance which could contain a revolutionary movement. The UAM at no point set itself the objective, however long-term, of political union. It was rather a diplomatic alliance and a vehicle for some economic cooperation. Thus, the UAM set up a number of specialized mechanisms: the Organisation Africaine et Malgache de Coopération Economique,[10] the Union Africaine et Malgache de Défense, the Union Africaine et Malgache de Postes et Télégraphes, and one related commercial enterprise, Air Afrique.[11]

We have already noted the role the UAM played in the period 1960–1963 up to the formation of the OAU. Quite apart from the ideological differences with the Casablanca powers,

[9] Even President Senghor, on September 21, asked Houphouet-Boigny to take the lead in convening a round table, though only of the independent states of former French West Africa. Senghor said: "Naturally, it could no longer be a question of a 'federation.' It would be a matter of a simple association, like that of the Conseil de l'Entente." Senghor thus conceded that Houphouet-Boigny had been right in his earlier opposition to the Federation of Mali.

[10] The OAMCE in its turn established two subordinate structures: the Union Africaine et Malgache de Banques pour le Developpement and the Office Africain et Malgache de la Propriété Industrielle.

[11] The Malagasy Republic did not participate in this enterprise, because sheer distance made it economically unfeasible.

it often served as an interest group at the U.N. demanding more equitable distribution of committee assignments or high Secretariat appointments between French-speaking and English-speaking Africa. During this period, there was an attempt by some of the young intellectuals who manned the bureaucracies of the UAM to push it beyond its limited self-contained existence and to bring it somewhat more in line with the movement for African unity. This was notably the case of its Secretary-General from November 1961 to March 1963, Albert Tevoedjré.[12] One effort was in the direction of including former Belgian Africa within the UAM. While for some this represented a strengthening of the UAM against revolutionary forces in Africa, for others, in the words of Tevoedjré, it was seen as "a great step toward an Africanization of the organization, a means of establishing a certain psychological distance vis-à-vis Paris . . ." A second effort was made in mid-1962, when the Secretariat tried to induce the UAM to undertake systematic action to aid liberation movements, somewhat along the lines which the OAU would undertake the following year. But this attempt was unsuccessful. The UAM heads of state showed great indecision, which was not surprising given their role in the Congo. At the very same meeting, the Secretariat also sought to encourage diplomatic links between the UAM states and the Communist states. The results were similarly negative.

The UAM was faced with a crisis of meaning following the creation of the OAU. We have discussed how "regionalism," meaning in fact the UAM, became an issue at the OAU's first Council of Ministers Meeting in Dakar in August 1963 and how OAU pressures mounted until the UAM agreed to dissolve itself in March 1964. It is important to see this process of dissolution from within the UAM. There had long been a politico-economic rivalry between the Ivory Coast and Sene-

[12] Tevoedjré was actually the second of four secretary-generals of the UAM. The other three, for various reasons, each held the post only briefly.

gal in French-speaking Africa despite the fact that their views on the larger African scene were not very different. When the Federation of Mali foundered, the Senegalese had no choice but to enter the UAM under Houphouet-Boigny's leadership and to accept the latter's formula of a very loose confederation. The rivalry remained, nonetheless.

The UAM was dissolved in March 1964, because by then neither the Ivory Coast nor Senegal desired to maintain it. The Ivory Coast simply wished to dissolve the UAM. In the quiet period following the creation of the OAU, the Ivory Coast had been lulled back into the isolationist stance (within Africa) that was the logical counterpart of its policy of separate economic development. The Ivory Coast fell back on the Conseil de l'Entente—and a reduced one at that, since Dahomey had virtually withdrawn from it at this point, following its revolution in October 1963. Senegal, on the other hand, was delighted to dissolve the UAM as a political structure but wished to replace it with a purely economic structure. This would allow Senegal to pursue its search for economic space without, however, the political encumbrance of the UAM. In that case, Senegal would be able to reinforce economic links with Mauritania, Guinea, and Mali (the latter two non-members of the UAM) in a regional economic structure for the development of the Senegal River. Thus Senegal was able to prevail upon the meeting to create as a successor structure the Union Africaine et Malgache de Coopération Economique (UAMCE), which was in fact the UAM's economic structures refurbished with the communications structure incorporated into it.[18] The strength of Senegal had increased because the various *coups d'état* within French-speaking Africa at this time had brought to power persons ready to go along with this new formula for diverse reasons. All that the Ivory Coast could do was to refuse to join UAMCE by not attending the May 26, 1964, meeting in Nouakchott, Mauritania,

[18] Thus, the defense structure disappeared altogether, but Air Afrique, an independent enterprise, was unaffected.

which was scheduled to adopt the charter.[14] As a result, the UAMCE was stillborn.

Nonetheless the UAM spirit had not disappeared. It had only become quiescent as part of the compromise of Addis Ababa. When the Congo had its second great crisis in 1964, the UAM was revived as a defense mechanism against revolutionary trends on the continent. Thus at Nouakchott in February 1965 the Organisation Commune Africaine et Malgache (OCAM) was born, inheriting the secretariat and structure of UAMCE but becoming a political organization once again. The Ivory Coast had emerged from its isolation, and Houphouet-Boigny once again asserted his *de facto* leadership of UAM/OCAM.[15] He consequently obtained the admission of Congo (L) to OCAM and got the hard core of OCAM to boycott the Accra meeting. This was not, however, without its weakening effect on the scope of OCAM. Mauritania withdrew from OCAM; and Senegal, Cameroon, Central African Republic, and Congo (B) attended Accra (as did Rwanda and Congo [L]).[16]

Thus UAM/OCAM could in no sense be considered a regional unity movement parallel to and rivaling an African unity movement, in the way that the movements for North African, French West African, and East African unity would be considered at certain stages of their development. UAM/OCAM has been a defensive political organization on the

[14] The Ivory Coast was joined in this refusal by her two close allies in the Conseil de l'Entente, Upper Volta and Niger, as well as by the Central African Republic.

[15] He also at this time drew Dahomey back into the Conseil de l'Entente and Togo into its orbit. The idea of "double nationality" first came under extensive discussion at this point.

[16] Soon after the Accra meeting—in fact, on November 12–13—the heads of state of Guinea, Mali, Mauritania, and Senegal held a meeting of their interstate economic structure. They decided to invite all the states of West Africa to form an economic grouping. This would, of course, have cut straight across the lines of OCAM. They emphasized this would be a grouping, not a group, the difference being that a grouping is a part of a whole, for in the words of President Ould Daddah, "the OAU comes before all else."

African continent designed to contain the movement for African unity and to undermine its revolutionary potential. Insofar as the OAU achieved the same end, which it seemed to the leaders of UAM to be doing for a while, the UAM was held in abeyance. When the OAU seemed, through the Congo Conciliation Commission and the activities of the Secretariat, to be moving in another direction, the UAM was revived (in the form of OCAM).

In effect, the three real movements for regional unity in Africa have not achieved political union or even survived as an effective political alliance, whereas the one regional grouping that has more or less continued to thrive as a political alliance, UAM/OCAM, was not in fact a movement for regional unity, wishing neither the form of political union nor the content of revolutionary transformation. What conclusions may we draw from this? It is often inferred that if regional unity movements seem to have little prospect in Africa today, the case against all-African political union is *a fortiori* obvious. Is this a valid inference?

There are some considerations that throw doubt on this simple equation. We must start by analyzing the objectives of these movements carefully. The movements for regional unity, like the movement for all-African unity, had two objectives, not one, and the two were often viewed in time sequence. These objectives were first liberation and secondly political unity which would make revolutionary transformation possible. But we have seen how the three regional unity movements did in fact contribute to liberation. It is true, of course, that they thereupon seemingly gave up on the second objective: political unity that would make revolutionary transformation possible. But in fact, we also saw that the revolutionary core of these three movements did not renounce the goal of larger unity but merely transferred it to a larger African scene. The reason seems obvious. They were faced with the enormous usual difficulties of creating new political unions. These are typically the fears of those in authority in the constituent units of loss of internal political power and the fears of the constituent units of loss of relative economic advantage. These difficulties can be overcome only by a movement motivated by a reasonable faith that the consequent union can in fact make a significant politico-economic difference. But in reality the relative smallness of the new "larger units" in question led rationally to a realization of the weak odds against a substantial gain. Hence, these movements simply expanded the boundary lines of their objectives.

It may then be demurred that a sufficiently large unit as the objective of a unity movement need not necessarily be the continent of Africa. It could be black Africa alone, or Africa plus the Middle East, or some other unit. This is true, to be sure, and it is in this sense "accidental" that in recent years (essentially since 1958) the people involved have concentrated their efforts on the unit which is the continent of Africa.

But this having been done, the continent of Africa rapidly acquired a social reality to which it is not too apposite to argue its historical newness. For history is a matter of contemporary vision and African politicians are refocusing the glasses with which their citizens see this history. Two examples from the border region between black Africa and Northern (or Arab) Africa will illustrate this well.

President Senghor was, as we know, one of the original spokesmen for the concept of negritude, of Negro-African culture. Yet when the Federation of Mali was a serious proposition, and it was hoped to include largely Arab Mauritania within it, Senghor began to talk of Negro-*Berber* culture. He wrote that: "The Berbers, who, in the Mesolithic era, invaded the [African] continent, intermarried with [the blacks]. This explains why the Berber and Egyptian languages are derived from both Semitic and Negro-African roots, as is the civilization of the men who spoke them." With this view of history, Senghor radically reduced the cultural separation of black and northern Africa.

A similar development has taken place in the Sudan, a country whose north is Arab but whose south is Nilotic in ethnic tradition. There P. E. H. Hair, an English historian, notes the revival of interest in the pre-Islamic Nubian past, "not least, perhaps, because the thousand years of Christian Nubia can be represented as an earlier installment of the role of the Sudan as a cultural bridge between the Middle East and Tropical Africa; and thus the Sudan tied in with the *pre-colonial* history of the countries to the south and west with whom the Sudan increasingly shares Pan-African aspirations." [17]

The only movement toward unity today in Africa is the movement toward continental unity. To be sure, those who envisage unity as alliance have continued to press forward with various kinds of regional economic cooperation, especially since such cooperation enjoys wide international support and encouragement. But the revolutionary core has remained largely indifferent to the successes and failures of these regional economic efforts. This results from the fact that the two groups have a different image of the economic, and hence social and political, consequences of such cooperation. It is to this subject, the economics of unity, that we must now turn.

[17] Hair adds: "Though politically generated, this view is not without much historical justification. . . ."

:VIII:

THE POLITICAL

IMPLICATIONS

OF ECONOMIC ANALYSIS

One of the basic justifications of African unity, no matter who speaks of it, is economic. It is argued that a larger unity means increased economic productivity and increased net income for the community. There is almost no one who is willing to say that these goals are not achievable, and very many who will argue that unity is a necessary step toward such an achievement. But within this very broad framework, the analyses of how in fact the goals may be achieved differ widely, and hence the political conclusions that derive from these analyses are not at all the same.

The basic economic situation of Africa is that today African economies are a mixture of subsistence farming and the production of certain raw-material products (coffee, cocoa, cotton, minerals) for export, principally to Western Europe and the United States, whence the Africans in turn import most of their manufactured goods. The state of the world economy is such that the primary products are sold at relatively low rates (in terms of reward for labor-power) and the manufactured goods are bought at relatively high rates, which is far less favorable for primary producers than the pattern of internal trade that has evolved in most industrialized countries. Furthermore, most African countries have essentially single-product export economies, which, given the tendency of the world market to fluctuate beyond the control of the producer countries, makes these economies (and the budgets of their governments) very vulnerable to sudden crises. Moreover, this classic pattern of trade, the colonial pact, has not disappeared with the independence of former colonial states. On the contrary, since the Second World War, the so-called gap between the industrialized and nonindustrialized countries has in fact grown. That is, given amounts of primary products have bought fewer manufactured goods.

The worsening terms of trade have not, however, meant that the absolute standards of living or that the national revenue has diminished. This is true in part because there has been a steady expansion of African production, which has found a market as a result of the expanding market in industrialized countries, and in part because the industrialized nations have transferred some income to the other nations in the form of grants, loans, subsidies, or free skilled manpower. However, the total of such income transfer or global aid since the Second World War is estimated to be approximately no more than the equivalent of income lost because of the worsening terms of trade. And the annual transfer, as a percentage of world revenue, has been diminishing since 1960. Hence, while African countries have been developing their infrastructures and their manpower potential, this development has been slow by comparison with the continued economic development of the already industrialized nations.

The problem as stated here is virtually universally recognized. The question is what to do about it. And the answer to that question is in large part a function of the analysis of what caused this growing gap in the world economy. Basically, and crudely, there are two schools of thought.

One school argues that economic development is the consequence of effort, initiative, and intelligence, and that the gap is a result of disproportionate input of these factors. The solution then, in principle, is clear. Obviously, such an analysis is congenial to persons favored by the present situation.

The other school argues that the gap is the consequence of the fact that groups which achieved an initial economic advantage for one reason or another have both the will and the power to perpetuate and expand this advantage. The solution then is somehow to break this power (and perhaps this will), an effect which can only be the consequence of action by those who are disadvantaged. Obviously, this analysis in turn is congenial to those who are not favored by the present situation.

While no doubt the nuances that each school of thought is capable of producing are manifold and impressively varied, the political actions of most governments and groups are clearly grounded in one analysis or the other.

The Euro-American viewpoint on economic development has not only determined Euro-American action in Africa, which is to be expected, but has also controlled the actions of international organizations such as the U.N. and especially the World Bank. There are, however, not one but three Euro-American views—what we might call the "official" view, the isolationist view, and the view of the left.

The official view, whatever the variations among the different Western powers, argues that African economies are in need of some immediate economic assistance, in various forms. The only serious possible source of such aid is the West, thus largely dismissing the potential role of the Soviet Union (and *a fortiori* China) and rejecting as economic folly the concept that Africa can dispense with such aid and still develop. Furthermore, the official view argues that the West has a moral obligation to give this aid. These moral obligations are in part owed to Africans, presumably as a legacy of colonial rule, and in part owed to the Western world itself, presumably to prevent the world-wide political consequences of African economic stagnation.

There have been two kinds of responses to this official view. One is the isolationist view, which argues that economic aid is largely wasted in the sense that it does not fulfill either of its ostensible objectives—economic development and political friendliness of Africa (and other nonindustrialized nations)—and that the moral obligations are overstated or misstated or can best be fulfilled by increased trade. The other response, similar in some ways, is that of the European left (a response which has been shared by Soviet analysts and by some African analysts). This is the view that economic aid in its present form does not fulfill the objective of economic development and was not in fact designed to do so. Rather it is a means of avoiding economic crisis in the West and of continuing to exploit African economies; in short, it is neo-colonialism. The true solution is through industrialization and trade diversification, both of which require planning and internal sacrifice.

One of the most sophisticated attempts to answer these two sets of criticisms of the official view was the Jeanneney Report, a report to the French government requested and received in 1963. Saying that the accusation of neo-colonialism "cannot be neglected," it stated that the complaint is over three asserted survivals of the colonial era: that of the colonial pact, of the dominating role of colonial companies, and of the continuation of colonial administration in the form of technical assistance. The report responded to these charges by talking of "ineluctable realities" and then asked what, given these, "can be done so that the most advanced peoples can give aid to the others without incurring the reproach of dominating them politically under the façade of independence or of exploiting them economically under the cover of good intentions"? The report found four principles of action to answer this need: "a state of mind," "avoiding excessive economic integration," "supporting the search for adapted structures," "thinking up procedures which will protect against the consequences of domination." These are pieties of course and they did not prevent the Algerian journal *Révolution Africaine* from dubbing the report "neo-neo-colonialism."

On the key question of unity, the Jeanneney Report is quite

clear. The Report is in favor of it, provided it is not all-African unity.

> In giving assistance, France ought to give preference to investments which take place in a regional framework, in conformity with agreements made between neighboring states. The optimal [1] dimension of this framework depends on the possible degree of integration of the economies, which is a function of the nature of their production and their transport facilities. To want to include in it a whole continent—all of Africa and Madagascar or all of South America for example—would be to increase the difficulties of establishment of common institutions, without being able to justify economically this giant size: within such a framework the distances between complementary or competing enterprises would be in fact, in a large number of cases, too big to permit effective specialization.

The logical conclusion is that the appropriate size-structure would be that of UAM/OCAM. This is reinforced by the Report's eulogy on the benefits of the franc zone which concludes with this paragraph:

> The existence of such cooperative institutions is so important for the development of the States of our former Empire that France should continue to reward, in its offers of cooperation, everything which moves against economic and monetary "balkanization." Even in the case of countries which might have renounced the disciplines and advantages of the franc zone,[2] France ought to favor everything which contributes to the cohesion of the aided countries among themselves. To do this, it ought to give preference to assistance which, channeled through multinational institutions

[1] Note that Jeanneney's appreciation of what is optimal is quite different, as we should expect, from that of Habib Niang when he cited Nkrumah, to which we referred in the last chapter.

[2] Guinea had done so, as had, partially but not entirely, Algeria, Morocco, and Tunisia. Mali had a special modified relationship with the franc zone.

constituted by aided countries, would contribute to the realization of regionally harmonized projects.

It should be noted that the French concern with "balkanization" is limited to economic and monetary matters.

Prime Minister Pompidou, in defending the Report in Parliament, explained that aid has many justifications: historic, political, cultural.

> Cooperation has equally its economic justifications . . . the industrial countries wish to be able to expand their sales in nonindustrial countries, and experience increasingly proves that in order to maintain or expand sales, we must furnish purchasing power to the buying countries, either by buying from them, lending them money, or even giving it to them.

The isolationist riposte to this analysis is called in France "Cartierism" after the French journalist Raymond Cartier, who has been attacking the official aid viewpoint since 1956. He has particularly stressed that the aid is ill-distributed and ill-used, while France has need of the money for internal development. The conclusion Cartier drew from this critique was curiously far-reaching in its implications, though he and others like him did not specify concrete steps that the alternative required. Cartier suggested that "the only efficient way to aid underdeveloped countries would be no doubt a general revalorization of tropical products. However, this must be a common action linked to the willingness of underdeveloped countries to aid themselves."

To one article by Cartier, a member of the French government, Michel Habib-Deloncle, responded by saying:

> Can we believe that [abandoning our former colonies] would be profitable for us? And can we believe that we would not in the end simply reinforce the camp of the have-nots of which certain countries, powerful because of their population size, would take the lead? And can we believe that in that case the consequences would not be

catastrophic for the position of the developed countries in the world, for their commerce, for their trade and especially for world equilibrium?

And in answering the criticism that aid would ruin France, the Gaullist journal *La Nation* stated somewhat baldly:

Can we count for nothing, for example, that it is a French polytechnician who has been drawing up, for the past two years, the economic plan of Madagascar? Can we believe that, knowing our possibilities, these experts do not orient in an intelligent manner certain projects toward our enterprises? And then it is clearly understood that from now on we shall not aid young states that abandon themselves to anarchy or those that, on their side, never bring us anything when they can.

While these statements have all been drawn from French sources, in fact the official view has been basically similar in all the Western countries, although American pronouncements may give slightly more space to anti-Communist justifications than French ones. The French point of view has been of particular importance in Africa because of France's extensive economic involvement on the continent and its key role in the Convention of Association between the European Economic Community (EEC) and the African associated states (eighteen in number, of which fourteen were former French colonies).

When the European Economic Community treaty was drawn up in Rome in 1957, none of France's African territories was as yet independent.[3] Under the treaty, the EEC assumed various special responsibilities in a number of colonial areas, and especially in Africa. The most important economic consequence was to open the market of French Africa to France's EEC partners (notably West Germany) in return for their contributing to an over-all development fund. France was doubtless more anxious for this exchange of advantages than some of its EEC partners that had important economic links

[3] This was true also of Belgian Africa. Italy was still administering the trust territory of Somalia.

with English-speaking Africa and Latin America, which might have been threatened by the preferential treatment offered to associated states.

After the expiration of the first convention five years later, on December 20, 1962, a new Convention of Association was signed between the EEC and the eighteen newly independent African countries covered by the previous accord.[4] It was ratified the following year. The central provisions of the Convention had to do with trade and with financial and technical cooperation. The Convention provided for the establishment of a European Development Fund, financed by the European members of the EEC, which disbursed grants to the associate members on request. This Fund was complemented by the European Investment Bank, which lent money at reduced interest rates to counteract violent fluctuations of prices of tropical products.

The provisions on trade, however, have been the most controversial and have had the clearest political implications. Basically there were three principal aspects to the provisions on trade. First, the African associated states were given access to the markets of the EEC, thus benefiting from the progressive abolition of customs duties and other restrictions. This provision was feared by other African states because of its possible negative impact on their own access to EEC markets. In terms of inter-African relations, it accentuated a competitive relationship between the EEC associates and the other African states.[5]

[4] Guinea was excluded from the workings of the Convention after its independence in 1958, but none of the other ex-colonies made, or was required to make, a similar break.

[5] This could be clearly seen when, later, some other African countries, such as Nigeria and the three East African states, considered entering into negotiations with the EEC for some kind of treaty relationship, which they hoped would overcome the negative effects of the preferential treatment for the eighteen. The latter were noticeably cool to such an accord, and France was reluctant (reinforced by the prompting of some of her former colonies) to allow it to proceed. Although Nigeria continued to press its negotiations with the EEC, which eventually ended

Secondly, in return, the markets of the eighteen associated states were to be progressively opened to EEC countries. This was immediately modified by the so-called Safeguard Clause which grants that in the case of "serious disturbances" in the economy of an associated state, that state may take "the necessary protective measures," provided there is consultation. There were reciprocal safeguards for the European members, although here it took a collective decision of EEC members to authorize their use.

Thirdly, and most relevant to our discussion, the Convention provided for the possibility of creating customs unions or free-trade areas between the Associated States or "between one or more Associated States and one or more third countries insofar as they neither are nor prove to be incompatible with the principles and provisions of said Convention." Leaving aside the issue of how incompatibility was defined, this provision was seriously limited by a most-favored-nation clause. The comment of the ECA Secretariat in 1960 on the only slightly less liberal provisions of the first Convention indicated a skepticism that was widespread in African circles outside the Associated States.

> Unlikely as it may be that [the EEC members] would regard a general raising of protective tariffs in the associated states as being in harmony with the spirit of the Rome Treaty, it is even less likely that they would tolerate discrimination against them in favour of African countries. The preferential arrangements of the Rome Treaty will tend to preserve and even strengthen the traditional features of African trade, namely concentration on industrialized markets to the exclusion of any significant trade flows between

---

successfully in 1966, Tanganyika took the lead in September 1962 in rejecting the idea. The then Premier, Rashidi Kawawa, said:

"It is obvious that if we join the Community we should cement ourselves to the Western bloc. Further, we believe that our association with the Community will be against the possibility of the promotion of African unity, which we highly value."

the various monetary zones of the continent. . . . There is therefore a danger that the Rome Treaty may tempt [the Associated States] to prefer the short-run advantage of tariff concessions [in EEC markets] to the long-run gains of industrial development.

This last suggestion, that the Convention might hinder the development of industrialization, has been a sensitive one and prompted a special memorandum from France to the ECA in 1962 to deny it. In the final section on recommendations, the ECA document suggested: "There may be some advantage for associated countries to aim at an arrangement covering a relatively short period (perhaps five years) and to avoid very general commitments with escape clauses which tend to work out at the disadvantage of the partner having a very weak bargaining position." The second half of this advice was in fact not heeded.

The presuppositions and analyses of the official Western view on economic development have not however been accepted by most Africans, certainly not by the revolutionary core of the movement for African unity, but not even by many of the leaders of the various Associated States of the EEC. For the initial premise of the Africans was different. Their initial premise was that the existing system of international trade has been based on nonequivalent exchanges. That is to say, the (majority) African assumption was that the existing price relationship between African exports and imports was not economically ineluctable but was in fact determined by the power relationships of the world social system. The prices were seen to be a function of a complex of political and economic calculations, only one of which was the marginal utility of a given product on the world market at a given time. If this was so, then changing other parts of this complex might be even more urgent than adjusting rates and nature of production. Since this involved a complex of political and economic calculations, there were various possibilities in the establishment of priorities. Here we come to the fundamental difference between the revolutionary core and those who believed in unity as alliance.

For the latter, Africa's political and economic weakness led to the conclusion that the West was the only immediate source of increased income by means of transfer of funds through loans, grants, and investments. This transfer of funds would then be used, it was argued, to transform the economic base of African society. At this point Africa would be able to afford more self-assertiveness. Militant positions involving sharp breaks with the West would weaken rather than strengthen Africa's bargaining position, since the most significant consequence of such militance would be to reinforce Cartierist tendencies in Western countries. The example often cited of such a consequence was the difficulties the Guinean economy has experienced as a result of breaking with France in 1958. This did not need to happen, say the proponents of unity as alliance. Precisely because the West has put higher priorities on developments in other continents, African lack of support for the West on various international issues of no direct concern to Africa has resulted in high negative sanctions. Conversely, African support on these issues has resulted in high rewards. Thus, the argument went on, Africa should maintain and even strengthen monetary and economic links with Europe and not pursue pan-African aspirations in a manner that would offend the West.

For the revolutionary core, this argument was at best deceptive and wrong, perhaps even dishonest, and an ideological justification of the small minority in power in most African states that were gaining advantage under the present system. For the solutions involving continued African reliance on Western aid were seen to be ineffective in their ostensible goal: transforming the base of African society. This aid, they argued, was carefully limited and was given in a form that would result in an expansion of African production of primary products needed by the West. But the nonequivalence of the exchange would remain fixed over time, and production for export would continue to be a disproportionately large segment of over-all production. On the other hand, they saw various openings in the present world system to strengthen Africa's hand. One was precisely neutralism, involving in a diplomatic and economic sense Russian and Chinese assistance. Such assistance did not need to match that from the West. Under the best of circumstances, at present, Communist aid and trade could not do so. But some Communist aid was far better than none. The increased leverage it gave to African recipients would make it possible to get better terms of aid and trade from the West, as well as increased support for liberation. But, this argument ran, since Africa continued to be weak, the West would try to subvert militant regimes, to which the effective answer could only be union. In Nkrumah's words, "As we examine the multifarious dangers to which the new states and all the freedom fighters of Africa are exposed, the more it becomes certain that our best, indeed our one protection is in unity."

We see then that seeking to transform the nature of Africa's economy and overcome "nonequivalence of exchange" led to two quite different conclusions as to strategy: what we have designated as unity as alliance and unity as movement. But let us be clear about what the difference was. It was about the ways of organizing all-African political activity. It was about the willingness to break out of the politico-economic circuit of the West. But it was not about accepting Western economic aid. There has been no African state thus far, however committed to a revolutionary ideology, that has been willing to make the kind of break with the West that China has made. Indeed, no African state, however socialist its ideology, has been unwilling to receive outside private investment. Perhaps this was because the African nations were all essentially too weak to make such a total break and survive.

The debate among Africans about strategy was a debate about the political implications of economic analysis, and the differences in strategy have been reflected in a series of specific issues. One of the basic economic ideas of the movement for unity has long been the idea of an African common market, often in opposition to the idea of Eurafrican integration as symbolized in the Convention of Association between the EEC and the Associated States. Corollary to the African common market has been the proposal to form an African payments union. A second basic idea has been coordinated industrial development, and its corollary, coordinated transport facilities. A third basic idea has been an African development bank. Both the ECA and OAU have been officially committed to these ideas and resolutions in their favor can be traced back to the second meeting of the AAPC in January 1960.

Thus far, the most tangible result of these commitments has been the creation of the African Development Bank (ADB). First proposed at the AAPC meeting, it was reproposed at the Conference of African Businessmen held in Monrovia in August of 1961. It was then taken up by ECA, which, at its fourth session in February–March 1962, created a nine-nation committee to work out the arrangements. As a result of its work, the ECA could convene in Khartoum, shortly after the creation of the OAU, from July 31 to August 4, 1963, a Conference of Finance Ministers on the Establishment of an African Development Bank. An Agreement was signed there by twenty-two of thirty-three eligible governments, and the agreement entered into force on September 10, 1964, with the requisite minimum number of ratifications, which have increased steadily to include almost all of Africa's independent nations.[6] The headquarters of the bank are in Abidjan, Ivory Coast. The Bank has two special features. It is exclusively African in membership, capital, and direction. But because, of course, this would necessarily limit its working funds, it is permitted to receive and administer Special Funds obtained elsewhere. Secondly, it is permitted far greater flexibility in the use of funds than most banking institutions.

[6] Despite Article 3 of the Agreement, which provides that "any African country which has the status of an independent State may become a member of the Bank," the Republic of South Africa has been expressly ruled ineligible by a special resolution of the Conference of Finance Ministers "until its Government has terminated its apartheid policies."

Despite the initial skepticism of world banking circles, including the World Bank, it is easy to see why this is the first major all-African economic institution to have been created.[7] It required at the outset no break of any kind with Western institutions nor did it seem to favor at the outset any particular African state. The flexibility of operation was seen by Africans as perhaps enabling them to obtain easier credit and by world banking institutions as perhaps relieving some of the pressure on them of African governments. For the world banking institutions, too, it was a matter of turning over difficult decisions about relatively small amounts of money to a group that had specialized local knowledge and which acted, in effect, as an agent. To help coordinate their actions, the World Bank has established a regional headquarters in Abidjan. The African Ministers of Finance have conversely organized themselves into an African group at the meetings of the World Bank, beginning with the Tokyo meeting of September 1964. In 1965 the group recorded a strong objection to the attitude of the industrialized countries, which considered the question of liquidity as the sole burning concern of the World Bank.

The future role of the ADB is uncertain. It began life amid admonitions. In his message to the Conference of Finance Ministers in 1963, George Woods, President of the World Bank, referred to Article 38 of the Agreement which provides that the Bank "shall not interfere in the political affairs of any member" or "be influenced in [its] decisions by the political character of the member concerned," for "only economic considerations shall be relevant to their decisions." Woods warned that "with or without supplemental resources, any departure from the principle of non-political and experienced management will frustrate the African Bank's basic objective." Quite the contrary, *The Spark* warned in an editorial the following week:

[7] There is one earlier institution, the African Institute of Economic Development and Planning, which was officially launched on February 18, 1963, and was located in Dakar, Senegal. It was, however, a training institution rather than a structure of actual economic cooperation.

The point must be emphasized that political direction is needed if the African Development Bank is to become a lever for promoting the economic independence of African states. To leave it either without political direction or with a conflict of political objectives will quite conceivably convert the bank into an instrument for the penetration and further enslavement of Africa by international finance oligarchies.

Joint economic development, such as coordinated industrial planning and new trans-African transportation networks, had been harder to achieve because the efforts were bound to favor some states more than others by the sheer decisions about location. Thus agreements have been very hard to come by without an over-all political framework. Here again the ECA has been the most active institution, sponsoring various industrial missions to different parts of Africa as well as conferences on industrial coordination.

ECA operated from a basic principle of regionalism, arguing that single African states are too small for industrial development, and the African continent as a whole too large at the present time. For most purposes it considered that there were five optimal regions. The ECA formally maintained four subregional offices:[8] Tangier (covering North Africa, including the U.A.R. and the Sudan); Niamey (for West Africa); Leopoldville (for Central Africa—that is, Congo [L], the four states of former French Equatorial Africa, and Cameroon); and Lusaka (for East Africa, including Ethiopia, Somalia, Rwanda, Burundi, Malawi, Zambia, and the Malagasy Republic).[9]

Thus far, the most ambitious project sponsored by the ECA

[8] In ECA terminology, the offices are subregional rather than regional since Africa is itself a region as far as the United Nations Economic and Social Council is concerned.

[9] Rhodesia is also included in the long-range planning, but the Rhodesian government has been induced not to try to participate in any sessions of the ECA for the present. The fifth region, or subregion, is South Africa, or southern Africa, but there is at this time no ECA activity or planning for that area at all.

has been the idea of a joint iron-and-steel complex for all of West Africa. This has run into difficulties because of competition for location sites, and the ECA subsequently widened the scope of proposed coordination to include other industries (chemicals and fertilizers, and engineering) in the hope of overcoming various resistances. Similarly the ECA has encouraged coordination in North Africa, but in this case limited to Morocco, Algeria, Tunisia, and Libya, which in the past have had, comparatively, the greatest number of economic links on the African continent.[10] There has also been a project for a trans-Saharan transport link, which has encountered similar difficulties of location.

The idea of the common market—at the very minimum the reduction or elimination of tariff barriers and other obstacles to intra-African trade—has always been central to the movement toward unity. But thus far, very little has been accomplished toward this end. The negative reasons are well known. African economies lacked complementarity of production,[11] and trans-African transport facilities were grossly uneconomic. This was the consequence of the colonial pattern of trade which left a legacy of tariff and monetary policies and various institutional arrangements that did not particularly encourage intra-African trade. Thus, as ECA says, "for intra-African trade to develop it is necessary to produce the things which can be traded among African countries." The positive advantages of greater economic integration are equally well known. The expanded internal market would permit economies of scale and would offer the opportunity of specialization, which would in turn permit a more widespread import substitution.

The advantages were of course so patent that it is clear there must have been some major obstacles to achieving such integration. There have been two in Africa, the classic pair of obstacles to economic integration: outside pressures which counted on the short-run interest of African governments, and

[10] The most important single instance of recorded intra-African trade is the reciprocal trade between Algeria and Morocco.

[11] ECA pointed out, however, that "there is a definite complementarity, both in climate and in soil, between various parts of Africa."

the difficulty of assuring an equitable share in the total progress as a result of integration. The first obstacle was clearly noted by the Executive Secretary of ECA, Robert Gardiner, when, in his statement on economic integration, he remarked: "It is difficult to reconcile the allegiance to the common market with that to an outside preferential system." But as we have seen, most African states were tied to an outside preferential system—and eighteen of them to a highly structured one, the EEC. There was no pressing reason why the outside powers that had preference in African markets should have encouraged the liquidation of this preference; and for the African states involved, the substitution of a new preference system for their old one might have entailed short-run difficulties for the economy.

Equally important as a restraint may have been the problem of equitable development within an African common market. The history of all economic development has been that of uneven growth. If this occurred in economic units that cross national boundaries, the political pressure for compensatory measures became very strong. And it became very difficult to guarantee such economic compensation without a political authority to ensure redistribution. This then returns us to the issue of political unification. The advocates of unity as alliance have often argued the virtue of economic cooperation as a practical first step, practical in that it is presumably easier to agree on cooperation than on political union, and cooperation creates over time the links of solidarity that would further the sentiment for political union. The advocates of unity as movement have long pointed to the practical difficulties (and positive disadvantages to some) of economic unity which preceded rather than grew out of political unification. The proposition for an African common market has thus far fallen between the two stools. For, in practice, the UAM/OCAM states, as proponents of a practical economic approach, have in fact found continued links with the EEC even more practical than ECA projects, in the sense of providing immediate national income. Those states which have looked to larger union have not in practice given high priority to an African common market, as they essentially consider it a consequence of political developments, not a prelude. The evolution of Tanzania's policies on these questions has demonstrated how easily an economically weak partner could become disillusioned with a formula of economic integration (in this case, the East African common market and common currency) that was not matched with a political structure that could guarantee redistribution of benefits.

A similar difficulty occurred with proposals to create an African payments union. On the one hand, the UAM/OCAM states did not seem to be willing to renounce the advantages of the guarantees of the franc zone for the uncertain effects of a payments union. On the other hand, many of the states that were willing to break, partially or totally, from monetary links with the West were also those states whose policies of internal economic development led them to impose severe import and currency controls which affected the world value of their currency. Entering into an African payments union could have negated much of the effect of these controls unless there were some mechanism to ensure the same controls on a continental level. But this would have presumed a political structure.

One of the reasons why these dilemmas were posed at all has been that the ECA and the OAU—though both emanations of the member governments (and for the two organizations the lists of full members were identical) and operating on the basis of resolutions passed by delegates from these governments—have achieved, as was inevitable, a certain autonomous life of their own, and as functional agencies they pursued functional goals. The OAU was in practice so absorbed in the more purely political functional tasks (aid to liberation movements, resolving border disputes, working out a convention on refugees, containing political differences between member-states, achieving national reconciliation in the Congo) that it expended relatively little time on economic projects.

This natural tendency to give priority to political questions, since the OAU is a political organization, was reinforced by the constant and total attention the older ECA gave to projects of economic cooperation. But the technicians of the ECA did not consider only African pressures. Financed by, and ultimately responsible to, the United Nations, they have functioned in a world context and been responsive to the pressures and views of international institutions which, almost by definition, have looked with favor on the emergence of new functional structures. ECA's semi-independent role emerged most clearly in its pressure toward regionalism, which pleased neither the UAM/OCAM states, because it placed them into three separate ECA subregions, nor the states which gave absolute priority to continental development.[12] Criticism of this pressure was nonetheless muted, in part because few real issues were posed and because the critics were bemused by how ECA's bias discomforted their opponents. Gardiner himself has argued: "The approach [to economic integration] is flexible, through small groups of countries, through subregions and in the case of some projects on a regional [that is, continental] basis. There is no conflict between the step by step, essentially sub-regional approach and the regional approach, with all-African integration as the ultimate objective." It is doubtful that the proponents of unity as movement would agree.

In this ambivalent situation, wherein the strategy of African economic development was not resolved, the fact that there were three separate organizations all bearing responsibility in this domain—the OAU, ECA, and the ADB—complicated the evolution of a unitary policy. This was even more complicated by the emergence of a fourth major institutional structure in which Africa invested much energy: the United Nations Conference on Trade and Development (UNCTAD).

The origins of UNCTAD were not in African problems at

[12] However, these states were not always consistent. Ghana, under Nkrumah, had been the most forthright opponent of regionalism. But, in 1963, in its own proposals for a military command, the Ghana government suggested organizing such a command in four regions which were very similar to ECA's economic subregions.

ail, but in the desire of the Soviet Union to establish more normal trading relations with the Western world. When the idea of a new world trade conference was first proposed, the warm support of the underdeveloped countries led the Western powers to accept such a conference, but also transformed its nature into one that would deal primarily with the problems of the economic development of the world, and in particular with barriers to trade and obstacles to industrialization as they specially affected underdeveloped countries. This focus was assured by designating as Secretary-General of UNCTAD Raúl Prebisch, former Executive Secretary of the Economic Commission for Latin America, where he had already made known his ideas for the reorganization of the world economy.

Prebisch, in his report to the Conference, which was held in Geneva from March 23 to June 16, 1964, started his analysis with the premise that there is a "persistent tendency towards external imbalance associated with the development process." Surveying the economic problems involved, he stated: "However, for the technical discussion to be profitable, it must be preceded by a political decision of the first importance, namely, a decision to transfer in one way or another, to the countries exporting primary commodities the extra income accruing to the industrial countries as a result of the deterioration in the terms of trade. . . . In other words, compensatory operations must be an integral part of a more rational policy for financing development." The detailed solutions he suggested amounted to cumulating the long list of solutions which had hitherto been considered by the Western world as alternative remedies: easy access to the markets of the developed world of both the primary products and the manufactured goods (hopefully much expanded in volume and diversity) of the underdeveloped nations; the maintenance of commodity prices, low priority on research for substitutes for primary products, compensatory schemes for over-all financial fluctuations, expansion of aid and easier terms of repayment, and development of trade within the underdeveloped world and between it and Communist nations.

This set of quite ambitious demands came at a moment when African solidarity was at a high point, the year following the founding of the OAU. And so it was possible, in the spirit of the compromise of Addis Ababa, to get the African countries to take a relatively unified and militant position on these questions. Indeed, in the end, the African group was more militant for these proposals than any other group or even than Prebisch himself. The OAU, at the first meeting of its Economic and Social Commission (in Niamey, Niger, December 9–13, 1963), devoted much time to the forthcoming UNCTAD and adopted a resolution urging that African states take a joint stand in favor of a series of measures designed to give the underdeveloped countries preferential treatment in meeting their economic needs. In its preparatory work, the secretariat of the ECA took a similar line. The ECA meeting in Addis Ababa on February 28, 1964, resolved to establish a coordinating committee of African states for the forthcoming conference, and invited the secretariat of the OAU to service the committee. Virtually simultaneously, the Council of Ministers of the OAU, meeting in Lagos from February 24 to 29, recommended the organization of a working party of African states for the conference.

The African group was not, however, the most significant grouping at the Conference. Rather, it was the Group of 77, composed of the countries from Asia, Africa, and Latin America and the Caribbean,[13] that set the pace for the meeting. This was the first time in the history of the world that a political group or alliance was formed of the underdeveloped nations, which have sometimes also been called the proletarian nations. The intention of this appellation has been to indicate the parallel of their struggle against the developed nations with that of the class struggle in nineteenth-century Europe, with corresponding implications for strategy. An editorial in *Jeune Afrique* argued that: "The nonaligned countries . . .

[13] Actually Israel and Cuba were excluded and Yugoslavia and Cyprus included. On many issues, New Zealand and Rumania, as well as Israel and Cuba, associated themselves with the 77.

are to the Third World what trade unionists are to the workers: an avant-garde force which organizes the solidarity of
the underprivileged class and poses the demands of this class
to the haves."

The African group worked with the Group of 77; and, in fact,
the Group of 77 showed more harmony at this Conference
than the opposite camp of the developed nations. Nonetheless,
harmony was not total, and it is worth noting that in one important difference on tactics—the extent of concessions to be
made to the Western nations on what kind of permanent structure would emerge from the Conference—the African group
was even more militant than the Group of 77, although it had
to concede finally. The West had wanted no continuing structure; the 77 had wanted a new world trade organization. The
latter did obtain a permanent conference, which would meet
every three years under the aegis of the General Assembly of
the U.N., and a permanent secretariat. This was no doubt their
essential victory. The resolutions, most of which reflected the
fact that the 77 were in the majority, often were passed without
a single affirmative vote by a Western nation. Their importance
lay, therefore, less in having done anything to change the
pattern of the world economy than in having psychologically
prepared the terrain for the future world negotiations.

The significance for African unity of this new major institution on the world scene has been contradictory. On the one
hand, it met one of the fundamental concerns of the pro-
tagonists of unity as movement, that of asserting the necessity
of united political action of underdeveloped nations vis-à-vis
the Western world in order to achieve a basic reallocation of
the world's resources. In this context, where the primacy of
their own immediate economic needs was bound to overcome
the ideological justifications that have linked the more conservative states to the Western world, many states became
committed to a political stance far more radical than they
would have assumed by themselves. One instance of this
could be seen in the pressure that was successfully brought on
the eighteen African Associated States, which were induced to

support a resolution calling upon the developed nations to eliminate, by December 31, 1965, all discriminatory preferences for access to their markets.[14] This kind of pull on reluctant nations to take a more militant line as a result of the atmosphere of united action is similar to the effect the creation of the OAU had on many of these same states in regard to support for liberation movements.

On the other hand, such a conference, being by its very nature based on negotiations, encouraged a reformist approach which was fundamentally the approach of the advocates of unity as alliance. Furthermore, it enhanced the fluidity of alliance, by creating a Group of 77 alongside, and overlapping, the group of independent African states. The more such alliances any one state is meaningfully involved in, the less total must be its commitment to any one given alliance.

UNCTAD thus has had the potential of both cementing and dissolving African unity. Whether it will ultimately do one or the other may depend less on whatever its own future course of development will be than on the degree to which purely African problems will retain the forefront of African attention. If they do, then the common efforts within the 77 will simply reinforce an already solid base. If they do not, Africa may recede into the background as a less meaningful unit to African states than a world class and/or ideological cleavage. But the only African issue that is likely to compete with the nature of the world economic system as a focus of Africa's energies for change is that of the liberation of southern Africa. It is to this problem that we must next turn our attention.

[14] This was achieved by inserting two compromise clauses in the proposal of the Group of 77. One subordinated the elimination of preferential treatment to the ability to assure equivalent advantages to those underdeveloped nations (e.g., the eighteen) that now have special relationships to developed nations. The second was a call to establish a group of experts to work out a scheme that would guarantee world commodity markets. The deadline was not in fact met.

:IX:

THE LIBERATION

OF SOUTHERN AFRICA

We have underlined the absolute primacy of the liberation of southern Africa for the revolutionary core of the movement toward African unity. It was the high priority they give to this objective that induced them to enter into the compromise of Addis Ababa which established the OAU, a compromise which seriously restrained their freedom of action. It was the lack of progress on this front as well as the second Congo crisis that led them during 1965 to have serious doubts about the wisdom of the compromise. It was the continued priority they gave to this objective that led them to be so conciliatory before and during the Accra meeting of the heads of state in October 1965. Yet for neither the core nor the periphery of the movement has the strategy of liberation proved a straightforward proposition. There have been two fundamental problems that have plagued the movement.

In the first place, the institutions of sovereignty, as we suggested earlier, put a serious crimp in the mode of operation of a movement. Specifically, the independent African states created a structure at Addis Ababa, the African Liberation Committee, to aid liberation. The relationship between this body which represented sovereign states and the freedom movements which claimed legitimacy but did not have sovereignty and the question as to which should have the right to decide on issues of strategy have been matters of contention from the beginning.

In the second place, whereas liberation was an essential aspect of the objectives of the revolutionary core, not all liberation movements could be considered part of this revolutionary core. For some their program was limited to the achievement of independence. Since in most cases there was more than one liberation movement in a given territory, decisions had to be made as to which to support, and these decisions were arrived at differently by the different African states, reflecting their ideological options and often narrow national interests.

These problems existed before 1963 but in a far less acute form, because up to that time the liberation of an African territory was to a very large degree a totally internal matter. To be sure, other African countries were interested in principle, and some mutual aid was available. Ghana created the Bureau of African Affairs, which aided movements in various countries and even organized conferences of freedom fighters. The U.A.R. created the African Association, which gave facilities in Cairo to various groups. Tunisia and Morocco housed the Algerian liberation army. Various other states undertook to assist specific movements at specific times. Freedom fighters met with leaders of independent states in such organizations as the AAPC. Various liberation movements created coordinating structures, the most important of these being PAFMECA.

Nonetheless the over-all situation was one of considerable laissez-faire. The liberation movements did what they wanted, sought aid from whom they wanted, and got it where they could. If an African country desired to give more advice than was welcome, the liberation movement simply turned to other allies. This laissez-faire policy succeeded fairly well as long as the objects of liberation were the relatively easy British, French, and Belgian colonies. But by 1963, especially in the light of the effects of the first Congo crisis, it was clear to all

Africans that the liberation of territories within the hard core of white domination—Portuguese Africa, Rhodesia, and South Africa—required new and more coordinated techniques. It was thus at the initiative of the liberation movements themselves, and to the great applause and relief of the independent states, that the founding conference of the OAU created the African Liberation Committee.

From the beginning the liberation movements made clear their desire to be treated as the equals, morally and juridically, of the independent African states. In their joint memorandum to the heads of state at Addis Ababa, which called for the creation of an African Liberation Bureau, the various liberation movements stated:

> No African country or nation is really free until all Africa is free. Accordingly, we urge most strongly that in all African countries no forms of discrimination or differentiation of status should ever be entertained among us African peoples. We are all African freedom fighters. The fact that we are not yet free is not due to any lack of revolutionary spirit in our movements. It is due to the oppressive tactics of the imperialists as well as some historical and political realities in our territories. We urge sincerely that in this Summit Conference we be accorded a status commensurate to our position as brothers and comrades of the other African freedom fighters who have already won their independence. We request that the opportunity be given to us to participate in and address the Summit Conference as associate members.

They were not in fact accorded such a status, at Addis Ababa or afterward.

The liberation movements did, however, obtain the creation of a permanent institution to coordinate aid to them. The Addis Ababa resolution, which established an ALC composed of nine nations with headquarters in Dar es Salaam, made it "responsible for harmonizing the assistance from African States and for managing the Special Fund to be set up for that purpose." The resolution further established two guidelines for the action of independent states and one guideline for the strategy of liberation. Independent states were enjoined "to receive on [their] territories . . . nationalists from liberation movements in order to give them training in all sectors" and "to promote in each State the transit of all material aid and the establishment of a body of volunteers in various fields, with a view to providing the various African national liberation movements with the assistance they need in the various sectors."

As for the strategy of liberation, all national liberation movements were invited "to co-ordinate their efforts by establishing common action fronts where necessary so as to strengthen the effectiveness of their struggle and the rational use of the concerted assistance given them." The theme of common action fronts was not a new one. It was an old and very understandable pressure from those who had already won their independence. Just three months prior to the Addis Ababa conference, the Third AAPSC meeting in Moshi, Tanganyika, from February 4 to 11, 1963, had listed as one of the most urgent tasks for Afro-Asian peoples "the formation of a united national front in any one country that is not liberated yet and the co-ordination of action amongst these different national fronts to make their struggle for independence more effective." But this understandable recommendation was easier to make than to realize, as was testified to by the history of the already independent nations, relatively few of which had achieved a total united national front before independence. The importance of the recommendation at that point, however, was that it would be taken by the new and powerful ALC as the very foundation of its action.

The ALC made three other decisions of principle from the very beginning. It decided that no kind of tactic, whether political, economic, or military, would be excluded *a priori* from consideration. This was implicit in the resolutions of Addis Ababa and in the accompanying debate, but the resolutions did stop short of an explicit endorsement of the use of vio-

lence. The ALC decided, nonetheless, and from the very beginning, that there were some colonial situations in southern
Africa where the use of violence was essential to achieving
change.

The second, and in a way most far-reaching, of the ALC
decisions on principle was that the committee had been established to be the organ of over-all African strategy on liberation. This meant an assertion of authority vis-à-vis African
independent states, requesting that they channel aid to liberation movements through the ALC. A *fortiori* this was an assertion of authority vis-à-vis friendly non-African states that might
wish to give aid. It was also to some extent an assertion of
authority vis-à-vis the OAU Secretariat, despite the "super-
visory control" the Cairo heads of state meeting gave the
Secretariat over the ALC, since the ALC was a political body
headed by a minister directly responsible to the Council of
Ministers of the OAU. It was, most controversially, an assertion of authority vis-à-vis the liberation movements themselves. How far the ALC was willing and able to assert its
primacy and to what degree others would accept the legitimacy of this assertion were to be continuing and critical issues.

Finally, the ALC delegated its own ultimate responsibility,
at least in part, to "neighboring countries." This meant that
aid to a liberation movement was to be administered to that
liberation movement through the independent African state
which shared its border, if one existed. To be sure, this system
was administratively convenient, but it also had the political
implication of allowing the neighboring state considerable
control over the liberation movement next door. And since almost all such neighboring states were members of the ALC,
this was powerful leverage. Tanganyika bordered Mozambique
(as well as Malawi and Zambia, which became independent
in 1964). The Congo (L) bordered Angola (and the Congo
[B], not a member of the ALC, bordered Cabinda, an enclave
that was part of Angola). Guinea and Senegal bordered Portuguese Guinea. Ethiopia bordered French Somaliland. At the
Accra meeting of the heads of state in 1965, two more mem-

bers were added to the ALC: Zambia, which bordered Rhodesia, Mozambique, Angola, South-West Africa, and Bechuanaland; and Somalia, which bordered French Somaliland. As we shall see, the policy of the ALC was heavily influenced by the policy of the neighboring states toward the various particular colonial situations.

When the ALC began its first session, which was held in Dar es Salaam from June 25 to July 4, 1963, its outlook was moderately optimistic. In British Africa, Kenya and Zanzibar had fixed dates for independence. Nyasaland (Malawi) had been permitted to withdraw from the Central African Federation and was certain to go forward to independence. That summer, Northern Rhodesia (Zambia) was placed in the same position by the decision to dissolve the Central African Federation, to be effective on January 1, 1964. There seemed to be reason to think that the British might be induced to complete this process of decolonization in the region by arranging for Southern Rhodesia to proceed sooner or later to independence under majority rule.

Portuguese Africa seemed somewhat more difficult, especially because whatever tentative moves were made to liberalize policy while Adriano Moreira was Minister of Overseas Provinces, the door had been definitely closed with his dismissal on December 3, 1962. But there were uprisings in Angola and Portuguese Guinea and a united liberation front had been established in Mozambique. It was felt that with an extra push, the Portuguese position might begin to crumble.

South Africa seemed the most difficult obstacle of all. But sabotage appeared to be on the increase, even if an armed uprising might have to await the day when a border state would be independent. In the meantime, the case on South-West Africa was proceeding in the International Court of Justice, and Britain seemed inclined to be firm with South Africa on the three High Commission Territories—Basutoland, Bechuanaland, and Swaziland—each of which could look forward to relatively rapid constitutional advance to independence.

In the euphoria of the compromise of Addis Ababa, it was easy to be optimistic. The careful balance of members of the ALC further ensured initial moderation. Of the nine, three were former Casablanca powers (Algeria, Guinea, and U.A.R.), four former Monrovia powers (Congo [L], Ethiopia, Nigeria, and Senegal), and two former PAFMECSA members (Tanganyika and Uganda).

Within the framework of the various decisions on principle noted above, the ALC made two important tactical decisions. One concerned Central Africa. It was decided that Rhodesia was likely to be the easiest of the major areas to liberate and that the best way to pursue the Rhodesian question was by having the African members of the Commonwealth place concerted diplomatic pressure on the United Kingdom. The objective of the pressure would be to induce the U.K. to convene a constitutional conference which would begin the transfer of power to the African majority. To bolster this effort, the ALC urged that the still united nationalist movement, the Zimbabwe African People's Union (ZAPU), undertake militant action. And to secure the flank, the ALC decided to give a considerable amount of money to the United National Independence Party of Northern Rhodesia (Zambia) to aid it to win the forthcoming preindependence elections. The ALC considered the opposition Northern Rhodesian African National Congress as highly compromised by its acceptance of financial support from Tshombe, when he headed the secessionist Katanga regime which bordered Northern Rhodesia.

The second important tactical decision was to try to reinforce the armed struggle in Portuguese Africa. Here there were three main areas of struggle and four "neighboring countries" on the ALC. In the case of Mozambique, where armed struggle had not yet begun, the neighboring country Tanganyika considered the Frente de Libertação de Moçambique (FRELIMO) a widely representative nationalist front and dismissed the two other groups as insignificant. Indeed the latter were not permitted to operate in Tanganyika and thus could not even argue their case before the ALC. The ALC

adopted Tanganyika's view and threw its support behind
FRELIMO.

In the case of Angola, we have already recounted how the
principal neighboring state, the Congo (L), whose government at that time was headed by Adoula, recognized the GRAE
in the very middle of the first session of the ALC. Nonetheless,
both Guinea and Algeria had long been supporters of the
MPLA, and the ALC decided to send a conciliation commission to Leopoldville to see if it could induce the two nationalist groups to get together. The commission was composed of Algeria, Congo (L), Guinea, Nigeria, Senegal, and
Uganda. Similarly, in Portuguese Guinea, the two neighboring states, Guinea and Senegal, each backed one of the rival
movements, respectively the PAIGC and the FLING. It was
decided to send the same commission on to Conakry and
Dakar to pursue a similar mission of unifying the rival movements.

We have already recounted above the outcome of these
missions. In each case, the ALC found conciliation impossible
and opted to throw exclusive support to the stronger movement, which they determined to be the GRAE and the PAIGC.
In the case of Angola, the supporters of the MPLA on the ALC
conceded the point, and the Dakar meeting of the Council
of Ministers recommended that all African states recognize the
GRAE. In the case of Portuguese Guinea, Senegal refused to
concede the point, carried her fight to the Council of Ministers,
and won there acceptance of shared aid to the two movements
(although the PAIGC was to receive more than FLING).
Thus the ALC invested its prestige heavily in two decisions:
the efficacy of African diplomatic pressure to obtain liberation in Rhodesia; the wisdom of granting all-out and exclusive
support to the GRAE in Angola. In the following two years
both decisions were considered, even by the Committee itself,
to have been in error, and the prestige of the ALC suffered
accordingly.

The ALC in the coming years largely disregarded the mandate that it should insist on the necessity of forming common

action fronts. In Northern Rhodesia it threw its weight behind one of two movements, as it did in Mozambique, Angola, and Portuguese Guinea (although in the last instance, its decision was reversed by the Council of Ministers). Nonetheless, as we shall see, the ALC did not abandon altogether the principle of common action fronts. It merely applied it selectively, according to its political preferences. Where it considered one of the two or more movements more nationalist, more militant, or simply stronger, it might opt for exclusive support for it, as it did in a number of cases. When it considered two or more movements as legitimate movements, it would share the aid between them. This would lead to subtle and changing judgments, reflected in the ratio of aid offered to each. The recognition of two movements could still lead to the refusal to recognize a third. Since these judgments had very immediate and very important political consequences, different members of the ALC continually stood for different solutions. Nor were the decisions of the ALC final. They could be reversed by the Committee itself, and were on a number of occasions. They could be overruled by the Council of Ministers, and were several times. They could be undermined by individual independent African states channeling money or support directly to movements not favored or less favored by the ALC. This too happened, although its occurrence was more difficult because the "neighboring country" could control such aid to some extent (but often there were several neighboring countries).

These initial decisions of the ALC led to several reactions. First of all, there was the reaction of the enemy, the colonial-settler powers in southern Africa. They began to move quickly, to make certain that the relative optimism of the ALC would have no justification. Their response was to increase internal repression, to make their basic political positions still more unyielding, and to tighten coordination of their plans. In short, they decided that a hard line would work, given the changed world political situation brought about in part as a consequence of the first Congo crisis and in part as a result of the

détente between the U.S.A. and the U.S.S.R. and the split between the U.S.S.R. and China. The colonial-settler powers estimated that a showdown would create more political havoc in
independent Africa than in their countries.

The second reaction came from the revolutionary core. Their
early uncertainty about the meaning of the creation of the
ALC turned into open attack when they observed the initial
mode of operation of the Committee. The strongest reaction
appeared in *The Spark* (October 25, 1963), which attacked
the ALC for assuming responsibility for over-all strategy, for
transferring the primary role in aiding liberation movements
to neighboring countries, and for having an overelaborate secretariat which took inadequate security precautions. Finally,
it attacked the strategy on Rhodesia because this strategy assumed that "colonialism seeks to prepare the peoples under
it for full self-government," because the ALC forgot "that
if the colonial power 'guides' the colonial territory to freedom
the end result is not complete independence but neo-colonialism," and because the ALC reintroduced the regional concept
by the back door in giving a special collective role to African
members of the Commonwealth. Finally, it attacked the decision on Angola, saying: "Through the formula of the 'neighboring' independent state having the big say in how the liberation movement next door is to be aided, the Liberation Committee succumbed to the blackmail of the Adoula government.
The result has been the virtual crippling of all revolutionary
liberation movements in Angola and the forcible acceptance
by all revolutionaries of [the GRAE's] (and U.S.A's) main line
of negotiations with Portugal."

The third reaction came from the liberation movements
themselves. In this case, of course, the reactions were varied
and depended to a considerable extent on the attitude of the
ALC toward the particular movement. But even in the best
situation, wherein a movement was recognized as the sole
legitimate recipient of aid for a given country, the liberation
movements tended to chafe at the concept that the ALC directed strategy, could mediate, even arbitrate internal di-

visions, and might even potentially intervene directly in the process of liberation.

We noted above how PAFMECSA was the predecessor in one sense of the ALC.[1] We noted, too, that, in 1962 PAFMECSA became transformed into an organization whose members were governments in independent countries and one or more liberation movements in nonindependent countries. Thus at the time of Addis Ababa it seemed to be implied that PAFMECSA should disappear along with the Casablanca and Monrovia groups. But there was some debate within PAFMECSA. Some wished to retain it as an East and Central African organization of independent states within OAU, just as others wished to preserve the UAM. Some of the member liberation movements wished to retain PAFMECSA as a counterbalance to the ALC. Finally, after consultations but without a plenary meeting, on September 24, 1963, the decision was taken to dissolve PAFMECSA by the then President of PAFMECSA, Kenneth Kaunda of Northern Rhodesia, whose country's independence was at that point clear and assured, and President Nyerere of Tanganyika, whose country held the chairmanship of the ALC. Only three months later, on December 20, 1963, a number of liberation movements tried to revive it in a different form. A meeting was held in Dar es Salaam to create a Union of Non-Independent African States (UNIAS). Among the aims they stated were "to plan strategy on problems confronting the African Liberation Movement" and "to uphold the independence of the Liberation Movement." In the memorandum they drafted to be submitted to the heads of state, they complained of the functioning of the ALC, its "red tape," and the attachment of conditions to aid which they found "reprehensible" because of the "insinuation of distrust and irresponsibility implied." They demanded full diplomatic recognition and hence seats in the plenary sessions of the OAU, four seats on the ALC, and a majority of the personnel on the secretariat of the ALC. The ALC argued that

[1] It is symbolic, if nothing more, that the building the ALC used for its headquarters in Dar es Salaam was previously used by PAFMECSA.

such proposals were unrealistic, since leaders of liberation movements lacked the responsibilities of power and since the question of whom to recognize was precisely the most difficult issue. Furthermore the ALC and the Tanganyika government made clear how unwelcome a creation UNIAS was and the whole structure was simply dropped.

This fundamental framework we have described—the basic outlook of the ALC, the hard line of white resistance, the unhappiness of the revolutionary core with the work of the ALC, the discomfort of many liberation movements with its claims to strategic control—remained constant throughout the following two years. But the ALC's particular stances on individual countries did evolve with the increase of its own detailed knowledge and the internal developments on the liberation front.

The evolution of the attitude of the ALC on Angola was perhaps the most dramatic. We have already related how at the Dakar Council of Ministers meeting, August 2–11, 1963, a unanimous recommendation of the ALC to accord exclusive and full diplomatic recognition of the GRAE was adopted. In the year to come, this recognition was to be accorded by virtually all the African states with two notable exceptions. One was Ghana. The other was Congo (B). The revolution in Congo (B) which overthrew Youlou took place less than a week after the Dakar OAU Council of Ministers meeting. The new government welcomed the MPLA which had been expelled from Congo (L), and the MPLA was able to begin slowly to rebuild its political force as well as to engage in military activity in the enclave of Cabinda.

On the one hand, the GRAE seemed to enjoy ever increasing political success. Not only had most African states recognized it, but in January 1964 the Chinese Foreign Minister met Holden Roberto, President of the GRAE, in Nairobi and invited him to Peking. In April 1964 Viriato da Cruz, leader of a wing of MPLA which had split with the main body in the summer of 1963, joined the political front of the GRAE. At the Cairo meeting of the heads of state in July 1964 Holden

Roberto was seated with full rights as a delegate. On the other hand, the end of the Adoula regime in the Congo (L) and his replacement by Tshombe in July 1964 meant that the GRAE's Congo base shifted from one controlled by Adoula, a close personal friend of Roberto's, to one controlled by Tshombe, a long-time political opponent of Roberto's and an ally of the Portuguese. At the very same Cairo meeting Jonas Savimbi, the Foreign Minister of the GRAE, publicly announced his resignation, charging the GRAE with inefficacy. The Cairo meeting reopened the Angola question and took a curiously contradictory position, which served to save the face of those who regretted what they now considered their hasty call for recognition of the GRAE. The heads of state at one and the same time called on all members who had not yet recognized the GRAE to do so and to accord it aid, and also called for the reconciliation of the GRAE and the MPLA. They asked the ALC to use its good offices toward this end, assisted by a committee composed of Congo (B), Ghana, and the U.A.R. The efforts of this committee of three, which included at least two nations openly sympathetic to the MPLA, led to a special session of the ALC in Dar es Salaam on November 24–25, 1964. There the ALC decided to divest the GRAE of its privilege of exclusivity and to accord aid to both the GRAE and the MPLA. The Nairobi Council of Ministers in March 1965 rejected the ALC's report on Angola but reiterated essentially the ambiguous Cairo decision. Once again, the OAU called on the GRAE and MPLA to form a common front, aided by the same committee of three.

By this point whatever lingering doubts the revolutionary core had had about the appropriate policy toward the Angolan movements were resolved. At the Winneba meeting of the AAPSC in May 1965 the UPA[2] of Holden Roberto was expelled from membership, leaving the MPLA as the sole Angolan representative. In June the GRAE's Minister of Defense,

[2] Since the AAPSC was composed of political parties, it was the UPA, Roberto's party, and not the GRAE, a government, which had been a member.

Alexander Taty, attempted a coup and, although unsuccessful, this was taken by the ALC to signal further disintegration of the military strength of the GRAE. The ALC thereupon increased its relative military support of the MPLA.

In the case of Portuguese Guinea, the ALC did not reverse itself. Rather, it proved unable during these two years to overcome the political objections of Senegal, a member and a "neighboring country," to the exclusive recognition of the PAIGC. Finally, the Nairobi meeting of the Council of Ministers decided to appoint a Military Commission of Enquiry composed of representatives of Cameroon, Mauritania, and Sierra Leone. This commission penetrated the interior of Portuguese Guinea in territory controlled and administered by the PAIGC and reported that only the PAIGC was engaged in effective military action. Nonetheless, Senegal still won its point that a portion of the aid of the ALC should continue to go to FLING.

In Mozambique the situation was different; the "neighboring country," Tanzania, stood solidly behind FRELIMO. When FRELIMO began its open insurrection on September 25, 1964, aid by the ALC increased. In June 1965 the various small opposition movements to FRELIMO combined to form the Comité Revolucionário de Moçambique (COREMO). The latter was formed in Lusaka virtually under the auspices of the Zambian government. But Zambia was not yet a member of the ALC, and the latter continued its exclusive support to FRELIMO.

Rhodesia, like Portuguese Guinea, was a source of great frustration to the ALC, not because the ALC could not dissuade one of its own members from a minority view, but because it could at no point impose its views on the stronger of the two nationalist movements. In July 1963 part of the leadership of the Zimbabwe African People's Union (ZAPU) split off and the next month formed the Zimbabwe African National Union (ZANU). The split soon hardened into unreconcilable and often violent opposition. ZAPU, led by Joshua Nkomo, demonstrated in the following two years that it had the clear support of the majority of the population. ZANU, led by the Reverend Ndabaningi Sithole, however, had the support not only of a majority of the intellectuals and students but the tacit encouragement of a large number of interested African independent states.

In the meantime, in Rhodesia the white population replaced Winston Field with Ian Smith as Prime Minister on April 13, 1964. Smith was notable for his more vigorous position vis-à-vis Britain and the nationalists. Both Nkomo and Sithole and most of their cadres were placed in confinement in the year that followed. With the independence of Zambia on October 24, 1964, Smith began to move toward the unilateral declaration of independence that was finally made on November 11, 1965.

The OAU reacted to these developments in two ways. On the one hand, the resolutions of the various meetings became ever more insistent and explicit in their collective demands to Britain. We have already described the results of this. On the other hand, the OAU never ceased trying to bring about a reconciliation of ZAPU and ZANU. The Cairo meeting asked the governments of Malawi and Tanzania[3] "to offer their good offices to the nationalist parties in Southern Rhodesia so as to bring about a united front of all the liberation movements for the rapid attainment of their common objective of independence." The trip on August 13 by the two Foreign Ministers of Malawi and Tanzania to Lusaka to achieve this end was a failure. On May 7, 1965, Smith won the elections in Rhodesia overwhelmingly. The special session of the Council of Ministers in Lagos, Nigeria, in June, was "deeply disturbed by the gulf which exists between the two nationalist movements in Southern Rhodesia, ZAPU and ZANU" and created a committee of six "neighboring[4] African States"—Malawi, Zambia, Tanzania, Uganda, Kenya, and Ethiopia—to "establish quickly a common front." This committee met in Nairobi,

[3] Actually, at the time of the meeting, the name of this country was still the United Republic of Tanganyika and Zanzibar.
[4] This in fact stretched the meaning of "neighboring."

Kenya, from July 20 to 22 in the presence of the OAU Secretary-General, Diallo Telli. The session was fruitless. The committee appointed a subcommittee of Tanzania, Kenya, and Zambia, which reported back to the larger committee on August 27–29. The ALC, meeting on August 7, appointed a subcommittee composed of Algeria, the U.A.R., and Nigeria to mediate. This ALC subcommittee also was unsuccessful; it met on August 29 to draft unanimously adopted recommendations which amounted to proposing the imposition of reconciliation. The Committee of Six of the Council of Ministers continued its work during the Accra meeting of the heads of state. It recommended that the ALC suspend all forms of aid to both movements until they acted to establish a common front.

In the end, however, all this effort had no effect. ZAPU, as the stronger movement (and the one from which ZANU had split), insisted that it receive exclusive recognition and that the individuals who had formed ZANU were free to rejoin ZAPU. ZANU was much more sympathetic to the mediation efforts since, being the weaker movement, it proclaimed the necessity for a united front. But ZANU never conceded the point the mediators insisted on—that Nkomo should head this united front. When Smith's unilateral declaration of independence was not followed by an insurrection inside Rhodesia, the OAU was unsure what attitude to take: whether to ignore both movements, which it more or less did at the extraordinary session convened in Addis Ababa in December 1965, or whether to recognize ZAPU, as some recommended at the following session in Addis Ababa in March, 1966. It remained to be seen how far the independent states could go toward remolding a liberation movement to their image and toward successfully operating within a colonial country other than through a liberation movement.[5]

[5] Even some of the stronger defendants of the autonomy of liberation movements vis-à-vis the ALC, like *The Spark*, showed impatience in this situation. In an editorial of June 26, 1964, *The Spark* stated: "We believe the liberation movements are experienced and mature and that the [ALC] should listen to their advice when they specify what help is

In South Africa and related territories, the ALC had less to do, since these areas were less immediately fronts of political and military action. (The resolutions of the various OAU meetings calling for various kinds of boycotts were administered by a Sanctions Bureau created within the Secretariat of the OAU, whose main task was to police enforcement by OAU members themselves of the sanctions collectively agreed upon. This police action was not notably successful.)

The ALC initially took a relatively neutral attitude toward the two principal South African liberation movements, the African National Congress (ANC) and the Pan-Africanist Congress (PAC), which were both banned inside the country. In the years following the creation of the ALC, the PAC—or at least that segment of it that has operated outside of South Africa—was dramatically split a number of times. This fact, combined with the evidence of ANC activity attested to by the so-called Rivonia Trial in South Africa,[6] led to increasing, though not exclusive, ALC support for the ANC. Both the ANC and the PAC successfully opposed the idea of aid to any third movement in South Africa, such as the All-African Convention.

In South-West Africa, similarly, the initial response of the ALC was to support both principal movements, the South-West African Peoples' Organization (SWAPO) and the South-West African National Union (SWANU). Indeed, under the pressure of the ALC, the two joined together in early October 1963 to form the South-West African National Liberation Front (SWANLIF). But SWANLIF was short-lived, and afterward SWANU's activity seemed to decline somewhat. There-

most needed in a given situation." But during the Accra meeting, on October 19, 1965, *The Spark* reported with sympathy, in an article on ZANU-ZAPU reconciliation entitled "OAU Must Take Firm Action," that the Committee of Six "is understood to have recommended that no member-state should allow its soil to be used by any party which thus defies the efforts of the OAU."

[6] The court condemned a number of South Africans for planning sabotage, including Nelson Mandela, Secretary-General of the African National Congress.

fore in mid-1965 the ALC moved toward exclusive support of SWAPO.

The ALC was most indecisive in the High Commission Territories. In Basutoland, Bechuanaland, and Swaziland it gave, in each case, some small support to two or more movements. In the case of Swaziland, it induced the separate movements to set up the Joint Council of Swaziland Political Parties.[7] All three territories had elections after the creation of the ALC: Swaziland on June 29, 1964; Bechuanaland on February 28, 1965; and Basutoland on April 29, 1965. In each case, conservative and traditionalist forces won the elections, albeit only narrowly in Basutoland, and the movements supported by the ALC lost. Furthermore, the winning parties were all committed in varying degrees to a policy of friendly diplomatic relations with the South African government after their own independence, achieved in 1966 by Lesotho (Basutoland) and Botswana (Bechuanaland). And still more upsetting to many Africans was the fact that the South African government seemed to have given some real pre-electoral support to the winners, most notably in Basutoland. This presented the ALC with the same kind of decision the CIAS had faced in 1959 with regard to Cameroon: to what degree were they prepared to favor militant or pan-African political movements in colonial territories in situations where, for whatever reasons, it seemed likely that the opponents of such movements would soon be the authorities of an independent state, with the full rights of a member of the OAU? Here, as in the case of the Cameroon, support for the more revolutionary movements was dropped in the interests of cohesion among the sovereign states. The ALC in 1965 decided on a virtual hands-off policy in the three countries. As in the case of the admission of Cameroon to membership in the CIAS, this was a victory for unity as alliance over unity as movement.

By the summer of 1965 discontent with the ALC was great,

---

[7] In addition, most of these groups in the three territories have been joined together in the Pan-African Solidarity Conference, whose existence predated the formation of the ALC and whose real activity was minimal.

especially among the revolutionary core and the liberation movements. Some of this discontent was a projection on the ALC of blame for the larger stalemate of the movement toward African unity, for which the ALC was only in part (perhaps in relatively small part) responsible. Oscar Kambona, chairman of the ALC, had stated the problem quite clearly in September 1964:

> The Congo situation had an unfortunate effect on the decolonization of Africa. It has temporarily halted the southward advance of free Africa and has enabled the imperialists to establish a defence line, from the Congo right through to Mozambique, in a vicious bid to hold Africa's attainment of political freedom. With this defence, the imperialists wish to encircle Dr. Kenneth Kaunda. Africa's only alternative is to break through this evil line and push Portugal, Southern Rhodesian minority settlers, and South Africa's whites into the defensive.

But one year later, they were not yet on the defensive.

The most promising front of action at that point seemed Portuguese Africa. From October 3 to 8, 1965, in Dar es Salaam, there was held the second meeting of the Conferência das Organizações Nacionalistas das Colonias Portuguesas (CONCP), which grouped FRELIMO, MPLA, PAIGC, and the Comité de Libertação de São Tomé e Principe (CLSTP). The CONCP had always made clear its participation in the revolutionary core. At its first conference in Casablanca, April 18–20, 1961, it had "noted with satisfaction" the resolutions of the heads of state of the Casablanca powers. The long-standing disputes between the MPLA and the UPA/GRAE and between PAIGC and FLING had made clear both the ideological commitment and the alliances within Africa.

The CONCP decided on a consolidated structure which would coordinate political and military strategy—a new departure in liberation tactics. It indicated support for the democratic Portuguese opposition and threatened that if the colonial wars continued, the war might be extended to Portugal itself.[8] In terms of the status of the movements themselves, it asked for exclusive recognition of the PAIGC and denounced "all maneuvers which tend to exercise pressure within the African Liberation Committee of the OAU to prevent the recognition of nationalist organizations which indisputably lead the struggle of their respective peoples." Similarly, it asked that recognition of the GRAE be withdrawn and that the MPLA be accorded exclusive recognition. This last demand was a sign of self-confidence, since previously the MPLA had only asked for equal recognition with the UPA/GRAE and had favored the creation of a common front, an idea the MPLA now rejected. The CONCP also called for a revision of the ALC's mode of operation in the interests of greater efficiency.

On the eve of the Accra meeting of the heads of state, President Nyerere stated in the interview he accorded to *Jeune Afrique:*

[The African Liberation Committee] was supposed to be, at its origin, an instrument of liberation and not a political committee having the power to pass resolutions. It was understood that resolutions on African liberation were the affair of the heads of state. An executive body was needed on the other hand to carry out effectively these decisions. What do we see at the present time? A committee, here in Dar es Salaam, which votes resolutions and more resolutions. I defended this committee on several occasions[9] but I'm now convinced that it has been a failure and that if Africa wishes to undertake a resolute action for the liberation of dependent territories and countries, it must consider the reorientation of this committee which is no longer the adequate instrument we hoped for.

[8] This tactic had been tried, but only briefly, by the FLN during the Algerian war of independence.
[9] President Nyerere refers most of all to his very vigorous defense of the ALC at the Cairo heads of state meeting when he reacted to the criticisms leveled by President Nkrumah.

Despite this strong criticism from the president of the host country of the ALC and a similar criticism by the Secretary-General of the OAU in his report, in fact very little actual change in either the terms of reference or the mode·of operation of the ALC was decided upon at Accra. In the resolution on Portuguese Africa the ALC was invited "to give assistance only to nationalist movements that are in fact fighting within the Portuguese colonies to be liberated," but this wording, by not naming movements, left open the question of its proper interpretation. The resolution on the High Commission Territories decided "to continue to support these movements which have so far been supported by the Organization of African Unity," but it failed to indicate how far such support should go.

In the ALC itself the only significant change was the addition of two "neighboring states": Zambia and Somalia. Zambia had become independent since the creation of the ALC and, apart from Tanzania, was the largest center of liberation activity in independent Africa. Somalia's status as a neighboring state had been passed over in 1963. However, beginning in 1964, the ALC began to concern itself actively with French Somaliland, and Somalia considered it unfair that Ethiopia, which held very different views about the disposition of French Somaliland, had a seat on the ALC and she did not.[10] Malawi too was a "neighboring state," bordering on both Mozambique

[10] The Somalis supported the Front de Libération des Côtes des Somalis with headquarters in Mogadiscio, Somalia. It stood for independence and incorporation in Somalia, and was the organization to raise the issue of French Somaliland before the ALC. The Ethiopians supported the Mouvement de Libération de Djibouti with headquarters in Dire Dawa, Ethiopia. It stood for independence and incorporation in Ethiopia. The Somalis claimed the organization was created by the Ethiopians only when the issue became an active one before the ALC. In mid-1964 the ALC created a commission of inquiry composed of Congo (L), Nigeria, and Senegal, which visited Somalia and Ethiopia in January 1965. One result of the formation of this committee was that a third group, a political party functioning legally inside French Somaliland, called the Parti du Mouvement Populaire, assumed a more nationalist stance. The commission recommended that the three parties form a common action front; however, this advice was not heeded.

and Rhodesia. The Council of Ministers at Accra had recommended adding Malawi as well to the ALC. When the heads
of state convened, President Nyerere denounced this proposal,
pointing out that Malawi had never contributed funds to the
ALC,[11] and charged that Malawi was in active collusion with
the Portuguese and Rhodesian authorities. He threatened to
withdraw Tanzania from the OAU if Malawi were added to
the ALC. Malawi was not in fact anxious to serve on the committee and the issue was dropped.

The net result of the growing unease about the strategy of
liberation as conducted by the ALC was inconclusive. During
the Accra meeting, thirteen liberation movements were called
together by the PAC. They strongly criticized the ALC, and
decided to hold a joint conference to set up an organization
that would represent their collective interests. Seven liberation movements refused to associate themselves with this
group, although they shared some of the criticisms. The seven
were the four groups in the CONCP, plus the ANC, ZAPU,
and SWAPO. These seven were the core of an emerging alliance[12] among liberation movements, recognizing one another
as the most representative and most revolutionary movements
in their respective countries. These seven all received aid from
the ALC, and in most cases they were the exclusive or majority recipients of such aid. Nonetheless, they were no less
critical.[13] In November 1965 the trade-union journal, *Revolution et Travail*, held a round-table conference in Algiers with
representatives of six of these seven groups (plus the National
Liberation Front of South Vietnam). The journal posed the
problem for the group in the following terms: "The present
international conjuncture is characterized by a world-wide im-

[11] Prime Minister Hastings Banda of Malawi had only the month before, in September 1965, on a visit to the Malagasy Republic, accused
the ALC of giving funds to his political opponents, exiled in Tanzania,
to subvert his regime. The ALC denied this charge.
[12] The membership of this alliance has shifted somewhat over time.
For example, in 1963 SWANU rather than SWAPO was part of it.
[13] The GRAE, another major recipient of aid, also and separately refused to go along with the public attack on the ALC.

perialist assault and by a retreat of the revolutionary movement as a result of what we have called 'the timidity of the
one and the aggressiveness of the other.'" The representative
of the MPLA agreed with this analysis and reminded the
group of the initiative of the liberation movements at Addis
Ababa for the creation of the ALC, adding: "in asking for the
creation of this organism, we wanted to be part of it and not
simply observers—we wanted to take part in the discussions."
As for the Accra meeting, he stated:

> As President Boumediene justly said, they managed at
> Accra to conclude sterile accords which do harm not only
> to the revolutionary movements of Africa but to the true
> unity of this continent. I recall, in passing, that at the time
> that we had the Casablanca group and the Monrovia group,
> things were more clear, most definite, as concerns the strug-
> gle for national liberation of the peoples still under colonial
> domination.

Let us recall once again that for the revolutionary core of
the movement for unity, the *raison d'être* of the compromise
of Addis Ababa was the fact that the creation of the OAU
might accelerate the process of the liberation of southern
Africa. The OAU chose as its main instrument the ALC, a
structure controlled by representatives of independent African
states. The operations of the ALC have led it into inevitable
discord with the liberation movements over the issue of who
ultimately should determine the strategy of liberation. For
the revolutionary core, the operations of the ALC were inherently ambiguous, but in essentially the same way as all
political activity of the OAU, because the ALC allowed a
large voice to those who did not share the core's revolutionary
aspirations. The assumption that the struggle for liberation
was a single uncomplicated operation on which advocates of
unity as movement and advocates of unity as alliance could
readily agree had proved to be false. Aid for liberation involved, first of all, deciding who should control this aid and
hence implied the entire range of political decisions that would

determine the future of the countries involved and thereby of Africa as a whole. The way the struggle for liberation in southern Africa would be conducted would thus largely determine the likelihood of achieving the objectives of the movement for African unity.

: X :

THE ROLE

OF THE AVANT-GARDE

A movement by definition is avant-garde, and it also has an avant-garde. That is, it seeks to change the social structure, and has within it those who push it to move still faster and harder toward its objectives. Avant-gardes are drawn from those segments of a society that are less integrated into a system and have least to lose by pursuing the logical consequences of their ideals. But avant-gardes, to be effective, must take organizational form and, to that extent, become involved in the compromises of a system. Thus there is a constant tension and a constant oscillation.

Furthermore, there are often several groups that have pretensions to being the avant-garde. And as one group becomes more moderate another may come forward to hold the banner high. In the movement toward African unity the pretendants have been many, and sometimes overlapping, since 1957. There have been the AAPC and the AAPSC, whose roles and limitations we discussed previously. There have been certain sovereign states that have at specific points taken the lead, some more consistently than others. There have been student organizations, particularly those of Africans studying in Europe. The latter might have been the major force except for two severe limitations: they were far removed from the scene and they were very ambivalent about being committed to African unity as an ideal. There have been the youth movements that played a major role in the earlier movement for French West African unity we discussed in a previous chapter.

The group that has had relatively the most solid claim to persistently avant-garde positions is the African trade-union movement. There are several reasons for this, rooted in the social structure of contemporary Africa. First of all, national trade-union leaders have also very often been second-level political leaders. It is important to understand what this has meant. In almost every case, they have been active participants in the political process, with ties to the nationalist parties, and they viewed their trade-union activities as part of their larger political commitment. As trade-unionists, however, they have not been the top political leaders, although trade-union leadership has often been a channel for political ascent. Yet once such men as Sékou Touré, Djibo Bakary, Rashidi Kawawa, and Tom Mboya became full-time political officeholders, they ceased to be in any meaningful sense trade-union leaders. They may have retained a certain legacy of thought, analysis, and sympathy (or they may not have), but there were now others who led the trade-unions. They were nonetheless second-level leaders and not third-level leaders. That is to say, in almost every African state, both before and after independence, the national trade-union leaders were men of political consequence whose views were heard and whose pressures were felt. In a few cases they helped to bring down governments. Their status as second-level political leaders, neither at the very top nor very far down, gave them power and perquisites in the system. But it also meant that they had peers who had greater power and privilege.

Secondly, they tended to represent a segment of the population that was in the same social situation as they themselves. Trade-unions, for the most part, represented skilled workers, schoolteachers, junior civil servants; in other words, those who had, in relation to the overwhelming majority of the population who were peasants, a high and regular income. But they were still relatively deprived in comparison with top politicians, senior civil servants, professional men, and, in some African countries, businessmen and the larger cash-crop farmers. They were, in many countries, a large enough group in the urban centers, to make their weight felt. Furthermore, the members of the trade-unions had, by and large, sufficient education and sophistication to appreciate the true nature of the distribution of goods in the society.

Thirdly, trade-unions were relatively strong and permanent structures, having in most cases their own bureaucracies. They had a network of transnational contacts, both among African nations and with the rest of the world, that were partially independent of other political or diplomatic channels. They were furthermore part of an international trade-union arena which had distinctive norms, which often placed pressure on African trade-unions, and which could in turn provide support for trade-union pressures upon national governments.

Fourthly, trade-unions were not given free political rein by nationalist parties or independent African governments. They were not allowed for the most part to function as organizations of political opposition. If they got too far out of line, either they were repressed or the political authorities arranged a change of trade-union leadership. But precisely because of this political control, trade unions rarely became total outsiders to the political system, and could therefore operate as forces within it. The result was that in many African countries the trade-union movement represented the major legitimate opposition, albeit constrained in its forms of public expression and its degree of deviation.

Fifthly, the existence of this subtle and legitimate opposition in many less radical African countries made possible organizational links of the movement for African unity in countries where it was otherwise difficult. We shall see how this operated in the attempt to create a pan-African trade-union structure.

To appreciate the difficulties of establishing such a structure, we must look at the early history of trade-unionism in Africa. When trade-unions began, they were much more closely tied into metropolitan structures than were their corresponding nationalist political parties. In British Africa, whereas the parties were scarcely in contact with British parties, the trade-unions were supported by the Trades Union Congress (TUC) and linked to the same international trade-union structure as the TUC, which from 1949 on was the International Confederation of Free Trade Unions (ICFTU). In French Africa, whereas the parties were at first affiliated on a parliamentary level (*apparenté*) to French political parties, the trade-unions were integral parts of the three French trade-union structures and therefore of the three internationals with which the French unions were affiliated. The three French trade-union structures in question were the Confédération Générale du Travail (CGT), by far the most important in French Africa, the Confédération Française des Travailleurs Chrétiens (CFTC) and the CGT–Force Ouvrière (FO). The internationals were respectively the World Federation of Trade Unions (WFTU), the International Federation of Christian Trade Unions (IFCTU), and the ICFTU. The situation in Belgian Africa was somewhat similar to that in French Africa. (In Portuguese Africa trade unions were not permitted.)

In general, therefore, there was an important difference between the trade-unions and the political parties in terms of their relations to their counterparts in the metropolitan countries. The trade-unions of the colonial powers played a relatively important role in the early development of African trade-unions, far larger than the role played by metropolitan parties in the early days of nationalist parties. Hence the metropolitan trade-unions and the international trade-union structures of which they were a part retained considerable influence for a long time in Africa.

The first trade-union structure in Africa to try to break out of the mold of metropolitan patronage was the Union Générale des Travailleurs Tunisiens (UGTT). In 1946, when it was relaunched, it sought direct affiliation to the WFTU (which at that time still included the trade-unions that later broke off to form the ICFTU). WFTU, dominated as it was by the European left, whose ambivalence toward African nationalism we discussed in the first chapter, was very reluctant to grant the UGTT full recognition because it suspected that the UGTT gave nationalist political objectives priority over syndical class objectives. These suspicions were, to be sure, not without basis. Finally, in January 1949, within days after the split of the Western trade unions from the WFTU, the latter hastened to admit the UGTT in addition to the previous member, the rival Union Syndicale des Travailleurs Tunisiens, which was the renamed Tunisian section of the CGT. The UGTT remained affiliated to the WFTU only briefly, since the latter still gave favored treatment to the USTT. After a major quarrel in the summer of 1949, the UGTT quit the WFTU to join shortly thereafter the newly formed and rival ICFTU.

At the congress of the UGTT in Tunis in April 1951, which confirmed the disaffiliation from the WFTU and the affiliation with the ICFTU, Mahjoub Ben Seddik, representing the nationalist fraction of the Moroccan trade-unions still affiliated to the CGT, publicly proclaimed the autonomy of the Moroccan trade-unions and indicated that their presence inside the CGT was provisional. This promise was fulfilled in 1955 with the creation of the Union Marocaine de Travail (UMT). In 1956, after the Algerian war of independence had begun, the Algerian trade-unionists similarly broke with the CGT and formed the Union Générale des Travailleurs Algériens (UGTA). Both the UMT and the UGTA followed the UGTT's path by entering the ICFTU.

Developments in North Africa had great influence on the trade-union movement in French West Africa. The WFTU convened in Dakar on April 9–10, 1947, a pan-African trade-union conference. This was the first major inter-African labor meeting ever held. It was, however, limited to French black Africa and it was under the auspices of the CGT, the delegates coming from various African sections of the CGT. The WFTU sought to hold a second such conference in Douala, French Cameroun, in February 1951. But the colonial authorities of the territory forbade it, since the WFTU had been banned in France the previous month. Instead, from October 22 to 28, 1951, the CGT, which was not banned, convened an African conference in Bamako, Mali. Here the lesson of North African experience led the CGT to accept the creation of two interterritorial coordinating committees, one for West Africa and one for Equatorial Africa. This was a gingerly taken step toward autonomy. In February 1953 the CFTC followed suit with two regional coordinating committees.

The next major step occurred in July 1955 at the meeting of the Coordinating Committee of the Rassemblement Démocratique Africain in Conakry, Guinea. Most, but not all, CGT leaders in Africa were also active in the RDA, and almost all RDA trade-unionists were in the CGT. At this meeting the trade-union report was made by Sékou Touré, who was at that time both the leader of the Guinea RDA and one of the three federal secretaries of the CGT for West Africa. The RDA decided, on the basis of Sékou Touré's recommendation, to push for disaffiliation of African trade unions from the CGT. The results of the RDA decision were not long in coming. In November 1955 the Senegal-Mauritania section of the CGT decided to break with both the CGT and WFTU and create a new structure. In January 1956 these unions plus the Guinea CGT and some others formed the Confédération Générale des Travailleurs Africains (CGTA) under the leadership of Sékou Touré and Diallo Seydou. The CGTA launched a call for a larger trade-union conference. In the light of this development, the so-called "orthodox" CGT held a meeting of its coordinating committee for French West Africa (minus, of course, those who had left). It too called for a trade-union conference to establish a new structure, "which would have the task of deciding upon its links with the French CGT." It was a small compromise and one that omitted all mention of the WFTU, but it was in any case three months too late. The world climate had changed and so had the African. It was 1956, the year of destalinization, the year of the spectacular break of Aimé Césaire with the French Communist Party, and the year of the Hungarian Revolution. In French Africa it was the year of the *loi cadre* which granted semiautonomy to the various territorial governments. Small concessions by the CGT and the WFTU were unacceptable.

In July 1956 the CFTC, responding to the new demand for autonomy, renamed itself at a meeting in Ouagadougou, Upper Volta, the Confédération Africaine des Travailleurs Croyants (CATC).[1] The position of the CGTA was becoming widely accepted. In October the autonomous railwaymen's union got the CGTA and the "orthodox" CGT to join them in a single call for a unity conference, which was then held in Cotonou, Dahomey, January 16–19, 1957. The CATC felt obliged to come. The conference ended in the formation of the Union Générale des Travailleurs d'Afrique Noire (UGTAN). UGTAN achieved its unity on the basis of nonaffiliation of its constituent to any international trade-union organization. This in fact affected only the WFTU which lost its West African affiliates. The CATC unions withdrew from UGTAN after the conference because participation involved disaffiliation from the IFCTU as well as unity on a territorial level. The tiny FO unions did not even attend the Cotonou meeting. Thus UGTAN represented essentially the old CGT plus some autonomous unions, but as UGTAN they were affiliated neither to CGT nor to WFTU.

WFTU had by now learned much from its North African fiasco and put on the bravest face it could, deciding to maintain fraternal relations with UGTAN. That the WFTU was nonetheless unhappy with the creation of UGTAN can be seen by how it dragged its feet in Equatorial Africa. In December 1956 the CGT affiliate in French Cameroun became the Confédération Générale du Travail du Kamerun (CGTK), which affiliated directly with the WFTU. The various CGT affiliates

[1] Not only did they change "Française" to "Africaine," but they changed "Chrétiens" to "Croyants" specifically in order to include Moslems.

in French Equatorial Africa did not even attend the Cotonou meeting. Instead, in April 1957 they formed along with the CGTK the Confédération Générale Aéfienne du Travail (CGAT). On their behalf, Jacques N'Gom, Secretary-General of the CGTK, declared to the 1957 world congress of the WFTU: "The trade-union organizations of French Equatorial Africa and the CGTK believe that trade-union unity at the level of a given region such as black Africa should not close the door to international trade-union solidarity and unity." This statement is very similar to statements made at later ICFTU congresses by men such as Ahmed Tlili of Tunisia and Tom Mboya of Kenya to justify continued affiliation to the ICFTU.

If the WFTU played its main role in French Africa[2] up to 1957 largely because of the CGT's influence, the ICFTU played its main role in British Africa largely because of the influence of the British TUC. The two main territories where ICFTU influence was at all in question before 1957 were the Gold Coast (Ghana) and Nigeria.

In Nigeria, where the trade-union movement came into existence during the Second World War, the Nigerian Trade Union Congress (NTUC) was a founding member of the WFTU. It also affiliated in 1946 to the major nationalist party, the National Council of Nigeria and the Cameroons (NCNC). With the split in the WFTU came a split in the NTUC. The split in Nigeria was healed by the creation in May 1950 of the Nigerian Labour Congress, which once again affiliated to the WFTU. The affiliation, however, was a continued source of discord. Consequently, the Congress withdrew from the WFTU in February 1951, but for this and other reasons the Congress disintegrated. It was replaced in 1953 by the All-Nigerian Trade Union Federation (ANTUF) which main-

[2] The one exception was the Sudan, where the Sudan Workers Trade Union Federation affiliated to the WFTU right after independence in 1956, having been prevented earlier from doing so by colonial legislation. When the military, under General Abboud, took over in November 1958, all trade-union activity was suspended and the leaders of the Federation were arrested.

THE PROBLEMS OF A MOVEMENT

tained its unity until 1957 by not having an international affiliation.

The Gold Coast history was somewhat different. The Gold
Coast Trades Union Congress (GCTUC) called a general
strike in January 1950 to support the political program of the
Convention People's Party (CPP). As a result, the GCTUC
was suppressed. It was reorganized as a trade-union that was
neutral in Gold Coast politics and affiliated to the ICFTU
rather than the WFTU. This led in 1952 to a split by CPP
members, who formed the Ghana TUC and attacked the affiliation of the GCTUC to the ICFTU. The two factions reunited
in 1953, on the basis of nonaffiliation, as the GCTUC. Thus
in August 1953 the GCTUC withdrew from the ICFTU.

The ICFTU began to be active in West Africa in 1951.
When the WFTU was refused permission to hold a meeting
in Douala in February 1951, the ICFTU proceeded to hold
one there in March. The ICFTU also sent a traveling team to
West Africa in conjunction with the meeting. The meeting included trade-unionists from the four territories of British West
Africa and from the relatively unimportant FO unions in
French black Africa. The visit of the ICFTU team and the
meeting were very successful in both Nigeria and the Gold
Coast, leading to the disaffiliation of their trade-unions from
the WFTU. The team was less successful in French West
Africa. The FO in France suspected any direct contact of its
affiliates with the ICFTU, and for the following year successfully negated the proposal for direct contact which had ema-
nated from the Douala conference. A compromise was reached,
and it was decided to establish a West African Trade Union
Information and Advisory Centre in Accra in 1954. It was
very inconvenient, therefore, that the reunited Gold Coast
TUC had disaffiliated. The British TUC put great pressure
on the Ghana TUC to rejoin the ICFTU. Since this pressure
was felt shortly after the British suspension of the British
Guiana constitution because of the alleged Communist leanings of the government, the Gold Coast political leadership
decided to purge two notorious leftist trade-unionists, and in

March 1954 the GCTUC rejoined the ICTFU.[3] An attempt by some trade-unionists linked to the political opposition to create a rival organization in 1955, which received support from the WFTU, was successfully fought.

Thus, when serious pan-African political developments began in 1957, African trade-unions had already had a very active experience with the issues of unity and the implications of international links. This early history was to mark the internecine struggle of African trade-unions after 1957 and was to make the issue of international affiliations a central one for those trade-unionists who constituted themselves as the avantgarde of the movement toward African unity.

At the beginning of 1957 the trade-union picture in Africa was as follows. The WFTU had made a series of major errors in Africa which largely involved their initial inability to appreciate the force of African nationalism, the inevitably close links of trade-union movements with nationalist parties, and the consequent drive for autonomy from metropolitan tradeunion organizations. Because the WFTU did not allow in time for the direct affiliation of nationalist trade-unions, by-passing in particular the CGT, the WFTU had lost its affiliates in North Africa and was in the process of losing them in French West Africa. Similarly, the tie was dropped in Nigeria under nationalist pressures and in the interests of internal unity. In Sudan alone it lost an affiliate through simple suppression by the authorities.

The ICFTU was able to profit from the errors of the WFTU in North Africa. But in the rest of French Africa the ICFTU had made scarcely any dent, principally because it sought to deal with the insignificant FO unions, and even there it was met by opposition from its own French affiliate. In British

[3] The sequence of events was as follows: August 1953—disaffiliation of GCTUC from ICFTU; October 9, 1953—suspension of British Guiana Constitution; late October—Turkson Ocran, Secretary-General of TUC, relieved of TUC duties and suspended from CPP, along with Anthony Woode, M.P., for alleged Communist leanings; February 12, 1954— Nkrumah defends before National Assembly a decree which denies Communists employment in the civil service; March 1954—reaffiliation of GCTUC to ICFTU.

East and Central Africa, where trade-unions came into existence for the most part only after the creation of the ICFTU and were heavily dependent for political as well as economic support on the British TUC, the ICFTU acquired affiliates. But in British West Africa they secured the Gold Coast's adherence only through external political pressure, which however was sweetened by the mistake of the WFTU in support- ing the opposition party's trade-union structure in 1955. In Nigeria ANTUF was neutral and was therefore considered hostile by the ICFTU, which was seeking to establish a structure that would affiliate to it.

Nonetheless, over-all, the position of the ICFTU was infinitely superior to that of the WFTU at the time the ICFTU convened its First African Regional Trade Union Conference in Accra from January 14 to 19, 1957. The chief organizer was John Tettegah, Secretary-General of the GCTUC and then the African member of the Executive Committee of the ICFTU. All the ICFTU affiliates in Africa came except the Moroccan UMT. Kwame Nkrumah, Prime Minister of the about-to-be-independent Ghana, opened its sessions. In his speech Nkrumah stressed a theme that was to underlie much subsequent trade-union history in Africa:

> We welcome the creation of trade unions and we welcome help from trade unions from abroad in assisting our unions to organize and to expand. But it is essential that trade unionism in Africa takes into account the particular conditions of Africa. It would be fatal if it was thought that trade unionism can be established merely by copying what has been done in Europe and America.

With this meeting the ICFTU was launched as a major force on the African continent. It was launched in Accra and, with the cooperation of the Ghana government, just at the moment when Ghana was about to begin the serious political activity that marked the renewal of the movement for African unity. But the ICFTU had two extremely strong biases which controlled its activities and led it into conflict with the movement toward African unity. One was bias of the European (and American) left, which saw trade-unions as structures that primarily fought employers, which in the case of Africa were primarily governments. This conflicted with the strong conviction of the majority of African trade-unionists that their objectives were primarily not class but national objectives which could be pursued best in close collaboration with the nationalist political party. The second bias, which derived from the very origin of the ICFTU, was a total commitment to the political primacy of anticommunism, and a consequent deep aversion to neutralism, whether of governments or of trade-unions.[4] This conflicted with the deep commitment to nonalignment which would emerge clearly in Africa, and the conviction of many Africans, certainly of the revolutionary core of the movement toward African unity, that the primary political obstacle to the achievement of African political and economic objectives lay in Africa's close links with the Western world. What started at the Accra trade-union meeting as a misunderstanding soon expanded into an opposition of principle, which led eventually to total conflict throughout the African continent. In the process of this evolving conflict the ICFTU managed to repeat most of the actions of the WFTU which had had such disastrous consequences. These actions led to similar, if less total, consequences for the ICFTU, which became in the eyes of the avant-garde of the movement for unity the leading element of the enemy forces.

Developments on the trade-union front paralleled those on the political front. Or rather, since trade-unions served as an avant-garde, they preceded and indeed in part shaped the political developments. The Accra Regional Conference had decided in principle on the creation of an African Regional Organization (AFRO) of the ICFTU. There was considerable European reluctance about the creation of this united struc-

---

[4] For example, in 1956, George Meany, President of the AFL-CIO, publicly accused Prime Minister Jawaharlal Nehru of India of being pro-Communist because of his neutralism, his hostility to President Syngman Rhee of Korea, and his opposition to the Southeast Asia Treaty Organization.

ture, the objections being put forward on technical grounds. It was decided therefore to create first three area committees and eventually to link them by an over-all council. The three areas were to be North Africa, West Africa, and East, Central, and Southern Africa. These were to be set up at the Fifth World Congress of the ICFTU in Tunis in July 1957. In July, however, the North Africans decided that they did not need an ICFTU label for their regional structure. This was the heyday of the movement toward Maghreb unity, and the assertion of relative independence fit in with North African sentiments. The Ghana TUC, the ICFTU's only really strong affiliate in West Africa, declined to proceed with a West African area committee until French West Africa could be effectively included, and by this they meant UGTAN. ICFTU was, however, highly suspicious of UGTAN's political philosophy and was still toying with the idea of working through FO.[5] Only the East, Central, and Southern African Area Committee was established, chaired by Tom Mboya. This fitted it in perfectly with the nascent PAFMECA; and unlike the North Africans, the East Africans needed the political protection the ICFTU and the British TUC would give them in their political struggles with the Colonial Office.

The Tunis meeting hinted at the nature of the ICFTU's future difficulties. However, those trade-unions that were the avant-garde of the movement toward unity were not represented there at all. Those unions were joined together in UGTAN, which was strongest in French West Africa. At this point it must be recalled that the drive for African unity in French West Africa was really a drive for regional unity. UGTAN reflected this spirit and indeed led this drive. The drive culminated in the De Gaulle Referendum of September

[5] In February 1958 the FO sections in French Africa finally cut their links with the French FO and, at a meeting in Abidjan, constituted themselves the Confédération Africaine des Syndicats Libres-Force Ouvrière (CASL-FO). The inclusion of FO in the title was a concession to the sentiments of the French FO. It was dropped shortly after in an effort to persuade the ICFTU to adopt CASL as its West African regional organization. But CASL was far too weak and the ICFTU rejected this strategy.

28, 1958. Most political parties called for a "yes" vote in the Referendum. UGTAN, at a special meeting in Bamako on September 10–11, 1958, called for a "no" vote, stating that the proposed constitution "consecrates the division of Africa in order to assure the permanence of colonization in its modern form." UGTAN stated as its minimum objective the setting up of two sovereign unified African states, one in (French) West Africa and one in (French) Equatorial Africa. UGTAN was joined in calling for a "no" vote by the Conseil de la Jeunesse d'Afrique, the Fédération des Etudiants d'Afrique Noire en France, and the Union Générale des Etudiants d'Afrique Occidentale. The two major political parties which called for a "no" vote were the Guinea RDA and the Niger Sawaba, led respectively by Sékou Touré and Djibo Bakary, both leaders of UGTAN.

Soon after the Referendum the first AAPC was held in Accra in December. Among the resolutions was one on African trade-union unity which called for the creation of a unified African trade-union structure. There was, however, disagreement as to its structure. After the meeting the pressure for a new organization mounted. From January 15 to 19, 1959, UGTAN held its first general congress in Conakry, in newly independent Guinea, whose President, Sékou Touré, was also the Secretary-General of UGTAN. In his report to the Congress he made very clear his conception of UGTAN's role:

> UGTAN has proclaimed itself the avant-garde element in the struggle for the liberation of Africa, and this is why it insists that its action be pursued in the awareness of the contradictions between African national independence and foreign domination. . . . If UGTAN constitutes the unified workers' movement, it is because the old trade unions had liberated themselves from the metropolitan trade-union structures to which they had been previously affiliated in order to create their own unity. It is with this clear notion on the best perspectives of the unity of the African father-land that UGTAN participated in the recent pan-African conference in Accra and hailed the Ghana-Guinea Union as

a dynamic element in the movement that will eventually lead to the United States of Africa.

At this meeting, John Tettegah, Secretary-General of the Ghana TUC, became Vice-President of UGTAN. UGTAN, as the avant-garde of the movement for French West African unity, had transformed itself into an element in the movement for continental unity. It would now begin to enter into relations with trade-union movements as far away as the Belgian Congo and Nyasaland. The Bureau of UGTAN was mandated at this congress to seek a pan-African meeting.

In April 1959 the Ghana TUC and the UMT of Morocco, both still members of the ICFTU, called at their respective national conferences for a pan-African meeting. Ghana ceased to cooperate with the ICFTU from early 1959, although its formal disaffiliation did not occur until December.[6] On August 23, 1959, the Ghana TUC visited the Nigerian TUC. They issued a joint statement supporting a pan-African meeting and also advocating the establishment of a Federation of West African Trade Unions that would include English-, French-, and Portuguese-speaking countries.[7] From September 8 to 12 a meeting of a preparatory committee in Casablanca was attended by the UMT of Morocco and the Algerian UGTA, both still members of the ICFTU, plus UGTAN and the Egyptian

[6] The ICFTU began to move its regional office *de facto* to Lagos in mid-1959, but again the Accra office was not formally closed until December.

[7] Nigerian trade-unions had become increasingly split after 1955 on the issue of affiliation to the ICFTU. In March 1959 they achieved temporary unity under the name of the Trades Union Congress of Nigeria (TUCN). However, apart from the President, Michael Imoudu, all the officers of the TUCN were drawn from the former ICFTU affiliates. In April 1959 the Executive voted to seek affiliation with the ICFTU. This led to a new split. At the time of the joint communiqué, however, the split was not yet formalized and the signer for Nigeria was Lawrence Borha, Secretary-General of the TUCN and leader of the pro-ICFTU faction. By November, at the meeting of the Preparatory Conference of AATUF at Accra, two representatives of the Borha faction were expelled in favor of four late-arriving members of the Imoudu faction. The latter took the name, at their constituent congress in 1960, of the Nigerian Trade Union Congress (NTUC).

TUC. The meeting called for a pan-African organization. The Steering Committee of the AAPC met from October 6 to 9 in Accra and decided to convene a Preparatory Conference for the trade-union organization. The chairman of the Committee, Tom Mboya, who might have opposed such a move, did not attend; he was severely criticized for his absence as well as for his point of view. The Secretary-General of the AAPC, Abdoulaye Diallo, himself an old trade-union leader, asked the Ghana TUC to constitute a convening secretariat for the Preparatory Conference to be held in Accra from November 4 to 9.

The dates of the Accra meeting clearly were chosen in relation to the proposed dates of the Second African Regional Conference of ICFTU. The latter was scheduled for Lagos from November 9 to 15, to be preceded by a seminar beginning on November 4. The objective was clearly to force a choice by unions between the two meetings. Both sides seemed interested in forcing the choice, and they succeeded. The Preparatory Conference in Accra decided to convene a constituent congress of the All-African Trade Union Federation (AATUF) in mid-May 1960 in Casablanca. It established a Preparatory Committee with headquarters in Accra and chose a bureau composed of Mahjoub Ben Seddik of the UMT as President and six secretaries representing the Ghanaian TUC, the Egyptian TUC, the Nigerian TUC, the Algerian UGTA, and two from the interterritorial UGTAN. In their appeal to African workers the Conference stated that "the influence of imported ideologies does not in any way meet the needs of the struggle for liberation, and that, on the contrary, the rivalries of international confederations, their interference with and pressures exerted upon African trade unions, have always been a source of division and diversion, prejudicial to the unity of the popular forces and their effective action." The Lagos regional meeting of the ICFTU, on the other hand, reaffirmed its loyalty to the AAPC but added: "We see no conflict in this stand with our continued support and affiliation with the ICFTU. On the contrary, we regard this as an opportunity to project the African personality." From this point forth, neither side was to budge substantially from its position on this key issue of affiliation.

In January 1960 the Second AAPC was held in Tunis and, in conjunction with it, the first meeting of the Preparatory Committee of AATUF. The Tunis conference was a moment of compromise, as we may recall. It was also a moment of optimism on the African scene, the beginning of the year during which so many African states were to become independent. As for the trade-unions, it was still hoped on both sides that the other would give way on the affiliation issue. The AAPC resolution hailed the forthcoming meeting of AATUF, but avoided all mention of the affiliation question. As a result of the continued negotiations, the May meeting that was to mark the formation of AATUF was postponed and was not held until one year later, in May 1961.

The postponement was to little avail. The summer of 1960 was the beginning of the first Congo crisis with all that it entailed in emphasizing the two basic differences in approach to questions of unity. From November 7 to 11 in Tunis the third Regional Conference of ICFTU was held. In the previous May Omer Becu had become the Secretary-General of ICFTU, replacing J. H. Oldenbroek, who had represented a point of view within ICFTU rather rigid in its attitude toward African trade-unions. The AFL-CIO was willing to support "nationalist" trade-unions provided they were "free" trade-unions. They fought not only for modification of ICFTU "rigidity" but for a freer hand for themselves in Africa, which they were reluctantly granted. As a result of this internal ICFTU controversy, the African Regional Organization (AFRO) was finally allowed to come into existence, with headquarters in Lagos. Like the CGT-WFTU about-face after the creation of the CGTA, this gesture by the ICFTU came too late to undo the drive for disaffiliation. AFRO at this point could command the loyalty of only a segment of Africa's significant trade unions: those of Tunisia and Libya, those in East and Central Africa, and one faction in Nigeria.

We have noted how the Congo crisis led to the creation of the Casablanca and Monrovia powers; we shall soon see parallel structures on the trade-union front. In the case of the two intergovernmental structures, PAFMECA took a somewhat middle-of-the-road position, still representing at that time the nonindependent states. Though the trade-unions within PAFMECA's region were almost all affiliated to the ICFTU, precisely as we have noted because their countries' primary battles were the anticolonial struggle for political sovereignty, it was natural for the leaders of AATUF to feel that this region represented a weak link in the chain of ICFTU affiliates. From this point forward East and Central African unions were to become a central arena of struggle between AATUF and ICFTU.

The opening move of AATUF was a gentle one. John Tettegah, representing the Ghana TUC, paid an official visit to Tom Mboya, who was then Secretary-General of the Kenya Federation of Labour (KFL). In a joint communiqué issued on November 11, 1960, which has since become quite famous, the two leaders said on behalf of their national trade unions: "It is agreed that AATUF should not be affiliated to any of the international trade union centres," and added that the "Kenya Federation of Labour and the Ghana TUC both recognize the right of each National Centre to decide on its international relations." The key word was "relations," the KFL taking this to include affiliation and the Ghana TUC presuming the opposite.

Thus the communiqué turned out to be quite meaningless and the honeymoon was brief. In December at Lagos the International Labor Organization convened the first meeting of African Ministers of Labour. At this meeting, Gogo Nzeribe, a Nigerian trade-unionist sympathetic to AATUF, distributed a pamphlet entitled *The Great Conspiracy*, which contained what was claimed to be a secret British cabinet document on African trade-unions indicating that the ICFTU was operating on behalf of Western powers. Tom Mboya, who was directly impugned, attacked this as a "subtle manoeuvre," by implication of Tettegah and AATUF.[8]

The third meeting of the Preparatory Committee of AATUF, held from April 20 to 23, 1961, in Conakry, convened the inaugural congress for Casablanca from May 25 to 28. One of the key issues was, of course, credentials, since in many African states there were competing trade unions, and in some independent states trade-unions-in-exile. The committee decided that eight trade-unions should be "foundation members" of AATUF and that they should decide on the credentials of the others. The eight were the Ghanaian TUC, the Egyptian TUC, the Confédération Nationale des Travailleurs Guinéens-UGTAN, the Union Nationale des Travailleurs Maliens, the UMT (Morocco), the UGTA (Algeria), the UGTT (Tunisia), and the KFL (Kenya). Of the eight, the last four were at that time members of ICFTU, but only the UGTT and the KFL were members of AFRO and committed to continued membership in ICFTU.

Virtually all African trade-unions came to Casablanca, including those affiliated both to the ICFTU and to the IFCTU as well as some in exile. Many of the IFCTU members, however, were denied more than observer status by the credentials committee. Mahjoub Ben Seddik in his Report of Doctrine and Orientation launched the slogan which incarnated the spirit of the meeting and which was adopted in the resulting Charter of AATUF: "The era of mother-countries (métropoles) is over." He concluded his analysis by summing up what he felt to be the two fundamental characteristics of the trade-union struggle: "radicalism, of a tough revolutionary sincerity; empiricism, difficult to classify or to identify with foreign ideologies." This is a pithy restatement of what had always been the main characteristics of the movement toward African unity.

---

[8] Secret documents continued to play a role. In 1962 the ICFTU distributed what it claimed was a secret letter from Ibrahim Zakaria, a Sudanese and a secretary of the WFTU, to Charles Heymann of the Ghana TUC, indicating secret financial support for AATUF by WFTU. AATUF decried the genuineness of the letter.

Adorning the hall of the meeting were pictures of the four martyrs under whose inspiration the meeting was held: Lumumba, Moumié, Ferhat Hached, and Aissat Idir (the last two were trade-union leaders of Tunisia and Algeria, respectively, who were killed during their countries' struggles for independence). But 1961 was not a moment of unity, least of all from the point of view of the avant-garde elements. These held firm on the issue of disaffiliation, considering it to be the key symbolic issue. For disaffiliation meant essentially the willingness to follow a path independent of the Western (colonial and neo-colonial) world, with which the ICFTU and IFCTU were identified. The split with the WFTU had already occurred, although there were and would remain a few groups still affiliated.[9] On this issue, there were three main positions at the Conference: that of Ghana, Guinea, Mali, and the U.A.R. calling for immediate disaffiliation; that of Tunisia and Kenya, calling for freedom of each national unit to decide its own affiliation; and that of Morocco and Algeria, both still affiliated to the ICFTU but in favor of everyone's disaffiliating. Morocco and Algeria tried to arrive at a compromise. They succeeded in having a clause adopted modifying the requirement for disaffiliation as follows: "Nevertheless, as a temporary measure, national trade-union organizations who belong to international trade-union federations at the time of this Congress are given a delay of ten months to achieve disaffiliation." Neither Tunisia nor Kenya nor their friends would accept this and they walked out of the Conference.

In its conception of the revolutionary role of trade unions, AATUF put the principle of international nonalignment and disaffiliation first. But it added two other principles: one was its firm position against trade-union pluralism in Africa and

[9] The trade-unions in Egypt, Libya, and the suppressed union in the Sudan also belonged to the International Confederation of Arab Trade Unions (ICATU), with headquarters in Cairo. For those most vigorously calling for disaffiliation, ICATU was never an issue since it was a Third World and not an international trade-union federation. Those who stayed with the ICFTU often pointed to continued affiliation with ICATU as violating the demand for nonaffiliation with extra-African bodies.

its consequent insistence on the creation of a single trade-union center in each country. This was aimed, on the one hand, at those countries, such as Nigeria or Kenya, where there were two unions, whose differences usually focused at this point on the question of disaffiliation. It was aimed also at the existence of the separate Christian trade unions and their African confederal structure, the Union Panafricaine des Travailleurs Croyants (UPTC),[10] which had been a continuing issue from the time of the original UGTAN Congress of Cotonou in January 1957.

The second principle was the rejection of apoliticism. The Charter of AATUF says: "Colonialism has made of all Africans exploited men. Also the workers and the peasants constitute the principal stratum of African society, the most awakened and the most dynamic Africa cannot achieve its ends without them nor even more against them. Their role is first of all a political one." But the Charter adds: "Trade-unions do not have to submit to dictation of political tutelage of any party: they occupy rather a leading position which confers certain rights upon them and assigns them certain duties." Those who stood against disaffiliation would make a central argument of their case against AATUF that its leading affiliates were all trade-unions subordinate to and controlled by their respective nationalist parties. This was the subject of a constant parade of allegations and counterallegations for years to come. In fact, most trade-unions, whether in AATUF or not, seemed to stand for the close collaboration of a trade-union organization with its political party or government, if they liked the dominant political power of that country, and against the

[10] The UPTC had been created in Brazzaville on January 11–14, 1959. Its affiliates were the unions in the two CATCs in West and Equatorial Africa, plus federations in the Malagasy Republic, Congo (L), and Nigeria. At its first Congress, May 2–5, 1960, in Cotonou, the UPTC in its resolution on African trade-union unity said that "unity achieved in confusion and contradiction would undoubtedly lead to the weakening of African trade-unionism." At the AATUF meeting in Casablanca, Ben Seddik refused the floor to Gilbert Pongault, Secretary-General of the UPTC, when he wished to speak in the name of the UPTC but gave it to him in his capacity as a trade-union representative from Congo (B).

subordination of trade unions in African countries other than their own if they did not happen to like its dominant political power. In any case, the most prominent instance of a dominant trade union in relatively open opposition to its own government, in an independent African country and not in exile, was the UMT in Morocco, whose Secretary-General, Ben Seddik, was the President of AATUF.

The AATUF Congress thus ended in an open split between the adherents of the revolutionary core of the movement for African unity and those who stood for a different concept of unity, which we have called unity as alliance. The only ones who seemed to regret the split were the Moroccan and Algerian federations and one of the Senegalese trade-union federations. AATUF established headquarters in Casablanca, elected Ben Seddik President, and chose seven secretaries, one each from Algeria, Ghana, Guinea, Mali, Morocco, Kenya, and the U.A.R. The list was the same as the list of eight founding members minus Tunisia. In Mboya's absence after he had left Casablanca, he was named secretary from Kenya, but he subsequently refused the position.

The ICFTU's reaction to the creation of AATUF was immediate and strong. An editorial entitled "Pan-Africanism and the ICFTU," which appeared in the July 1961 issue of its journal, *Free Labour World*, made clear the nature of the suspicions which led it into open opposition to AATUF: "The Communist-controlled WFTU knows only too well that it will never get the affiliation of any responsible African labor body; the best it can hope for is their isolation from the free world labor movement. It has consequently gone all out to encourage separatist and isolationist tendencies under the mask of neutralism." In short, for the ICFTU, AATUF was inspired by, and was a front for, the WFTU. The ICFTU rejected the credibility of AATUF's main claim for existence, its quest for African autonomy and African revolutionary values.

The KFL in Kenya issued a statement on July 8, 1961, in which it attacked the undemocratic nature of the organization of the congress, but accepted nonetheless many of the slogans of AATUF, and suggested a minor concession by agreeing that "international affiliation could, unless it is constantly and vigilantly watched, constitute a danger to national independence." But it wished to leave the actual decision to each national center. It coupled this with a call for a new conference, which was to become the theme of the opposition. The AATUF Secretariat denounced this proposal as "not only negative and futile but an action purported to create doubt and confusion and to engender division."

Strong counterpressures by the ICFTU led to hesitations on the part of North Africa. The East African situation was uncertain. The combination caused AATUF to slow down and postpone two secretariat meetings. The meeting of the Trade Union Council of the UAS (Ghana-Guinea-Mali), on November 6–8, 1961, had the air of a retrenchment operation.

From January 9 to 14, 1962, in Dakar a rival pan-African conference was held, organized by the Union Nationale des Travailleurs Sénégalais (UNTS), itself unaffiliated internationally,[11] but supported both by the ICFTU and IFCTU. The placard in the hall read INDEPENDENT AND AUTHENTIC TRADE-UNIONISM, with the clear implication that AATUF was neither independent (of WFTU) nor authentic (because the unions were government-controlled).

The conference drew a large number of delegates. All the Christian unions came, but here, as in Casablanca, as individual national unions and not collectively as the UPTC. Most of the ICFTU unions came, but neither Morocco nor Algeria did. The ICFTU group included East and Central Africa, Tunisia, Libya, and the TUC-Nigeria. Some unaffiliated unions came. Besides Senegal, they included notably groups from Mauritania, the Ivory Coast, and Niger, and some from other UAM states. The assembled delegates decided to create a new organization called the African Trade Union Confederation (ATUC). The President was to be Ahmed Tlili of Tunisia and the headquarters were to be in Dakar, Senegal.

[11] It derived historically from a split in the union that was part of UGTAN and hence unaffiliated.

On paper, the differences between AATUF and ATUC were small. The most significant difference was on affiliation. While ATUC itself was to be unaffiliated, its members retained freedom of action, thus emphasizing the concept of unity as alliance. On trade-union pluralism, ATUC accepted the principle that there should be only one trade-union center per country and that therefore, where there were two, they should seek to unite, but accepted as a transitional measure multiple membership per country. This permitted the UPTC unions to join ATUC on the assumption of early national unity efforts, but in the following years very little national trade-union unity took place under the aegis of ATUC. When it did occur, it resulted from pressure from the national government rather than from ATUC for such trade-union unity. Most of the political resolutions were similar to those AATUF might have passed. A few were not. For example, ATUC condemned Moroccan ambitions to annex Mauritania. On the Congo, ATUC gave strong support to the central government in its political struggles, explicitly against the Katanga regime, implicitly also against the supporters of Vice-Premier Gizenga, who was in fact dismissed from his post right after the ATUC meeting on January 16. Prime Minister Adoula had been himself a trade-unionist, active in a union that was affiliated to the ICFTU and a member of ATUC.[12]

One of the first actions taken by ATUC after its establishment was to send a delegation to the meeting of the Monrovia Group in Lagos, Nigeria, January 25–31. ATUC indeed formally requested "observer" status in the organization. The request was, however, rejected on the grounds that if ATUC was permitted observer status, with access to closed meetings, similar requests from liberation movements would have to be entertained. Here we see once more the reflex action of the sov-

---

[12] Similarly, in Angola the affiliate of ICFTU and member of ATUC was the Liga General das Trabalhadores Angolanas, linked politically to the UPA. The other union was the União Nacional das Trabalhadores Angolanas, which was linked to the MPLA and was a member of AATUF.

ereign states—to close the door to any action which might remove them from their collective political pre-eminence.

The creation of ATUC served as a counterbalance to
AATUF. After Casablanca John Tettegah of the Ghana TUC
had declared "total war" on those African trade-unionists who
remained affiliated and criticized the proposed Dakar Conference as "another Monrovia in Dakar." After Dakar the
Secretariat of AATUF met on February 3–7 in Casablanca
and stated that it "considers the recent Dakar conference the
work of external intrigue and manoeuvres which do not respond to any African needs but was engineered to divide the
African labour front." But when March 1962 came and the
ten-month disaffiliation limit was up, neither Morocco nor
Algeria, both active members of the AATUF Secretariat, had
disaffiliated from the ICFTU. The reason lay in internal considerations. Both trade unions were engaged in very difficult
internal political struggles in which neither was anxious to
add to its burdens by making an active enemy of the ICFTU.
The Moroccan UMT had been for a long time a key element
in the opposition to the king, and it was felt that removing
Western support for the UMT, even though it was minimal,
might lead to an increased dependence on the monarchy. The
Algerians had been involved in their war for independence
(the truce not being signed until that same month of March
1962), and AFL-CIO support helped to create some American pressure on the French Government to negotiate. Both
the Moroccan and Algerian trade-unions were, however, by
the nature of their political commitments pulled to participate in AATUF. For the moment, they resolved this strain by
being active in AATUF without disaffiliating from the ICFTU.
This could not continue, however, for too long.

On May 5, the Nigerians tried once again to achieve trade-
union unity. The TUCN and the NTUC merged into the
United Labour Congress (ULC) which promptly voted 659–
407 to affiliate with the ICFTU. Thereupon the losers created
the Independent United Labour Congress (IULC), which in

time once again took on the name NTUC. This abortive attempt at trade-union unity came just before the beginning of Nigeria's first major crisis in the Western Region on May 21, 1962, which would continue to fester and would culminate in the military overthrow of the Nigerian government in January 1966.

Essentially, however, neither AATUF nor ATUC did very much during 1962. They were beset by the uncertainties that surrounded the diplomatic maneuvers involved in the search for intergovernmental unity that year. From January 4 to 6, 1963, the UMT held its Third Congress in Casablanca. Seeking to resolve the counterpressures upon it, and somewhat dismayed by political developments on the continent as a whole and on the trade-union front in particular, the UMT voted a very nuanced resolution on international relations. They analyzed the existing situation, explained that "the affiliation of the UMT to the ICFTU in 1955 had permitted the Moroccan trade-union movement to emerge from its isolation," noted the support of the ICFTU "during the difficult periods through which the Moroccan working class had passed," but observed that "nonetheless because of the hostility manifested by a part of the Arab and African trade-union movement to international organizations as a result of their past behavior in the Middle East and black Africa, the UMT is drawn between the needs of a useful international solidarity and the exigencies of the Arab and African trade-union movement." The conclusion of the UMT, therefore, was that "taking note of the fluidity of the situation and the probable changes that will take place, [the Congress] decides the immediate suspension of organic membership of the UMT in all international and continental trade-union federations and authorizes the National Council to decide finally at the right moment between the possible courses of action."

Thus the UMT suspended its affiliation both to ICFTU and to AATUF, a solution that was to find favor elsewhere. In the case of the UMT, however, the move was transitional and the National Council in April decided to withdraw from the ICFTU and to reaffirm participation in AATUF. In the meantime, in late January at the UGTA Congress in Algiers, Ben Seddik brought greetings on behalf of both the UMT and AATUF.[13]

May marked the compromise of Addis Ababa and the creation of the OAU. In anticipation, the projected second Congress of AATUF, scheduled for March 1963 in Bamako, had been postponed. This was to be the case also for the fourth Regional Conference of AFRO, scheduled for Nairobi for July. The immediate expectation, in the optimistic atmosphere of Addis Ababa, was that AATUF and ATUC would follow Casablanca and Monrovia into oblivion. On July 4, 1963, ten prominent trade-unionists associated with the ICFTU and ATUC met in Geneva during the International Labour Conference under the leadership of Lawrence Borha, Secretary-General of the ULC of Nigeria, and called on the Secretariats of ATUC and AATUF "to take steps to convene, at an early date, a meeting of representatives of all bona fide and democratic African national trade-union centres with a view to set up an All-African Trade Union Action Committee and to determine a 'positive action programme' aimed at the complete eradication of apartheid and other forms of racial discrimination on the African continent." Thus it was hoped to form trade-union unity around the issue which brought the states together at Addis Ababa, the liberation of southern Africa.

In July ICFTU lost three important affiliates. The Tanganyika Federation of Labor voted to disaffiliate as did the Zanzibar and Pemba Federation of Labor.[14] And finally, on July 25, the Algerian UGTA withdrew from the ICFTU at the very moment that President Nyerere of Tanganyika was

---

[13] In conjunction with the Third Congress, the UMT issued a communiqué along with a number of nonaligned trade-unions from Algeria, Ceylon, Chile, Guinea, Japan, Mali, U.A.R., and Yugoslavia, in which it called for mutual consultation (but not a new trade-union structure) among the unions of the Third World.

[14] This was one of two federations in Zanzibar. But the rival group had already affiliated with AATUF at Casablanca.

paying a state visit to Algeria.[15] The UGTA reaffirmed its "attachment to the African revolutionary idea" and pledged itself to work for an "Addis Ababa" of African trade-unionism. The reaction of the ICFTU to the UGTA step was strong and led to the UGTA's issuing a clarification in its journal:

> The UGTA considers that its primary duty is to work for the unity of African trade-unionism. . . . The present leaders of the ICFTU hold tight to lost illusions and their attitude is not a proof of wisdom, still less of solidarity. How many errors, false steps, needless impasses would the ICFTU have spared itself had its leaders been ready to understand that Africa is grown up and knows how to determine her true friends.

On July 26, 1963, the Secretariat of AATUF, meeting in Bamako, appealed for a meeting with ATUC. This proposal met resistance within the Secretariat among those who looked with considerable suspicion on the compromise of Addis Ababa and with consequently greater suspicion on an AATUF-ATUC merger, which they felt might vitiate the role of trade-unions as an avant-garde. Nonetheless, the appeal was issued, the ATUC Secretariat responded favorably, and the two groups met in their one and only joint meeting, in Dakar, October 17–19, 1963. The meeting was on the face of it successful. The two groups issued a joint communiqué calling for a single unaffiliated African trade-union center and recommended "to all existing trade-union organizations to unite on a national basis and free themselves of any international affiliations." Toward this end they decided on the creation of a joint preparatory committee to convene a meeting in late 'April or early May 1964, for which the joint committee would prepare the

[15] The year to come was to see the disaffiliation of the Northern Rhodesian affiliate from the ICFTU and the disintegration of the Southern Rhodesian affiliate. In September 1965 the Kenya government imposed a legislated fusion between the KFL, affiliated to the ICFTU and ATUC, and its rival affiliated to AATUF. The Kenya government ordained that the resulting structure, the Central Organization of Trade Unions, could not affiliate to any extra-Kenya organization.

agenda and the documents and determine the basis of representation.

This unity did not last long. On his return home to Tunis from Dakar, Ahmed Tlili, the Tunisian President of ATUC, held a press conference in which he criticized AATUF's sole interest in the question of affiliation and said, "To force disaffiliation as a prerequisite to reunification is not in accordance with the principle of noninterference in the internal affairs of each national center." ATUC thereupon sent a circular to all affiliated organizations criticizing the "exaggerated importance" given to the key sentence in the Dakar communiqué on national disaffiliation, criticizing the "rigid as well as arrogant position" of the AATUF delegation on the question of affiliation, and saying:

In summary, it must be held from the sum total of the proceedings that no commitment was taken limiting the liberty of the centers affiliated with ATUC. The latter, desirous of strengthening trade-unionism in Africa and going ahead along the road of economic expansion, the struggle against underdevelopment and raising the workers' standard of living, unfortunately was not followed by AATUF which, as one can see, limits itself strictly to questions of formality which have no relation to the future of the African working masses. . . . If our delegation has conceded to its partner over formalities, that is to say, over the editorial aspect of the text it is solely with the purpose of not giving its partner an excuse to cause a cleavage which would be exploited in a spectacular and exaggerated way by the enemies whose intentions we well know.

On January 6–9, 1964, the UPTC held its second Congress in Brazzaville. The Secretary-General, Gilbert Pongault, in his Report of Orientation and Action summed up the existing trade-union situation quite well:

There is not the slightest doubt that everyone is in favor of a pan-African trade-union structure in the image of Addis

Ababa. But it is the doctrinal problem which leads to serious reservations. The nub of the problem, we should have the courage to admit, is not that of international disaffiliation, but rather that of the conception of the new trade-union structure that would be created. The truth is that in the discussion of pan-African trade-union unity, the partners trained in different schools each wish to achieve unity around and behind their ideological conception.

The meeting of the joint committee of AATUF and ATUC scheduled for Algiers in January 1964 was postponed to February 24 at the request of ATUC. The AATUF delegation showed up in February but ATUC did not, sending instead a telegram requesting a second postponement to March 23. ATUC gave AATUF the choice of site and the latter chose Dakar. It also decided to hold a meeting of its Secretariat on March 9–14 in Accra on the occasion of the Second International Trade Union Conference for Solidarity with the workers and people of South Africa, sponsored by the Ghana TUC and the WFTU. On March 9 AATUF received a telegram requesting a third postponement to May. Since the fourth Regional Conference of AFRO was scheduled for April, AATUF rejected this third call for a postponement and announced instead the convocation of its own second Congress in Bamako, adding that "it condemns the neo-colonialist position of the ATUC and denounces it as an organ representing the cause of imperialism in Africa." Later ATUC cited the fact that AATUF's rejection was made during this meeting, sponsored in part by WFTU, as proof of the WFTU's "interference" in African affairs and of AATUF's "very close relations" with WFTU.

From April 8 to 12, 1964, AFRO held its fourth Regional Conference in Addis Ababa. The chairman of the Conference, Alhaji Adebola of Nigeria, set the tone:

> Efforts made in the past to achieve unity have been hampered by the controversial question of international affiliation. This issue has been made the scapegoat. It is not affilia-

tion that has brought about the present controversy in the trade-union movement. The friction rather centers around whether the trade-union leaders are prepared to accept international principles and standards entrenched in the ILO Conventions and the United Nations Declaration of Human Rights, before moving toward the desired unity. [16]

The delegates reaffirmed their adherence to the ICFTU.

The AFRO meeting seemed to mark the end of the negotiations that grew out of the October joint meeting of the AATUF and ATUC. Nevertheless, in May 1964 the Algerian UGTA tried one last effort at mediation. Along with the Tunisian UGTT and the Senegalese UNTS, they called for a joint meeting in Algiers on May 12. AATUF would not come. The Algerians then tried, but failed, to convince the Tunisians and Senegalese to attend the AATUF meeting as observers without leaving the ICFTU. Hence it was as a conference of the avant-garde and not of compromise that AATUF held its second Conference in Bamako from June 10 to 14, 1964.

The President of AATUF, Mahjoub Ben Seddik, attacked ATUC as a "Tshombist" trade-union movement and declared that there were three Africas: "that of the struggle for national independence and against racism; that which is setting out increasingly firmly on the revolutionary and popular road; that which is politically liberated but which is still linked with a neo-colonialist development characterized above all by the political and military domination on the part of backward national elements supported by outside neo-colonialist forces."

The concept of the three Africas with three separate roles for trade-unions now became a focal theme of AATUF's eval-

[16] Just a month later, however, Adebola and his union, the ULC-Nigeria, were ready to join with AATUF-affiliated groups in Nigeria in a Joint Action Committee, which conducted a general strike from May 31 to June 13 and won major wage concessions from the Nigerian government. The Joint Action Committee did not long survive the general strike, since the ideological differences remained among the members. Thus, once again, the attempt to achieve Nigerian trade-union unity was abortive.

uation of its position. John Tettegah applied this theme to an analysis of the OAU:

> The Charter signed at Addis Ababa is only a document no matter how sacred its contents, how solemn and sincere were the intentions of its signatories. A document alone cannot unite a continent of two hundred and fifty million people. . . . The difficulties of the [African Liberation Committee], the open hostilities over border disputes, the lack of coordination on major issues of Africa's foreign policy, underestimation of the neo-colonialist policy of former Metropolitan powers and the existence of foreign military bases on African soil have offered enough evidence on the inadequacy of the OAU for the needs of Africa and African Unity. . . . The corollary of this view is that the rallying ground for African Unity is above all the common ideology. We have learned only too well that any close association of African States, one of which follows the path of socialism and the other is a client state of imperialism, would break down whenever and wherever it comes to the real test of African Unity. This has been exactly the case of the OAU, which is too fragile then to withstand the trend of the African Revolution, the main stream of which is still to come.

Bamako established AATUF as a firm and continuing structure. The Charter was formally adopted. The headquarters moved to Accra. Ben Seddik was renamed President and Tettegah was given the newly created post of full-time Secretary-General. The seven vice-presidents were chosen from Algeria, Congo (B), Guinea, Mali, Nigeria (NTUC), Tanganyika, and the U.A.R. If one compared the delegates at Bamako with those present at the founding of ATUC in Dakar, one would find several differences. Among independent states, AATUF had members in Algeria, Burundi, Ghana, Guinea, Mali, Morocco, Sudan, Tanganyika, U.A.R., and Zanzibar; and ATUC, members in Liberia, Libya, Malagasy Republic, Niger, and Tunisia. In most of the other independent states, they each had members, in most cases competing trade-union centers, but in a few cases the same center was affiliated to both groups or went to one as a member and the other as an observer: Cameroon, Central African Republic, Chad, Congo (B),[17] Congo (L), Dahomey, Gabon, Gambia, Ivory Coast, Kenya, Malawi, Mauritania, Nigeria, Senegal, Sierra Leone, Somalia, Togo, Uganda, Upper Volta. In nonindependent countries the situation was similar, but AATUF had groups from more countries than ATUC. In the Portuguese territories, AATUF had unions that supported the political parties in the CONCP.[18] In Rhodesia AATUF had the union that was linked to ZAPU. In South Africa AATUF had both the South African Council of Trade Unions (linked to the ANC) and the Federation of Free African Trade Unions (linked to the PAC). In this special case, AATUF broke its rule of a single member per country and admitted both. AATUF was thus reasonably well satisfied with its progress organizationally, the most important shift since the first AATUF meeting being that of Tanganyika and Zanzibar, reflecting the political developments in that area.[19]

Late 1964 saw Africa once again preoccupied with the Congo and this concern accentuated the now quite rigid division between AATUF and ATUC. From January 16 to 22, 1965, the Economic and Social Commission of the OAU met in Cairo. It had been charged by the Council of Ministers as early as February 1964 with studying how to implement the resolution of the Addis Ababa founding meeting of the OAU

[17] On December 17, 1964, the CATC, the only remaining member-group of ATUC in Congo (B), was dissolved by the government by virtue of a law which permitted only one trade-union center. It continued to be carried on ATUC's list as a union-in-exile.

[18] ATUC/AFRO had their counterparts. Emmanuel Kounzika, then Vice-Premier of the GRAE, addressed the fourth AFRO meeting in Addis Ababa.

[19] On March 31, 1965, AATUF announced they would establish a regional office for East and Central Africa with Michael Kamaliza, Secretary-General of the National Union of Tanzania Workers and the Minister of Labor of Tanzania, as Executive Director.

that called for the establishment of an African trade-union organization. The Commission had before them a report of the Secretary-General of the OAU which argued that, on paper at least, the charters of AATUF and ATUC took very similar positions on two important questions: the independence of trade-unions vis-à-vis governments, and the objective of a socialist society fitting the needs of Africa. He noted further that the key issue dividing them was that of international affiliations of African national trade-union centers. He concluded that the OAU should convene both groups to a meeting which would concentrate on spelling out the details of the points on which they agreed, in the hopes of coming to an ultimate accord on the questions which divided them. The Commission authorized the Secretary-General to proceed to organize such a meeting, including in the resolution its conviction "that the existing split in the African trade-union movement is due solely to the problems of affiliation to the trade-union organizations outside Africa," and adding that the logic of this argument applied to national organizations as well as to continental ones.

To counteract the effect of this resolution, which was criticized by the ATUC journal for its ambiguous terminology, ATUC submitted a long memorandum first to the OCAM meeting in Nouakchott, February 10–12, 1965, and then to the Nairobi meeting of the Council of Ministers of the OAU on February 18. In this memorandum, ATUC recapitulated the history of its relations with AATUF as it saw it, renewed its appeal for a joint meeting, asked the OAU and the International Labour Organization to help arrange it, and said that the problem of disaffiliation was outdated since the joint AATUF-ATUC meeting in Dakar in October 1963 had "recommended to all African trade-union organizations to free themselves from [the] tutelage [of international trade-union organizations] as soon as the new single pan-African trade-union organization shall have been constituted." At the same time, in Accra from February 10 to 13, the first Executive Bureau meeting of AATUF was held and turned its attention not to ATUC but to the general political situation in Africa. In particular, "confronted with the machinations of the imperialists which tend to hinder the march of the African peoples towards unity and obstruct their efforts at the Organization of African Unity," AATUF sounded "a warning to all African Governments and entreat[ed] them to do all in their power to defeat the plots of the colonialists and their agents." AATUF then stated that the "logical conclusion [of African Unity] is the creation of a continental union Government."

From October 5 to 8, 1965, the First Regular Congress of ATUC met in Lagos. It met without its President, Ahmed Tlili, whose mandate had been withdrawn by the UGTT [20] as a result of his suspension from both the UGTT and the only political party in Tunisia, the Parti Socialiste Destourien, of which Tlili had been a member of the Political Bureau. The Congress called once again for a meeting with AATUF. Despite this call, ATUC rejected a request of the Secretary-General of the OAU to meet with AATUF under his auspices in Accra just before the meeting of the heads of state. ATUC pleaded for a more neutral site.

Thus a stalemate seemed to have been reached, at least temporarily, at the end of 1965. The reason was quite simple. AATUF on the one hand and ATUC and AFRO on the other had two fundamentally different concepts of unity. John Tettegah of AATUF had said:

We should not lose sight of the fact that the struggle for unity is loaded with undesirable possibilities. While we are relentlessly fighting to achieve a genuine unity that will make us truly free and united, the neo-colonialists will stop at nothing to make sure we only realize a fake Unity—Unity without purpose, Unity without substance, Unity devoid of dynamic organizing will and power—which will eventually be instruments in the hands of neo-colonialism.

[20] This fact was "noted" by the Secretariat of ATUC in a communiqué on September 9, 1965.

But conversely, H.M. Luande of Uganda, Chairman of AFRO since the Fourth Conference, said:

> We believe that the only pan-African trade union unity worth achieving is the unity which respects the diversity and the autonomy of the individual trade-union centers which constitute it and which includes all the national centers of Africa. Any pan-African trade union movement which aims at subversion, subjugation, and interference in the internal and external relations of properly constituted individual national centers can neither be tolerated nor supported by AFRO.

One could not express more vividly the difference between unity as movement and unity as alliance.

If the trade-unions constituted the key popular organizations in the avant-garde of the movement toward African unity, they were not alone. There were the Pan-African Youth Movement (headquarters, Conakry), the Pan-African Students Movement (headquarters, Algiers), the All-African Women's Conference (headquarters, Bamako), the Pan-African Union of Journalists (headquarters, Accra), the African Cooperative Alliance (headquarters, Dar es Salaam), the All-African Farmers Union (headquarters, Accra), the Union of African Veterans Organizations (headquarters, Cairo), and the Encyclopaedia Africana (headquarters, Accra). It is no accident, of course, that the headquarters of all these groups were so well distributed among the capitals of what were, in the period we are discussing, the radical-nationalist states in Africa. None of these groups has played the important role that the trade unions have, but the collective effect of their existence has served to provide organizational sustenance to the avant-garde.[21]

[21] In addition to the pan-African structures, a number of popular organizations held meetings in 1961–1962 within the framework of the Union of African States: political parties, trade unions, youth, and women. But all these structures disappeared with the dissolution of the UAS in 1963.

These groups must be distinguished from various church, educational, and professional organizations which have emerged on the pan-African level in recent years. The fact that these latter groups developed a pan-African structure is more a reflection of the impact of pan-African ideology than an expression of impulses in active support of it. Nonetheless, the rapidly growing network of what might be called technical pan-African structures could come to be an important under-pinning for the OAU. Such structures, however, tended to strengthen the concept of unity as alliance, whereas the avant-garde popular organizations tended to strengthen the concept of unity as movement. The distinction between the two types of nongovernmental structures was never perfect, and border-line groups might move back and forth from one category to another. One of the characteristics which distinguished the two kinds of groups was the attitude toward international affiliations. The avant-garde groups tended to be nonaffiliated and to make this an ideological issue,[22] whereas the others tended to be constituted as the African regional structure of an international body, which, however, seldom had members in the Communist world.

Like AATUF, the Pan-African Youth Movement (PAYM) had its ancestry in one of the organizations involved in the movement for French West African unity, in this case the Conseil de la Jeunesse d'Afrique. The latter, despite its name, had been limited to French West Africa and found it even harder than UGTAN to survive the political crisis in French West Africa which resulted from the Referendum and the consequent independence of Guinea. At the meeting in August 1960 of the World Assembly of Youth (headquarters, Brussels) in Accra, the African delegates and observers met on the side at a meeting convened by Abdoulaye Diallo, Secretary-General of the AAPC, in pursuance of the resolution passed at the

[22] The major exception was the African Cooperative Alliance, which was affiliated to the International Cooperative Alliance. The latter, how-ever, was one of the rare international nongovernmental organizations which had members from both the Western world and the Communist world. Hence affiliation in this case did not mean alignment.

First and Second AAPC's. From the deliberations of this group came the decision to establish a Preparatory Committee of the Pan-African Youth Conference, which eventually met in Accra from October 13 to 17, 1961. The principle of nonaffiliation was adopted after considerable debate. One of the strongest opponents was a Senegalese delegate active in the World Federation of Democratic Youth (headquarters, Budapest). It was agreed that the new organization should be a wing of the AAPC.

The Pan-African Youth Conference was held in Conakry from April 26 to 30, 1962, and the PAYM was launched. Prior to it, there was a contretemps. Under the inspiration of PAFMECSA, a Pan-African Youth Regional Conference was held in Moshi, Tanganyika, March 16–19, 1962. Delegates came from the eastern half of Africa. This was an expression of the growing discomfort of PAFMECSA at that time with the leadership of the AAPC.[23] In the letter of invitation to the conference at Moshi, the proposed list of delegates to the Conakry meeting was criticized as being distorted for ideological motives. Reference was made to the difference between the Casablanca and Monrovia groups. Any tendency to make permanent this East-West split on the youth level was quashed by Julius Nyerere himself when he addressed the Moshi meeting, and the meeting confined itself to proposing amendments to the constitution to be adopted in Conakry instead of creating a rival organization.

The East African fears were, however, ill-founded since the Guinean organizers were already themselves moving toward reconciliation. The Guineans sought diligently to acquire the attendance of the official youth movements of the UAM countries. The delegation from the youth section of the governing party of the Ivory Coast played a prominent role in the meeting. The resulting organization convened only two meetings of its new Executive, both in 1962, an abortive one in

[23] John Tettegah and Abdoulaye Diallo had just criticized the regionalism which PAFMECSA represented at its meeting in Addis Ababa on February 2–10, 1962.

Lagos and in Dakar from December 11 to 14, to which the
UAM sent an observer. The PAYM then lapsed into inactivity,
having helped to create some of the atmosphere that preceded
the compromise of Addis Ababa. It nonetheless took its place
in the roster of avant-garde organizations because of its formal
adoption of the principle of nonaffiliation and because of its
early history.

The Pan-African Students Movement had a somewhat more
complex history. The largest concentration of African students,
up until 1960 at least, was in Britain and in France. There
grew up in these two countries two important African students' organizations with a long tradition of radicalism: the
West African Students Union (WASU), which was founded
in 1925, and the Fédération des Etudiants d'Afrique Noire en
France (FEANF), which dated from 1950. At the seventh
meeting of the International Student Conference (headquarters, Leiden) held in Ibadan, Nigeria, in September 1957, the
African delegates decided to convene a Pan-African Students
Congress (PASC) at Kampala, Uganda, in July 1958. The
meeting of PASC was rent by debate over links with the West;
the debate was focused on the formal issue of whether or not
to grant FEANF delegate status. The technical problem was
that FEANF was not a student union functioning in Africa.
The real political issue, however, was FEANF's affiliation to
the International Union of Students (headquarters, Prague).
The Conference was rather evenly split. The split largely
paralleled linguistic lines. The same issue arose once again at
the Second PASC in Tunis, August 1–7, 1959. The struggle
again focused on the formal issue of the seating of FEANF,
and this time WASU and the Union Nationale des Etudiants
Kamerunais (linked to the UPC) as well. Once again the
PASC was fairly evenly split.

In 1959 FEANF issued a pamphlet entitled *African Students
and African Unity* in which it criticized the methods of the
AAPC as "little short of political reformism" and said that
"the thesis of unity for unity's sake has to be ruled out." As a
consequence, it called on student organizations to "contemp-

tuously reject" neutralism on the international student or political front. In 1960, at the Twelfth Congress, FEANF said
that "the unity of Africa necessarily requires first that its independence be total and unconditional, that is to say: a) rup-
ture of all organic and institutional links with the former colonial powers and the imperialist powers; b) liquidation of
all foreign bases on national soil; c) liquidation of monopolies;
d) organization of democratic institutions assuring control by
the popular masses of national construction to the full satisfaction of their aspirations and their legitimate interests."

In March 1958 a number of African student groups and
liberation movements founded in London the Committee of
African Organizations (CAO), in which a number of subsequently leading African politicians were active. In October
1960 the CAO convened an African youth conference in London, and at its Easter meeting in 1962 it decided to convene
a conference of African students' organizations in Europe and
America. This conference was held in Belgrade from August
29 to September 1, 1962, and included not only WASU and
FEANF, but similar organizations in Western and Eastern
Europe and in the Americas. The meeting decided to establish
an All-African Students Union (in Europe). The Preamble
to the Charter that was adopted contained almost verbatim
a reproduction of the 1960 FEANF four-point program for
African unity. The communiqué supported the decisions of
the Belgrade Conference of Heads of State and Government of
Non-Aligned Countries, and threw the students' weight behind AATUF, "the continent's only true independent and
Africa-orientated federation of trade-unions." Its analysis of
unity is summarized in the affirmation "that a united Africa is
more than a Union of African Governments." The Conference
called for a continuing structure and established its headquarters in London. Later two coordinating committees, one for
Western Europe (headquarters, Paris) and one for Eastern
Europe (headquarters, Prague), were established. The third
meeting was held in Moscow in March 1964. At this meeting,
the students proclaimed African youth the avant-garde of the

struggle for liberation and African unity. They reaffirmed their
support for a pan-African youth structure, "condemn[ed] energetically the reactionary utilization of this idea by certain
African governments" and warned that the subordination of
youth movements to these reactionary governments held back
"the struggle for national liberation."

These developments in Europe and the internal developments on the African scene created quite a different atmosphere for the Third PASC, held in Nairobi, August 3–7, 1964.
The formal question of credentials was this time settled clearly
and permanently in favor of the Europe-based students' organizations. The Conference decided on the establishment of
a Pan-African Students Movement (PASM) and in its preamble included, again almost verbatim, the four-point program of the 1960 FEANF Congress. PASM took on a very
militant tone and at the meeting of its Executive Committee
in Algiers from January 15 to 17, 1965, it "stigmatiz[ed] the
appeal of the OAU for 'national reconciliation' [in the Congo]
as playing the imperialist game and tending to demobilize
Congolese patriots." This attack on the OAU followed one
made by FEANF at its Seventeenth Congress, December 27–
30, 1964, in which it said: "Objectively, the OAU has transformed itself into a powerful break on the advance of the
African liberation movement, and is under the dominant influence of international imperialism and the reactionary African states who are devoted to it."

The Pan-African Union of Journalists (PAUJ) came into
existence in Bamako at a meeting on May 19–23, 1961, immediately before the founding of AATUF. It expressed its
clear belief in "committed journalism," but led a desultory existence until the second PAUJ Conference in Accra from November 11 to 15, 1963, when the headquarters of PAUJ was
moved from Bamako to Accra and Kofi Batsa, editor of *The
Spark,* became Secretary-General. The Second Conference of
PAUJ declared that: "There is no short-cut for our Revolution.
We must first clean our political houses, so that our inde-

pendent states will be ready for the political sacrifices which the achievement of African Unity entails."

The PAUJ has been paralleled in two technical fields. There were the Union of National Radio and Television Organizations of Africa and the Union of Africa News Agencies. Both these groups, being more technical, had a more universal African membership than PAUJ. However, both of them and the PAUJ were encouraged by the OAU to come together in the Coordinating Committee of African Unions in the Field of Mass Communications. This enterprise was the most successful of the attempts by the' OAU to bring the various pan-African nongovernmental structures under its wing.

The All-African Women's Conference like the PAYM evolved out of a French West African background, an organization called the Union des Femmes de l'Ouest Africain. Partially for this reason, some groups from UAM countries came to the founding conference in Dar es Salaam from July 27 to August 1, 1962, and the subsequent meetings were held in Abidjan and Monrovia. The meeting in Dar es Salaam called for disaffiliation from international organizations whose aims and objectives were in conflict with the Conference, a somewhat ambiguous formula. The All-African Farmers Union was established as a result of a meeting called by the farmers' wing of the Ghana CPP in Accra from March 19 to 27, 1962. Similarly, the African Cooperative Alliance grew out of a meeting convened by the cooperative organization affiliated to the ruling political party of Tanganyika in Moshi, Tanganyika, from November 14 to 21, 1964. The work and membership of the two groups overlapped to some extent. The Union of African Veterans Organizations held its constituent meeting from April 6 to 9, 1964, in Cairo. All four of these inter-African organizations tended to draw their members from radical-nationalist African states and from only some of the other African countries, thus giving the former a greater weight within these organizations than within the OAU.

Finally, a word should be said about the Encyclopaedia Africana. This was not an organization but a cultural project originated by Dr. W. E. B. DuBois and later controlled by an all-African Editorial Board which held its first meeting in Accra September 24–29, 1964. The Encyclopaedia was conceived as an attempt to make a global assessment of the African past by African scholars with an Afro-centric viewpoint. It was a long-range scholarly project supported at first by the Ghana government and later endorsed by the OAU.

Thus, through a multiorganizational framework, the avant-garde created a force with which it could place pressures on the movement for African unity. But because African organizations were ultimately so dependent, politically and financially, on their governments, the avant-garde could never proceed too far ahead, at least not too far ahead of the radical-nationalist governments. But as we have noted, this constraint was its strength since it kept the avant-garde, and most notably AATUF, near enough to the political views of the radical-nationalist governments to be in a position to have some influence on them.

Unity and Modernization

—Achievement

and Perspective

:XI:

AN IDEOLOGY

FOR A MOVEMENT

We have distinguished two different concepts of unity—unity as movement and unity as alliance. And we have tried throughout the earlier sections of this book to indicate how these two views have been in constant dialogue and often conflict with each other, and how bearing in mind this distinction helps to clarify the real differences behind sometimes confusing terminological similarities. In the light of this distinction, we may now return to the problem raised in the opening chapter. Why has there been such a discrepancy between the positive connotations of unity for Africans and the skeptical, if not negative, connotations for outsiders?

Africans in their response to the theme of African unity have been paying tribute to the ideological force of unity as movement, very often even when they are not themselves supporters of the movement. One of the marks of an effective social movement is that it often can induce others within its social milieu to share its rhetoric, pay lip service to its ideals, and even applaud its victories. The ideas incarnate too many hopes and aspirations, assuage too many frustrations for them to be scorned publicly.

Outsiders, on the other hand, are subject to this social pressure to a far smaller degree. They tend in their responses to evaluate the prospects of unity as alliance. The consequent skepticism may perhaps not be a measured judgment, but since outsiders are not committed to the objectives of the movement, they are also usually not directly affected by the accuracy of their judgments. A skeptical judgment may well be nugatory and not neutral in its effects, and for some this may be the point. The real source of the discrepancy is that a rose is not a rose is not a rose.

Many of those involved in the movement toward unity are therefore reluctant to discuss differences within the movement for fear this will serve the purposes of its opponents. However functional such a refusal may be for the participants, the contrast between the two views of unity remains a real one. Of course, the antinomy of the two views is not new, nor does it apply only to the question of African unity. It is the antinomy of what has been termed in France the party of movement and the party of order. This does not mean that those who believe in movement do not believe in order, or vice versa. It simply implies that each group has a consistent bias, or a normal priority in its approach to social action.

Behind these two approaches may lie conflicting interests and correlated conflicting ultimate values. But they are intellectualized into competing theories of social structure and of the process of modernization. We have already discussed this in the context of its very important application to theories of economic development. It is useful, however, to spell out its more general application, particularly for the party of movement, since inherently those who stand for movement have more articulated concepts of the social system. To defend order, one needs power and authority. But to change a system, one needs a rational hypothesis of how the system operates and how it is therefore possible to change it.

In this specific case, that of the movement toward African unity, the theory of society starts with the now classic assumption found in much of modern social science, that men and groups operate to optimize self-interest. It therefore follows that if the present world political and economic structure is disadvantageous to Africans and advantageous to others (say, collectively the Western developed nations or influential elements within them), it is natural that the former will work to change the structure and that the latter will oppose such attempts. The end-goal of change is equality—political, economic, and cultural—with the currently more developed regions of the world. Such equality can only be achieved by the modernization of African societies. The question then is: How is it possible to modernize such societies in the face of the expected opposition of developed countries? The movement toward African unity contends that continental unity is required before there can be successful modernization.

The concept of unity as a prerequisite to modernization is derived from a series of assumptions: Only with considerable self-discipline and self-denial can societies manage to place a sufficient amount of their current production income into the long-range investments which will multiply growth and hence enable these societies to "narrow the gap" with developed societies. Such a program leads inevitably to considerable internal resistance on the part of almost all the slightly advantaged segments of the citizenry. Massive investment therefore requires political self-control, and perhaps considerable social isolation in order to diminish the sense of relative deprivation among those who are asked to make sacrifices.

It is further assumed that outside powers, for reasons of both short-run and long-run interest, will oppose, if they can, both self-discipline and isolation. President Nyerere summed up as early as 1961 what he thought was happening:

I believe that the second scramble for Africa has begun in real earnest. And it is going to be a much more dangerous scramble than the first one. . . . No imperialist power is going to fight another imperialist power for the control of Africa: that would be too crude a method in the context of 1961, 1962. No, this time, . . . African brother is going to slaughter African brother—not in the interests of Africa, but in the interests of the imperialists, both old and new! . . . That is why, during the difficulties in the Congo, when the idea of an African Command was first proposed, I was very taken with it.

The question then becomes: What kind of societies are able to achieve the necessary self-control and isolation to prevent external manipulation of internal politics? The answer is given first of all in terms of size. Unless a unit is sufficiently large in area and population, it has neither the potential physical strength to withstand outside threats nor the economic resources to survive relative isolation. If, however, the unit is sufficiently large, then it could develop, provided it adopted two further policies: the establishment of a strong central political network capable of enforcing the self-control and minimizing outside influence; the adoption of a policy of noninvolvement in the outside world in order to neutralize exterior influences. The former is sought through such mechanisms as the one-party state. The latter is achieved through nonalignment. Nonalignment, to be realistic, takes into perspective an over-all social accounting of outside influence. Hence at present it leans more closely in Africa to the Communist world in order to counterbalance the effects of the network of inherited structures and relationships permeating contemporary Africa which provide the means whereby the West still exercises considerable influence on internal developments.

There is one last assumption. It is that ideology reflects interest. Hence, on the one hand, it is essential to develop a coherent ideology that will legitimate and therefore render possible the program of the revolutionary core. On the other hand, it is equally essential to prevent the opponents from undermining this ideological drive by diluting its slogans. H. M. Basner expressed this view in the *Ghanaian Times* in 1965:

For neo-colonialism in contradiction to the needs of direct colonialism, the appearance of unity without real unity is

as important as the appearance of independence without
real independence on the continent of Africa. That is the
political technique which serves the United States best in
controlling the Latin American continent and with which it
wishes to control Africa.

Hence for the revolutionary core of the movement toward
African unity the concept of neo-colonialism is central—neo-
colonialism, which in Nkrumah's words is "the worst form of
imperialism." The reason is simple. "For those who practice
it, it means power without responsibility and for those who
suffer from it, it means exploitation without redress." African
unity is seen as the only significant way in which neo-colonialism can be checked. Even if small individual governments are
not under neo-colonialist control, they are unable alone to
change significantly the world balance of power and trade, and
furthermore they are politically vulnerable, for, in Nkrumah's
analysis, "in any continent where neo-colonialism exists on a
wide scale the same social pressures which can produce revolts in neo-colonial territories will also affect those states
which have refused to accept the system and therefore neo-
colonialist nations have a ready-made weapon with which they
can threaten their opponents if they appear successfully to be
challenging the system."

It is precisely because the dangers of unity are so great to
the existing world system that the obstacles to unity are so
great. What, then, can in fact bring about a reversal of this
situation in which the cards seem to be stacked on the side of
the *status quo?* True to the voluntarist tradition of modern
revolutionary causes, the answer is given in terms of organized
social action, the establishment of a social movement—which
from time to time will take different organizational forms—
sometimes represented by particular governments, but usually
remaining a social force that is more amorphous and larger
than any of these. This amorphousness is its weakness. A
social movement is vulnerable to sudden and unpredictable
political waves, the semispontaneous support that erupts and

dies down. It is bound by a sense of communion among cadres but not one of mutual obligation. But its amorphousness can also be its strength, provided the movement is linked to, but not totally controlled by, responsible and continuing social organizations. This has thus far been the nature of this movement.

We have seen how from 1957 to 1965 the movement found its locus in several different places. One was in Nkrumah's Ghana, which was a key center of the movement but by no means its only one. Ghana provided some of the organizational base and some of the money, and it contributed significantly to the beginnings of an ideology—but it was not, of course, the only active participant. An over-all view of the revolutionary core reveals that it came to consist of four separate segments, interlinked but each having power in its own right, and each offering its own particular perspective.

The first and most powerful segment was comprised of the radical-nationalist states. The list of these states has varied over the years. The ardor of the governments of these states has certainly gone up and down according to internal exigencies and external pressures. None of these states could claim it has never made compromises that it would not criticize in others. But on the whole, at the end of 1965, the revolutionary core could be said to have included Algeria, Congo (B), Ghana, Guinea, Mali, Tanzania, and the U.A.R.[1] The governments of these countries provided stability, money, and international respectability to the revolutionary core. They also contributed prudence and compromise.

The second major segment was the All-African Trade Union Federation (AATUF). This provided a force with membership in many independent African states in addition to the radical-nationalist states, one that had semilegitimate access to the other independent states. This force was somewhat

[1] Along with Mauritania, Somalia, and Sudan, these were the only states to break diplomatic relations with the United Kingdom in accordance with the resolution of the Sixth Extraordinary Session of the Council of Ministers of the OAU in Addis Ababa on December 3, 1965. It was to Algeria, Ghana, Guinea, Mali, and the U.A.R. that Gbenye made his appeal for aid to the Stanleyville regime in late 1965.

but not totally independent of the governments of the radical-nationalist states. It was sufficiently independent to apply a radicalizing pressure, but sufficiently controlled to be considered a part of the system, and hence able to exert an influence on these governments. Thus AATUF was slightly less stable, less well financed, and less respectable than these governments, but also less prudent and less prone to compromise.

The third major segment was made up of the radical opposition parties in independent states—such as the Sawaba of Niger, the UPC of Cameroon, the UNFP of Morocco. This segment was the weakest in real strength. Often living in exile, and dependent on financial support from the radical-nationalist states, the leaders led peripatetic lives and were subject to the vicissitudes of exile politics. None of these opposition parties had come to power by the end of 1965 (although one might consider the participation of the Umma party in the Zanzibari revolution as an exception). On the other hand, their freedom from immediate responsibility made it unnecessary for them to compromise. Indeed, it made it impossible, for in their case a compromise involved a relinquishment of revolutionary goals. Furthermore, it allowed them the leisure and the perspective to function as the intellectual critics within the revolutionary core. Insofar as they were permitted to express their views, their analyses were the most intellectually rigorous if not always the most influential.

The fourth segment was composed of certain of the liberation movements. In particular, it seems to have been built at the end of 1965 around the emerging alliance of the four movements in Portuguese Africa grouped in the CONCP, plus ZAPU of Southern Rhodesia, SWAPO of South West Africa, and the ANC of South Africa. This listing was itself very controversial and its chief justification was the self-image and mutual support of the seven movements involved.[2] Other

[2] In late 1965 a leader of FRELIMO (Mozambique) stated that:

As far as liberation movements are concerned, we saw at Accra [OAU heads of state meeting] a clear split between those who are truly engaged in revolutionary action and those which are liberation movements in name only. For us Mozambicans this clarification is very important for the pursuit of the struggle.

segments of the revolutionary core have often made other judgments as to which liberation movements were revolutionary. The most debated instance was the claim made by the PAC of South Africa to be more revolutionary than ANC. Some African states at one time acknowledged this claim. AATUF in 1964 refused to choose between ANC and PAC. In Southern Rhodesia, ZANU made a similar claim in regard to ZAPU, but its lack of mass support stood in its way. In South-West Africa, SWANU was at first given the recognition which seemed later to shift to SWAPO. One of the factors that complicated the evaluation and image of these movements was the Russian-Chinese split. As liberation movements emerged in the 1950s, the Soviet Union and the United States often tendered support to opposing groups. When the Chinese began to play a separate role from the Soviet Union, they often supported groups that opposed those supported by the Soviet Union. This led to a very large number of curious instances in which, by 1965, the same liberation movement was being supported by, and seeking support in, the United States and China.

If the movement for African unity was amorphous and complex and without centralized direction, it was nonetheless by no means weak. It was, in fact, the most important indigenous political force on the African continent, the only one that at all competed in impact with the strength of the Western world. Its power lay in part in the basic popularity of its themes and its analyses and their appeal to politically conscious cadres throughout the continent. And its power also derived in part from the basic instability of independent African states because of the constant social and economic pressures they were unable to meet. This instability therefore provided a constant occasion for using revolutionary ideas as the intellectual justification of new power. The movement's power lay also in its very motion, in its faith that history was with it both because the movement would alert and make conscious its own troops and because the enemy would ultimately collapse. Nkrumah said in 1965:

Neo-colonialism, like colonialism is an attempt to export the social conflicts of the capitalist countries. The temporary success of this policy can be seen in the ever-widening gap between the richer and the poorer nations of the world. . . . [But] neo-colonialism is a mill-stone around the necks of the developed countries which practice it. Unless they can rid themselves of it, it will drown them.

The immediate power of the movement was of constant concern to it and led to continual debates over the tactics of unity. There were those who warned of "wanting to be too united." Bechir Ben Yahmed once argued in an editorial in *Jeune Afrique:* "By wanting monolithism, you get a split. This is the teaching of history." And in support he cited Fidel Castro: "Revolutionaries who are divided and who insult each other can not efficiently fight the imperialist enemy." But, on the other hand, the Algerian trade-union journal *Révolution et Travail* argued:

"Unity at any price" is an argument, nothing but an argument, an instrument which the stronger faction of the movement uses. When the conjuncture is favorable to the revolution, "unity at any price" is an instrument of revolutionary policy. When the conjuncture is unfavorable to the revolution, "unity at any price" becomes an instrument of conservative and reactionary policy.

Thus, after the Accra OAU meeting at the end of 1965, a representative of one of the revolutionary liberation movements, the PAIGC, drew the following conclusion:

The penetration of imperialists in Africa is not a consequence of the loss of terrain they are suffering, as in Asia, but it constitutes a veritable implantation gradually made in a favorable terrain. . . . Faced with this situation, our duty is clear. We must at all cost revise our policy of unity and combat the colonialist and neo-colonialist forces which constitute the base of imperialist penetration.

If tactics determine the immediate power of a movement, the long-range power is determined by an even thornier question, that of ideology. For although Nkrumah has said that "a movement without an ideology is lost from its inception," the movement for African unity did not at first evolve a consistent, systematic ideology. We have already discussed how in its origins as a doctrine pan-Africanism was highly ambivalent on the relationship of class and race. It was not sure to what extent Marxian analysis was in fact a valid basis for the understanding of African problems. Therefore, pan-Africanism neither accepted nor rejected Marxian analysis. Rather it tried to do both simultaneously.

Nonetheless, at the time of the Fifth Pan-African Congress at Manchester in 1945 many pan-Africanists thought of themselves as Marxists. Yet in the development of the struggle for independence, the pendulum seemed to swing in the other direction. In 1956 George Padmore, often referred to before his death as the "theoretician of pan-Africanism," wrote his major work, which he entitled *Pan-Africanism or Communism? The Coming Struggle for Africa*. That same year, as we have mentioned, Aimé Césaire broke with the French Communist party, *Présence Africaine* convened the First World Congress of Writers and Artists dedicated to the celebration of African ideas, and Sékou Touré formed the UGTA, which when it became UGTAN in 1957 explicitly rejected the idea of the class struggle as not relevant to Africa.

These events marked the beginning of a major intellectual trend in Africa which went by the generic name of African socialism. The essential elements in the argument were the classless nature of contemporary African society, the communitarian nature of African traditional society, the consequent inapplicability of Marxian analysis to the internal politics of independent African states, and the feasibility of a transition to modern socialism without passing through a bourgeois, capitalist phase. This ideology spread throughout the continent, although the exact term used to describe it varied.

The reasons for its rapid emergence and widespread adoption are both external and internal. On the world scene, African socialism represented for some a liberation from Western intellectual tutelage, of which Marxism was considered to be but one variant. We have mentioned the ambivalences of Western leftist parties on colonial questions and the particular difficulties this generated on the trade-union scene. For others, from the beginning, the adjective "African" placed before socialism was a plea for respectability in Western official circles. However, we are here concerned with the attitudes of the revolutionary core. African socialism also had an internal advantage in that it reinforced the sense of national integrity of new nations. As we saw previously, the earliest independent nations in Africa tended to be more radical-nationalist in their orientation than most of the nations that emerged in what might be thought of as the 1960 wave. Hence in the beginning the use of African socialism to reinforce national stability seemed to serve the revolutionary cause.

But when more and more African nations became independent, those states considered to be neo-colonial by the revolutionary core used liberally the concept of African socialism both to strengthen themselves internally against radical opposition movements and to abjure internationally policies which would involve any systematic rejection of the West and its replacement by new links with the Communist world. As this occurred, the revolutionary core became more and more chary of the concept of African socialism. In time the concept was repudiated, then denounced. Disavowal was voiced most notably in Mali, Algeria, and Ghana.

Mali was the first. After the split in 1960 with Senegal, Mali rejected the elaborately developed notion of African socialism as stated by President Senghor of Senegal. The extraordinary congress of Mali's party in September 1960 called for an economic policy which was "within the framework of socialist planning founded on African realities." This was to become the new formula, as distinguished, on the one hand, from African (or other regionally specific) socialism and, on the other hand, from the unqualified formula of "scientific socialism" espoused by a few, primarily African students in Europe. President Modibo Keita of Mali warned in early 1962: "Let us not be deceived by word-magic. Most of [the other African] states speak of African socialism. Even Senghor speaks of African socialism. If we don't watch out, the word socialism will be emptied of its content, and the most capitalist systems and the most reactionary bourgeois can hide themselves behind the slogan of socialism." Nonetheless, that same year, in welcoming President Diori of Niger to Bamako, he noted: "Our [Party] Congress opted for socialism enriched by African and Malian values." And one of his ministers, speaking at a party seminar specified: "If our objectives . . . are those of Scientific Socialism, we have always felt that our context is a specific context, that we must take it into account in the interest of these very ends." The key nuance revolved around the issue of the existence of classes. The minister spoke of the absence of classes but of the presence, nonetheless, of contradictions. And President Keita spoke of "divergencies of interest" which, having been "shelved" during the colonial struggle, "reappeared" after independence. He added that "Marxism is not a dogma" but "a method of research, analysis, and action from which we must draw maximum profit but which we cannot use in the same way as other societies, in view of our specific situation."

A similar evolution of language may be seen in Algeria, following independence in 1962. Here, however, it was a bit more muted because internal political struggles focused around this very issue of ideological terminology. President Ben Bella tried to find a delicate balance. He spoke in 1962 of "a revolutionary socialism taking account of our Arabo-Islamic traditions." Similarly, addressing the students in 1963, he insisted:

Scientific socialism is being widely praised [à l'honneur]. Our socialism is scientific, but it takes into account our Arabo-Islamic background. We are for scientific socialism.

We only ask one thing that we be left our God, our Allah! Apart from that, we are ready to go further than any scientific socialism whatever. I told this to Fidel Castro and other Communist leaders.

A like argument made by an Egyptian analyst and published in *Al Gomourhia* was translated and reprinted in the Algerian journal *Révolution Africaine* (and also in *L'Etincelle* published in Accra). The article criticized the conflict artificially created between Islam and scientific socialism, saying that "scientific socialism is not the exclusive monopoly of the Communists but a reserve common to all sincere revolutionaries" and that "to accept scientific socialism does not necessarily mean embracing philosophical materialism."

When Boumediene came to power in Algeria in 1965, this discussion stopped and the subtle position was no longer argued. Boumediene and his supporters had opposed those who wished to reinforce the emphasis on "scientific socialism," and threw their weight behind the "Arabo-Islamic" basis of socialism, which thus returned Algeria to a variant of the formula of African socialism.

It was in Ghana once again that the ideological position was elaborated in greatest detail. This can be found in Nkrumah's book *Consciencism* and throughout the various issues of *The Spark* and *L'Etincelle*. On the one hand, African socialism was denounced categorically: "The historic mission of 'African socialism' is to combat and, if possible, defeat scientific socialism firstly by introducing elements alien to socialist thought, and secondly by denying some of the foundations of socialist ideology." That this represents an ideological evolution can be seen from the fact that it is only in late 1965 that the Constitution of the CPP was rewritten to expunge references to African socialism.[3] In particular, the concept of

[3] In 1961, Kofi Baako had written:

In order to distinguish it from socialism practiced in other places, which in its entirety may not be suitable or applicable to the conditions and circumstances of Africa, [Nkrumahism] has been described as 'African socialism.' This should not be interpreted to mean a re-

African communalism was attacked. It was not that communalism never existed. But "since the inescapable fact of history
is that our communal life has largely given way to colonialism
and neo-colonialism (both variants of capitalism), the transformation of colonial Africa to socialist Africa can only be
by way of revolution."

On the other hand, if Nkrumahism was not African socialism, it was also not "synonymous with Communism" (nor was
it conversely a "negation of scientific socialism"). Habib Niang, one of the leading expositors of Nkrumahism, argued
in 1965 that "Nkrumah thinks, and he has said so publicly,
that there exists a contradiction between the international
Communist movement and nationalism" and that "Marxism
ceases to be a sure guide from the moment the liberation
movement has caused the outspurt from universal interiority
of exteriorities (national and zonal entities)." [4] One of the
key differences seen between Marxism and Nkrumahism was
that the latter was not atheist but "able to take a coldly objective view of religion," this view not being a "mere tactical
view" but deriving "logically from its philosophical stand point
of rejecting the sole reality of matter while upholding its
primacy."

In summary, then, the "revolutionary ideology of Nkrumahism [was defined as] scientific socialism applied to the historical conditions and aspiration of Africa." In Nkrumah's
own words: "It is essential that socialism should include over-
riding regard to the experience and consciousness of a people,
for if it does not do so, it will be serving an idea and not a
people. It will generate a contradiction. It will become dog-
matic." But there was another contrary danger. "A clever and
unscrupulous neo-colonialism can pervert and corrupt this

---

striction of its application only to Africa; it only means that as a socialist nondoctrinaire philosophy, it is primarily designed to solve the
peculiar social, economic, and political problems imposed by imperialism and colonialism on our continent.

[4] But in the same article, Niang criticized both Padmore and DuBois
for not having appreciated the teachings of Lenin in *Imperialism: The
Highest Stage of Capitalism*.

relativist aspect of specific socialism and use it in fact to re-
colonize a people. It is essential that socialism in its specific
form should at every point and every level be justified only
by reference to *socialist* general principles."

We have dwelled on these ideological statements because
they represented an important element of the strategy that was
emerging for the movement toward African unity. The movement was determined to distinguish itself intellectually from
non-African Communist doctrine, since one of the key objectives of the movement was to re-establish African cultural
and intellectual autonomy in the world system. It did this by
emphasis of the need to specify the application of a general
doctrine to particular historical conditions. It did this further
by emphasizing one key doctrinal distinction from classical
Marxism: the rejection of doctrinaire atheism, which was
seen as an historically rooted reaction to the particular place
and role of the Christian churches in Western societies.

However, the revolutionary core was also very concerned
with the vacuity of the concept of African socialism, a concept which this same revolutionary core was largely responsible for originating in the late 1950s. In its view, the term had
been taken over by the opponents of the African revolution as
an ideological cover for their own surrender to the acceptance
of combined Western hegemony in Africa.

The difficulty with the ideological position that emerged
between 1960 and 1965 was its very subtlety, and therefore
the ease with which it could be distorted, whether deliberately
or innocently. Hence it was in need of constant reinterpretation. But the movement for African unity, unlike the world
Communist movement from 1917–1956, had no central organizational structure and no clear intellectual hierarchy. This
meant that such reinterpretation had to be done collectively,
and consequently it was done with less rigor and promptitude
than might otherwise have been the case. This led in time to
increased conflicts between different segments of the movement, as their interests began to move apart. In particular, the
interests of the radical-nationalist states had begun to diverge

by the end of 1965 from the interests of the liberation movements, and even more from the opposition parties in the independent states. AATUF, being a meeting ground of the radical-nationalist states on the one hand and the liberation movements and opposition parties on the other, was caught in the
middle.

With the fall of Nkrumah in February 1966 this phase of
the history of the movement had come to an end. To appraise
the future prospects of the movement, we must place it in the
larger world perspective.

:XII:

AFRICAN UNITY

IN THE WORLD CONTEXT

The success of a social movement requires more than an interested group and an appropriate ideology. It also needs a social climate which allows the movement freedom to organize, to propagate its ideas among its followers and its opponents, and ultimately to bargain in the political arena. The movement toward African unity did enjoy such freedom in the period 1957–1965. It was, however, declining toward the end of that period, and the fall of President Nkrumah in February 1966 may be said to have marked its effective end, at least for the moment.

The field of action of the movement toward African unity was not Africa but the world, for its objectives were not simply to transform Africa, but to transform Africa by transforming the world. Its enemies were internal to be sure, but the internal enemies were seen as agents of foreign powers—the essence of the concept of "neo-colonialism." We must accordingly analyze the emergence of the movement for African unity in terms of the world system, for it was the changing state of this system that made it possible for the movement to gain and then to lose its freedom of maneuver.

The world system has been built since World War II around a tension between the dominant world power, the United States, and a revolutionary world power, the U.S.S.R. The United States has been the dominant world power by virtue of its unmatched economic and military, and hence political, strength. This inherent dominance has been increased by the fact that the U.S. has organized and led a coalition of nations that included most of the other industrialized countries. One of the important symbolic structures of this coalition has been the North Atlantic Treaty Organization. To be sure, the nations in NATO share for the most part a common cultural heritage (Western Christianity), mixed economies based on relatively free markets, and a common ideology (pluralistic representational structures and welfare state legislation). But even more fundamentally, they share a common interest in defending the relatively high standards of living of their societies and in preserving the internal compromise on the distribution of rewards so painfully worked out in the period 1848–1945. While the responses of Western leaders to the demands of revolutionaries fluctuate between the classical alternatives of stern refusal and timely but minimal concessions, they nevertheless share a strong basic interest in preserving a world *status quo*.

In contrast, the U.S.S.R. is—or was—a revolutionary state in the sense that it has demanded a larger share of world income and world power, and has done so in the name of an ideology which has seemed to challenge most of the fundamental values of the West. In pursuing its own claims, it has simultaneously concentrated on internal development and the weakening of Western dominance in the world system. Toward the latter end, it has historically offered aid and comfort to any movement anywhere which also seemed to challenge the dominant powers in the world system. This policy it has termed "anti-imperialism."

Only with the end of World War II did the U.S.S.R. achieve a sufficient degree of internal economic and military development to enable it seriously—that is, more than verbally—to challenge the Western countries in the world arena. The immediate consequence of its postwar strength was an ability to expand the Soviet role by installing friendly regimes ("peoples' democracies") in Eastern Europe. The world upheaval also made it possible for revolutionary forces, under a Communist label, to attain power in Yugoslavia and China.

What Soviet military occupation made possible in Eastern Europe (where the Communist movements were in fact weak, except in Yugoslavia) could not be repeated in Western Europe, even in France and Italy (where the Communist parties were large and well organized), for the Western governments successfully organized to counter the threat. The most important weapon was the Marshall Plan, which ensured to Western European countries the rapid restoration of a large share in the world's wealth. Indeed, the standard of living of these countries has been raised so high that, for the first time, the skilled workers of Europe have begun to enter the market of luxury consumption.

The Cold War, as the U.S.-U.S.S.R. tension came to be called, centered around the disposition of Germany, the defeated world power. During this period, neutralism was impossible. Any country which sought to shift its position from alignment to neutrality had in fact to seek the military support of its former enemy, as the Yugoslav example demonstrated. The high point of the Cold War was the Berlin blockade of 1948–1949, when the Western world successfully demonstrated its technical superiority to the Communist countries and thus fixed European boundaries for some time to come. The Berlin blockade led directly to the formal organization of NATO.

Then came the North Korean invasion of South Korea in 1950, which was less a manifestation of continued Soviet expansionism than a consequence of Moscow's inability to control the revolutionary forces its protective strength had permitted to develop in East Asia. In fact, the Korean War was an embarrassment to both sides, for in military terms it was an unsatisfactory stalemate. Moreover, the U.S.S.R. had begun to consider that the development of its atomic bomb in 1949 might enable it to gain a larger share in the control of the world polity by negotiations, a possibility endangered by peripheral wars. For its part, the United States feared the debilitating long-run consequences of permanent conflicts.

The stage was thus set for a thaw in the Cold War—first as a result of the truce in Korea, speeded by the death of Stalin and the advent of Eisenhower to the U.S. Presidency. Stalin's successors saw to it that the thaw, which was in fact an armed truce, developed rapidly. The first sign of willingness to effect a truce could be seen in the refusal of the Eisenhower Administration to support in any significant way the anti-Russian uprising in East Germany in June 1953, despite the President's verbal commitment to "liberation." The Geneva Conference of 1954, which ended the Indochina war and enabled France to liquidate its onerous commitments in Southeast Asia, was followed by the Geneva Summit Conference of 1955, at which the U.S. and the U.S.S.R. created "the spirit of Geneva"—a euphemism for the rejection of violence in political intercourse, particularly in Europe. Concretely, the "Geneva spirit" resulted in the Austrian state treaty, and indirectly in the *de facto* armistice in the Quemoy-Matsu dispute in the Formosa Straits.

The state of armed truce also permitted developments on three other fronts. At the Bandung Conference of 1955, the Third World asserted its existence as a unit separate from the Western and Communist worlds, and proclaimed the limited and quite formal ideology of nonalignment. The meaning of Bandung can be seen in two acts. One was the decision in 1955 to admit the long waiting list of applicants for membership in the United Nations, which opened the way to a numerical reorganization of the U.N. which led to a Third World majority and symbolized the willingness of the U.S. and the U.S.S.R. to court the Third World's favor. The second was the Suez conflict of 1956, in which the U.S. and the U.S.S.R. demonstrated their willingness to court Third World favor at the expense of the immediate interests of the Western European powers, if need be. The U.S. and the U.S.S.R. remained competitive world powers, but they were now competing for advantage within a framework of antagonistic cooperation rather than a framework of total enmity.

The second front of development occurred in the Communist world itself. In 1956 Chairman Khrushchev made his myth-breaking report to the Twentieth Party Congress of the Communist Party of the Soviet Union, which was to result both in "destalinization" within the U.S.S.R., the Eastern European countries, and within Communist parties elsewhere in the world; and "desatellization," or the reassertion of nationalism in the various countries of the Communist world, not least of all in China.

A third line of development opened in the West, where the state of armed truce permitted a loosening of the bonds of unity within the Western World. One symptom of this that followed the coming to power in France of Charles de Gaulle was his attempt to delineate a French policy clearly separate from that of the United States. Another was the ideological evolution of the Western position represented by the evolving concept of the industrial society, of which the Western and Soviet models were two varieties. Ideological change could also be seen in the decline of the primacy of the anti-Communist creed, and in the remarkably rapid reformulation of Roman Catholic theology called the *aggiornamento*. A third symptom was John F. Kennedy's dedication to the principle that the primary objective of U.S. foreign policy should be an amelioration of relations with the U.S.S.R.

Kennedy's concern was to transform the armed truce into a full *détente*, a *détente* in which the Soviet Union would accept the rough outlines of the world *status quo* in return for a gradually increasing share in international decisions, along with other developed nations. Gradualism was not merely a function of prudence, but also of Kennedy's wish to encourage the Soviet Union to bring along with it the bulk of the forces that supported it as a world revolutionary power. Thus, the Kennedy policy combined an increase in U.S. military superiority over the U.S.S.R. with an increase in trade between the

West and the Soviet bloc. It combined firmness on Berlin with an agreement to support middle-of-the-road forces in Southeast Asia, Africa, and Latin America. When the Soviet Union tested the limits of these concessions by attempting to establish missile bases in Cuba, Kennedy was outraged by the overreaching. His firm response to the attempt led to the compromise of Soviet military withdrawal from Cuba in return for American abstention from invasion. Kennedy's concession was simply an affirmation of his middle-of-the-road policy, whereas Russian withdrawal was a renunciation of its revolutionary role. Had Castro not proclaimed himself in 1961 a "Marxist-Leninist" and thus placed the U.S.S.R. in an embarrassing ideological bind, the U.S.S.R. might have withdrawn totally from Cuba in 1962 instead of maintaining its expensive economic aid to Cuba, at least for the time being.

The Kennedy policy reached its apogee in the nuclear test-ban treaty of 1963, an agreement that would have been ideologically unthinkable ten years earlier. In the new atmosphere the *détente* created, China was the immediate loser—a fact clearly perceived in Peking, whose current ideological dispute with Moscow had emerged with the death of Stalin and the subsequent Soviet decision to increase internal consumption levels and relax political controls. Economic decentralization within the U.S.S.R. had as a counterpart a lessening of Soviet aid to the rest of the Communist world, and most of all to China. The issue was whether the Soviet Union was or was not under an obligation to help China to industrialize before increasing its own consumption levels. The debate ended, as might have been expected, in the Soviet decision to give priority to its own internal economic development, a choice made possible in part by the willingness of the West to begin moving toward *détente*. China increasingly drew the conclusion that it must turn inward for its own economic development, and that it must organize support for its effort throughout the Third World by becoming the new world revolutionary center. By 1963, the year of the test-ban treaty, the ideological split in the Communist world was virtually complete. The Johnson Administration was free to harden its position in the Vietnamese war.

This is the context in which Africa has emerged since World War II. As we have seen, the world system has passed through three stages, the defining feature of each being the state of relations between the dominant power, the U.S., and the erstwhile world revolutionary power, the U.S.S.R. The first stage was cold war, and its core period was 1946–1949. The second stage was armed truce; its core period was 1953–1960. The third stage is *détente*. Its core period began in 1963. The politics of Africa reflected the opportunities for maneuver afforded by these three periods, always, of course, after the delay necessary for men to perceive changes in the limits on their political action that resulted from changes in the world system.

If World War II weakened colonial power in Asia, the Western European metropoles envisaged no comparable decolonization of Africa in the immediate postwar period. At first, the colonial government simply suppressed the African nationalist movements. The U.S.S.R., literally forbidden entry into and communication with the African colonies, was unable in any serious way to affect the balance of forces. In any event, Africa was of low priority to the Soviet Union; the issues in Central Europe, East Asia, and the Middle East were of much more pressing concern. The main contact of the world Communist movement with Africa therefore occurred through the Western European Communist parties. This liaison had the advantage of facility, but over time it had the great defect of offending African nationalist sentiment. As for the United States, it showed only the most limited concern for African affairs during this period. The U.S. was more than willing to allow colonial matters to remain in the hands of the Western European powers, albeit with some misgiving lest Western Europe was being too lenient with incipient African Communist elements.

In a situation characterized by colonial repression, the relative unconcern of the U.S.S.R., and indifference on the part of the United States, the nascent African nationalist movements drew the only plausible conclusion. If they were to survive at all, they had to break their links with the world Communist movement. This was most spectacularly true of French West Africa, though instances abounded in British Africa as well. Since their commitments had been largely verbal and in large part opportunistic, the break was relatively easy. Moreover, it had the enormous advantage of placing the African nationalists in a position to profit by the next change in the world system.

When the U.S. and the U.S.S.R. moved into a stance of armed truce, the attitudes of both powers toward the Third World, including Africa, changed radically. For one thing, they both abandoned the position—first the U.S.S.R. and later the United States—that neutralism, in the words of John Foster Dulles, was immoral. From a cold war assumption that he who is not with us is against us, they moved to an appreciation that during negotiations it is a positive advantage to have neutrals, and that he who is not against us is preserving for us the possibility of maneuver. It was now seen that there could be several varieties of neutrals along a continuous scale. The difference during this period between the U.S. and the U.S.S.R. was not in their policies but in their language. Suez demonstrated that the two powers had the same real policy, but until President Kennedy assumed office the U.S. was unwilling to concede that it was in fact pursuing a policy of accepting the legitimacy of nonalignment by the Third World.

The African nationalists sensed their opportunity and seized it. The U.S.S.R. had become willing to give active aid to African anticolonial movements without demanding a certificate of ideological allegiance in return. They gave money and scholarships and diplomatic support. Soviet aid was less important in itself than in the fact that, in the context of armed truce, it led to active U.S. assistance to very largely the same groups in order to deflect any growing sentiment of appreciation to the U.S.S.R. The aid was sometimes given directly but more often through the international voluntary organizations of labor unions, youth, students, women, etc., which

one or the other major power controlled and influenced. The
Western European powers paid the price of this U.S.-U.S.S.R.
competition for African favor, as they often bitterly observed.
Nonetheless, from an African point of view, it was a boon
that contributed greatly to the rapid and relatively bloodless
drive toward independence which reached its peak in 1960.
It was also during this period that the movement toward
African unity emerged as an effort to channel the released
energy, to bring it firmly under African control, and enable
it to function as a force independent of the continued favors
of the U.S. and the U.S.S.R.

Thus, during the period 1953–1960, African nationalist
movements were vocal supporters of *détente* between the U.S.
and the U.S.S.R. They saw in their declarations the bolstering
of an advantageous competition for their favor, and the promise of continued support. Their position was also one way of
asserting Africa's presence on the world scene. From 1960 on,
the nationalists were to eat the fruit, not always sweet, of
the *détente* they had so ardently advocated.

Although the movement toward African unity was the single
strongest indigenous political force on the African continent
from 1957 on, it remained far weaker in real political strength
than the Western world as a whole—weaker even than the
U.S. alone, when the latter found it necessary or desirable to
assert its strength. The disparity passed unnoticed as long as
the U.S. policy was aimed at supporting African nationalism
against the colonial powers. But with the Congo crisis of 1960,
U.S. priorities shifted toward preventing the consolidation of
a revolutionary movement on the African continent which
might seriously affect the balance of forces in the world.

The first Congo crisis coincided with a Soviet decision to
withdraw from active political provocation, a choice that reflected its judgment that the U.S.S.R. had more to gain for
the present from improving its relations with the U.S. than
from courting African support. The key incident occurred
early. When Mobutu ordered Soviet Embassy personnel to
quit the Congo on September 17, 1960, in the wake of Kasa-

vubu's dismissal of Lumumba, the U.S.S.R. complied instantly, though it continued to refuse to recognize the legitimacy of the regime that gave the order. Since that era, the Lumumbist forces in the Congo have enjoyed little more than sporadic verbal encouragement from Russia, which ceased to be a source of effective aid.

As the external equation changed, the U.S.S.R. ceased or diminished its active support to revolutionary forces elsewhere on the continent, whereas U.S. support to more conservative elements was growing steadily. China had not yet developed the resources or central world position needed to insert itself in the role the U.S.S.R. had played in 1953–1960. Thus the United States no longer had the impetus of significant Communist aid to African revolutionary forces to spur it on. The Congo crisis, furthermore, reawoke a latent fear of, and contempt for, Africans throughout the West. Without the goad of Soviet pressure, the U.S. adopted an increasingly cautious attitude toward liberation movements in southern Africa. At the same time it began to displace the European colonial powers as the principal Western political force in Africa.

By the time the second Congo crisis arose in 1964, the new situation had become clear. There was no external influence on the African continent to equal that of the United States, and the U.S. concluded that it would be necessary to use its force to maintain certain interests no matter how unpalatable its moves were to the Africans. The expansion of the war in Vietnam reinforced this attitude. Thus the U.S. moved to support the Kasavubu-Tshombe government with material and moral aid when it feared that the anti-American rebel forces would come to power in July 1964. It sanctioned Tshombe's use of South African mercenaries and transported them in U.S. planes. The Stanleyville paratroop drop aroused enormous African resentment, but the politically significant fact is that African indignation changed nothing. The U.S.S.R. was virtually mute, and the U.S. won its point—the maintenance of a pro-Western regime in Leopoldville.

The impotence of African states in the face of Rhodesia's

unilateral declaration of independence on November 11, 1965, was hence not unexpected. It was easily predictable, given the world context, and was probably taken into account in the planning of the Rhodesian whites; the British and U.S. response was also tempered by the knowledge that Africans themselves could not act. This assessment of Africa's present inability to maneuver in the world situation will continue to play a part in the calculations of all powers with an interest in southern Africa for some time to come.

As we have seen, the change in the world system from armed truce to *détente* has had a direct effect on Africa by enabling the interested outside powers to influence the course of events. Indirectly, the change has had an even greater impact on the domestic affairs of the independent countries, and on the movement for African unity.

Most of the recently independent African states have three characteristics in common. The first is a fragility that results from unformed national communities, the weakness of national political structures, and the consequent absence of widespread loyalty to the existing political system. The most common means of overcoming this weakness has been the installation of a one-party regime. In the absence of a coherent ideology and cadres hardened by shared suffering over a long period, the parties have tended to slide into inanition soon after their initial triumph. In a number of countries, military forces have sought to substitute themselves for failing party regimes, but in the long run they are unlikely to succeed in channeling political energy more effectively than the one-party systems they replaced. Indeed, they are more likely to become way stations on the road to avowedly oligarchic, anti-revolutionary regimes.

The second feature common to these states is the non-existence of a national economy. Typically, they are geared into a larger world economic complex (usually of a Eurafrican variety) in which the relative openness of trade contributes to an ever-increasing economic gap between Africa and Europe. The gap is widened by Africa's growing population and is far from offset by international aid, which is, furthermore, diminishing as a result of the *détente* between the U.S. and the U.S.S.R.

The third common feature is a social stratification system in which the number of individuals with middle-class aspirations, acquired as a result of expanding educational opportunities, far exceeds the ability of the currently underdeveloped economies to offer jobs and status commensurate with their expectations.

Thus we have political weakness, intensified poverty relative to a world reference scale, and an increasing number of educated unemployables. Inevitably, discontent is rife, and, in the words of Chou En-lai, Africa is "ripe for revolution." That is to say, some of the necessary, though scarcely the sufficient, conditions for revolution are there. Whether revolutions will in fact occur is likely to depend on whether the world situation again moves in a direction that will allow freedom of maneuver to African revolutionary forces.

In these circumstances, there are two possible choices for contemporary African governments. One is to go along with the realities of the present world situation as best they can, and make bilateral aid agreements that are as profitable as they can arrange. Such agreements sometimes benefit the national communities as a whole, but more often they profit only a small stratum of cadres. Sooner or later, such regimes are likely to undergo internal coups when discontent with cultural subordination and the lack of international militancy of the regime becomes too galling and the profiteering too great. But in the present world context, such coups do little to improve the basic situation, as the new regimes face the same external realities and the same internal difficulties as did their predecessors.

Alternatively, the governing elite may attempt to establish a tight internal political regime and begin to cut the ties binding the country to the world economic complex of which it is a part. This course has been followed by the radical-nationalist states that form part of the revolutionary core of the movement toward African unity. These states have further sought to create a political bloc that could collectively renegotiate the terms by which trade is conducted in the present world economic system, and they have seen in the rapid liberation of southern Africa an essential element in making possible such a renegotiation.

In terms of internal stability, the second line of action has been little more successful than the first, as witness the ouster of Ahmed Ben Bella in Algeria and the overthrow of President Nkrumah's regime in Ghana. Domestically, the policies of the radical-nationalist governments have generated as much discontent as the policies of less "radical" regimes, and for reasons differing mainly in degree. The more systematic economic and political controls imposed by the "radical" governments antagonized as many of the middle cadres of the country as did the more cavalier repressions and misappropriations of the other regimes. Furthermore, although the "radical" regimes knew corruption too, it was less the corruption that caused discontent than the sealing off of certain kinds of profiteering to the nascent bourgeoisie. And the break with international economic complexes led inevitably to severe and irritating short-run shortages of consumers' goods.

There is, however, a second factor in the instability of the radical-nationalist states. No longer protected by U.S.-Soviet competition for their favor, they are now more fully exposed to pressures arising in the world economy of which they are an appendage. Since one of the central objectives of the movement toward African unity is to compel the developed (that is, for the most part, Western) world to accept a reallocation of world income through new covenants to govern commerce, it is to be expected that the Western world would discourage the movement from coalescing and becoming an effective international force. Since the U.S.S.R. is now likely to lose as much as it might gain from such a reorganization of the world system, the West is more free than it was to act in terms of its own interests on the African continent.

For the revolutionary core of the African unity movement,

the immediate future is rather dim, and the prospects for an early liberation of southern Africa quite remote. Indeed, it might be said that southern Africa is in full counteroffensive, seeking with increasing success to obtain the installation of relatively docile buffer states around its periphery. The prospects for stability in many independent African states is low, even in the relatively stronger radical-nationalist states. The future of the Organization of African Unity is uncertain, though the important question is not whether the OAU survives in its present form, but the extent to which it or a successor organization can serve as a vehicle for the movement toward unity.

This negative prognosis does not mean that the movement toward African unity will disappear. Far from it, the ultimate fate of the movement will be greatly affected by political developments in three key African countries that harbor unfulfilled nationalist revolutions: South Africa, Congo, and Nigeria. All three are large in size, population, and resources. All have relatively important economies and considerable long-run potential. They also have a long history of internal divisions among the nationalists on a combination of politico-ethnic grounds. In each, the key sectors of the economy are heavily influenced or controlled by foreign interests, or by persons perceived as agents of foreign interests by the nationalists. Of course, these circumstances are common throughout Africa, but the geographical and economic importance of the countries cited lends weight to political events within them. In none of the three do the politically aware inhabitants believe that real power, either within their boundaries or throughout Africa, rests in the hands of a strong centralized indigenous political authority that is relatively independent of world forces, nor do they believe that their governments are undertaking economic programs that will achieve rapid national transformation of the standard of living.

It is therefore quite possible that in each case there will eventually be a major political revolution, after a long process of growth of a structured revolutionary movement with a strong ideology. When and if such explosions occur, their impact on the movement toward African unity will depend in large part on whether the revolutions receive at least tacit support from the majority of African states (perhaps through the OAU), or whether these revolutions will cause a major split among African states, as happened in the first Congo crisis. The African reaction will in turn depend to a large extent on the world conjuncture and the array of pressures— or lack of pressures—to which the relatively weak independent African governments will be exposed. In the case of South Africa, for a radical nationalist movement to succeed it must evict from power a militarily strong and tightly organized repressive caste-group and successfully substitute for it a new and strong central administration. For a radical-nationalist movement to succeed in the Congo or Nigeria it must counter both political lethargy and entrenched interests, and reorganize national politics from the ground up. None of these tasks would be easy, nor likely to be accomplished rapidly. Moreover, even if a coherent political party came into being in any of these countries and proved able to keep the reins of power, its external impact on the movement toward African unity would probably depend on links between the revolutionaries and the unity movement established before the seizure of power, and hence on the political themes used in organizing the revolution. This leads to the old idea of a continental mass party, which has never been seriously pursued, although some nationalists had wished to develop the All-African Peoples' Conference along these lines.

Aside from its strengthening the forces involved in the separate nationalist struggles, coordination between the revolutionaries in these three countries and the unity movement elsewhere on the continent would imply the emergence of a common ideology more elaborate and inclusive than the present radical-nationalist position. The ideological statements of the revolutionary core of the unity movement have in fact been moving toward a subtle and perhaps cumbersome *via media*. They place sufficient emphasis on the class basis of

Africa's internal divisions to legitimate action against domestic groups that are considered agents of neo-colonialism—groups unwilling to move with sufficient strength and speed against Western hegemony in Africa. On the other hand, the emerging ideology also includes sufficient emphasis on the particularity of African society to sustain the goal of continental autonomy and achieve international recognition, if not acceptance. It seems thereby to pose no short-run threat to the world balance of power, though of course the revolutionary objective is to shift the world balance in the long run.

Some areas in which this inchoate ideology may develop more concrete theses are already apparent. Various suggestions that the Marxian analysis of economic development is in some respects outdated may call forth a fresh appraisal of the entire development process. If the movement is to present a coordinated front toward the rest of the world, and avoid splits that arise from differing appreciations of Sino-Soviet doctrinal divisions or French and American tactics, there could also be a fresh analysis of the direction of change in the international politico-economic system. Of course, it is not certain that the ideologists will discover solutions to these problems, or that they will build a coordinated movement even if they succeed. The latent theme of pan-African romantic particularism may once again come to hold the center of attention, unbalanced by any universalist class analysis.

There is a third possibility. Africa may not see the maturation of either a more elaborate revolutionary ideology or a reinforced romantic ideology. There could be an ideological void. Africa would then be unlikely to achieve the kind of political organization that would enable it to transform itself significantly, or to gain the relative political, economic, and cultural autonomy in the world that is the prime objective of the movement toward African unity.

Outside the continent, the emergence of China as a revolutionary power, and eventually as a great power, could initiate a sequence of Sino-American relations rather comparable to U.S.-Soviet relations following World War II: cold war, armed truce, and *détente*. Perhaps the two powers are already approaching the stage of cold war. Africa's revolutionary forces might find a new opportunity to develop swiftly during a projected period of Chinese-U.S. armed truce, with both powers competing for Africa's favor. If the continental unifiers were to seize their opportunity before *détente* set in, African unity might then be achieved.

Since a movement is judged by its results, to assess the movement toward African unity requires consideration of its real objective: the attainment of equality with the rest of the world in terms of economy, political power, and cultural recognition. A continental government is not the goal per se, but a symbolic rallying point and a major element of strategy. The real goal is far more revolutionary, for the attainment of continental equality would in fact mean a basic transformation of African society and thereby of world society. If the movement succeeds in winning equality, or brings Africa closer to winning it, the movement will have attained its goals, even though it may not have attained the formal objective of a continental union government.

Its messianic faith was expressed by President Modibo Keita of Mali when he cited Renan: "Nothing great is achieved without chimeras. Ah! Hope never deceives, and I am sure that all the hopes of the 'believer' will come to be and more. Humanity achieves perfection in wishing for it and hoping for it."

EPILOGUE

LOOKING AT AFRICAN INDEPENDENCE
TEN YEARS LATER

Books should be read and assessed as a reflection of their time. My own book is very much a book of the early 1960s. I wrote it for the most part in the fall of 1960 and I had a chance to make corrections up through the late spring of 1961.

I remember 1960 as a moment of great optimism and renewal, both in Africa and in the United States. In Africa, 1960 was the Year of Independence, the year in which the All-African Peoples' Conference meeting in Tunis had set 1963 as a deadline for the total liberation of Africa. Africans did not think this date fanciful, and I for one shared their optimism. One of the most egregious errors of the book occurs on page 6, where I said: "As of the writing of this book, it seems likely that the remaining nonindependent states will become independent within several years." The year 1963 was chosen as the deadline, incidentally, because it marked the 100th anniversary of the Emancipation Proclamation—which tells us something of Africa's relationship to the United States in 1960.

In the United States, 1960 was the year John F. Kennedy was elected President. It is easy now to see the Kennedy era as simply one more step in a long and consistent march of American politics. I myself have recently argued this in an article in *Africa Report* on American foreign policy in Africa. But at the time, Kennedy seemed to promise a breath of fresh air in the musty atmosphere of Cold War thinking. Those of us who lived through the 1950s—whose oppressiveness was more intellectual and less physical than that of some other eras—thought there was a chance for significant social change in America through peaceful means. It was not that we had any blind faith in Kennedy as an individual—the Kennedy myth starts largely with his assassination—but that Kennedy's regime seemed to reflect some social changes that were occurring elsewhere in the country and the world: de-Stalinization in the USSR, Castro's coming to power in Cuba, the civil rights movement in the United States.

No doubt all of this facile optimism was unfounded and led us into error. But I find it easy to understand how both Africa and the United States could have jumped so eagerly and enthusiastically on this bandwagon of hope after difficult years of struggle both had known just before, and I put forth no *mea culpa* for being optimistic and acting politically and intellectually in terms of it.

So much for background. What of the book? Do I still defend its theses, now that I am more sober about what was going on then, now that I have revised my judgment of many events that happened between 1945 and 1960, both in Africa and in the United States?

Let me start by outlining the three most important lacunae or underemphases in the book which I have thought about and written about in the years since 1961. The first concerns the colonial period in its prime; the second, the period of decolonization; the third, the politics of the immediate postindependence period.

My discussion of social change in the colonial era placed too little emphasis on the widespread, continuing phenomenon of rural discontent. One or two critics and colleagues, particularly Herbert Weiss, picked me up on this, in print and in private. But my critics were surprisingly few in number. It is easy now to see why this should have been so. Because my generation of American scholars were so upset by how the early (British) anthropologists had concentrated their attention on the rural areas, in a search for pristine, ahistorical tribal cultures, and ignored, along with the colonial administrators, the new educated classes, we failed to notice that the error of the anthropologists was not that they studied the rural areas, but *how* they studied them. It became the destiny of a subsequent wave of social science writing, especially that of the new breed of Afrocentric historians, such as the so-called Dar es Salaam school of Terence Ranger and his colleagues, to begin to rectify this particular imbalance.

It seems clear to me now, as I have since stated, that the colonial order was very disorderly indeed; that peasant rebelliousness, if sporadic, was unceasing; and that the discontent of the urban educated classes can neither be understood nor evaluated properly without putting it in the context of rural turmoil.

The second way in which my book was deficient grows out of the first limitation. I presented the process of decolonization in Africa as a political compromise, entered into by the two main parties represented at the negotiating tables: the metropolitan governments and the nationalist leadership. I argued that there came a point where each side, in its calculus of interests, perceived such a compromise as beneficial. I still believe this to be correct. However, what I did not stress sufficiently at the time, and have since made explicit in later work, is the degree to which this compromise was made at the expense of lower strata of the society (that is, small farmers, landless agricultural labor, unskilled and semiskilled urban workers, the unemployed school-leavers). Not only was this compromise made at their expense. It was intended to be at their expense. The metropolitan powers were making concessions in order to separate the nationalist leadership from these strata and prevent a more coherent and conscious degree of radical political activity; most of the nationalist elite were either indifferent to the needs of these strata or explicitly frightened of the potential threat to their own positions. In partial self-defense, I might say that in 1960 most of the more radical members of the African elites were not yet able or willing to openly criticize their peers. They feared that a split in the African "united front" could set back the granting of independence. Neocolonial compromise though some thought it to be, these same persons preferred obtaining the legal appurtenances of sovereignty to remaining still longer under colonial rule. And I have always felt that it is wrong to be more royalist than the king.

The third limitation to my argument is that my picture of the one-party system and the national hero is somewhat rosy, as many said at the time of first publication. Only, I'm not sure I mean rosy in the same way many of my critics did. The way I feel it was rosy is precisely the consequence of the second lacuna. I did not stress the degree to which the single-party system, in most cases, was, in Fanon's phrase, a dictatorship of the bourgeoisie. I have since done so. I have also since stressed the degree to which the party in the one-party state tends to become a ceremonial institution subordinate to the state machinery.

In addition, I overestimated the staying power of national heroes— even those who were real ones, in the sense both of their historic role and strength of personality. It is encouraging morally and intellectually to see that even men of impressive acumen, foresight and political courage—I count Nkrumah among them—are creatures rather than creators of their society, and that once, for whatever reason, they no longer reflect the confluence of social forces, once they make too many "mistakes," they fall. I am not applauding their fall. On the contrary. But I am noting that the element of personal strength which they intrude on the political equation—their "charisma," if you will, that now perhaps discarded phrase—is fragile and conjunctural.

Having noted the ways in which I would amend or add to my arguments as I originally presented them, let me underline the aspects of the book I would most emphatically reaffirm. I will do this in tandem with the lacunae: one concerning the colonial period in its prime; one concerning the period of decolonization; one concerning the politics of the immediate postindependence period.

I presented the colonial period as a "colonial situation," that is, as one in which the territory (and, I should add, at another level of analysis, the empire) was a single arena of power and social action, within which the phenomena we studied took place. Moreover, this arena, this system, was beset by flagrant and inherent contradictions that led to its early demise. J. F. Ade Ajayi and other African historians are now reminding us regularly how short the colonial period was. They are trying to place into a longer African time-perspective the importance of the impact of the colonial rule. But the shortness points to a second truth: how deeply unstable the particular form of social organization of a territory known as colonial rule really is. Today, this way of looking at the colonial system as an interacting totality is so widespread as to be often implicit and unself-conscious. In 1960 the shadow of Malinowski still loomed large.

I presented the process of decolonization as a sort of carefully articulated minuet with a few surprises and little violence—which I still feel is a correct description of what happened (outside of southern Africa). Even Algeria and Kenya do not invalidate this description, as the violence there was an integral part of the continent-wide minuet. The two wars were intensive but, in important ways, constrained and predictable in their evolution. I attributed the phenomenon of rapid, relatively easy decolonization to a conjuncture of the world system, the Cold War between the United States and the Soviet Union. The impact of this international context on the principal negotiators of decolonization was, it seemed to me and still does, clear and direct—and indeed conscious and visible. To be sure, this conjuncture came to an end. In my second volume, *Africa: The Politics of Unity*, I dated the end as 1963, and explained how the end of the Cold War had very negatively affected the movement for African unity, the liberation of southern Africa and the economic development of the continent.

Finally, I presented the politics of the early post-independence period as one in which the one-party state was a central political mechanism. One colleague told me that the most "outrageous" statement I had made in my book was that found on page 96: "The choice has not been between one-party and multi-party states; it has been between one-party states and either anarchy or military regimes or various combinations of the two." Ten years later, this statement does not strike me as the least bit outrageous. I would say it has proved to be very accurate. I would go further. The only useful political analysis is to uncover what alternatives are in fact available for the actors in a given system at a given point of time. I argued then and would argue now that among the possible political forms which African states can take in the *present* era—that is, let us say, from 1957–1975—is neither the bourgeois liberal state (despite the romantic notions of the framers of the post-Nkrumah Ghana constitution), nor a state which would cut off all its economic links with the capitalist world (despite the wistful critiques of some non-African Marxists). I do not suggest that the latter is not possible in the foreseeable future. In fact, I have several times suggested that Nigeria, Congo/K and a post-revolution South Africa are all prime candidates for such a regime—not *now*, but *perhaps* ten to twenty years from now. I believed and believe that in the present period the one-party system, to the extent that it can be effectively established, is more viable and more beneficial to Africa and to the world than any present alternative—this despite all its shortcomings, cruelties and deceptions.

There is one other statement I made about the one-party state which I should like to reaffirm and which partially compensates for some of the lacunae I have discussed. It is on page 161: "The image of a small elite imposing their will, through the party structure, on an inert mass fails to take account of the real dispersion of power that still exists in every African country." Everything we have seen since 1960 reinforces this point. But it is well perhaps to underline once more its theoretical importance. We talk of systems, of institutions, of influence. All these words exaggerate the articulation of the structures and do not sufficiently evoke the image of rumbling forces beneath the surface which are far more determinative of the present and the future than the things that are immediately apparent.

APPENDIX A

A GLOSSARY OF INITIALS

GENERAL NOTE: *When the initials do not make clear the geographic locus of the organization, this is specifically indicated under the title. The affiliations of the organization most relevant to the discussion in this book are indicated as well. In a number of instances, nonetheless, organizations changed their affiliations in the course of their history, as the text often indicates.*

AAPC	All-African People's Conference
AAPSC	Afro-Asian People's Solidarity Conference
AATUF	All-African Trade Union Federation
ADB	African Development Bank
AFRO	African Regional Organization —ICFTU
ALC	African Liberation Committee —also, Committee of Nine
ANC	African National Congress —South Africa
ANTUF	All-Nigerian Trade Union Federation
ATUC	African Trade Union Confederation
CAO	Committee of African Organizations
CASL(-FO)	Confédération Africaine des Syndicats Libres (-Force Ouvrière) —French black Africa —member of ICFTU
CATC	Confédération Africaine des Travailleurs Croyants —French black Africa —member of UPTC and IFCTU
CCTA	Commission for Technical Cooperation in Africa (South of the Sahara)
CFTC	Confédération Française des Travailleurs Chrétiens —member of IFCTU

CGAT	Confédération Générale Aéfienne du Travail
	—French Equatorial Africa
	—member of WFTU
CGT	Confédération Générale du Travail
	—France
	—member of WFTU
CGTA	Confédération Générale des Travailleurs Africains
	—French West Africa
CGTK	Confédération Générale du Travail du Kamerun
	—French Cameroon
	—member of WFTU
CIAS	Conference of Independent African States
CLSTP	Comité de Libertaçáó de Sao Tomé e Principe
	—member of CONCP
CNL	Conseil National de Libération
	—Congo (L)
CONCP	Conferência das Organizacões Nacionalistas das Colonias Portuguesas
CPP	Convention People's Party
	—Ghana
ECA	Economic Commission for Africa
	—United Nations
ECOSOC	Economic and Social Commission
	—United Nations
FAO	Food and Agriculture Organization
	—United Nations
FEANF	Fédération des Etudiants d'Afrique Noire en France
FLING	Frente de Libertaçáo de la Independência Nacional da Guiné
	—Portuguese Guinea
FLN	Front de Libération Nationale
	—Algeria
FO	Confédération Générale du Travail-Force Ouvrière
	—France
	—member of ICFTU
FRELIMO	Frente de Libertaçáo de Moçambique
	—member of CONCP
GCTUC	Gold Coast Trades Union Congress
	—member of ICFTU
GPRA	Gouvernement Provisoire de la République Algérienne
GRAE	Govêrno Revolucionário da Angola em Exilo
	—see UPA

IAMO	Inter-African and Malagasy States Organization
	—also, Monrovia Powers
ICATU	International Confederation of Arab Trade Unions
ICFTU	International Confederation of Free Trade Unions
IFCTU	International Federation of Christian Trade Unions
ILO	International Labor Organization
	—United Nations
IULC	Independent United Labour Congress
	—Nigeria
	—member of AATUF
	—also, NTUC
KFL	Kenya Federation of Labour
	—member of ATUC
	—member of ICFTU
MPLA	Movimento Popular para Libertação da Angola
	—member of CONCP
NCNC	National Congress of Nigeria and the Cameroons
NTUC	Nigerian Trade Union Congress
	—member of AATUF
OAU	Organization of African Unity
OCAM	Organisation Commune Africaine et Malgache
	—successor to UAM
PAC	Pan-Africanist Congress
	—South Africa
PAFMEC(S)A	Pan-African Freedom Movement of East, Central (and Southern) Africa
PAIGC	Partido Africano para Independência da Guiné e Cabo Verde
	—Portuguese Guinea and Cape Verde Islands
	—member of CONCP
PASC	Pan-African Students Conference
PASM	Pan-African Students Movement
	—outgrowth of PASC
PAUJ	Pan-African Union of Journalists
PAYM	Pan-African Youth Movement
RDA	Rassemblement Démocratique Africain
	—French black Africa
SWANLIF	South-West Africa National Liberation Front
	—comprised SWAPO and SWANU
SWANU	South-West Africa National Union
SWAPO	South-West Africa Peoples' Organization
TUC	Trades Union Congress

	—United Kingdom
	—member of ICFTU
TUCN	Trades Union Congress—Nigeria
	—member of ATUC
	—member of ICFTU
UAM	Union Africaine et Malgache
	—also, Brazzaville Group
UAMCE	Union Africaine et Malgache de Coopération Economique
	—comprised of some members of UAM
UAS	Union of African States
	—also, Ghana-Guinea-Mali Union
UGTA	Union Générale des Travailleurs Algériens
	—member of AATUF
UGTAN	Union Générale des Travailleurs d'Afrique Noire
	—predecessor of AATUF
UGTT	Union Générale des Travailleurs Tunisiens
	—member of ATUC
	—member of ICFTU
ULC	United Labour Congress
	—Nigeria
	—member of ATUC
	—member of ICFTU
	—successor of TUCN
UMT	Union Marocaine de Travail
	—member of AATUF
UNCTAD	United Nations Conference on Trade and Development
UNESCO	United Nations Educational, Scientific, and Cultural Organization
UNFP	Union Nationale des Forces Populaires
	—Morocco
UNIAS	Union of Non-Independent African States
UNTS	Union Nationale des Travailleurs Sénégalais
	—member of ATUC
UPA	União das Populações da Angola
	—member of GRAE
UPC	Union des Populations du Cameroun
	—(French) Cameroon
	—not to be confused with Uganda People's Congress

UPTC	Union Panafricaine des Travailleurs Croyants —member of IFCTU
WASU	West African Students Union
WFTU	World Federation of Trade Unions
ZANU	Zimbabwe African National Union —Rhodesia
ZAPU	Zimbabwe African People's Union —Rhodesia

APPENDIX B

RESOLUTION ON NEO-COLONIALISM

ALL-AFRICAN PEOPLES'
CONFERENCE
CAIRO, MARCH 23–31, 1961

The third All-African Peoples' Conference meeting in Cairo from the 25th to the 31st of March, 1961, having carefully reviewed the current situation in Africa:

Considers that Neo-Colonialism, which is the survival of the colonial system in spite of formal recognition of political independence in emerging countries which become the victims of an indirect and subtle form of domination by political, economic, social, military or technical, is the greatest threat to African Countries that have newly won their independence or those approaching this status.

Emphasises the examples of the Congo, the French Community, the Federation of Rhodesia and Nyasaland, which indicate that the colonial system and international imperialism, realising their failure in facing the development of revolutionary movements in Africa, make use of many means to safeguard the essential of their economic and military power.

When the recognition of national independence becomes inevitable, they try to deprive these countries of their essence of real independence. This is done by imposing unequal economic, military and technical conventions; by creating puppet governments following false elections, or by inventing some so-called constitutional formulas of multi-national co-existence intended only to hide the racial discrimination favouring settlers.

Whenever such machinations appear insufficient to hamper the combativity and determination of popular liberation movements, dying colonialism tries, under the cover of Neo-Colonialism or through the guided intervention of the United Nations, the balkanisation of newly-independent States or the systematic division of the political or syndical vivid forces, and in desperate cases, like in the Congo, colonialism goes as far as plots, repressive measures by army and police, and murder in cold-blood.

Conscious that Neo-Colonialism manifests itself through economic and political intervention, intimidation and blackmail in order to prevent African States from directing their political, social and economic policies towards the exploitation of their natural wealth for the benefit of their peoples.

Considers that such countries as the United States, Federal Germany, Israel, Britain, Belgium, Holland, South Africa and France are the main perpetrators of Neo-Colonialism.

Manifestations of Neo-Colonialism

This Conference denounces the following manifestations of Neo-Colonialism in Africa:

(a) Puppet governments represented by stooges and even fabricated elections, based on some chiefs, reactionary elements, anti-popular politicians, big bourgeois compradores or corrupted civil or military functionaries.

(b) Regrouping of States, before or after independence by an imperial power in federation or communities linked to that imperial power.

(c) Balkanisation as a deliberate political fragmentation of States by creation of artificial entities, such as, for example, the case of Katanga, Mauritania, Buganda, etc.

(d) The economic entrenchment of the colonial power before independence and the continuity of economic dependence after formal recognition of National sovereignty.

(e) Integration into colonial economic blocks which maintain the underdeveloped character of African economy.

(f) Economic infiltration by a foreign power after independence, through capital investments, loans and monetary aids or technical experts of unequal concessions, particularly those extending for long periods.

(g) Direct monetary dependence, as in those emergent independent States whose finances remain in the hands of and directly controlled by colonial powers.

(h) Military bases sometimes introduced as scientific research stations or training schools, introduced either before independence or as a condition for independence.

Agents of Neo-Colonialism

The Third All-African Peoples' Conference exposes the following active agents of Neo-Colonialism:

(a) Colonial embassies and missions serving as nerve centres of espionage and pressure points on the local African governments directly or through their civil or military technicians.

(b) So-called foreign and United Nations technical assistants who ill-advise and sabotage national political, economical, educational and social development.

(c) Military personnel in armed forces and police, as officers or advisers who serve above all, the colonial interests directly, or through local officers who remain loyal to their former masters.

(d) The representatives from imperialist and colonial countries under the cover of religion. Moral Re-armament, cultural, Trade Union and Youth or Philanthropic Organisations.

(e) The malicious propaganda by radio, press, literature controlled by imperial and colonial countries, as well as in some independent African Countries where press and radio are still owned by im-perialist powers.

(f) Puppet Governments in Africa being used by imperialists in the furtherance of Neo-Colonialism, such as the use of their good offices by the neo-colonial powers to undermine the sovereignty and aspira-tions of other African States.

Means of Fighting Neo-Colonialism

The Third All-African Peoples' Conference, whose very reason of exist-ence is the mobilisation of African masses for the liberation of Africa, is firmly convinced that it is by intensifying this mobilisation that Africa will find the most efficient way to fight Neo-Colonialism and to extract the last roots of imperialism.

It is the duty of popular, political, syndical, youth and women's organ-isations, not only to inspire and to wage the struggle against Neo-Colonialism, but also, and above all to be vigilant, to control the correct application of the general outline and to denounce all those who attempt to deviate it from its real objectives.

The Conference realises that the struggle against Neo-Colonialism must be associated with the struggle against all forms of opportunism which is the mask of the accomplices of imperialism.

It is therefore by awakening of the conscience of the masses by the establishment of landmarks of real liberation, that the masses will be freed from the power of certain slogans and formulas that only serve as a camouflage for colonialism.

That is why, the Conference:

(a) Condemns the balkanisation of emerging States, whether dependent or independent, as a way to perpetuate Neo-Colonialism in Africa (Congo, Mauritania, Northern Rhodesia, Buganda, etc.)

(b) Condemns the federations and communities created before in-dependence under the patronage of colonial States.

(c) Invites all independent African States to give aid and assistance to liberate the African countries still under foreign domination.

(d) Urges all independent African States which still retain foreign military and para-military bases, to liquidate these bases as soon as possible.

(e) This Conference re-affirms its determination to continue to mobilise popular mass opinion to denounce enemies of true independence and agents of Neo-Colonialism, camouflaged in all possible forms.

(f) This Conference denounces aid with expressed or unexpressed strings attached.

(g) This Conference urges the Independent African States to intensify their efforts for the creation of an effective form of cooperation among the African States in the Economic, Social and Cultural domains, in order to frustrate Neo-Colonialism.

(h) This Conference deplores the attitude of some independent African States who, under the guise of neutrality, are passive even on vital matters affecting the whole of Africa, and who, by their passive activities in fact promote the cause of Neo-Colonialism.

(i) This Conference calls for the immediate launching of the All-African Trade Union Federation as an effective means of counter-acting Neo-Colonialism.

INDEX